CCNA INTRO: Introduction to Cisco Networking Technologies Study Guide

CCNA INTRO Exam Objectives

OBJECTIVE	CHAPTER
Design and Support	
Use a subset of Cisco IOS commands to analyze and report network problems	8
Use embedded layer 3 through layer 7 protocols to establish, test, suspend, or disconnect connectivity to remote devices from the router console	8
Determine IP addresses	2, 3, 8
Implementation and Operation	
Establish communication between a terminal device and the router IOS, and use IOS for system analysis	4, 8
Manipulate system image and device configuration files	8
Perform an initial configuration on a router and save the resultant configuration file	4
Use commands incorporated within IOS to analyze and report network problems	8
Assign IP addresses	4
Describe and install the hardware and software required to be able to communicate via a network	1
Use embedded data link layer functionality to perform network neighbor discovery and analysis from the router	8
Use embedded layer 3 through layer 7 protocols to establish, test, suspend, or disconnect connectivity to remote devices from the router console	8
Technology	
Demonstrate the mathematical skills required to work seamlessly with integer decimal, binary, and hexadecimal numbers and simple binary logic	1
Define and describe the structure and technologies of computer networks	1
Describe the hardware and software required to be able to communicate via a network	1
Describe the physical, electrical, and mechanical properties and standards associated with optical, wireless, and copper media used in networks	1
Describe the topologies and physical issues associated with cabling common	

Sybex®
An Imprint of
WILEY

OBJECTIVE	CHAPTER
Identify the key characteristics of common wide area networking (WAN) configurations and technologies, and differentiate between these and common LAN technologies	9
Describe the purpose and fundamental operation of the Internetwork Operating System (IOS)	4, 8
Describe the role of a router in a WAN	9
Identify the major internal and external components of a router, and describe the associated functionality	8
Identify and describe the stages of the router boot-up sequence	8
Describe how the configuration register and boot system commands modify the router boot-up sequence	8
Describe the concepts associated with routing, and the different methods and protocols used to achieve it	5, 6
Describe how an IP address is associated with a device interface, and the association between physical and employ IPaddressing techniques	3, 4, 5
Employ IP addressing techniques	3, 4, 5
Compare and contrast collision and broadcast domains, and describe the process of network segmentation	1, 5
Describe the principles and practice of switching in an Ethernet network	1, 7
Explain how collisions are detected and handled in an Ethernet system	1
Explain the fundamental concepts associated with the Ethernet media access technique	1
Describe how the protocols associated with TCP/IP allow host communication to occur	2, 5, 6
Describe the operation of the Internet Control Message Protocol (ICMP) and identify the reasons, types, and format of associated error and control messages	2
Describe the principles and practice of packet switching utilizing the Internet Protocol (IP)	5, 6

NOTE Exam objectives are subject to change at any time without prior notice and at Cisco's sole discretion. Please visit Cisco's website (www.cisco.com) for the most current listing of exam objectives.

Sybex®
An Imprint of
WILEY

CCNA® INTRO
Introduction to Cisco® Networking Technologies
Study Guide

Todd Lammle

Wiley Publishing, Inc.

Acquisitions and Development Editor: Jeff Kellum
Technical Editor: Patrick Bass
Production Editor: Martine Dardignac
Copy Editor: Judy Flynn
Production Manager: Tim Tate
Vice President and Executive Group Publisher: Richard Swadley
Vice President and Executive Publisher: Joseph B. Wikert
Vice President and Publisher: Neil Edde
Permissions Editor: Laura Carpenter VanWinkle
Media Development Specialist: Steven Kudirka
Book Designers: Judy Fung and Bill Gibson
Compositor: Craig Woods, Happenstance Type-O-Rama
Proofreader: Nancy Riddiough
Indexer: Nancy Guenther
Cover Designer: Ryan Sneed

Copyright © 2006 by Wiley Publishing, Inc., Indianapolis, Indiana
Published simultaneously in Canada

ISBN-13: 978-0-470-06850-2
ISBN-10: 0-470-06850-7

Sybex®
An Imprint of
WILEY

To Our Valued Readers:

Thank you for looking to Sybex for your CCNA Introduction to Cisco Networking Technologies (INTRO) exam prep needs. We at Sybex are proud of our reputation for providing certification candidates with the practical knowledge and skills needed to succeed in the highly competitive IT marketplace. Certification candidates have come to rely on Sybex for accurate and accessible instruction on today's crucial technologies and business skills.

Just as Cisco is committed to establishing measurable standards for certifying Cisco Certified Network Administrators (CCNAs), Sybex is committed to providing those individuals with the knowledge needed to meet those standards.

The author and editors have worked hard to ensure that this edition of *CCNA INTRO: Introduction to Cisco Networking Technologies Study Guide* you hold in your hands is comprehensive, in depth, and pedagogically sound. We're confident that this book will exceed the demanding standards of the certification marketplace and help you, the CCNA candidate, succeed in your endeavors.

As always, your feedback is important to us. If you believe you've identified an error in the book, please send a detailed e-mail to support@wiley.com. And if you have general comments or suggestions, feel free to drop me a line directly at nedde@wiley.com. At Sybex we're continually striving to meet the needs of individuals preparing for certification exams. Good luck in pursuit of your CCNA certification!

Neil Edde
Vice President and Publisher
Sybex, an Imprint of Wiley

To all the great food and friends at Bone Daddy's Barbeque in Dallas, Texas!
All my thanks!

Acknowledgments

For trying to keep me going in a straight line, I need to thank Neil Edde. It is no small accomplishment, and I applaud him for his patience and dedication to our vision.

Jeff Kellum was instrumental in the success of this book. Without his hard work and focused attention to producing a flawless product, it would never have come together as quickly as it did. Jeff has an almost magical ability to keep me working even under immense pressure at times and has been a solid asset in making this a powerful, high-quality book. Thank you!

In addition, Martine Dardignac and Judy Flynn made the editorial process a breeze! I'll work with this team any time!

I also want to thank my technical editor, Patrick Bass. His dedicated, concise comments have been invaluable and have made this a better book.

Thanks also to the CD team, whose hard work has resulted in a power-packed, good-looking CD test engine. Thanks also to the proofreader, Nancy Riddiough; the indexer, Nancy Guenther; and the compositor Craig Woods of Happenstance Type-O-Rama.

Contents at a Glance

Contents

Introduction

Welcome to the exciting world of Cisco certification! You have picked up this book because you want something better—namely, a better job with more satisfaction. Rest assured that you have made a good decision. Cisco certification can help you get your first networking job or more money and a promotion if you are already in the field.

Cisco certification can also improve your understanding of the internetworking of more than just Cisco products: You will develop a complete understanding of networking and how different network topologies work together to form a network. This is beneficial to every networking job and is the reason Cisco certification is in such high demand, even at companies with few Cisco devices.

Cisco is the king of routing and switching. The Cisco certifications reach beyond popular certifications such as the Microsoft Certified System Engineer (MCSE) and other operating system certifications to provide you with an indispensable factor in understanding today's network—insight into the Cisco world of internetworking. By deciding that you want to become Cisco certified, you are saying that you want to be the best—the best at routing and the best at switching. This book will lead you in that direction.

 For updates covering additions or modifications to the CCNA certification exams, as well as additional study tools for other Cisco certifications, be sure to visit the Todd Lammle website at www.lammle.com.

Cisco's Network Support Certifications

Initially, to secure the coveted Cisco certification, you took only one test and then you were faced with the (extremely difficult) Routing and Switching CCIE hands-on lab, an all-or-nothing approach that made it tough to succeed.

In response to repeated failures from CCIE candidates, Cisco created a series of new certifications to help you get the coveted Cisco Certified Internetwork Expert (CCIE), as well as aid prospective employers in measuring skill levels even if you are not. With these new written certifications, which make for a better approach to preparing for that almighty lab, Cisco opened doors that few were allowed through before.

Cisco Certified Network Associate (CCNA)

The CCNA certification is the first in the new line of Cisco certifications and is the precursor to all current Cisco certifications. Now you can become a Cisco Certified Network Associate a couple different ways, but two written exams is what this book was designed for. And you don't have to stop there—you can choose to continue with your studies and achieve a higher certification, called the Cisco Certified Network Professional (CCNP). Someone with a CCNP has all the skills and knowledge they need to attempt the Routing and Switching CCIE lab. Just becoming a CCNA can land you that job you've dreamed about.

Why Become a CCNA?

Cisco, not unlike Microsoft, has created the certification process to give administrators a set of skills and to equip prospective employers with a way to measure skills or match certain criteria. Becoming a CCNA can be the initial step of a successful journey toward a new, highly rewarding, and sustainable career.

The CCNA program was created to provide a solid introduction not only to the Cisco Internetwork Operating System (IOS) and Cisco hardware, but also to internetworking in general, making it helpful to you in areas that are not exclusively Cisco's. At this point in the certification process, it's not unrealistic that network managers—even those without Cisco equipment—require Cisco certifications for their job applicants.

If you make it through the CCNA and are still interested in Cisco and internetworking, you're headed down a path to certain success.

What Skills Do You Need to Become a CCNA?

To meet the CCNA certification skill level, you must be able to understand or do the following:

- Install, configure, and operate LAN, WAN, and dial access services for small networks (100 nodes or fewer).
- Use the following protocols: IP, IGRP, Serial, Frame Relay, IP RIP, VLANs, Ethernet, and access lists.

How Do You Become a CCNA?

The way to become a CCNA is to pass two little tests (CCNA INTRO exam 640-801 and CCNA ICND 640-811). Then—poof!—you're a CCNA. (Don't you wish it were that easy?) True, it can be just one test (640-801), but you have to possess enough knowledge to understand what the test writers are asking, and they ask some really hard questions in all three of these tests.

This book was written specifically for the two-step CCNA certification process, but is a great introduction if you are interested in landing a job in internetworking. These tests are as follows:

- Exam 640-811: Interconnecting Cisco Networking Devices (ICND)
- Exam 640-821: Introduction to Cisco Networking Technologies (INTRO)

I can't stress this enough: it's critical that you have some hands-on experience with Cisco routers. If you can get ahold of some 2500 or 2600 series routers, you're set. But if you can't, we've worked hard to provide hundreds of configuration examples throughout this book to help network administrators (or people who want to become network administrators) learn what they need to know to pass the CCNA exam.

For hands-on training with Todd Lammle, please see www.globalnettraining .com. Each student will get hands-on experience by configuring at least three routers and two switches—no sharing of equipment!

What Does This Book Cover?

This book covers everything you need to know in order to pass the CCNA INTRO exam. However, taking the time to study and practice with routers or a router simulator is the real key to success.

The information you will learn in this book is listed in the following bullet points:

- Chapter 1 introduces you to internetworking. You will learn the basics of the Open Systems Interconnection (OSI) model the way Cisco wants you to learn it. Ethernet networking and standards are discussed in detail in this chapter as well. There are written labs and plenty of review questions to help you. Do not skip the written labs in this chapter!

- Chapter 2 provides you with the background necessary for success on the exam as well as in the real world by discussing TCP/IP. This in-depth chapter covers the very beginnings of the Internet Protocol stack, goes all the way to IP addressing and understanding the difference between a network address and broadcast address, and ends with network troubleshooting.

- Chapter 3 introduces you to subnetting. You will be able to subnet a network in your head after reading this chapter. In addition, you'll learn about Variable Length Subnet Masks (VLSMs) and how to troubleshoot IP networks. Plenty of help is found in this chapter if you do not skip the written lab and review questions.

- Chapter 4 introduces you to the Cisco Internetwork Operating System (IOS) and command-line interface (CLI). In this chapter you will learn how to turn on a router and configure the basics of the IOS, including setting passwords, banners, and more. IP configuration will be discussed and a hands-on labs will help you gain a firm grasp of the concepts taught in the chapter. Before you go through the hands-on labs, be sure to complete the written lab and review questions.

- Chapter 5 teaches you about IP routing. This is a fun chapter because you will begin to build your network, add IP addresses, and route data between routers. Written and hands-on labs will help you understand IP routing to the fullest. You will also learn about static and default routing.

- Chapter 6 dives into dynamic routing using RIP and IGRP (more advanced routing protocols are covered in the CCNA Study Guide 640-801). The written lab, hands-on labs, and review questions will help you master these two routing protocols.

- Chapter 7 gives you a background on layer 2 switching and how switches perform address learning and make forwarding and filtering decisions. Network loops and how to avoid them with the Spanning Tree Protocol (STP) will be discussed, as well as the different LAN switch types used by Cisco switches. Be sure to go through the written lab and review questions in this chapter.

- Chapter 8 provides you with the management skills needed to run a Cisco IOS network. Backing up and restoring the IOS and router configuration are covered, as are the troubleshooting tools necessary to keep a network up and running. Before performing the hands-on labs in this chapter, complete the written lab and review questions.

- Chapter 9 concentrates on Cisco wide area network (WAN) protocols. This chapter covers the basics of WAN protocols and goes into detail about HDLC, and PPP. Do not skip the written lab, review questions, and hands-on labs found in this chapter.

- The glossary is a handy resource for Cisco terms. This is a great tool for understanding some of the more obscure terms used in this book.

How to Use This Book

If you want a solid foundation for the serious effort of preparing for the Cisco Certified Network Associate (CCNA) INTRO exam, then look no further. I have spent hundreds of hours putting together this book with the sole intention of helping you to pass the CCNA INTRO exam and learn how to configure Cisco routers and switches.

This book is loaded with valuable information, and to help you get the most out of your studying time, I recommend the following study method:

1. Take the assessment test immediately following this introduction. (The answers are at the end of the test.) It's okay if you don't know any of the answers; that is why you bought this book! Carefully read over the explanations for any question you get wrong and note which chapters the material comes from. This information should help you plan your study strategy.

2. Study each chapter carefully, making sure that you fully understand the information and the test objectives listed at the beginning. Pay extra-close attention to chapters from which questions you missed in the assessment test were taken.

3. Complete each written lab at the end of each chapter. Do *not* skip the written exercises because they directly relate to the CCNA INTRO exam and what you must glean from the chapter you just read. Do not just skim these labs! Make sure you understand completely the reason for each answer.

4. Complete all hands-on labs in the chapter, referring to the text of the chapter so that you understand the reason for each step you take. If you do not have Cisco equipment available, go to www.routersim.com for a router simulator that will cover all the labs needed for all your Cisco certification needs.

5. Answer all of the review questions related to each chapter. (The answers appear at the end of the chapters.) Note the questions that confuse you and study the corresponding sections of the book again. Do not just skim these questions! Make sure you understand completely the reason for each answer.

6. Try your hand at the bonus exams that are included on the companion CD. The questions in these exams appear only on the CD. This will give you a complete overview of the type of questions you can expect to see on the real CCNA INTRO exam. Check out www.lammle.com for more Cisco exam prep questions.

7. Also on the companion CD is the first module from my complete CCNA video series, which covers internetworking and basic networking. This is critical for the CCNA INTRO exam. In addition, as an added bonus, I have included an audio section from my CCNA audio program. Do not skip the video and audio section!

8. Test yourself using all the flashcards on the CD. These are brand new and include an updated flashcard programs to help you prepare for the CCNA INTRO exam. This is a great study tool!

To learn every bit of the material covered in this book, you'll have to apply yourself regularly and with discipline. Try to set aside the same time period every day to study, and select a comfortable and quiet place to do so. If you work hard, you will be surprised at how quickly you learn this material.

If you follow these steps and really study and practice the review questions, the bonus exams, the Todd Lammle video/audio sections, the electronic flashcards, and all the written and hands-on labs, it would be hard to fail the CCNA INTRO exam.

What's on the CD?

We worked hard to provide some really great tools to help you with your certification process. All of the following tools should be loaded on your workstation when studying for the test. As a fantastic bonus, I was able to add both a section from my CCNA video and a section from my audio series to the CD included with this book!

The Sybex Test Preparation Software

The test preparation software prepares you to pass the CCNA INTRO exam. In the test engine, you will find all the review and assessment questions from the book, plus two additional bonus exams that appear exclusively on the CD.

Electronic Flashcards for PC, Pocket PC, and Palm Devices

To prepare for the exam, you can read this book, study the review questions at the end of each chapter, and work through the practice exams included in the book and on the companion CD. But wait, there's more! You can also test yourself with the flashcards included on the CD. If you can get through these difficult questions and understand the answers, you'll know you're ready for the CCNA INTRO exam.

The flashcards include over 125 questions specifically written to hit you hard and make sure you are ready for the exam. Between the review questions, bonus exams, and flashcards on the CD, you'll be more than prepared for the exam.

CCNA: Cisco Certified Network Associate Study Guide in PDF

Sybex offers the *CCNA INTRO: Introduction to Cisco Networking Technologies Study Guide* in PDF on the CD so you can read the book on your PC or laptop. (Acrobat Reader 7 is also included on the CD.)

To get up-to-the-minute CCNA INTRO and other Cisco exam information, please see www.lammle.com.

Todd Lammle Videos

I have created a full CCNA series of videos that can be purchased in either DVD or downloadable format from www.lammle.com. However, as a bonus included with this book, the first module of this series is included on the CD in its entirety. The video is over one hour of informative CCNA INTRO information. This module alone has a value of $149! Do not skip this video as it covers the internetworking objectives, which are very important to the CCNA INTRO exam.

Todd Lammle Audios

In addition to the section of videos included for free on the CD, I have included one full section from my CCNA audio series—almost one hour of audio! The full CCNA audio series has a value of $199 and can be found at www.lammle.com. This is a great tool to add to your arsenal of study material to help you pass the CCNA INTRO exam.

> To find more Todd Lammle videos and audios, as well as other Cisco study material, please see www.lammle.com.

Minimum System Requirements

You will need Windows 98, Second Edition or higher, as well as a 233 megahertz (MHz) processor, such as an Intel Pentium II or Advanced Micro Devices (AMD) processor. In addition, you will need 128 MB of RAM, and Windows Media Player 9 or higher.

Where Do You Take the Exams?

You may take the CCNA INTRO exam at any of the more than 800 Prometric Authorized Testing Centers around the world (www.2test.com), or call 800-204-EXAM (3926). You can also register and take the exams at a Pearson VUE authorized center (www.vue.com) or call (877) 404-EXAM (3926).

Here's how to register for a Cisco Certified Network Associate exam:

1. Determine the number of the exam you want to take. (The CCNA INTRO exam number is 640-821.)

2. Register with the nearest Prometric Registration Center or Pearson VUE testing center. At this point, you will be asked to pay in advance for the exam. At the time of this writing, the exams are $100 each and must be taken within one year of payment. You can schedule exams up to six weeks in advance or as late as the same day you want to take it—but if you fail a Cisco exam, you must wait five days before you will be allowed to retake it. If something comes up and you need to cancel or reschedule your exam appointment, contact Prometric or Pearson VUE at least 24 hours in advance.

3. When you schedule the exam, you'll get instructions regarding all appointment and cancellation procedures, the ID requirements, and information about the testing-center location.

Tips for Taking Your CCNA INTRO Exam

The CCNA INTRO exam test contains about 45 to 55 questions and must be completed in 75 minutes or less. This information can change per exam. You must get a score of about 85 percent to pass this exam, but again, each exam can be different.

Many questions on the exam have answer choices that at first glance look identical—especially the syntax questions! Remember to read through the choices carefully because close doesn't cut it. If you get commands in the wrong order or forget one measly character, you'll get the question wrong. So, to practice, do the hands-on exercises at the end of this book's chapters over and over again until they feel natural to you.

Also, never forget that the right answer is the Cisco answer. In many cases, more than one appropriate answer is presented, but the *correct* answer is the one that Cisco recommends. On the exam, it always tells you to pick one, two, or three, never "choose all that apply." The CCNA INTRO 640-821 exam may include the following test formats:

- Multiple-choice single answer
- Multiple-choice multiple answer
- Drag-and-drop
- Fill-in-the-blank
- Router simulations

In addition to multiple choice and fill-in response questions, Cisco Career Certifications exams may include performance simulation exam items.

   Check RouterSim's router and switch simulator at www.routersim.com.

Router simulations in Cisco proctored exams will not show the steps to follow in completing a router interface configuration. They do allow partial command responses. For example, show config or sho config or sh conf would be acceptable. Router#show ip protocol or Router#show ip prot would be acceptable.

Here are some general tips for exam success:

- Arrive early at the exam center so you can relax and review your study materials.
- Read the questions *carefully*. Don't jump to conclusions. Make sure you're clear about *exactly* what each question asks.
- When answering multiple-choice questions that you're not sure about, use the process of elimination to get rid of the obviously incorrect answers first. Doing this greatly improves your odds if you need to make an educated guess.
- You can no longer move forward and backward through the Cisco exams, so double-check your answer before clicking Next since you can't change your mind.

After you complete an exam, you'll get immediate, online notification of your pass or fail status, a printed Examination Score Report that indicates your pass or fail status, and your exam results by section. (The test administrator will give you the printed score report.) Test scores are automatically forwarded to Cisco within five working days after you take the test, so you don't need to send your score to them. If you pass the exam, you'll receive confirmation from Cisco, typically within two to four weeks.

About the Author

Todd Lammle, CCNA/CCNP/CCSP/CCVP, CEH/CHFI, is the authority on Cisco certification networking. He is a world renowned author, speaker, and trainer. Todd has over 25 years of experience working with LANs, WANs, and Wireless Networks. He is president of GlobalNet Training, a network integration and training firm based in Dallas, and CEO of RouterSim, LLC. You can reach Todd through www.lammle.com.

Assessment Test

1. You have 10 users plugged into a hub running 10Mbps half duplex. There is a server connected to the switch running 10Mbps half duplex as well. How much bandwidth does each host have to the server?

    A. 100kbps

    B. 1Mbps

    C. 2Mbps

    D. 10Mbps

2. What does the command `routerA(config)#line cons 0` allow you to perform next?

    A. Set the Telnet password.

    B. Shut down the router.

    C. Set your console password.

    D. Disable console connections.

3. Which of the following is the valid host range for the subnet on which the IP address 192.168.168.188 255.255.255.192 resides?

    A. 192.168.168.129–190

    B. 192.168.168.129–191

    C. 192.168.168.128–190

    D. 192.168.168.128–192

4. What does the `passive` command provide to dynamic routing protocols?

    A. Stops an interface from sending or receiving periodic dynamic updates.

    B. Stops an interface from sending periodic dynamic updates but not from receiving updates.

    C. Stops the router from receiving any dynamic updates.

    D. Stops the router from sending any dynamic updates.

5. Which protocol does Ping use?

    A. TCP

    B. ARP

    C. ICMP

    D. BootP

6. How many collision domains are created when you segment a network with a 12-port switch?

    A. 1

    B. 2

    C. 5

    D. 12

7. Which of the following commands will allow you to set your Telnet password on a Cisco router?

    A. `line telnet 0 4`

    B. `line aux 0 4`

    C. `line vty 0 4`

    D. `line con 0`

8. If you wanted to delete the configuration stored in NVRAM, what would you type?

    A. `erase startup`

    B. `erase nvram`

    C. `delete nvram`

    D. `erase running`

9. Which protocol is used to send a Destination Network Unreachable message back to originating hosts?

    A. TCP

    B. ARP

    C. ICMP

    D. BootP

10. Which class of IP address has the most host addresses available by default?

    A. A

    B. B

    C. C

    D. A and B

11. What LAN switch mode keeps CRC errors to a minimum but still has a fixed latency rate?

    A. STP

    B. Store and forward

    C. Cut-through

    D. FragmentFree

12. How many broadcast domains are created when you segment a network with a 12-port switch?

    A. 1

    B. 2

    C. 5

    D. 12

13. What PDU is at the Transport layer?

    A. User data

    B. Session

    C. Segment

    D. Frame

14. What is a stub network?

   A. A network with more than one exit point

   B. A network with more than one exit and entry point

   C. A network with only one entry and no exit point

   D. A network that has only one entry and exit point

15. Where is a hub specified in the OSI model?

   A. Session layer

   B. Physical layer

   C. Data Link layer

   D. Application layer

16. What does the command `show controllers s 0` provide?

   A. The type of serial port connection (e.g., Ethernet or Token Ring)

   B. The type of connection (e.g., DTE or DCE)

   C. The configuration of the interface, including the IP address and clock rate

   D. The controlling processor of that interface

17. What is the main reason the OSI model was created?

   A. To create a layered model larger than the DoD model

   B. So application developers can change only one layer's protocols at a time

   C. So different networks could communicate

   D. So Cisco could use the model

18. Which layer of the OSI model creates a virtual circuit between hosts before transmitting data?

   A. Application

   B. Session

   C. Transport

   D. Network

   E. Data Link

19. Which protocol does DHCP use at the Transport layer?

   A. IP

   B. TCP

   C. UDP

   D. ARP

20. How do you copy a router IOS to a TFTP host?

   A. `copy run starting`

   B. `copy start running`

   C. `copy running tftp`

   D. `copy flash tftp`

21. If your router is facilitating a CSU/DSU, which of the following commands do you need to use to provide the router with a 64kbps serial link?

   A. RouterA(config)#**bandwidth 64**

   B. RouterA(config-if)#**bandwidth 64000**

   C. RouterA(config)#**clockrate 64000**

   D. RouterA(config-if)#**clock rate 64**

   E. RouterA(config-if)#**clock rate 64000**

22. Which of the following commands will set your prompt so you can set your Telnet password on a Cisco router?

   A. line telnet 0 4

   B. line aux 0 4

   C. line vty 0 4

   D. line con 0

23. What command do you use to set the enable secret password on a Cisco router to *todd*?

   A. RouterA(config)#**enable password todd**

   B. RouterA(config)#**enable secret todd**

   C. RouterA(config)#**enable secret password todd**

   D. RouterA(config-if)#**enable secret todd**

24. Which protocol is used to find an Ethernet address from a known IP address?

   A. IP

   B. ARP

   C. RARP

   D. BootP

25. Which command is used to enable RIP on a Cisco router?

   A. copy tftp rip

   B. router rip on

   C. router rip

   D. on rip routing

Answers to Assessment Test

1. D. Each device has10Mpbs to the server. See Chapter 1 for more information.

2. C. The command `line console 0` places you at a prompt where you can then set your console user-mode password. See Chapter 4 for more information.

3. A. 256 – 192 = 64. 64 + 64 = 128. 128 + 64 = 192. The subnet is 128, the broadcast address is 191, and the valid host range is the numbers in between, or 129–190. See Chapter 3 for more information.

4. B. The `passive` command, short for `passive-interface`, stops regular updates from being sent out an interface. However, the interface can still receive updates. See Chapter 5 for more information.

5. C. Internet Control Message Protocol (ICMP) is the protocol at the Network layer that is used to send echo requests and replies. See Chapter 2 for more information.

6. D. Layer 2 switching creates individual collision domains. See Chapter 7 for more information.

7. C. The command `line vty 0 4` places you in a prompt that will allow you to set or change your Telnet password. See Chapter 4 for more information.

8. A. The command `erase-startup-config` deletes the configuration stored in NVRAM. See Chapter 4 for more information.

9. C. ICMP is the protocol at the Network layer that is used to send messages back to an originating router. See Chapter 2 for more information.

10. A. Class A addressing provides 24 bits for hosts addressing. See Chapter 3 for more information.

11. D. FragmentFree LAN switching checks into the data portion of the frame to make sure no fragmentation has occurred. See Chapter 7 for more information.

12. A. By default, switches break up collision domains but are one large broadcast domain. See Chapter 1 for more information.

13. C. Segmentation happens at the Transport layer. See Chapter 1 for more information.

14. D. Stub networks have only one connection to an internetwork. Only default routes can be set on a stub network or network loops may occur. See Chapter 5 for more information.

15. B. A hub is a Physical layer device. See Chapter 1 for more information.

16. B. The command `show controllers s 0` tells you what type of serial connection you have. If it is a DCE, you need to provide the clock rate. See Chapter 4 for more information.

17. C. The primary reason the OSI model was created was so that different networks could interoperate. See Chapter 1 for more information.

18. C. The Transport layer creates virtual circuits between hosts before transmitting any data. See Chapter 1 for more information.

19. C. User Datagram Protocol is a connection network service at the Transport layer and DHCP uses this connectionless service. See Chapter 2 for more information.

20. D. The command used to copy a configuration from a router to a TFTP host is `copy flash tftp`. See Chapter 8 for more information.

21. E. The clock rate command is two words, and the speed of the line is in bits per second (bps). See Chapter 5 for more information.

22. C. The command `line vty 0 4` places you in a prompt that will allow you to set or change your Telnet password. See Chapter 4 for more information.

23. B. The command `enable secret todd` sets the enable secret password to *todd*. See Chapter 4 for more information.

24. B. If a device knows the IP address of where it wants to send a packet but doesn't know the hardware address, it will send an ARP broadcast looking for the hardware address or, in this case, the Ethernet address. See Chapter 2 for more information.

25. C. To enable RIP routing on a Cisco router, use the `global config` command `router rip`. See Chapter 6 for more information.

Chapter

1

Internetworking

THE CCNA INTRO EXAM TOPICS COVERED IN THIS CHAPTER INCLUDE THE FOLLOWING:

✓ **Implementation and Operation**

- Describe and install the hardware and software required to be able to communicate via a network

✓ **Technology**

- Demonstrate the mathematical skills required to work seamlessly with integer decimal, binary, and hexadecimal numbers and simple binary logic

- Define and describe the structure and technologies of computer networks

- Describe the hardware and software required to be able to communicate via a network

- Describe the physical, electrical, and mechanical properties and standards associated with optical, wireless, and copper media used in networks

- Describe the topologies and physical issues associated with cabling common LANs

- Compare and contrast collision and broadcast domains, and describe the process of network segmentation

- Describe the principles and practice of switching in an Ethernet network

- Explain how collisions are detected and handled in an Ethernet system

- Explain the fundamental concepts associated with the Ethernet media access technique

Welcome to the exciting world of internetworking. This first chapter will really help you understand the basics of internetworking by focusing on how to connect networks together using Cisco routers and switches. First, you need to know exactly what an internetwork is, right? You create an internetwork when you connect two or more LANs or WANs via a router and configure a logical network addressing scheme with a protocol such as IP.

I'll be covering these four topics in this chapter:

- Internetworking basics
- Network segmentation
- How bridges, switches, and routers are used to physically segment a network
- How routers are employed to create an internetwork

I'm also going to dissect the Open Systems Interconnection (OSI) model and describe each part to you in detail, because you really need a good grasp of it for the solid foundation you'll build your networking knowledge upon. The OSI model has seven hierarchical layers that were developed to enable different networks to communicate reliably between disparate systems. It's crucial for you to understand the OSI model as Cisco sees it, so that's how I'll be presenting the seven layers to you.

Since there's a bunch of different types of devices specified at the different layers of the OSI model, it's also very important to understand the many types of cables and connectors used for connecting all those devices to a network. We'll go over cabling Cisco devices, discussing how to connect to a router or switch (along with Ethernet LAN technologies) and even how to connect a router or switch with a console connection.

We'll finish the chapter by discussing the three-layer hierarchical model that was developed by Cisco to help you design, implement, and troubleshoot internetworks.

After you finish reading this chapter, you'll encounter 20 review questions and three written labs. These are given to you to really lock the information from this chapter into your memory. So don't skip them!

It is important to remember that this is not an "intro" book to networking but an introduction book to Cisco internetworking. For a beginning look at networking, please see *CompTIA Network+ Study Guide* (Sybex, 2005).

Internetworking Basics

Before we explore internetworking models and the specifications of the OSI reference model, you've got to understand the big picture and learn the answer to the key question, why is it so important to learn Cisco internetworking?

Networks and networking have grown exponentially over the last 15 years—understandably so. They've had to evolve at light speed just to keep up with huge increases in basic mission-critical user needs such as sharing data and printers as well as more advanced demands such as videoconferencing. Unless everyone who needs to share network resources is located in the same office area (an increasingly uncommon situation), the challenge is to connect the sometimes many relevant networks together so all users can share the networks' wealth.

Starting with a look at Figure 1.1, you get a picture of a basic LAN network that's connected together using a hub. This network is actually one collision domain and one broadcast domain—but no worries if you have no idea about what this means because I'm going to talk about both collision and broadcast domains so much throughout this whole chapter, you'll probably even dream about it!

Okay, about Figure 1.1... How would you say the PC named Bob communicates to the PC named Sally? Well, they're both on the same LAN connected with a multiport repeater (a hub). So does Bob just send out a data message, "Hey Sally, you there?" or does Bob use Sally's IP address and put things more like, "Hey 192.168.0.3, are you there?" Hopefully, you picked the IP address option, but even if you did, the news is still bad—both answers are wrong! Why? Because Bob is actually going to use Sally's MAC address (known as a hardware address), which is burned right into the network card of Sally's PC, to get ahold of her.

FIGURE 1.1   The basic network

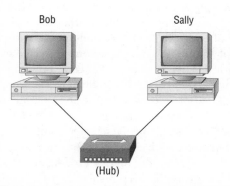

Bob   Sally

(Hub)

The basic network allows devices to share information.
The term computer language refers to binary code (0s or 1s).
The two hosts above communicate using hardware or MAC addresses.

Great, but how does Bob get Sally's MAC address since Bob knows only Sally's name and doesn't even have her IP address yet? Bob is going to start with name resolution (hostname to IP address resolution), something that's usually accomplished using Domain Name Service (DNS). And of note, if these two are on the same LAN, Bob can just broadcast to Sally asking her for the information (no DNS needed)—welcome to Microsoft Windows!

Here's an output from an network analyzer depicting a simple name resolution process from Bob to Sally:

Time   Source   Destination   Protocol   Info
53.892794 192.168.0.2 192.168.0.255 NBNS   Name query NB **SALLY**<00>

As I already mentioned, since the two hosts are on a local LAN, Windows will just broadcast to resolve the name Sally (the destination 192.168.0.255 is a broadcast address). Let's take a look at the rest of the information:

Ethernet II, Src: 192.168.0.2 (00:14:22:be:18:3b), Dst: Broadcast (ff:ff:ff:ff:ff:ff)
What this output shows is that Bob knows his own MAC address and source IP address but not Sally's IP address or MAC address, so Bob sends a broadcast address of all *f*s for the MAC address (a Data Link layer broadcast) and an IP LAN broadcast of 192.168.0.255. Again, don't freak—you're going to learn all about broadcasts in Chapter 3, "IP Subnetting and Variable Length Subnet Masks (VLSMs) and Troubleshooting IP."

Before the name is resolved, the first thing we've got to do is broadcast on the LAN to get Sally's MAC address so we can communicate to her PC and resolve her name to an IP address:
Time   Source   Destination   Protocol Info
5.153054 192.168.0.2 Broadcast   ARP   Who has 192.168.0.3? Tell 192.168.0.2

Next, check out Sally's response:
Time   Source   Destination   Protocol   Info
5.153403 192.168.0.3   192.168.0.2   ARP   192.168.0.3 is at 00:0b:db:99:d3:5e
5.53.89317 192.168.0.3 192.168.0.2 NBNS   Name query response NB **192.168.0.3**

Okay sweet—we now have both Sally's IP address and her MAC address! These are both listed as the source address at this point because this information was sent from Sally back to Bob. So, *finally*, Bob has the all goods he needs to communicate with Sally. And just so you know, I'm going to tell you all about ARP and show you exactly how Sally's IP address was resolved to a MAC address a little later in Chapter 5, "IP Routing."

By the way, I want you to understand that Sally still had to go through the same resolution processes to communicate back to Bob—sounds crazy, huh? Consider this a welcome to IPv4 and basic networking with Windows (and we haven't even added a router yet!).

To complicate things further, it's also likely that at some point you'll have to break up one large network into a bunch of smaller ones because user response will have dwindled to a slow crawl as the network grew and grew. And with all that growth, your LAN's traffic congestion has reached epic proportions. The answer to this is breaking up a really big network into a number of smaller ones—something called *network segmentation*. You do this by using devices like *routers*, *switches*, and *bridges*. Figure 1.2 displays a network that's been segmented with a switch so each network segment connected to the switch is now a separate collision domain. But make note of the fact that this network is still one broadcast domain.

FIGURE 1.2   A switch replaces the hub, breaking up collision domains.

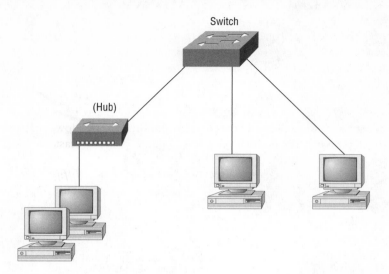

Keep in mind that the hub used in Figure 1.2 just extended the one collision domain from the switch port. Here's a list of some of the things that commonly cause LAN traffic congestion:

- Too many hosts in a broadcast domain
- Broadcast storms
- Multicasting
- Low bandwidth
- Adding hubs for connectivity to the network
- A bunch of ARP or IPX traffic (IPX is a Novell routing protocol that is like IP, but really, really chatty.)

Take another look at Figure 1.2—did you notice that I replaced the main hub from figure 1.1 with a switch? Whether you did or didn't, the reason I did that is because hubs don't segment a network; they just connect network segments together. So basically, it's an inexpensive way to connect a couple of PCs together, which is great for home use but that's about it!

Routers are used to connect networks together and route packets of data from one network to another. Cisco became the de facto standard of routers because of its high-quality router products, great selection, and fantastic service. Routers, by default, break up a *broadcast domain*—the set of all devices on a network segment that hear all the broadcasts sent on that segment. Figure 1.3 shows a router in our little network that creates an internetwork and breaks up broadcast domains:

FIGURE 1.3   Routers create an internetwork.

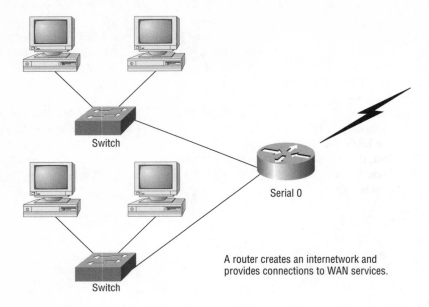

Switch

Serial 0

Switch

A router creates an internetwork and
provides connections to WAN services.

Figure 1.3 is a pretty cool network. Each host is connected to its own collision domain, and the router has created two broadcast domains. And don't forget that the router provides connections to WAN services as well! The router uses something called a serial interface, specifically, a V.35 physical interface on a Cisco router.

Breaking up a broadcast domain is important because when a host or server sends a network broadcast, every device on the network must read and process that broadcast—unless you've got a router. When the router's interface receives this broadcast, it can respond by basically saying, "Thanks, but no thanks," and discard the broadcast without forwarding it on to other networks. Even though routers are known for breaking up broadcast domains by default, it's important to remember that they break up collision domains as well.

There are two advantages of using routers in your network:

- They don't forward broadcasts by default.

- They can filter the network based on layer 3 (Network layer) information (e.g., IP address).

Four router functions in your network can be listed as follows:

- Packet switching

- Packet filtering

- Internetwork communication

- Path selection

Remember that routers are really switches; they're actually what we call layer 3 switches (we'll talk about layers later in this chapter). Unlike layer 2 switches, which forward or filter frames, routers (layer 3 switches) use logical addressing and provide what is called packet switching. Routers can also provide packet filtering by using access lists (which are not discussed in this book), and when routers connect two or more networks together and use logical addressing (IP), this is called an internetwork. Last, routers use a routing table (map of the internetwork) to make path selections and to forward packets to remote networks.

Conversely, switches aren't used to create internetworks (they do not break up broadcast domains by default); they're employed to add functionality to a network LAN. The main purpose of a switch is to make a LAN work better—to optimize its performance—providing more bandwidth for the LAN's users. And switches don't forward packets to other networks as routers do. Instead, they only "switch" frames from one port to another within the switched network. Okay, you may be thinking, "Wait a minute, what are frames and packets?" I'll tell you all about them later in this chapter, I promise!

By default, switches break up *collision domains*. This is an Ethernet term used to describe a network scenario wherein one particular device sends a packet on a network segment, forcing every other device on that same segment to pay attention to it. At the same time, a different device tries to transmit, leading to a collision, after which both devices must retransmit, one at a time. Not very efficient! This situation is typically found in a hub environment where each host segment connects to a hub that represents only one collision domain and only one broadcast domain. By contrast, each and every port on a switch represents its own collision domain.

Switches create separate collision domains but a single broadcast domain. Routers provide a separate broadcast domain for each interface.

The term *bridging* was introduced before routers and hubs were implemented, so it's pretty common to hear people referring to bridges as switches. That's because bridges and switches basically do the same thing—break up collision domains on a LAN (in reality, you cannot buy a physical bridge these days, only LAN switches, but they use bridging technologies, so Cisco still calls them multiport bridges).

So what this means is that a switch is basically just a multiple-port bridge with more brainpower, right? Well, pretty much, but there are differences. Switches do provide this function, but they do so with greatly enhanced management ability and features. Plus, most of the time, bridges only had 2 or 4 ports. Yes, you could get your hands on a bridge with up to 16 ports, but that's nothing compared to the hundreds available on some switches!

You would use a bridge in a network to reduce collisions within broadcast domains and to increase the number of collision domains in your network. Doing this provides more bandwidth for users. And keep in mind that using hubs in your network can contribute to congestion on your Ethernet network. As always, plan your network design carefully!

Figure 1.4 shows how a network would look with all these internetwork devices in place. Remember that the router will not only break up broadcast domains for every LAN interface, but break up collision domains as well.

When you looked at Figure 1.4, did you notice that the router is found at center stage and that it connects each physical network together? We have to use this layout because of the older technologies involved—bridges and hubs. On the top network in Figure 1.4, you'll notice that a bridge was used to connect the hubs to a router. The bridge breaks up collision domains, but all the hosts connected to both hubs are still crammed into the same broadcast domain. Also, the bridge only created two collision domains, so each device connected to a hub is in the same collision domain as every other device connected to that same hub. This is actually pretty lame, but it's still better than having one collision domain for all hosts. Notice something else: The three hubs at the bottom that are connected also connect to the router, creating one humongous collision domain and one humongous broadcast domain. This makes the bridged network look much better indeed!

FIGURE 1.4   Internetworking devices

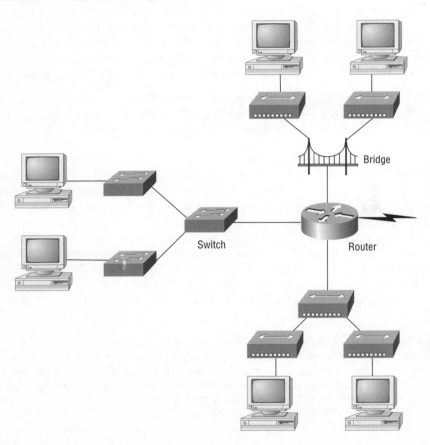

> Although bridges/switches are used to segment networks, they will not isolate broadcast or multicast packets.

The best network connected to the router is the LAN switch network on the left. Why? Because each port on that switch breaks up collision domains. But it's not all good—all devices are still in the same broadcast domain. Do you remember why this can be a really bad thing? Because all devices must listen to all broadcasts transmitted, that's why. And if your broadcast domains are too large, the users have less bandwidth and are required to process more broadcasts, and network response time will slow to a level that could cause office riots.

Once we have only switches in our network, things change a lot! Figure 1.5 shows the network that is typically found today.

FIGURE 1.5   Switched networks creating an internetwork

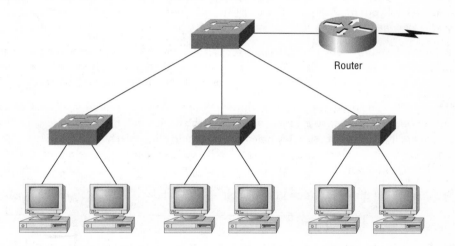

Router

Okay, here I've placed the LAN switches at the center of the network world so the routers are connecting only logical networks together. If I implemented this kind of setup, I've created virtual LANs (VLANs) something I'm going to tell you about soon, in Chapter 7, "LAN Switching." So don't stress. But it is really important to understand that even though you have a switched network, you still need a router to provide your inter-VLAN communication, or internetworking. Don't forget that!

Obviously, the best network is one that's correctly configured to meet the business requirements of the company it serves. LAN switches with routers, correctly placed in the network, are the best network design. This book will help you understand the basics of routers and switches so you can make tight, informed decisions on a case-by-case basis.

Let's go back to Figure 1.4 again. Looking at the figure, how many collision domains and broadcast domains are in this network? Hopefully, you answered nine collision domains and three broadcast domains! The broadcast domains are definitely the easiest to see because only routers break up broadcast domains by default. And since there are three connections, that gives you three broadcast domains. But do you see the nine collision domains? Just in case that's a no, I'll explain. The all-hub network is one collision domain; the bridge network equals three collision domains. Add in the switch network of five collision domains—one for each switch port—and you've got a total of nine.

In Figure 1.5, each port on the switch is a separate collision domain and each VLAN is a separate broadcast domain. But you still need a router for routing between VLANs. How many collision domains do you see here? I'm counting 10—remember that connection between the switches is considered a collision domain!

 Real World Scenario

Should I Just Replace All My Hubs with Switches?

You're a network administrator at a large company in San Jose. The boss comes to you and says that he got your requisition to buy a switch and is not sure about approving the expense; do you really need it?

Well, if you can, sure—why not? Switches really add a lot of functionality to a network that hubs just don't have. But most of us don't have an unlimited budget. Hubs still can create a nice network—that is, of course, if you design and implement the network correctly.

Let's say that you have 40 users plugged into four hubs, 10 users each. At this point, the hubs are all connected together so that you have one large collision domain and one large broadcast domain. If you can afford to buy just one switch and plug each hub into a switch port, as well as the servers into the switch, then you now have four collision domains and one broadcast domain. Not great, but for the price of one switch, your network is a much better thing.

So, go ahead! Put that requisition in to buy all new switches. What do you have to lose?

So now that you've gotten an introduction to internetworking and the various devices that live in an internetwork, it's time to head into internetworking models.

Internetworking Models

When networks first came into being, computers could typically communicate only with computers from the same manufacturer. For example, companies ran either a complete DECnet solution or an IBM solution—not both together. In the late 1970s, the *Open Systems Interconnection (OSI) reference model* was created by the International Organization for Standardization (ISO) to break this barrier.

The OSI model was meant to help vendors create interoperable network devices and software in the form of protocols so that different vendor networks could work with each other. Like world peace, it'll probably never happen completely, but it's still a great goal.

The OSI model is the primary architectural model for networks. It describes how data and network information are communicated from an application on one computer through the network media to an application on another computer. The OSI reference model breaks this approach into layers.

In the following section, I am going to explain the layered approach and how we can use this approach in helping us troubleshoot our internetworks.

The Layered Approach

A *reference model* is a conceptual blueprint of how communications should take place. It addresses all the processes required for effective communication and divides these processes into logical groupings called *layers*. When a communication system is designed in this manner, it's known as *layered architecture*.

Think of it like this: You and some friends want to start a company. One of the first things you'll do is sit down and think through what tasks must be done, who will do them, what order they will be done in, and how they relate to each other. Ultimately, you might group these tasks into departments. Let's say you decide to have an order-taking department, an inventory department, and a shipping department. Each of your departments has its own unique tasks, keeping its staff members busy and requiring them to focus on only their own duties.

In this scenario, I'm using departments as a metaphor for the layers in a communication system. For things to run smoothly, the staff of each department will have to trust and rely heavily upon the others to do their jobs and competently handle their unique responsibilities. In your planning sessions, you would probably take notes, recording the entire process to facilitate later discussions about standards of operation that will serve as your business blueprint, or reference model.

Once your business is launched, your department heads, each armed with the part of the blueprint relating to their own department, will need to develop practical methods to implement their assigned tasks. These practical methods, or protocols, will need to be compiled into a standard operating procedures manual and followed closely. Each of the various procedures in your manual will have been included for different reasons and have varying degrees of importance and implementation. If you form a partnership or acquire another company, it will be imperative that its business protocols—its business blueprint—match yours (or at least be compatible with it).

Similarly, software developers can use a reference model to understand computer communication processes and see what types of functions need to be accomplished on any one layer. If they are developing a protocol for a certain layer, all they need to concern themselves with is that specific layer's functions, not those of any other layer. Another layer and protocol will handle the other functions. The technical term for this idea is *binding*. The communication processes that are related to each other are bound, or grouped together, at a particular layer.

Advantages of Reference Models

The OSI model is hierarchical, and the same benefits and advantages can apply to any layered model. The primary purpose of all such models, especially the OSI model, is to allow different vendors' networks to interoperate.

Advantages of using the OSI layered model include, but are not limited to, the following:

- It divides the network communication process into smaller and simpler components, thus aiding component development, design, and troubleshooting.

- It allows multiple-vendor development through standardization of network components.

- It encourages industry standardization by defining what functions occur at each layer of the model.

- It allows various types of network hardware and software to communicate.

- It prevents changes in one layer from affecting other layers, so it does not hamper development.

The OSI Reference Model

One of the greatest functions of the OSI specifications is to assist in data transfer between disparate hosts—meaning, for example, that they enable us to transfer data between a Unix host and a PC or a Mac.

The OSI isn't a physical model, though. Rather, it's a set of guidelines that application developers can use to create and implement applications that run on a network. It also provides a framework for creating and implementing networking standards, devices, and internetworking schemes.

The OSI has seven different layers, divided into two groups. The top three layers define how the applications within the end stations will communicate with each other and with users. The bottom four layers define how data is transmitted end-to-end. Figure 1.6 shows the three upper layers and their functions, and Figure 1.7 shows the four lower layers and their functions.

FIGURE 1.6   The upper layers

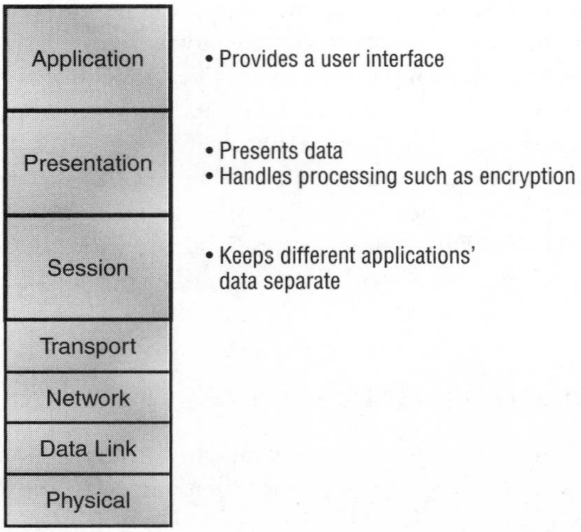

When you study Figure 1.6, understand that the user interfaces with the computer at the Application layer and also that the upper layers are responsible for applications communicating between hosts. Remember that none of the upper layers knows anything about networking or network addresses. That's the responsibility of the four bottom layers.

In Figure 1.7, you can see that it's the four bottom layers that define how data is transferred through a physical wire or through switches and routers. These bottom layers also determine how to rebuild a data stream from a transmitting host to a destination host's application.

The following network devices operate at all seven layers of the OSI model:

- Network management stations (NMSs)
- Web and application servers
- Gateways (not default gateways)
- Network hosts

FIGURE 1.7 The lower layers

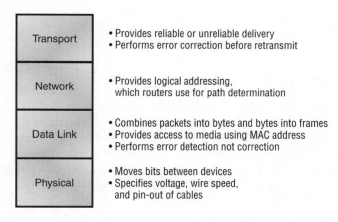

Basically, the ISO is pretty much the Emily Post of the network protocol world. Just as Ms. Post wrote the book setting the standards—or protocols—for human social interaction, the ISO developed the OSI reference model as the precedent and guide for an open network protocol set. Defining the etiquette of communication models, it remains today the most popular means of comparison for protocol suites.

The OSI reference model has seven layers:

- Application layer (layer 7)
- Presentation layer (layer 6)
- Session layer (layer 5)
- Transport layer (layer 4)
- Network layer (layer 3)
- Data Link layer (layer 2)
- Physical layer (layer 1)

Figure 1.8 shows a summary of the functions defined at each layer of the OSI model. With this in hand, you're now ready to explore each layer's function in detail.

FIGURE 1.8   Layer functions

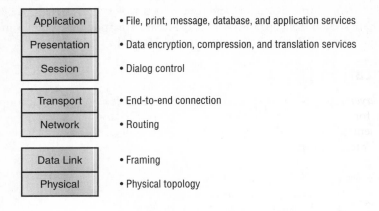

The Application Layer

The *Application layer* of the OSI model marks the spot where users actually communicate to the computer. This layer only comes into play when it's apparent that access to the network is going to be needed soon. Take the case of Internet Explorer (IE). You could uninstall every trace of networking components from a system, such as TCP/IP, NIC card, and so on, and you could still use IE to view a local HTML document—no problem. But things would definitely get messy if you tried to do something like view an HTML document that must be retrieved using HTTP or nab a file with FTP or TFTP. That's because IE will respond to requests such as those by attempting to access the Application layer. And what's happening is that the Application layer is acting as an interface between the actual application program—which isn't at all a part of the layered structure—and the next layer down by providing ways for the application to send information down through the protocol stack. In other words, IE doesn't truly reside within the Application layer—it interfaces with Application layer protocols when it needs to deal with remote resources.

The Application layer is also responsible for identifying and establishing the availability of the intended communication partner and determining whether sufficient resources for the intended communication exist.

These tasks are important because computer applications sometimes require more than only desktop resources. Often, they'll unite communicating components from more than one network application. Prime examples are file transfers and email, as well as enabling remote access, network management activities, client/server processes, and information location. Many network applications provide services for communication over enterprise networks, but for present and future internetworking, the need is fast developing to reach beyond the limits of current physical networking.

It's important to remember that the Application layer is acting as an interface between the actual application programs. This means that Microsoft Word, for example, does not reside at the Application layer but instead interfaces with the Application layer protocols. Chapter 2 will present some programs that actually reside at the Application layer—for example, FTP and TFTP.

The Presentation Layer

The *Presentation layer* gets its name from its purpose: It presents data to the Application layer and is responsible for data translation and code formatting.

This layer is essentially a translator and provides coding and conversion functions. A successful data-transfer technique is to adapt the data into a standard format before transmission. Computers are configured to receive this generically formatted data and then convert the data back into its native format for actual reading (for example, EBCDIC to ASCII). By providing translation services, the Presentation layer ensures that data transferred from the Application layer of one system can be read by the Application layer of another one.

The OSI has protocol standards that define how standard data should be formatted. Tasks like data compression, decompression, encryption, and decryption are associated with this layer. Some Presentation layer standards are involved in multimedia operations too.

The Session Layer

The *Session layer* is responsible for setting up, managing, and then tearing down sessions between Presentation layer entities. This layer also provides dialogue control between devices, or nodes. It coordinates communication between systems and serves to organize their communication by offering three different modes: *simplex*, *half duplex*, and *full duplex*. To sum up, the Session layer basically keeps different applications' data separate from other applications' data.

The Transport Layer

The *Transport layer* segments and reassembles data into a data stream. Services located in the Transport layer both segment and reassemble data from upper-layer applications and unite it onto the same data stream. They provide end-to-end data transport services and can establish a logical connection between the sending host and destination host on an internetwork.

Some of you are probably familiar with TCP and UDP already. (But if you're not, no worries—I'll tell you all about them in Chapter 2.) If so, you know that both work at the Transport layer and that TCP is a reliable service and UDP is not. This means that application developers have more options because they have a choice between the two protocols when working with TCP/IP protocols.

The Transport layer is responsible for providing mechanisms for multiplexing upper-layer applications, establishing sessions, and tearing down virtual circuits. It also hides details of any network-dependent information from the higher layers by providing transparent data transfer.

 The term *reliable networking* can be used at the Transport layer. It means that acknowledgments, sequencing, and flow control will be used.

The Transport layer can be connectionless or connection-oriented. However, Cisco is mostly concerned with you understanding the connection-oriented portion of the Transport layer. The following sections will provide the skinny on the connection-oriented (reliable) protocol of the Transport layer.

Flow Control

Data integrity is ensured at the Transport layer by maintaining *flow control* and by allowing users to request reliable data transport between systems. Flow control prevents a sending host on one side of the connection from overflowing the buffers in the receiving host—an event that can result in lost data. Reliable data transport employs a connection-oriented communications session between systems, and the protocols involved ensure that the following will be achieved:

- The segments delivered are acknowledged back to the sender upon their reception.

- Any segments not acknowledged are retransmitted.

- Segments are sequenced back into their proper order upon arrival at their destination.

- A manageable data flow is maintained in order to avoid congestion, overloading, and data loss.

 The purpose of flow control is to provide a means for the receiver to govern the amount of data sent by the sender.

Connection-Oriented Communication

In reliable transport operation, a device that wants to transmit sets up a connection-oriented communication with a remote device by creating a session. The transmitting device first establishes a connection-oriented session with its peer system, which is called a *call setup* or a *three-way handshake*. Data is then transferred; when the transfer is finished, a call termination takes place to tear down the virtual circuit.

Figure 1.9 depicts a typical reliable session taking place between sending and receiving systems. Looking at it, you can see that both hosts' application programs begin by notifying their individual operating systems that a connection is about to be initiated. The two operating systems communicate by sending messages over the network confirming that the transfer is approved and that both sides are ready for it to take place. After all of this required synchronization takes place, a connection is fully established and the data transfer begins (this virtual circuit setup is called overhead!).

FIGURE 1.9   Establishing a connection-oriented session

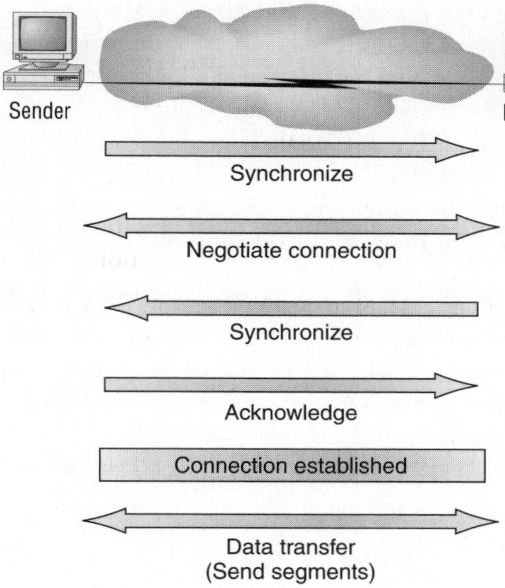

While the information is being transferred between hosts, the two machines periodically check in with each other, communicating through their protocol software to ensure that all is going well and that the data is being received properly.

Let me sum up the steps in the connection-oriented session—the three-way handshake—pictured in Figure 1.9:

- The first "connection agreement" segment is a request for synchronization.

- The second and third segments acknowledge the request and establish connection parameters—the rules—between hosts. The receiver's sequencing is requested to be synchronized here as well, so that a bidirectional connection is formed.

- The final segment is also an acknowledgment. It notifies the destination host that the connection agreement has been accepted and that the actual connection has been established. Data transfer can now begin.

Sounds pretty simple, but things don't always flow so smoothly. Sometimes during a transfer, congestion can occur because a high-speed computer is generating data traffic a lot faster than the network can handle transferring. A bunch of computers simultaneously sending datagrams through a single gateway or destination can also botch things up nicely. In the latter case, a gateway or destination can become congested even though no single source caused the problem. In either case, the problem is basically akin to a freeway bottleneck—too much traffic for too small a capacity. It's not usually one car that's the problem; there are simply too many cars on that freeway.

Okay, so what happens when a machine receives a flood of datagrams too quickly for it to process? It stores them in a memory section called a *buffer*. But this buffering action can only solve the problem if the datagrams are part of a small burst. If not, and the datagram deluge continues, a device's memory will eventually be exhausted, its flood capacity will be exceeded, and it will react by discarding any additional datagrams that arrive.

No huge worries here, though. Because of the transport function, network flood control systems really work quite well. Instead of dumping resources and allowing data to be lost, the transport can issue a "not ready" indicator to the sender, or source, of the flood (as shown in Figure 1.10). This mechanism works kind of like a stoplight, signaling the sending device to stop transmitting segment traffic to its overwhelmed peer. After the peer receiver processes the segments already in its memory reservoir—its buffer—it sends out a "ready" transport indicator. When the machine waiting to transmit the rest of its datagrams receives this "go" indictor, it resumes its transmission.

In fundamental, reliable, connection-oriented data transfer, datagrams are delivered to the receiving host in exactly the same sequence they're transmitted—and the transmission fails if this order is breached! If any data segments are lost, duplicated, or damaged along the way, a failure will transmit. This problem is solved by having the receiving host acknowledge that it has received each and every data segment.

A service is considered connection-oriented if it has the following characteristics:

- A virtual circuit is set up (e.g., a three-way handshake).
- It uses sequencing.
- It uses acknowledgments.
- It uses flow control.

FIGURE 1.10   Transmitting segments with flow control

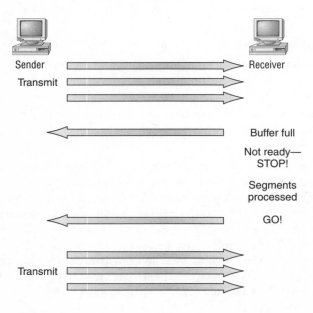

The types of flow control are buffering, windowing, and congestion avoidance.

Windowing

Ideally, data throughput happens quickly and efficiently. And as you can imagine, it would be slow if the transmitting machine had to wait for an acknowledgment after sending each segment. But because there's time available *after* the sender transmits the data segment and *before* it finishes processing acknowledgments from the receiving machine, the sender uses the break as an opportunity to transmit more data. The quantity of data segments (measured in bytes) that the transmitting machine is allowed to send without receiving an acknowledgment for them is called a *window*.

 Windows are used to control the amount of outstanding, unacknowledged data segments.

So the size of the window controls how much information is transferred from one end to the other. While some protocols quantify information by observing the number of packets, TCP/IP measures it by counting the number of bytes.

As you can see in Figure 1.11, there are two window sizes—one set to 1 and one set to 3.

FIGURE 1.11   Windowing

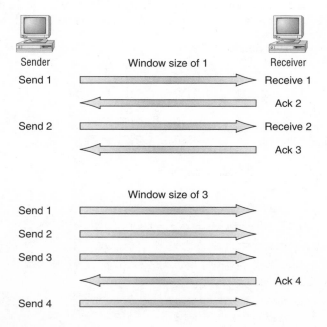

When you've configured a window size of 1, the sending machine waits for an acknowledgment for each data segment it transmits before transmitting another. If you've configured a window size of 3, it's allowed to transmit three data segments before an acknowledgment is received.

In our simplified example, both the sending and receiving machines are workstations. In reality this is not done in simple numbers but in the amount of bytes that can be sent.

 If a receiving host fails to receive all the segments that is should acknowledge, the host can improve the communication session by decreasing the window size.

Acknowledgments

Reliable data delivery ensures the integrity of a stream of data sent from one machine to the other through a fully functional data link. It guarantees that the data won't be duplicated or lost. This is achieved through something called *positive acknowledgment with retransmission*—a technique that requires a receiving machine to communicate with the transmitting source by sending an acknowledgment message back to the sender when it receives data. The sender documents each segment it sends and waits for this acknowledgment before sending the next segment. When it sends a segment, the transmitting machine starts a timer and retransmits if it expires before an acknowledgment is returned from the receiving end.

In Figure 1.12, the sending machine transmits segments 1, 2, and 3. The receiving node acknowledges it has received them by requesting segment 4. When it receives the acknowledgment, the sender then transmits segments 4, 5, and 6. If segment 5 doesn't make it to the destination, the receiving node acknowledges that event with a request for the segment to be resent. The sending machine will then resend the lost segment and wait for an acknowledgment, which it must receive in order to move on to the transmission of segment 7.

FIGURE 1.12   Transport layer reliable delivery

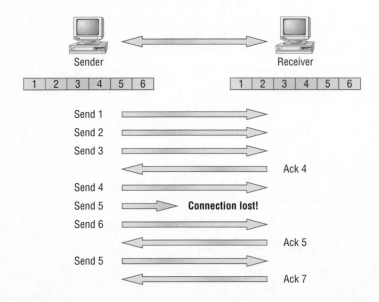

The Network Layer

The *Network layer* (also called layer 3) manages device addressing, tracks the location of devices on the network, and determines the best way to move data, which means that the Network layer must transport traffic between devices that aren't locally attached. Routers (layer 3 devices) are specified at the Network layer and provide the routing services within an internetwork.

It happens like this: First, when a packet is received on a router interface, the destination IP address is checked. If the packet isn't destined for that particular router, it will look up the destination network address in the routing table. Once the router chooses an exit interface, the packet will be sent to that interface to be framed and sent out on the local network. If the router can't find an entry for the packet's destination network in the routing table, the router drops the packet.

Two types of packets are used at the Network layer: data and route updates.

Data packets   Used to transport user data through the internetwork. Protocols used to support data traffic are called *routed protocols*; examples of routed protocols are IP and IPX. You'll learn about IP addressing in Chapter 2 and Chapter 3.

Route update packets   Used to update neighboring routers about the networks connected to all routers within the internetwork. Protocols that send route update packets are called routing protocols; examples of some common ones are RIP, EIGRP, and OSPF. Route update packets are used to help build and maintain routing tables on each router.

In Figure 1.13, I've given you an example of a routing table. The routing table used in a router includes the following information:

Network addresses   Protocol-specific network addresses. A router must maintain a routing table for individual routing protocols because each routing protocol keeps track of a network with a different addressing scheme. Think of it as a street sign in each of the different languages spoken by the residents that live on a particular street. So, if there were American, Spanish, and French folks on a street named Cat, the sign would read Cat/Gato/Chat.

FIGURE 1.13   Routing table used in a router

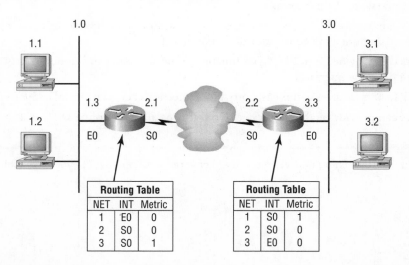

Interface   The exit interface a packet will take when destined for a specific network.

Metric   The distance to the remote network. Different routing protocols use different ways of computing this distance. I'm going to cover routing protocols in Chapter 5 and 6, but for now, know that some routing protocols use something called a *hop count* (the number of routers a packet passes through en route to a remote network), while others use bandwidth, delay of the line, or even tick count (1/18 of a second).

And as I mentioned earlier, routers break up broadcast domains, which means that by default, broadcasts aren't forwarded through a router. Do you remember why this is a good thing? Routers also break up collision domains, but you can also do that using layer 2 (Data Link layer) switches. Because each interface in a router represents a separate network, it must be assigned unique network identification numbers, and each host on the network connected to that router must use the same network number. Figure 1.14 shows how a router works in an internetwork.

FIGURE 1.14   A router in an internetwork

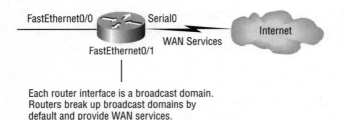

Each router interface is a broadcast domain.
Routers break up broadcast domains by
default and provide WAN services.

Here are some points about routers that you should really commit to memory:

- Routers, by default, will not forward any broadcast or multicast packets.
- Routers use the logical address in a Network layer header to determine the next hop router to forward the packet to.
- Routers can use access lists, created by an administrator, to control security on the types of packets that are allowed to enter or exit an interface.
- Routers can provide layer 2 bridging functions if needed and can simultaneously route through the same interface.
- Layer 3 devices (routers in this case) provide connections between virtual LANs (VLANs).
- Routers can provide quality of service (QoS) for specific types of network traffic.

Switching and VLANs and are covered in Chapter 7, "Layer 2 Switching."

The Data Link Layer

The *Data Link layer* provides the physical transmission of the data and handles error notification, network topology, and flow control. This means that the Data Link layer will ensure that messages are delivered to the proper device on a LAN using hardware addresses and translates messages from the Network layer into bits for the Physical layer to transmit.

The Data Link layer formats the message into pieces, each called a *data frame*, and adds a customized header containing the hardware destination and source address. This added information forms a sort of capsule that surrounds the original message in much the same way that engines, navigational devices, and other tools were attached to the lunar modules of the Apollo project. These various pieces of equipment were useful only during certain stages of space flight and were stripped off the module and discarded when their designated stage was complete. Data traveling through networks is similar.

Figure 1.15 shows the Data Link layer with the Ethernet and IEEE specifications. When you check it out, notice that the IEEE 802.2 standard is used in conjunction with and adds functionality to the other IEEE standards.

FIGURE 1.15   Data Link layer

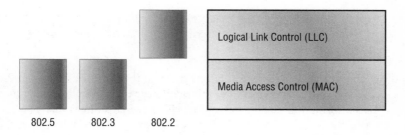

It's important for you to understand that routers, which work at the Network layer, don't care at all about where a particular host is located. They're only concerned about where networks are located and the best way to reach them—including remote ones. Routers are totally obsessive when it comes to networks. And for once, this is a good thing! It's the Data Link layer that's responsible for the actual unique identification of each device that resides on a local network.

For a host to send packets to individual hosts on a local network as well as transmitting packets between routers, the Data Link layer uses hardware addressing. Each time a packet is sent between routers, it's framed with control information at the Data Link layer, but that information is stripped off at the receiving router and only the original packet is left completely intact. This framing of the packet continues for each hop until the packet is finally delivered to the correct receiving host. It's really important to understand that the packet itself is never altered along the route; it's only encapsulated with the type of control information required for it to be properly passed on to the different media types.

The IEEE Ethernet Data Link layer has two sublayers:

Media Access Control (MAC) 802.3   Defines how packets are placed on the media. Contention media access is "first come/first served" access where everyone shares the same bandwidth—hence the name. Physical addressing is defined here, as well as logical topologies. What's a logical topology? It's the signal path through a physical topology. Line discipline, error notification (not correction), ordered delivery of frames, and optional flow control can also be used at this sublayer.

Logical Link Control (LLC) 802.2   Responsible for identifying Network layer protocols and then encapsulating them. An LLC header tells the Data Link layer what to do with a packet once a frame is received. It works like this: A host will receive a frame and look in the LLC header to find out where the packet is destined—say, the IP protocol at the Network layer. The LLC can also provide flow control and sequencing of control bits.

The switches and bridges I talked about near the beginning of the chapter both work at the Data Link layer and filter the network using hardware (MAC) addresses. We will look at these in the following section.

Switches and Bridges at the Data Link Layer

Layer 2 switching is considered hardware-based bridging because it uses specialized hardware called an *application-specific integrated circuit (ASIC)*. ASICs can run up to gigabit speeds with very low latency rates.

Latency is the time measured from when a frame enters a port to the time it exits a port.

Bridges and switches read each frame as it passes through the network. The layer 2 device then puts the source hardware address in a filter table and keeps track of which port the frame was received on. This information (logged in the bridge's or switch's filter table) is what helps the machine determine the location of the specific sending device. Figure 1.16 shows a switch in an internetwork.

The real estate business is all about location, location, location, and it's the same way for both layer 2 and layer 3 devices. Though both need to be able to negotiate the network, it's crucial to remember that they're concerned with very different parts of it. Primarily, layer 3 machines (such as routers) need to locate specific networks, whereas layer 2 machines (switches and bridges) need to eventually locate specific devices. So, networks are to routers as individual devices are to switches and bridges. And routing tables that "map" the internetwork are for routers as filter tables that "map" individual devices are for switches and bridges.

After a filter table is built on the layer 2 device, it will only forward frames to the segment where the destination hardware address is located. If the destination device is on the same segment as the frame, the layer 2 device will block the frame from going to any other segments. If the destination is on a different segment, the frame can be transmitted only to that segment. This is called *transparent bridging*.

When a switch interface receives a frame with a destination hardware address that isn't found in the device's filter table, it will forward the frame to all connected segments. If the unknown device that was sent the "mystery frame" replies to this forwarding action, the switch updates its filter table regarding that device's location. But in the event the destination address of the transmitting frame is a broadcast address, the switch will forward all broadcasts to every connected segment by default.

FIGURE 1.16   A switch in an internetwork

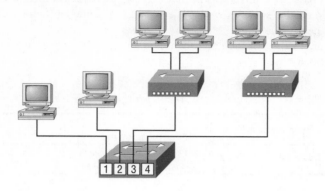

Each segment has its own collision domain.
All segments are in the same broadcast domain.

All devices that the broadcast is forwarded to are considered to be in the same broadcast domain. This can be a problem; layer 2 devices propagate layer 2 broadcast storms that choke performance, and the only way to stop a broadcast storm from propagating through an internetwork is with a layer 3 device—a router.

The biggest benefit of using switches instead of hubs in your internetwork is that each switch port is actually its own collision domain. (Conversely, a hub creates one large collision domain.) But even armed with a switch, you still can't break up broadcast domains. Neither switches nor bridges will do that. They'll typically simply forward all broadcasts instead.

Another benefit of LAN switching over hub-centered implementations is that each device on every segment plugged into a switch can transmit simultaneously—at least, they can as long as there is only one host on each port and a hub isn't plugged into a switch port. As you might have guessed, hubs allow only one device per network segment to communicate at a time.

Each network segment connected to the switch must have the same type of devices attached. What this means to you and me is that you can connect an Ethernet hub into a switch port and then connect multiple Ethernet hosts into the hub but you can't mix Token Ring hosts in with the Ethernet gang on the same segment. Mixing hosts in this manner is called *media translation*, and Cisco says you've just got to have a router around if you need to provide this service, although I have found this not to be true in reality—but remember, we're studying for the CCNA exam here, right?

Binary to Decimal and Hexadecimal Conversion

It's really important for you to truly understand the differences between binary, decimal, and hexadecimal numbers and how to convert one format into the other. So we'll start with binary numbering. It's pretty simple, really. The digits used are limited to either a 1 (one) or a 0 (zero), with each digit being called 1 bit (short for *bi*nary digi*t*). Typically, you count either 4 or 8 bits together, with these being referred to as a nibble or a byte, respectively.

What interests us in binary numbering is the value represented in a decimal format—the typical decimal format being the base-10 number scheme that we've all used since kindergarten. The binary numbers are placed in a value spot: starting at the right and moving left, with each spot having double the value of the previous spot.

Table 1.1 shows the decimal values of each bit location in a nibble and a byte. Remember, a nibble is 4 bits and a byte is 8 bits.

TABLE 1.1   Binary Values

Nibble values	Byte values
8 4 2 1	128 64 32 16 8 4 2 1

What all this means is that if a one digit (1) is placed in a value spot, then the nibble or byte takes on that decimal value and adds it to any other value spots that have a 1. And if a zero (0) is placed in a bit spot, then you don't count that value.

Let me clarify things. If we have a 1 placed in each spot of our nibble, we would then add up 8 + 4 + 2 + 1, to give us a maximum value of 15. Another example for our nibble values would be 1010, which means that the 8 bit and the 2 bit are turned on, which equals a decimal value of 10. If we have a nibble binary value of 0110, then our decimal value would be 6, because the 4 and 2 bits are turned on.

But the byte values can add up to a value that's significantly higher than 15. This is how: If we counted every bit as a one (1), then the byte binary value would look like this (remember, 8 bits equal a byte):

11111111

We would then count up every bit spot because each is turned on. It would look like this, which demonstrates the maximum value of a byte:

128 + 64 + 32 + 16 + 8 + 4 + 2 + 1 = 255

There are plenty of other decimal values that a binary number can equal. Let's work through a few examples:

10010110

Which bits are on? The 128, 16, 4, and 2 bits are on, so we'll just add them up: 128 + 16 + 4 + 2 = 150.

01101100

Which bits are on? The 64, 32, 8, and 4 bits are on, so we just need to add them up: 64 + 32 + 8 + 4 = 108.

11101000

Which bits are on? The 128, 64, 32, and 8 bits are on, so just add the values up: 128 + 64 + 32 + 8 = 232

Table 1.2 is a table you should memorize before braving the IP sections in Chapters 2 and 3.

TABLE 1.2   Binary to Decimal Memorization Chart

Binary Value	Decimal Value
10000000	128
11000000	192
11100000	224
11110000	240
11111000	248
11111100	252
11111110	254
11111111	255

Hexadecimal addressing is completely different than binary or decimal—it's converted by reading nibbles, not bytes. By using a nibble, we can convert these bits to hex pretty simply. First, understand that the hexadecimal addressing scheme uses only the numbers 0 through 9. And since the numbers 10, 11, 12, and so on can't be used (because they are two digits), the letters *A*, *B*, *C*, *D*, *E*, and *F* are used to represent 10, 11, 12, 13, 14, and 15, respectively.

Table 1.3 shows both the binary value and the decimal value for each hexadecimal digit.

TABLE 1.3   Hex to Binary to Decimal Chart

Hexadecimal Value	Binary Value	Decimal Value
0	0000	0
1	0001	1
2	0010	2
3	0011	3
4	0100	4
5	0101	5

TABLE 1.3   Hex to Binary to Decimal Chart *(continued)*

Hexadecimal Value	Binary Value	Decimal Value
6	0110	6
7	0111	7
8	1000	8
9	1001	9
A	1010	10
B	1011	11
C	1100	12
D	1101	13
E	1110	14
F	1111	15

Did you notice that the first 10 hexadecimal digits (0–9) are the same value as the decimal values? If not, look again. This handy fact makes those values super easy to convert.

So suppose you have something like this: 0x6A. (Sometimes Cisco likes to put *0x* in front of characters so you know that they are a hex value. It doesn't have any other special meaning.) What are the binary and decimal values? All you have to remember is that each hex character is one nibble and two hex characters together make a byte. To figure out the binary value, we need to put the hex characters into two nibbles and then put them together into a byte. 6 = 0110 and A (which is 10 in hex) = 0101, so the complete byte would be 01101010.

To convert from binary to hex, just take the byte and break it into nibbles. Here's what I mean.

Say you have the binary number 01010101. First, break it into nibbles—0101 and 0101—with the value of each nibble being 5 since the 1 and 4 bits are on. This makes the hex answer 55. And in decimal format, the binary number is 01101010, which converts to 64 + 32 + 8 + 2 = 106.

Here's another binary number:

11001100

Your answer would be 1100 = 12 and 1100 = 12 (therefore, it's converted to CC in hex). The decimal conversion answer would be 128 + 64 + 8 + 4 = 204.

One more example, then we need to get working on the Physical layer. Suppose you had the following binary number:

10110101

The hex answer would be 0xB5, since 1011 converts to B and 0101 converts to 5 in hex value. The decimal equivalent is 128 + 32 + 16 + 4 + 1 = 181.

The Physical Layer

Finally arriving at the bottom, we find that the *Physical layer* does two things: It sends bits and receives bits. Bits come only in values of 1 or 0—a Morse code with numerical values. The Physical layer communicates directly with the various types of actual communication media. Different kinds of media represent these bit values in different ways. Some use audio tones, while others employ *state transitions*—changes in voltage from high to low and low to high. Specific protocols are needed for each type of media to describe the proper bit patterns to be used, how data is encoded into media signals, and the various qualities of the physical media's attachment interface.

The Physical layer specifies the electrical, mechanical, procedural, and functional requirements for activating, maintaining, and deactivating a physical link between end systems. This layer is also where you identify the interface between the *data terminal equipment (DTE)* and the *data communication equipment (DCE)*. Some old-phone-company employees still call DCE data circuit-terminating equipment. The DCE is usually located at the service provider, while the DTE is the attached device. The services available to the DTE are most often accessed via a modem or *channel service unit/data service unit (CSU/DSU)*.

The Physical layer's connectors and different physical topologies are defined by the OSI as standards, allowing disparate systems to communicate. The CCNA exam is only interested in the IEEE Ethernet standards.

Hubs at the Physical Layer

A *hub* is really a multiple-port repeater. A repeater receives a digital signal and reamplifies or regenerates that signal and then forwards the digital signal out all active ports without looking at any data. An active hub does the same thing. Any digital signal received from a segment on a hub port is regenerated or reamplified and transmitted out all ports on the hub. This means all devices plugged into a hub are in the same collision domain as well as in the same broadcast domain. Figure 1.17 shows a hub in a network.

Hubs, like repeaters, don't examine any of the traffic as it enters and is then transmitted out to the other parts of the physical media. Every device connected to the hub, or hubs, must listen if a device transmits. A physical star network—where the hub is a central device and cables extend in all directions out from it—is the type of topology a hub creates. Visually, the design really does resemble a star, whereas Ethernet networks run a logical bus topology, meaning that the signal has to run from end to end of the network.

FIGURE 1.17   A hub in a network

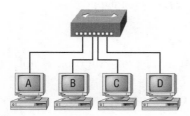

All devices in the same collision domain.
All devices in the same broadcast domain.
Devices share the same bandwidth.

Hubs and repeaters can be used to enlarge the area covered by a single LAN segment.

Ethernet Networking

Ethernet is a contention media access method that allows all hosts on a network to share the same bandwidth of a link. Ethernet is popular because it's readily scalable, meaning that it's comparatively easy to integrate new technologies, such as Fast Ethernet and Gigabit Ethernet, into an existing network infrastructure. It's also relatively simple to implement in the first place, and with it, troubleshooting is reasonably straightforward. Ethernet uses both Data Link and Physical layer specifications, and this section of the chapter will give you both the Data Link and Physical layer information you need to effectively implement, troubleshoot, and maintain an Ethernet network.

Ethernet networking uses *Carrier Sense Multiple Access with Collision Detection (CSMA/CD)*, a protocol that helps devices share the bandwidth evenly without having two devices transmit at the same time on the network medium. CSMA/CD was created to overcome the problem of those collisions that occur when packets are transmitted simultaneously from different nodes. And trust me—good collision management is crucial, because when a node transmits in a CSMA/CD network, all the other nodes on the network receive and examine that transmission. Only bridges and routers can effectively prevent a transmission from propagating throughout the entire network!

So, how does the CSMA/CD protocol work? Let's start by taking a look at Figure 1.18.

When a host wants to transmit over the network, it first checks for the presence of a digital signal on the wire. If all is clear (no other host is transmitting), the host will then proceed with its transmission. But it doesn't stop there. The transmitting host constantly monitors the wire to make sure no other hosts begin transmitting. If the host detects another signal on the wire, it sends out an extended jam signal that causes all nodes on the segment to stop sending data (think busy signal). The nodes respond to that jam signal by waiting a while before attempting to transmit again. Backoff algorithms determine when the colliding stations can retransmit. If collisions keep occurring after 15 tries, the nodes attempting to transmit will then timeout. Pretty clean!

When a collision occurs on an Ethernet LAN, the following happens:

- A jam signal informs all devices that a collision occurred.

- The collision invokes a random backoff algorithm.

- Each device on the Ethernet segment stops transmitting for a short time until the timers expire.

- All hosts have equal priority to transmit after the timers have expired.

FIGURE 1.18   CSMA/CD

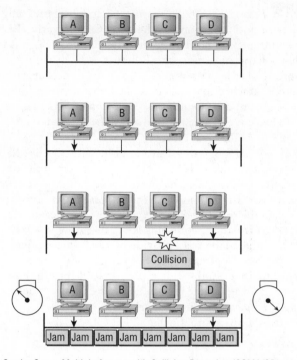

Carrier Sense Multiple Access with Collision Detection (CSMA/CD)

The following are the effects of having a CSMA/CD network sustaining heavy collisions:

- Delay
- Low throughput
- Congestion

Backoff on an 802.3 network is the retransmission delay that's enforced when a collision occurs. When a collision occurs, a host will resume transmission after the forced time delay has expired. After this backoff delay period has expired, all stations have equal priority to transmit data.

In the following sections, I am going to cover Ethernet in detail at both the Data Link layer (layer 2) and the Physical layer (layer 1).

Half- and Full-Duplex Ethernet

Half-duplex Ethernet is defined in the original 802.3 Ethernet; Cisco says it uses only one wire pair with a digital signal running in both directions on the wire. Certainly, the IEEE specifications discuss the process of half duplex somewhat differently, but what Cisco is talking about is a general sense of what is happening here with Ethernet.

It also uses the CSMA/CD protocol to help prevent collisions and to permit retransmitting if a collision does occur. If a hub is attached to a switch, it must operate in half-duplex mode because the end stations must be able to detect collisions. Half-duplex Ethernet—typically 10BaseT—is only about 30 to 40 percent efficient as Cisco sees it, because a large 10BaseT network will usually only give you 3 to 4Mbps—at most.

But full-duplex Ethernet uses two pairs of wires instead of one wire pair like half duplex. And full duplex uses a point-to-point connection between the transmitter of the transmitting device and the receiver of the receiving device. This means that with full-duplex data transfer, you get a faster data transfer compared to half duplex. And because the transmitted data is sent on a different set of wires than the received data, no collisions will occur.

The reason you don't need to worry about collisions is because now it's like a freeway with multiple lanes instead of the single-lane road provided by half duplex. Full-duplex Ethernet is supposed to offer 100 percent efficiency in both directions—for example, you can get 20Mbps with a 10Mbps Ethernet running full duplex or 200Mbps for Fast Ethernet. But this rate is something known as an aggregate rate, which translates as "you're supposed to get" 100 percent efficiency. No guarantees, in networking as in life.

Full-duplex Ethernet can be used in three situations:

- With a connection from a switch to a host
- With a connection from a switch to a switch
- With a connection from a host to a host using a crossover cable

Full-duplex Ethernet requires a point-to-point connection when only two nodes are present. You can run full-duplex with just about any device except a hub.

Now, if it's capable of all that speed, why wouldn't it deliver? Well, when a full-duplex Ethernet port is powered on, it first connects to the remote end and then negotiates with the other end of the Fast Ethernet link. This is called an *auto-detect mechanism*. This mechanism first decides on the exchange capability, which means it checks to see if it can run at 10 or 100Mbps. It then checks to see if it can run full duplex, and if it can't, it will run half duplex.

Remember that half-duplex Ethernet shares a collision domain and provides a lower effective throughput than full-duplex Ethernet, which typically has a private collision domain and a higher effective throughput.

Lastly, remember these important points:

- There are no collisions in full-duplex mode.
- A dedicated switch port is required for each full-duplex node.
- The host network card and the switch port must be capable of operating in full-duplex mode.

Now let's take a look at how Ethernet works at the Data Link layer.

Ethernet at the Data Link Layer

Ethernet at the Data Link layer is responsible for Ethernet addressing, commonly referred to as hardware addressing or MAC addressing. Ethernet is also responsible for framing packets received from the Network layer and preparing them for transmission on the local network through the Ethernet contention media access method.

Ethernet Addressing

Here's where we get into how Ethernet addressing works. It uses the *Media Access Control (MAC) address* burned into each and every Ethernet network interface card (NIC). The MAC, or hardware, address is a 48-bit (6-byte) address written in a hexadecimal format.

Figure 1.19 shows the 48-bit MAC addresses and how the bits are divided.

FIGURE 1.19   Ethernet addressing using MAC addresses

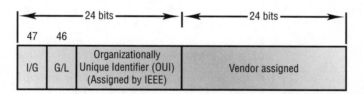

The *organizationally unique identifier (OUI)* is assigned by the IEEE to an organization. It's composed of 24 bits, or 3 bytes. The organization, in turn, assigns a globally administered address (24 bits, or 3 bytes) that is unique (supposedly, again—no guarantees) to each and every adapter it manufactures. Look closely at the figure. The high-order bit is the Individual/Group (I/G) bit. When it has a value of 0, we can assume that the address is the MAC address of a device and may well appear in the source portion of the MAC header. When it is a 1, we can assume that the address represents either a broadcast or multicast address in Ethernet or a broadcast or functional address in TR and FDDI (who really knows about FDDI?). The next bit is the G/L bit (also known as U/L, where *U* means *universal*). When set to 0, this bit represents a globally administered address (as by the IEEE). When the bit is a 1, it represents a locally governed and administered address (as in DECnet). The low-order 24 bits of an Ethernet address represent a locally administered or manufacturer-assigned code. This portion commonly starts with 24 0s for the first card made and continues in order until there are 24 1s for the last (16,777,216th) card made. You'll find that many manufacturers use these same six hex digits as the last six characters of their serial number on the same card.

Ethernet Frames

The Data Link layer is responsible for combining bits into bytes and bytes into frames. Frames are used at the Data Link layer to encapsulate packets handed down from the Network layer for transmission on a type of media access.

The function of Ethernet stations is to pass data frames between each other using a group of bits known as a MAC frame format. This provides error detection from a cyclic redundancy check (CRC). But remember—this is error detection, not error correction. The 802.3 frames and Ethernet frame are shown in Figure 1.20.

 Encapsulating a frame within a different type of frame is called *tunneling*.

FIGURE 1.20 802.3 and Ethernet frame formats

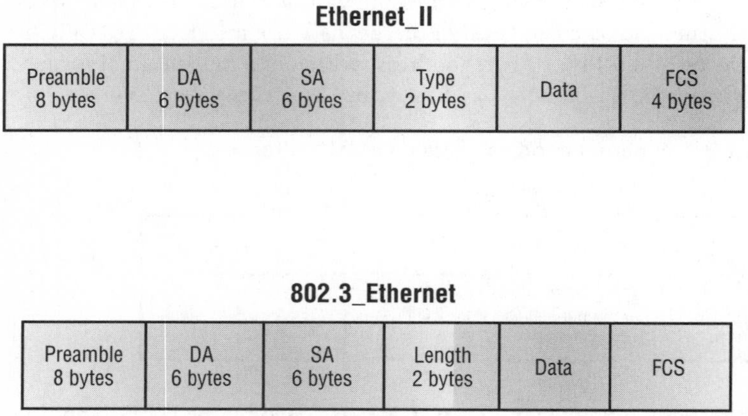

Ethernet_II

Preamble 8 bytes	DA 6 bytes	SA 6 bytes	Type 2 bytes	Data	FCS 4 bytes

802.3_Ethernet

Preamble 8 bytes	DA 6 bytes	SA 6 bytes	Length 2 bytes	Data	FCS

Following are the details of the different fields in the 802.3 and Ethernet frame types:

Preamble An alternating 1,0 pattern provides a 5MHz clock at the start of each packet, which allows the receiving devices to lock the incoming bit stream.

Start Frame Delimiter (SFD)/Synch The preamble is seven octets and the SFD is one octet (synch). The SFD is 10101011, where the last pair of 1s allows the receiver to come into the alternating 1,0 pattern somewhere in the middle and still synch up and detect the beginning of the data.

Destination Address (DA) This transmits a 48-bit value using the least significant bit (LSB) first. The DA is used by receiving stations to determine whether an incoming packet is addressed to a particular node. The destination address can be an individual address or a broadcast or multicast MAC address. Remember that a broadcast is all 1s (or *F*s in hex) and is sent to all devices but a multicast is sent only to a similar subset of nodes on a network.

Hex is short for *hexadecimal,* which is a numbering system that uses the first six letters of the alphabet (*A* through *F*) to extend beyond the available 10 digits in the decimal system. Hexadecimal has a total of 16 digits.

Source Address (SA)   The SA is a 48-bit MAC address used to identify the transmitting device, and it uses the LSB first. Broadcast and multicast address formats are illegal within the SA field.

Length or Type   802.3 uses a Length field, but the Ethernet frame uses a Type field to identify the Network layer protocol. 802.3 cannot identify the upper-layer protocol and must be used with a proprietary LAN—IPX, for example.

Data   This is a packet sent down to the Data Link layer from the Network layer. The size can vary from 64 to 1500 bytes.

Frame Check Sequence (FCS)   FCS is a field at the end of the frame that's used to store the CRC.

Let's pause here for a minute and take a look at some frames caught on our trusty Etherpeek network analyzer. You can see that the frame below has only three fields: Destination, Source, and Type (shown as Protocol Type on this analyzer):

```
Destination:   00:60:f5:00:1f:27
Source:        00:60:f5:00:1f:2c
Protocol Type: 08-00 IP
```

This is an Ethernet_II frame. Notice that the type field is IP, or 08-00 in hexadecimal.
The next frame has the same fields, so it must be an Ethernet_II frame too:

```
Destination:   ff:ff:ff:ff:ff:ff Ethernet Broadcast
Source:        02:07:01:22:de:a4
Protocol Type: 81-37 NetWare
```

I included this one so you could see that the frame can carry more than just IP—it can also carry IPX, or 81-37h. Did you notice that this frame was a broadcast? You can tell because the destination hardware address is all 1s in binary, or all *F*s in hexadecimal.
Now, pay special attention to the Length field in the next frame; this must be an 802.3 frame:

```
Flags:          0x80 802.3
Status:         0x00
Packet Length:  64
Timestamp:      12:45:45.192000 06/26/1998
Destination:    ff:ff:ff:ff:ff:ff Ethernet Broadcast
Source:         08:00:11:07:57:28
Length:         34
```

The problem with this frame is this: How do you know which protocol this packet is going to be handed to at the Network layer? It doesn't specify in the frame, so it must be IPX. Why? Because when Novell created the 802.3 frame type (before the IEEE did and called it 802.3 Raw), Novell was pretty much the only LAN server out there. So, Novell assumed that if you were running a LAN, it must be IPX, and it didn't include any Network layer protocol field information in the 802.3 frame.

Ethernet at the Physical Layer

Ethernet was first implemented by a group called DIX (Digital, Intel, and Xerox). They created and implemented the first Ethernet LAN specification, which the IEEE used to create the IEEE 802.3 Committee. This was a 10Mbps network that ran on coax and then eventually twisted-pair and fiber physical media.

The IEEE extended the 802.3 Committee to two new committees known as 802.3u (Fast Ethernet) and 802.3ab (Gigabit Ethernet on category 5) and then finally 802.3ae (10Gbps over fiber and coax).

Figure 1.21 shows the IEEE 802.3 and original Ethernet Physical layer specifications.

When designing your LAN, it's really important to understand the different types of Ethernet media available to you. Sure, it would be great to run Gigabit Ethernet to each desktop and 10Gbps between switches, and although this might happen one day, justifying the cost of that network today would be pretty difficult. But if you mix and match the different types of Ethernet media methods currently available, you can come up with a cost-effective network solution that works great.

FIGURE 1.21   Ethernet Physical layer specifications

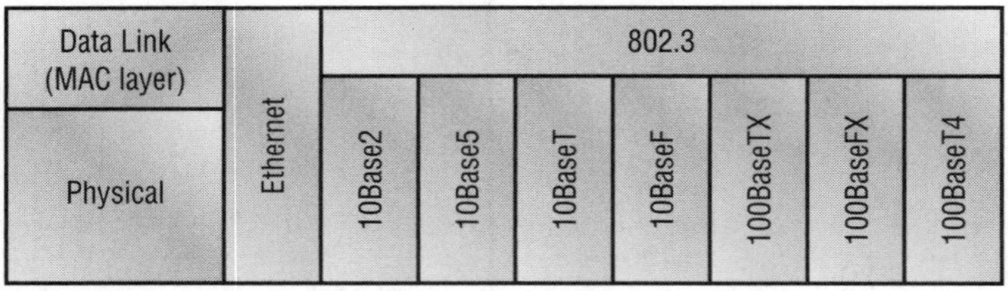

The EIA/TIA (Electronic Industries Association and the newer Telecommunications Industry Alliance) is the standards body that creates the Physical layer specifications for Ethernet. The EIA/TIA specifies that Ethernet uses a *registered jack (RJ) connector* with a 4 5 wiring sequence on *unshielded twisted-pair (UTP)* cabling (RJ-45). However, the industry is moving toward calling this just an 8-pin modular connector.

Each Ethernet cable type that is specified by the EIA/TIA has inherent attenuation, which is defined as the loss of signal strength as it travels the length of a cable and is measured in decibels (dB). The cabling used in corporate and home markets is measured in categories. A higher-quality cable will have a higher-rated category and lower attenuation. For example, category 5 is better than category 3 because category 5 cables have more wire twists per foot and therefore less crosstalk. Crosstalk is the unwanted signal interference from adjacent pairs in the cable.

Here are the original IEEE 802.3 standards:

10Base2   10Mbps, baseband technology, up to 185 meters in length. Known as *thinnet* and can support up to 30 workstations on a single segment. Uses a physical and logical bus with AUI connectors. The 10 means 10Mbps, Base means baseband technology, and the 2 means almost 200 meters. 10Base2 Ethernet cards use BNC (British Naval Connector, Bayonet Neill Concelman, or Bayonet Nut Connector) and T-connectors to connect to a network.

10Base5   10Mbps, baseband technology, up to 500 meters in length. Known as *thicknet*. Uses a physical and logical bus with AUI connectors. Up to 2,500 meters with repeaters and 1,024 users for all segments.

10BaseT   10Mbps using category 3 UTP wiring. Unlike with the 10Base2 and 10Base5 networks, each device must connect into a hub or switch, and you can have only one host per segment or wire. Uses an RJ-45 connector (8-pin modular connector) with a physical star topology and a logical bus.

The *Base* in the preceding network standards means *baseband*, which is a signaling method for communication on the network.

Each of the 802.3 standards defines an Attachment Unit Interface (AUI), which allows a one-bit-at-a-time transfer to the Physical layer from the Data Link media access method. This allows the MAC to remain constant but means the Physical layer can support any existing and new technologies. The original AUI interface was a 15-pin connector, which allowed a transceiver (transmitter/receiver) that provided a 15-pin–to–twisted-pair conversion.

The thing is, the AUI interface cannot support 100Mbps Ethernet because of the high frequencies involved. So 100BaseT needed a new interface, and the 802.3u specifications created one called the Media Independent Interface (MII), which provides 100Mbps throughput. The MII uses a *nibble*, defined as 4 bits. Gigabit Ethernet uses a Gigabit Media Independent Interface (GMII) and transmits 8 bits at a time.

802.3u (Fast Ethernet) is compatible with 802.3 Ethernet because they share the same physical characteristics. Fast Ethernet and Ethernet use the same maximum transmission unit (MTU), use the same MAC mechanisms, and preserve the frame format that is used by 10BaseT Ethernet. Basically, Fast Ethernet is just based on an extension to the IEEE 802.3 specification, except that it offers a speed increase of 10 times that of 10BaseT.

Here are the expanded IEEE Ethernet 802.3 standards:

100BaseTX (IEEE 802.3u)   EIA/TIA category 5, 6, or 7 UTP two-pair wiring. One user per segment; up to 100 meters long. It uses an RJ-45 connector with a physical star topology and a logical bus.

100BaseFX (IEEE 802.3u)   Uses fiber cabling 62.5/125-micron multimode fiber. Point-to-point topology; up to 412 meters long. It uses an ST or SC connector, which are media-interface connectors.

1000BaseCX (IEEE 802.3z)   Copper twisted-pair called twinax (a balanced coaxial pair) that can only run up to 25 meters.

1000BaseT (IEEE 802.3ab)   Category 5, four-pair UTP wiring up to 100 meters long.

1000BaseSX (IEEE 802.3z)   MMF using 62.5- and 50-micron core; uses a 850nano-meter laser and can go up to 220 meters with 62.5-micron, 550 meters with 50-micron.

1000BaseLX (IEEE 802.3z)   Single-mode fiber that uses a 9-micron core and 1300 nano-meter laser and can go from 3 kilometers up to 10 kilometers.

If you want to implement a network medium that is not susceptible to EMI, fiber-optic cable provides a more secure, long-distance cable that is not susceptible to EMI interference at high speeds.

Ethernet Cabling

Ethernet cabling is an important discussion, especially if you are planning on taking the Cisco exams. Three types of Ethernet cables are available:

- Straight-through cable
- Crossover cable
- Rolled cable

We will look at each in the following sections.

Straight-Through Cable

The *straight-through cable* is used to connect

- Host to switch or hub
- Router to switch or hub

Four wires are used in straight-through cable to connect Ethernet devices. It is relatively simple to create this type; Figure 1.22 shows the four wires used in a straight-through Ethernet cable.

FIGURE 1.22   Straight-through Ethernet cable

```
Hub/Switch                                Host

      1  ←————————————————→  1
      2  ←————————————————→  2
      3  ←————————————————→  3
      6  ←————————————————→  6
```

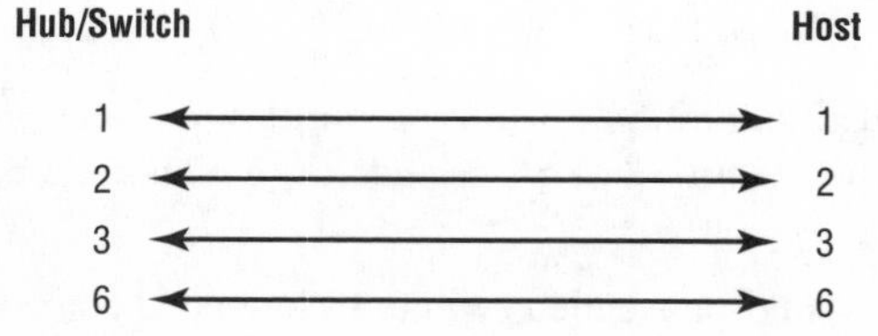

Notice that only pins 1, 2, 3, and 6 are used. Just connect 1 to 1, 2 to 2, 3 to 3, and 6 to 6 and you'll be up and networking in no time. However, remember that this would be an Ethernet-only cable and wouldn't work with Voice, Token Ring, ISDN, and so on.

Crossover Cable

The *crossover cable* can be used to connect

- Switch to switch
- Hub to hub
- Host to host
- Hub to switch
- Router direct to host

The same four wires are used in this cable as in the straight-through cable; we just connect different pins together. Figure 1.23 shows how the four wires are used in a crossover Ethernet cable.

Notice that instead of connecting 1 to 1, 2 to 3, and so on, here we connect pins 1 to 3 and 2 to 6 on each side of the cable.

FIGURE 1.23   Crossover Ethernet cable

Rolled Cable

Although *rolled cable* isn't used to connect any Ethernet connections together, you can use a rolled Ethernet cable to connect a host to a router console serial communication (com) port.

If you have a Cisco router or switch, you would use this cable to connect your PC running HyperTerminal to the Cisco hardware. Eight wires are used in this cable to connect serial devices, although not all eight are used to send information, just as in Ethernet networking. Figure 1.24 shows the eight wires used in a rolled cable.

These are probably the easiest cables to make because you just cut the end off on one side of a straight-through cable, turn it over and put it back on (with a new connector, of course).

FIGURE 1.24 Rolled Ethernet cable

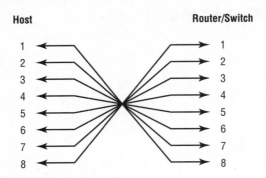

Once you have the correct cable connected from your PC to the Cisco router or switch, you can start HyperTerminal to create a console connection and configure the device. Set the configuration as follows:

1. Open HyperTerminal and enter a name for the connection. It is irrelevant what you name it, but I always just use Cisco. Then click OK.

2. Choose the communications port—either COM1 or COM2, whichever is open on your PC.

3. Now set the port settings. The default values (2400bps and no flow control hardware) will not work; you must set the port settings as shown in Figure 1.25.

Notice that the bit rate is now set to 9600 and the flow control is set to none. At this point, you can click OK and press the Enter key, and you should be connected to your Cisco device console port.

We've taken a look a look at the various RJ45 unshielded twisted pair (UTP) cables. Keeping this in mind, what cable is used between the switches in Figure 1.26?

FIGURE 1.25   Port settings for a rolled cable connection

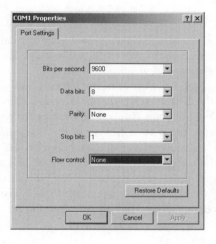

FIGURE 1.26   RJ45 UTP cable question #1

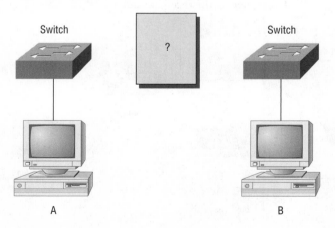

In order for host A to ping host B, you need a crossover cable to connect the two switches together. But what types of cables are used in the network shown in Figure 1.27?

In Figure 1.27 there's a variety of cables in use. For the connection between the switches, we'd obviously use a crossover cable like we saw in Figure 1.23. The trouble is, we have a console connection that uses a rolled cable. Plus, the connection from the router to the switch is a straight-through cable, as is also true for the hosts to the switches. Keep in mind that if we had a serial connection (which we don't), it would be a V.35 that we'd use to connect us to a WAN.

Data Encapsulation

When a host transmits data across a network to another device, the data goes through *encapsulation*: it is wrapped with protocol information at each layer of the OSI model. Each layer communicates only with its peer layer on the receiving device.

To communicate and exchange information, each layer uses *Protocol Data Units (PDUs)*. These hold the control information attached to the data at each layer of the model. They are usually attached to the header in front of the data field but can also be in the trailer, or end, of it.

Each PDU is attached to the data by encapsulating it at each layer of the OSI model, and each has a specific name depending on the information provided in each header. This PDU information is read only by the peer layer on the receiving device. After it's read, it's stripped off, and the data is then handed to the next layer up.

Figure 1.28 shows the PDUs and how they attach control information to each layer. This figure demonstrates how the upper-layer user data is converted for transmission on the network. The data stream is then handed down to the Transport layer, which sets up a virtual circuit to the receiving device by sending over a synch packet. Next, the data stream is broken up into smaller pieces, and a Transport layer header (a PDU) is created and attached to the header of the data field; now the piece of data is called a segment. Each segment is sequenced so the data stream can be put back together on the receiving side exactly as it was transmitted.

FIGURE 1.27   RJ45 UTP cable question #2

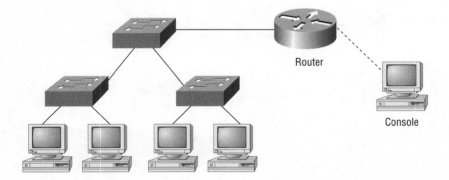

FIGURE 1.28   Data encapsulation

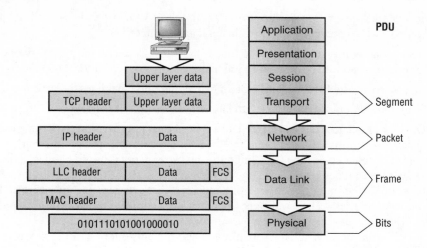

Each segment is then handed to the Network layer for network addressing and routing through the internetwork. Logical addressing (for example, IP) is used to get each segment to the correct network. The Network layer protocol adds a control header to the segment handed down from the Transport layer, and what we have now is called a *packet* or *datagram*. Remember that the Transport and Network layers work together to rebuild a data stream on a receiving host, but it's not part of their work to place their PDUs on a local network segment—which is the only way to get the information to a router or host.

It's the Data Link layer that's responsible for taking packets from the Network layer and placing them on the network medium (cable or wireless). The Data Link layer encapsulates each packet in a *frame*, and the frame's header carries the hardware address of the source and destination hosts. If the destination device is on a remote network, then the frame is sent to a router to be routed through an internetwork. Once it gets to the destination network, a new frame is used to get the packet to the destination host.

To put this frame on the network, it must first be put into a digital signal. Since a frame is really a logical group of 1s and 0s, the Physical layer is responsible for encoding these digits into a digital signal, which is read by devices on the same local network. The receiving devices will synchronize on the digital signal and extract (decode) the 1s and 0s from the digital signal. At this point the devices build the frames, run a CRC, and then check their answer against the answer in the frame's FCS field. If it matches, the packet is pulled from the frame and what's left of the frame is discarded. This process is called *de-encapsulation*. The packet is handed to the Network layer, where the address is checked. If the address matches, the segment is pulled from the packet and what's left of the packet is discarded. The segment is processed at the Transport layer, which rebuilds the data stream and acknowledges to the transmitting station that it received each piece. It then happily hands the data stream to the upper-layer application.

At a transmitting device, the data encapsulation method works like this:

1. User information is converted to data for transmission on the network.

2. Data is converted to segments and a reliable connection is set up between the transmitting and receiving hosts.

3. Segments are converted to packets or datagrams, and a logical address is placed in the header so each packet can be routed through an internetwork.

4. Packets or datagrams are converted to frames for transmission on the local network. Hardware (Ethernet) addresses are used to uniquely identify hosts on a local network segment.

5. Frames are converted to bits, and a digital encoding and clocking scheme is used.

6. To explain this in more detail using the layer addressing, I'll use Figure 1.29.

Remember that a data stream is handed down from the upper layer to the Transport layer. As technicians, we really don't care who the data stream comes from because that's really a programmer's problem. Our job is to rebuild the data stream reliably and hand it to the upper layers on the receiving device.

Before we go further in our discussion of Figure 1.30, let's discuss port numbers and make sure we understand them. The Transport layer uses port numbers to define both the virtual circuit and the upper-layer process, as you can see from Figure 1.30.

The Transport layer takes the data stream, makes segments out of it, and establishes a reliable session by creating a virtual circuit. It then sequences (numbers) each segment and uses acknowledgments and flow control. If you're using TCP, the virtual circuit is defined by the source port number. Remember, the host just makes this up starting at port number 1024 (0 through 1023 are reserved for well-known port numbers). The destination port number defines the upper-layer process (application) that the data stream is handed to when the data stream is reliably rebuilt on the receiving host.

FIGURE 1.29   PDU and layer addressing

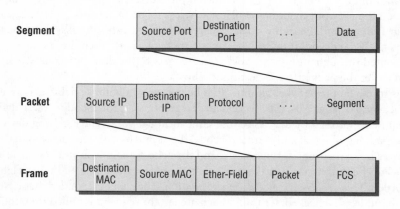

FIGURE 1.30   Port numbers at the Transport layer

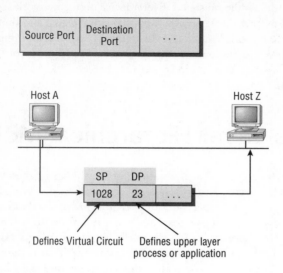

Now that we understand port numbers and how they are used at the Transport layer, let's go back to Figure 1.30. Once the Transport layer header information is added to the piece of data, it becomes a segment and is handed down to the Network layer along with the destination IP address. (The destination IP address was handed down from the upper layers to the Transport layer with the data stream, and it was discovered through a name resolution method at the upper layers—probably DNS.)

The Network layer adds a header, and adds the logical addressing (IP addresses), to the front of each segment. Once the header is added to the segment, the PDU is called a packet. The packet has a protocol field that describes where the segment came from (either UDP or TCP), so it can hand the segment to the correct protocol at the Transport layer when it reaches the receiving host.

The Network layer is responsible for finding the destination hardware address that dictates where the packet should be sent on the local network. It does this by using the Address Resolution Protocol (ARP)—something I'll talk about more in Chapter 2. IP at the Network layer looks at the destination IP address and compares that address to its own source IP address and subnet mask. If it turns out a local network request, the hardware address of the local host is requested via an ARP request. If the packet is destined for a remote host, IP will look for the IP address of the default gateway (router) instead.

The packet, along with the destination hardware address of either the local host or default gateway, is then handed down to the Data Link layer. The Data Link layer will add a header to the front of the packet and the piece of data then becomes a frame. (We call it a frame because both a header and a trailer are added to the packet, which makes the data resemble bookends or a frame, if you will.) This is shown in Figure 1.29. The frame uses an Ether-Type field to describe which protocol the packet came from at the Network layer. Now a cyclic redundancy check (CRC) is run on the frame, and the answer to the CRC is placed in the Frame Check Sequence field found in the trailer of the frame.

The frame is now ready to be handed down, one bit at a time, to the Physical layer, which will use bit timing rules to encode the data in a digital signal. Every device on the network segment will synchronize with the clock and extract the 1s and 0s from the digital signal and build a frame. After the frame is rebuilt, a CRC is run to make sure the frame is okay. If everything turns out to be all good, the hosts will check the destination address to see if the frame is for them.

If all this is making your eyes cross and your brain freeze, don't freak. I'll be going over exactly how data is encapsulated and routed through an internetwork in Chapter 5.

The Cisco Three-Layer Hierarchical Model

Most of us were exposed to hierarchy early in life. Anyone with older siblings learned what it was like to be at the bottom of the hierarchy. Regardless of where you first discovered hierarchy, today most of us experience it in many aspects of our lives. It is *hierarchy* that helps us understand where things belong, how things fit together, and what functions go where. It brings order and understandability to otherwise complex models. If you want a pay raise, for instance, hierarchy dictates that you ask your boss, not your subordinate. That is the person whose role it is to grant (or deny) your request. So basically, understanding hierarchy helps us discern where we should go to get what we need.

Hierarchy has many of the same benefits in network design that it does in other areas of life. When used properly, it makes networks more predictable. It helps us define which areas should perform certain functions. Likewise, you can use tools such as access lists at certain levels in hierarchical networks and avoid them at others.

Let's face it: Large networks can be extremely complicated, with multiple protocols, detailed configurations, and diverse technologies. Hierarchy helps us summarize a complex collection of details into an understandable model. Then, as specific configurations are needed, the model dictates the appropriate manner to apply them.

The Cisco hierarchical model can help you design, implement, and maintain a scalable, reliable, cost-effective hierarchical internetwork. Cisco defines three layers of hierarchy, as shown in Figure 1.31, each with specific functions.

The following are the three layers and their typical functions:

- The core layer: backbone
- The distribution layer: routing
- The access layer: switching

Each layer has specific responsibilities. Remember, however, that the three layers are logical and are not necessarily physical devices. Consider the OSI model, another logical hierarchy. The seven layers describe functions but not necessarily protocols, right? Sometimes a protocol maps to more than one layer of the OSI model, and sometimes multiple protocols communicate within a single layer. In the same way, when we build physical implementations of hierarchical networks, we may have many devices in a single layer, or we might have a single device performing functions at two layers. The definition of the layers is logical, not physical.

Now, let's take a closer look at each of the layers.

FIGURE 1.31   The Cisco hierarchical model

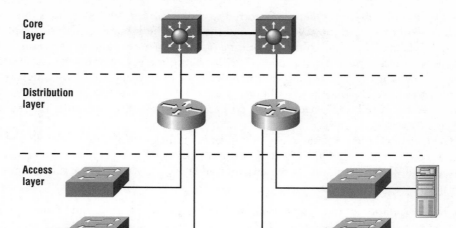

The Core Layer

The *core layer* is literally the core of the network. At the top of the hierarchy, the core layer is responsible for transporting large amounts of traffic both reliably and quickly. The only purpose of the network's core layer is to switch traffic as fast as possible. The traffic transported across the core is common to a majority of users. However, remember that user data is processed at the distribution layer, which forwards the requests to the core if needed.

If there is a failure in the core, *every single user* can be affected. Therefore, fault tolerance at this layer is an issue. The core is likely to see large volumes of traffic, so speed and latency are driving concerns here. Given the function of the core, we can now consider some design specifics. Let's start with some things we don't want to do:

- Don't do anything to slow down traffic. This includes using access lists, routing between virtual local area networks (VLANs), and packet filtering.

- Don't support workgroup access here.

- Avoid expanding the core (i.e., adding routers) when the internetwork grows. If performance becomes an issue in the core, give preference to upgrades over expansion.

Now, there are a few things that we want to do as we design the core. They include the following:

- Design the core for high reliability. Consider data-link technologies that facilitate both speed and redundancy, such as FDDI, Fast Ethernet (with redundant links), or even ATM.

- Design with speed in mind. The core should have very little latency.

- Select routing protocols with lower convergence times. Fast and redundant data-link connectivity is no help if your routing tables are shot!

The Distribution Layer

The *distribution layer* is sometimes referred to as the *workgroup layer* and is the communication point between the access layer and the core. The primary functions of the distribution layer are to provide routing, filtering, and WAN access and to determine how packets can access the core, if needed. The distribution layer must determine the fastest way that network service requests are handled—for example, how a file request is forwarded to a server. After the distribution layer determines the best path, it forwards the request to the core layer if needed. The core layer then quickly transports the request to the correct service.

The distribution layer is the place to implement policies for the network. Here you can exercise considerable flexibility in defining network operation. There are several actions that generally should be done at the distribution layer. They include the following:

- Routing
- Implementation of tools (such as access lists), of packet filtering, and of queuing
- Implementation of security and network policies, including address translation and firewalls
- Redistribution between routing protocols, including static routing
- Routing between VLANs and other workgroup support functions
- Definitions of broadcast and multicast domains

Things to avoid at the distribution layer are limited to those functions that exclusively belong to one of the other layers.

The Access Layer

The *access layer* controls user and workgroup access to internetwork resources. The access layer is sometimes referred to as the *desktop layer*. The network resources most users need will be available locally. The distribution layer handles any traffic for remote services. The following are some of the functions to be included at the access layer:

- Continued (from distribution layer) access control and policies
- Creation of separate collision domains (segmentation)
- Workgroup connectivity into the distribution layer

Technologies such as DDR and Ethernet switching are frequently seen in the access layer. Static routing (instead of dynamic routing protocols) is seen here as well.

As already noted, three separate levels does not imply three separate routers. There could be fewer, or there could be more. Remember, this is a *layered* approach.

Summary

Whew! I know this seemed like the chapter that wouldn't end, but it did—and you made it through! You're now armed with a ton of fundamental information; you're ready to build upon it and are well on your way to certification.

We started by discussing simple, basic networking and the differences between collision and broadcast domains. I also discussed the various devices used in an internetwork.

We then discussed the OSI model—the seven-layer model used to help application developers design applications that can run on any type of system or network. Each layer has its special jobs and select responsibilities within the model to ensure that solid, effective communications do, in fact, occur. I provided you with complete details of each layer and discussed how Cisco views the specifications of the OSI model.

In addition, each layer in the OSI model specifies different types of devices. I described the different devices, cables, and connectors used at each layer. Remember that hubs are Physical layer devices and repeat the digital signal to all segments except the one it was received from. Switches segment the network using hardware addresses and break up collision domains. Routers break up broadcast domains (and collision domains) and use logical addressing to send packets through an internetwork.

Last, this chapter covered the Cisco three-layer hierarchical model. I described in detail the three layers and how each is used to help design and implement a Cisco internetwork. We are now going to move on to IP addressing in the next chapter.

Exam Essentials

Remember the possible causes of LAN traffic congestion.   Too many hosts in a broadcast domain, broadcast storms, multicasting, and low bandwidth are all possible causes of LAN traffic congestion.

Understand the difference between a collision domain and a broadcast domain.   *Collision domain* is an Ethernet term used to describe a network collection of devices in which one particular device sends a packet on a network segment, forcing every other device on that same segment to pay attention to it. A broadcast domain is where a set of all devices on a network segment hear all broadcasts sent on that segment.

Understand the difference between a hub, a bridge, a switch, and a router.   Hubs create one collision domain and one broadcast domain. Bridges break up collision domains but create one large broadcast domain. They use hardware addresses to filter the network. Switches are really just multiple port bridges with more intelligence. They break up collision domains but create one large broadcast domain by default. Switches use hardware addresses to filter the network. Routers break up broadcast domains (and collision domains) and use logical addressing to filter the network.

Remember the difference between connection-oriented and connectionless network services. Connection-oriented services use acknowledgments and flow control to create a reliable session. More overhead is used than in a connectionless network service. Connectionless services are used to send data with no acknowledgments or flow control. This is considered unreliable.

Remember the OSI layers.   You must remember the seven layers of the OSI model and what function each layer provides. The Application, Presentation, and Session layers are upper layers and are responsible for communicating from a user interface to an application. The Transport layer provides segmentation, sequencing, and virtual circuits. The Network layer provides logical network addressing and routing through an internetwork. The Data Link layer provides framing and placing of data on the network medium. The Physical layer is responsible for taking 1s and 0s and encoding them into a digital signal for transmission on the network segment.

Remember the types of Ethernet cabling and when you would use them.   The three types of cables that can be created from an Ethernet cable are straight-through (to connect a PC's or a router's Ethernet interface to a hub or switch), crossover (to connect hub to hub, hub to switch, switch to switch, or PC to PC), and rolled (for a console connection from a PC to a router or switch).

Understand how to connect a console cable from a PC to a router and start HyperTerminal. Take a rolled cable and connect it from the COM port of the host to the console port of a router. Start HyperTerminal and set the BPS to 9600 and flow control to None.

Remember the three layers in the Cisco three-layer model.   The three layers in the Cisco hierarchical model are the core, distribution, and access layers.

Written Lab 1

In this section, you'll complete the following labs to make sure you've got the information and concepts contained within them fully dialed in:

- Lab 1.1: OSI Questions
- Lab 1.2: Defining the OSI Layers and Devices
- Lab 1.3: Identifying Collision and Broadcast Domains

Written Lab 1.1: OSI Questions

Answer the following questions about the OSI model:

1. Which layer chooses and determines the availability of communicating partners, along with the resources necessary to make the connection; coordinates partnering applications; and forms a consensus on procedures for controlling data integrity and error recovery?

2. Which layer is responsible for converting data packets from the Data Link layer into electrical signals?

3. At which layer is routing implemented, enabling connections and path selection between two end systems?

4. Which layer defines how data is formatted, presented, encoded, and converted for use on the network?

5. Which layer is responsible for creating, managing, and terminating sessions between applications?

6. Which layer ensures the trustworthy transmission of data across a physical link and is primarily concerned with physical addressing, line discipline, network topology, error notification, ordered delivery of frames, and flow control?

7. Which layer is used for reliable communication between end nodes over the network and provides mechanisms for establishing, maintaining, and terminating virtual circuits; transport-fault detection and recovery; and controlling the flow of information?

8. Which layer provides logical addressing that routers will use for path determination?

9. Which layer specifies voltage, wire speed, and pinout cables and moves bits between devices?

10. Which layer combines bits into bytes and bytes into frames, uses MAC addressing, and provides error detection?

11. Which layer is responsible for keeping the data from different applications separate on the network?

12. Which layer is represented by frames?

13. Which layer is represented by segments?

14. Which layer is represented by packets?

15. Which layer is represented by bits?

16. Put the following in order of encapsulation:

- Packets
- Frames
- Bits
- Segments

17. Which layer segments and reassembles data into a data stream?

18. Which layer provides the physical transmission of the data and handles error notification, network topology, and flow control?

19. Which layer manages device addressing, tracks the location of devices on the network, and determines the best way to move data?

20. What is the bit length and expression form of a MAC address?

Written Lab 1.2: Defining the OSI Layers and Devices

Fill in the blanks with the appropriate layer of the OSI or hub, switch, or router device.

Description   **Device or OSI Layer**

This device sends and receives information about the Network layer.

This layer creates a virtual circuit before transmitting between two end stations.

This layer uses service access points.

This device uses hardware addresses to filter a network.

Ethernet is defined at these layers.

This layer supports flow control and sequencing.

This device can measure the distance to a remote network.

Logical addressing is used at this layer.

Hardware addresses are defined at this layer.

This device creates one big collision domain and one large broadcast domain.

This device creates many smaller collision domains, but the network is still one large broadcast domain.

This device can never run full duplex.

This device breaks up collision domains and broadcast domains.

Written Lab 1.3: Identifying Collision and Broadcast Domains

In the following exhibit, identify the number of collision domains and broadcast domains in each specified device. Each device is represented by a letter:

1. Hub
2. Bridge
3. Switch

4. Router

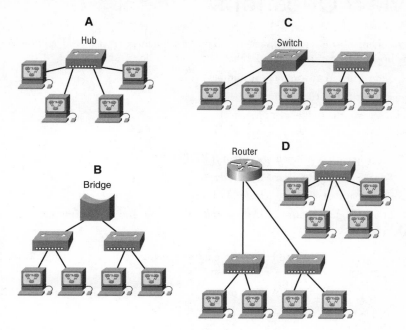

(The answers to the written labs can be found following the answers to the review questions for this chapter.)

Review Questions

1. A receiving host has failed to receive all of the segments that it should acknowledge. What can the host do to improve the reliability of this communication session?

    A. Send a different source port number.

    B. Restart the virtual circuit.

    C. Decrease the sequence number.

    D. Decrease the window size.

2. Which fields are contained within an IEEE Ethernet frame header? (Choose two.)

    A. Source and destination MAC address

    B. Source and destination network address

    C. Source and destination MAC address and source and destination network address

    D. FCS field

3. Which layer 1 devices can be used to enlarge the area covered by a single LAN segment? (Choose two.)

    A. Switch

    B. NIC

    C. Hub

    D. Repeater

    E. RJ-45 transceiver

4. Segmentation of a data stream happens at which layer of the OSI model?

    A. Physical

    B. Data Link

    C. Network

    D. Transport

5. Which of the following describe router functions? (Choose four.)

    A. Packet switching

    B. Collision prevention

    C. Packet filtering

    D. Broadcast domain enlargement

    E. Internetwork communication

    F. Broadcast forwarding

    G. Path selection

6. Routers operate at layer __. LAN Switches operates at layer __. Ethernet hubs operate at layer __. Word processing operates at layer __.

   A. 3, 3, 1, 7

   B. 3, 2, 1, none

   C. 3, 2, 1, 7

   D. 2, 3, 1, 7

   E. 3, 3, 2, none

7. When data is encapsulated, which is the correct order?

   A. Data, frame, packet, segment, bit

   B. Segment, data, packet, frame, bit

   C. Data, segment, packet, frame, bit

   D. Data, segment, frame, packet, bit

8. Why does the data communication industry use the layered OSI reference model? (Choose two.)

   A. It divides the network communication process into smaller and simpler components, thus aiding component development, design, and troubleshooting.

   B. It enables equipment from different vendors to use the same electronic components, thus saving research and development funds.

   C. It supports the evolution of multiple competing standards, and thus provides business opportunities for equipment manufacturers.

   D. It encourages industry standardization by defining what functions occur at each layer of the model.

   E. It provides a framework by which changes in functionality in one layer require changes in other layers.

9. What are two purposes for segmentation with a bridge?

   A. Add more broadcast domains.

   B. Create more collision domains.

   C. Add more bandwidth for users.

   D. Allow more broadcasts for users.

   E. Reduce collisions within a broadcast domain.

   F. Increase the number of collision domains.

10. Which of the following are unique characteristics of half-duplex Ethernet when compared to full-duplex Ethernet? (Choose two.)

   A. Half-duplex Ethernet operates in a shared collision domain.

   B. Half-duplex Ethernet operates in a private collision domain.

   C. Half-duplex Ethernet has higher effective throughput.

   D. Half-duplex Ethernet has lower effective throughput.

   E. Half-duplex Ethernet operates in a private broadcast domain.

11. You want to implement a network medium that is not susceptible to EMI. Which type of cabling should you use?

   A. Thicknet coax

   B. Thinnet coax

   C. Category 5 UTP cable

   D. Fiber-optic cable

12. Acknowledgments, sequencing, and flow control are characteristic of which OSI layer?

   A. Layer 2

   B. Layer 3

   C. Layer 4

   D. Layer 7

13. Which of the following are types of flow control? (Choose all that apply.)

   A. Buffering

   B. Cut-through

   C. Windowing

   D. Congestion avoidance

   E. VLANs

14. Which of the following types of connections can use full duplex? (Choose three.)

   A. Hub to hub

   B. Switch to switch

   C. Host to host

   D. Switch to hub

   E. Switch to host

15. What is the purpose of flow control?

   A. To ensure data is retransmitted if an acknowledgment is not received

   B. To reassemble segments in the correct order at the destination device

   C. To provide a means for the receiver to govern the amount of data sent by the sender

   D. To regulate the size of each segment

16. Which three statements are true about the operation of a full-duplex Ethernet network?

   A. There are no collisions in full-duplex mode.

   B. A dedicated switch port is required for each full-duplex node.

   C. Ethernet hub ports are preconfigured for full-duplex mode.

   D. In a full-duplex environment, the host network card must check for the availability of the network media before transmitting.

   E. The host network card and the switch port must be capable of operating in full-duplex mode.

17. What type of RJ45 UTP cable is used between switches?

  A. Straight-through

  B. Crossover cable

  C. Crossover with a CSU/DSU

  D. Crossover with a router in between the two switches

18. How does a host on an Ethernet LAN know when to transmit after a collision has occurred?

  A. In a CSMA/CD collision domain, multiple stations can successfully transmit data simultaneously.

  B. In a CSMA/CD collision domain, stations must wait until the media is not in use before transmitting.

  C. You can improve the CSMA/CD network by adding more hubs.

  D. After a collision, the station that detected the collision has first priority to resend the lost data.

  E. After a collision, all stations run a random backoff algorithm. When the backoff delay period has expired, all stations have equal priority to transmit data.

  F. After a collision, all stations involved run an identical backoff algorithm and then synchronize with each other prior to transmitting data.

19. What type of RJ45 UTP cable do you use to connect a PC's COM port to a router or switch console port?

  A. Straight-through

  B. Crossover cable

  C. Crossover with a CSU/DSU

  D. Rolled

20. You have the following binary number:

  10110111

  What is the decimal and hexadecimal equivalent?

  A. 69/0x2102

  B. 183/B7

  C. 173/A6

  D. 83/0xC5

Answers to Review Questions

1. D. A receiving host can control the transmitter by using flow control (TCP uses Windowing by default). By decreasing the window size, the receiving host can slow down the transmitting host so the receiving host does not overflow its buffers.

2. A, D. An Ethernet frame has source and destination MAC addresses, an Ether-Type field to identify the Network layer protocol, the data, and the FCS field that holds the answer to the CRC.

3. C, D. Not that you really want to enlarge a single collision domain, but a hub (multiport repeater) will provide this for you.

4. D. The Transport layer receives large data streams from the upper layers and breaks these up into smaller pieces called segments.

5. A, C, E, G. Routers provide packet switching, packet filtering, internetwork communication, and path selection.

6. B. Routers operate at layer 3. LAN switches operates at layer 2. Ethernet hubs operate at layer 1. Word processing applications communicate to the Application layer interface, but do not operate at layer 7, so the answer would be none.

7. C. The encapsulation method is data, segment, packet, frame, bit.

8. A, D. The main advantage of a layered model is that it can allow application developers to change aspects of a program in just one layer of the layer model's specifications. Advantages of using the OSI layered model include, but are not limited to, the following: It divides the network communication process into smaller and simpler components, thus aiding component development, design, and troubleshooting; allows multiple-vendor development through standardization of network components; encourages industry standardization by defining what functions occur at each layer of the model; allows various types of network hardware and software to communicate; and prevents changes in one layer from affecting other layers, so it does not hamper development.

9. B, C. Bridges break up collision domains, which allow more bandwidth for users.

10. A, D. Unlike full duplex, half-duplex Ethernet operates in a shared collision domain, and it has a lower effective throughput than full duplex.

11. D. Fiber-optic cable provides a more secure, long-distance cable that is not susceptible to EMI interference at high speeds.

12. C. A reliable Transport layer connection uses acknowledgments to make sure all data is transmitted and received reliably. A reliable connection is defined by a virtual circuit that uses acknowledgments, sequencing, and flow control, which are characteristics of the Transport layer (layer 4).

13. A, C, D. The common types of flow control are buffering, windowing, and congestion avoidance.

14. B, C, E. Hubs cannot run full-duplex Ethernet. Full duplex must be used on a point-to-point connection between two devices capable of running full duplex. Switches and hosts can run full duplex between each other, but a hub can never run full duplex.

15. C. Flow control allows the receiving device to control the transmitter so the receiving devices buffer does not overflow.

16. A, B, E. Full-duplex means you are using both wire pairs simultaneously to send and receive data. You must have a dedicated switch port for each node, which means you will not have collisions. Both the host network card and the switch port must be capable and set to work in full-duplex mode.

17. B. To connect two switches together, you would use a RJ45 UTP crossover cable.

18. B, E. Once transmitting stations on an Ethernet segment hear a collision, they send an extended jam signal to ensure that all stations recognize the collision. After the jamming is complete, each sender waits a predetermined amount of time, plus a random time. After both timers expire, they are free to transmit, but the must make sure the media is clear before transmitting and that they all have equal priority.

19. D. To connect to a router or switch console port, you would use a RJ45 UTP rolled cable.

20. B. You must be able to take a binary number and convert it into both decimal and hexadecimal. To convert to decimal, just add up the 1s using their value. The values that are turned on with the binary number of 10110111 are 128 + 32 + 16 + 4 + 2 + 1 = 183. To get the hexadecimal equivalent, you need to break the eight binary digits into nibble (four bits). 1011 and 0111. By adding up these values, you get 11 and 7. In hexadecimal, 11 is *B*, so the answer is 0xB7.

Answers to Written Lab 1

1. The Application layer is responsible for finding the network resources broadcast from a server and adding flow control and error control (if the application developer chooses).

2. The Physical layer takes frames from the Data Link layer and encodes the 1s and 0s into a digital signal for transmission on the network medium.

3. The Network layer provides routing through an internetwork and logical addressing.

4. The Presentation layer makes sure that data is in a readable format for the Application layer.

5. The Session layer sets up, maintains, and terminates sessions between applications.

6. PDUs at the Data Link layer are called frames. As soon as you see *frame* in a question, you know the answer.

7. The Transport layer uses virtual circuits to create a reliable connection between two hosts.

8. The Network layer provides logical addressing, typically IP addressing and routing.

9. The Physical layer is responsible for the electrical and mechanical connections between devices.

10. The Data Link layer is responsible for the framing of data packets.

11. The Session layer creates sessions between different hosts' applications.

12. The Data Link layer frames packets received from the network layer.

13. The Transport layer segments user data.

14. The Network layer creates packets out of segments handed down from the Transport layer.

15. The Physical layer is responsible for transporting 1s and 0s in a digital signal.

16. Segments, packets, frames, bits

17. Transport

18. Data Link

19. Network

20. 48 bits (6 bytes) expressed as a hexadecimal number

Answer to Written Lab 1.2

Description	Device or OSI Layer
This device sends and receives information about the Network layer.	Router
This layer creates a virtual circuit before transmitting between two end stations.	Transport
This layer uses service access points.	Data Link (LLC sublayer)
This device uses hardware addresses to filter a network.	Bridge or switch
Ethernet is defined at these layers.	Data Link and Physical
This layer supports flow control and sequencing.	Transport
This device can measure the distance to a remote network.	Router
Logical addressing is used at this layer.	Network
Hardware addresses are defined at this layer.	Data Link (MAC sublayer)
This device creates one big collision domain and one large broadcast domain.	Hub
This device creates many smaller collision domains, but the network is still one large broadcast domain.	Switch or bridge
This device can never run full duplex.	Hub
This device breaks up collision domains and broadcast domains.	Router

Answers to Written Lab 1.3

1. Hub: One collision domain, one broadcast domain
2. Bridge: Two collision domains, one broadcast domain
3. Switch: Four collision domains, one broadcast domain
4. Router: Three collision domains, three broadcast domains

Chapter

2

Internet Protocols

THE CCNA INTRO EXAM TOPICS COVERED IN THIS CHAPTER INCLUDE THE FOLLOWING:

✓ **Design and Support**

- Determine IP addresses

✓ **Technology**

- Describe how the protocols associated with TCP/IP allow host communication to occur

- Describe the operation of the Internet Control Message Protocol (ICMP) and identify the reasons, types, and format of associated error and control messages

The *Transmission Control Protocol/Internet Protocol (TCP/IP)* suite was created by the Department of Defense (DoD) to ensure and preserve data integrity, as well as maintain communications in the event of catastrophic war. So it follows that if designed and implemented correctly, a TCP/IP network can be a truly dependable and resilient one. In this chapter, I'll cover the protocols of TCP/IP, and throughout this book, you'll learn how to create a marvelous TCP/IP network—using Cisco routers, of course.

We'll begin by taking a look at the DoD's version of TCP/IP and then compare this version and its protocols with the OSI reference model discussed in Chapter 1, "Internetworking."

Once you understand the protocols used at the various levels of the DoD model, I'll cover IP addressing and the different classes of addresses used in networks today.

Subnetting will be covered in Chapter 3, "IP Subnetting and Variable Length Subnet Masks (VLSMs) and Troubleshooting IP."

TCP/IP and the DoD Model

The DoD model is basically a condensed version of the OSI model—it's composed of four, instead of seven, layers:

- Process/Application layer
- Host-to-Host layer
- Internet layer
- Network Access layer

Figure 2.1 shows a comparison of the DoD model and the OSI reference model. As you can see, the two are similar in concept, but each has a different number of layers with different names.

When the different protocols in the IP stack are discussed, the layers of the OSI and DoD models are interchangeable. In other words, the Internet layer and the Network layer describe the same thing, as do the Host-to-Host layer and the Transport layer.

FIGURE 2.1   The DoD and OSI models

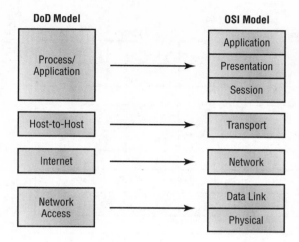

A vast array of protocols combine at the DoD model's *Process/Application layer* to integrate the various activities and duties spanning the focus of the OSI's corresponding top three layers (Application, Presentation, and Session). We'll be looking closely at those protocols in the next part of this chapter. The Process/Application layer defines protocols for node-to-node application communication and also controls user-interface specifications.

The *Host-to-Host layer* parallels the functions of the OSI's Transport layer, defining protocols for setting up the level of transmission service for applications. It tackles issues such as creating reliable end-to-end communication and ensuring the error-free delivery of data. It handles packet sequencing and maintains data integrity.

The *Internet layer* corresponds to the OSI's Network layer, designating the protocols relating to the logical transmission of packets over the entire network. It takes care of the addressing of hosts by giving them an IP (Internet Protocol) address, and it handles the routing of packets among multiple networks.

At the bottom of the DoD model, the *Network Access layer* monitors the data exchange between the host and the network. The equivalent of the Data Link and Physical layers of the OSI model, the Network Access layer oversees hardware addressing and defines protocols for the physical transmission of data.

The DoD and OSI models are alike in design and concept and have similar functions in similar layers. Figure 2.2 shows the TCP/IP protocol suite and how its protocols relate to the DoD model layers.

In the following sections, we will look at the different protocols in more detail, starting with the Process/Application layer protocols.

FIGURE 2.2   The TCP/IP protocol suite

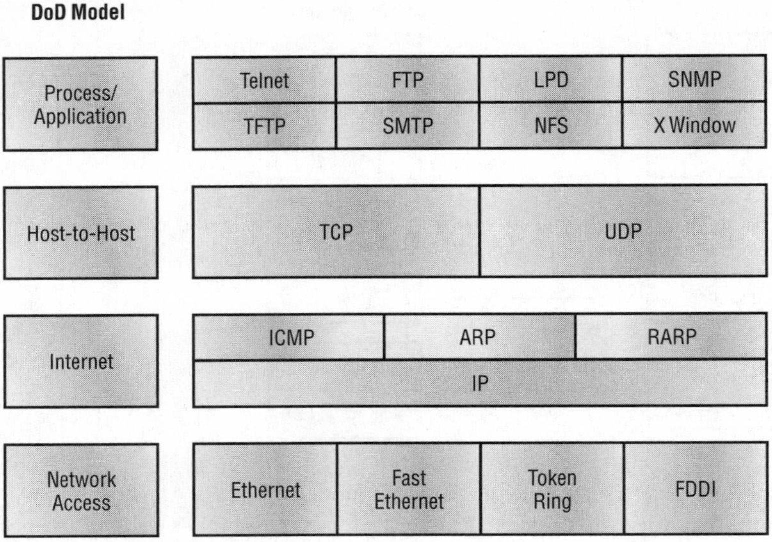

DoD Model

| Process/
Application | Telnet | FTP | LPD | SNMP |
| | TFTP | SMTP | NFS | X Window |

| Host-to-Host | TCP | UDP |

| Internet | ICMP | ARP | RARP |
| | IP | | |

| Network
Access | Ethernet | Fast
Ethernet | Token
Ring | FDDI |

The Process/Application Layer Protocols

In this section, I'll describe the different applications and services typically used in IP networks. The different protocols and applications covered in this section include the following:

- Telnet
- FTP
- TFTP
- NFS
- SMTP
- LPD
- X Window
- SNMP
- DNS
- DHCP/BootP

Telnet

Telnet is the chameleon of protocols—its specialty is terminal emulation. It allows a user on a remote client machine, called the Telnet client, to access the resources of another machine, the Telnet server. Telnet achieves this by pulling a fast one on the Telnet server and making the client machine appear as though it were a terminal directly attached to the local network. This projection is actually a software image—a virtual terminal that can interact with the chosen remote host.

These emulated terminals are of the text-mode type and can execute refined procedures such as displaying menus that give users the opportunity to choose options and access the applications on the duped server. Users begin a Telnet session by running the Telnet client software and then logging into the Telnet server.

 The name *Telnet* comes from "telephone network," which is how most Telnet sessions used to occur.

File Transfer Protocol (FTP)

File Transfer Protocol (FTP) is the protocol that actually lets us transfer files, and it can accomplish this between any two machines using it. But FTP isn't just a protocol; it's also a program. Operating as a protocol, FTP is used by applications. As a program, it's employed by users to perform file tasks by hand. FTP also allows for access to both directories and files and can accomplish certain types of directory operations, such as relocating into different ones. FTP teams up with Telnet to transparently log you into the FTP server and then provides for the transfer of files.

Accessing a host through FTP is only the first step, though. Users must then be subjected to an authentication login that's probably secured with passwords and usernames implemented by system administrators to restrict access. But you can get around this somewhat by adopting the username *anonymous*—though what you'll gain access to will be limited.

Even when employed by users manually as a program, FTP's functions by its users are limited to listing and manipulating directories, typing file contents, and copying files between hosts. It can't execute remote files as programs.

Trivial File Transfer Protocol (TFTP)

Trivial File Transfer Protocol (TFTP) is the stripped-down, stock version of FTP, but it's the protocol of choice if you know exactly what you want and where to find it, plus it's so easy to use and it's fast too! It doesn't give you the abundance of functions that FTP does, though. TFTP has no directory-browsing abilities; it can do nothing but send and receive files. This compact little protocol also skimps in the data department, sending much smaller blocks of data than FTP, and there's no authentication as with FTP, so it's insecure. Few sites support it because of the inherent security risks.

Network File System (NFS)

Network File System (NFS) is a jewel of a protocol specializing in file sharing. It allows two different types of file systems to interoperate. It works like this: Suppose the NFS server software is running on an NT server and the NFS client software is running on a Unix host. NFS allows for a portion of the RAM on the NT server to transparently store Unix files, which can, in turn,

---

Real World Scenario

When Should You Use FTP?

Your San Francisco office needs a 50MB file emailed to them right away. What do you do? Most email servers would reject the email because they have size limits. Even if there's no size limit on the server, it still would take a while to send this big file to SF. FTP to the rescue!

If you need to give someone a large file or you need to get a large file from someone, FTP is a nice choice. Smaller files (less than 5MB) can just be sent via email if you have the bandwidth of DSL or a cable modem. However, most ISPs don't allow files larger than 5MB to be emailed, so FTP is an option you should consider if you are in need of sending and receiving large files (who isn't these days?). To do this, you will need to set up an FTP server on the Internet so that the files can be shared.

Besides, FTP is faster than email, which is another reason to use FTP for sending or receiving large files. In addition, because it uses TCP and is connection-oriented, if the session dies, FTP can sometimes start up where it left off. Try that with your email client!

---

be used by Unix users. Even though the NT file system and Unix file system are unlike—they have different case sensitivity, filename lengths, security, and so on—both Unix users and NT users can access that same file with their normal file systems, in their normal way.

Simple Mail Transfer Protocol (SMTP)

Simple Mail Transfer Protocol (SMTP), answering our ubiquitous call to email, uses a spooled, or queued, method of mail delivery. Once a message has been sent to a destination, the message is spooled to a device—usually a disk. The server software at the destination posts a vigil, regularly checking this queue for messages. When it detects them, it proceeds to deliver them to their destination. SMTP is used to send mail; POP3 is used to receive mail.

Line Printer Daemon (LPD)

The Line Printer Daemon (LPD) protocol is designed for printer sharing. The LPD, along with the Line Printer (LPR) program, allows print jobs to be spooled and sent to the network's printers using TCP/IP.

X Window

Designed for client/server operations, *X Window* defines a protocol for writing client/server applications based on a graphical user interface (GUI). The idea is to allow a program, called a client, to run on one computer and have it display things through a window server on another computer.

Simple Network Management Protocol (SNMP)

Simple Network Management Protocol (SNMP) collects and manipulates this valuable network information. It gathers data by polling the devices on the network from a management station at fixed or random intervals, requiring them to disclose certain information. When all is well, SNMP receives something called a *baseline*—a report delimiting the operational traits of a healthy network. This protocol can also stand as a watchdog over the network, quickly notifying managers of any sudden turn of events. These network watchdogs are called *agents*, and when aberrations occur, agents send an alert called a *trap* to the management station.

Domain Name Service (DNS)

Domain Name Service (DNS) resolves hostnames—specifically, Internet names, such as www.routersim.com. You don't have to use DNS; you can just type in the IP address of any device you want to communicate with. An IP address identifies hosts on a network and the Internet as well. However, DNS was designed to make our lives easier. Think about this: What would happen if you wanted to move your web page to a different service provider? The IP address would change and no one would know what the new one was. DNS allows you to use a domain name to specify an IP address. You can change the IP address as often as you want and no one will know the difference.

DNS is used to resolve a *fully qualified domain name (FQDN)*—for example, www.lammle .com or todd.lammle.com. An FQDN is a hierarchy that can logically locate a system based on its domain identifier.

If you want to resolve the name *todd*, you either must type in the FQDN of todd.lammle.com or have a device such as a PC or router add the suffix for you. For example, on a Cisco router, you can use the command ip domain-name lammle.com to append each request with the lammle.com domain. If you don't do that, you'll have to type in the FQDN to get DNS to resolve the name.

An important thing to remember about DNS is that if you can ping a device with an IP address but cannot use its FQDN, then you might have some type of DNS configuration failure.

Dynamic Host Configuration Protocol (DHCP)/ Bootstrap Protocol (BootP)

Dynamic Host Configuration Protocol (DHCP) gives IP addresses to hosts. It allows easier administration and works well in small to even very large network environments. All types of hardware can be used as a DHCP server, including a Cisco router.

DHCP differs from BootP in that BootP gives an IP address to a host but the host's hardware address must be entered manually in a BootP table. You can think of DHCP as a dynamic BootP. But remember that BootP is also used to send an operating system that a host can boot from. DHCP can't do that.

But there is a lot of information a DHCP server can provide to a host when the host is requesting an IP address from the DHCP server. Here's a list of the information a DHCP server can provide:

- IP address
- Subnet mask
- Domain name
- Default gateway (routers)
- DNS
- WINS information

A DHCP server can give us even more information than this, but the items in the list are the most common.

A client that sends out a DHCP Discover message in order to receive an IP address sends out a broadcast at both layer 2 and layer 3. The layer 2 broadcast is all *F*s in hex, which looks like this: FF:FF:FF:FF:FF:FF. The layer 3 broadcast is 255.255.255.255, which means all networks and all hosts. DHCP is connectionless, which means it uses User Datagram Protocol (UDP) at the Transport layer, also known as the Host-to-Host layer, which we'll talk about next.

In case you don't believe me, here's an example of output from my trusty Ethereal analyzer:

```
Ethernet II, Src: 192.168.0.3 (00:0b:db:99:d3:5e), Dst: Broadcast
➥(ff:ff:ff:ff:ff:ff)
Internet Protocol, Src: 0.0.0.0 (0.0.0.0), Dst: 255.255.255.255
➥(255.255.255.255)
```

The Data Link and Network layer are both sending out "all hands" broadcasts saying, "Help—I don't know my IP address!"

The Host-to-Host Layer Protocols

The main purpose of the Host-to-Host layer is to shield the upper-layer applications from the complexities of the network. This layer says to the upper layer, "Just give me your data stream, with any instructions, and I'll begin the process of getting your information ready to send."

The following sections describe the two protocols at this layer:

- Transmission Control Protocol (TCP)
- User Datagram Protocol (UDP)

In addition, we'll look at some of the key host-to-host protocol concepts, as well as the port numbers.

Remember, this is still considered layer 4, and Cisco really likes the way layer 4 can use acknowledgments, sequencing, and flow control.

Transmission Control Protocol (TCP)

Transmission Control Protocol (TCP) takes large blocks of information from an application and breaks them into segments. It numbers and sequences each segment so that the destination's TCP protocol can put the segments back into the order the application intended. After these segments are sent, TCP (on the transmitting host) waits for an acknowledgment of the receiving end's TCP virtual circuit session, retransmitting those that aren't acknowledged.

Before a transmitting host starts to send segments down the model, the sender's TCP protocol contacts the destination's TCP protocol to establish a connection. What is created is known as a *virtual circuit*. This type of communication is called *connection-oriented*. During this initial handshake, the two TCP layers also agree on the amount of information that's going to be sent before the recipient's TCP sends back an acknowledgment. With everything agreed upon in advance, the path is paved for reliable communication to take place.

TCP is a full-duplex, connection-oriented, reliable, and accurate protocol, but establishing all these terms and conditions, in addition to error checking, is no small task. TCP is very complicated and, not surprisingly, costly in terms of network overhead. And since today's networks are much more reliable than those of yore, this added reliability is often unnecessary.

TCP Segment Format

Since the upper layers just send a data stream to the protocols in the Transport layers, I'll demonstrate how TCP segments a data stream and prepares it for the Internet layer. When the Internet layer receives the data stream, it routes the segments as packets through an internetwork. The segments are handed to the receiving host's Host-to-Host layer protocol, which rebuilds the data stream to hand to the upper-layer applications or protocols.

Figure 2.3 shows the TCP segment format. The figure shows the different fields within the TCP header.

FIGURE 2.3   TCP segment format

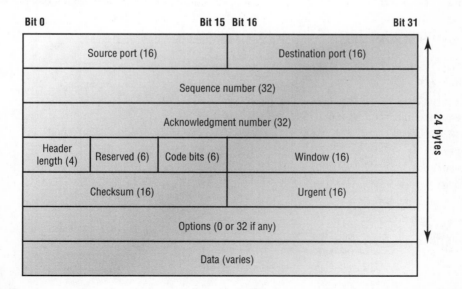

The TCP header is 20 bytes long, or up to 24 bytes with options. You need to understand what each field in the TCP segment is. The TCP segment contains the following fields:

Source port   The port number of the application on the host sending the data. (Port numbers will be explained a little later in this section.)

Destination port   The port number of the application requested on the destination host.

Sequence number   Puts the data back in the correct order or retransmits missing or damaged data, a process called *sequencing*.

Acknowledgment number   Defines which TCP octet is expected next.

Header length   The number of 32-bit words in the TCP header. This indicates where the data begins. The TCP header (even one including options) is an integral number of 32 bits in length.

Reserved   Always set to zero.

Code bits   Control functions used to set up and terminate a session.

Window   The window size the sender is willing to accept, in octets.

Checksum   The cyclic redundancy check (CRC), because TCP doesn't trust the lower layers and checks everything. The CRC checks the header and data fields.

Urgent   A valid field only if the Urgent pointer in the code bits is set. If so, this value indicates the offset from the current sequence number, in octets, where the first segment of non-urgent data begins.

Options   May be 0 or a multiple of 32 bits, if any. What this means is that no options have to be present (option size of 0). However, if any options are used that do not cause the option field to total a multiple of 32 bits, padding of 0s must be used to make sure the data begins on a 32-bit boundary.

Data   Handed down to the TCP protocol at the Transport layer, which includes the upper-layer headers.

Let's take a look at a TCP segment copied from a network analyzer:

```
TCP - Transport Control Protocol
  Source Port:       5973
  Destination Port: 23
  Sequence Number:  1456389907
  Ack Number:        1242056456
  Offset:            5
  Reserved:          %000000
  Code:              %011000
       Ack is valid
       Push Request
  Window:            61320
  Checksum:          0x61a6
```

```
Urgent Pointer:    0
No TCP Options
TCP Data Area:
vL.5.+.5.+.5.+.5   76 4c 19 35 11 2b 19 35 11 2b 19 35 11
  2b 19 35 +. 11 2b 19
Frame Check Sequence: 0x0d00000f
```

Did you notice that everything I talked about earlier is in the segment? As you can see from the number of fields in the header, TCP creates a lot of overhead. Application developers may opt for efficiency over reliability to save overhead, so User Datagram Protocol was also defined at the Transport layer as an alternative.

User Datagram Protocol (UDP)

If you were to compare *User Datagram Protocol (UDP)* with TCP, the former is basically the scaled-down economy model that's sometimes referred to as a thin protocol. Like a thin person on a park bench, a thin protocol doesn't take up a lot of room—or in this case, much bandwidth on a network.

UDP doesn't offer all the bells and whistles of TCP either, but it does do a fabulous job of transporting information that doesn't require reliable delivery—and it does so using far fewer network resources. (UDP is covered thoroughly in Request for Comments 768.)

The Requests for Comments (RFCs) form a series of notes, started in 1969, about the Internet (originally the ARPAnet). The notes discuss many aspects of computer communication, focusing on networking protocols, procedures, programs, and concepts but also including meeting notes, opinion, and sometimes humor.

There are some situations in which it would definitely be wise for developers to opt for UDP rather than TCP. Remember the watchdog SNMP up there at the Process/Application layer? SNMP monitors the network, sending intermittent messages and a fairly steady flow of status updates and alerts, especially when running on a large network. The cost in overhead to establish, maintain, and close a TCP connection for each one of those little messages would reduce what would be an otherwise healthy, efficient network to a dammed-up bog in no time!

Another circumstance calling for UDP over TCP is when reliability is already handled at the Process/Application layer. Network File System (NFS) handles its own reliability issues, making the use of TCP both impractical and redundant. But ultimately, it's up to the application developer to decide whether to use UDP or TCP, not the user who wants to transfer data faster.

UDP does *not* sequence the segments and does not care in which order the segments arrive at the destination. But after that, UDP sends the segments off and forgets about them. It doesn't follow through, check up on them, or even allow for an acknowledgment of safe arrival—complete abandonment. Because of this, it's referred to as an unreliable protocol. This does not mean that UDP is ineffective, only that it doesn't handle issues of reliability.

Further, UDP doesn't create a virtual circuit, nor does it contact the destination before delivering information to it. Because of this, it's also considered a *connectionless* protocol. Since UDP assumes that the application will use its own reliability method, it doesn't use any. This gives an application developer a choice when running the Internet Protocol stack: TCP for reliability or UDP for faster transfers.

So if you're using Voice over IP (VoIP), for example, you really don't want to use UDP, because if the segments arrive out of order (very common in IP networks), they'll just pass the segments up to the next OSI (DoD) layer in whatever order they're received, resulting in some seriously garbled data. On the other hand, TCP sequences the segments so they get put back together in exactly the right order—something UDP just can't do.

UDP Segment Format

Figure 2.4 clearly illustrates UDP's markedly low overhead as compared to TCP's hungry usage. Look at the figure carefully—can you see that UDP doesn't use windowing or provide for acknowledgments in the UDP header?

It's important for you to understand what each field in the UDP segment is. The UDP segment contains the following fields:

Source port   Port number of the application on the host sending the data.

Destination port   Port number of the application requested on the destination host.

Length   Length of UDP header and UDP data.

Checksum   Checksum of both the UDP header and UDP data fields.

Data   Upper-layer data.

UDP, like TCP, doesn't trust the lower layers and runs its own CRC. Remember that the Frame Check Sequence (FCS) is the field that houses the CRC, which is why you can see the FCS information.

The following shows a UDP segment caught on a network analyzer:

```
UDP - User Datagram Protocol
 Source Port:       1085
 Destination Port: 5136
 Length:            41
 Checksum:          0x7a3c
 UDP Data Area:
 ..Z......00 01 5a 96 00 01 00 00 00 00 00 11 0000 00
 ...C..2._C._C  2e 03 00 43 02 1e 32 0a 00 0a 00 80 43 00 80
Frame Check Sequence: 0x00000000
```

Notice that low overhead! Try to find the sequence number, ack number, and window size in the UDP segment. You can't because they just aren't there!

FIGURE 2.4   UDP segment

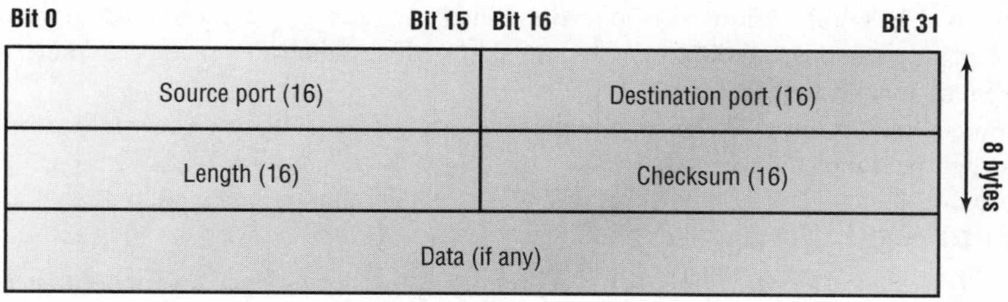

Bit 0		Bit 15	Bit 16		Bit 31
Source port (16)			Destination port (16)		
Length (16)			Checksum (16)		
Data (if any)					

8 bytes

Key Concepts of Host-to-Host Protocols

Since you've seen both a connection-oriented (TCP) and connectionless (UDP) protocol in action, it would be good to summarize the two here. Table 2.1 highlights some of the key concepts that you should keep in mind regarding these two protocols. You should memorize this table.

TABLE 2.1   Key Features of TCP and UDP

TCP	UDP
Sequenced	Unsequenced
Reliable	Unreliable
Connection-oriented	Connectionless
Virtual circuit	Low overhead
Acknowledgments	No acknowledgment
Windowing flow control	No windowing or flow control

A telephone analogy could really help you understand how TCP works. Most of us know that before you speak to someone on a phone, you must first establish a connection with that other person—wherever they are. This is like a virtual circuit with the TCP protocol. If you were giving someone important information during your conversation, you might say, "You know?" or ask, "Did you get that?" Saying something like this is a lot like a TCP acknowledgment—it's designed to get you verification. From time to time (especially on cell phones), people also ask, "Are you still there?" They end their conversations with a "Goodbye" of some kind, putting closure on the phone call. TCP also performs these types of functions.

Alternately, using UDP is like sending a postcard. To do that, you don't need to contact the other party first. You simply write your message, address the postcard, and mail it. This is analogous to UDP's connectionless orientation. Since the message on the postcard is probably not a matter of life or death, you don't need an acknowledgment of its receipt. Similarly, UDP does not involve acknowledgments.

Let's take a look at another figure, one that includes TCP, UDP, and the applications associated to each protocol, figure 2.5.

Port Numbers

TCP and UDP must use *port numbers* to communicate with the upper layers because they're what keeps track of different conversations crossing the network simultaneously. Originating-source port numbers are dynamically assigned by the source host and will equal some number starting at 1024. 1023 and below are defined in RFC 3232 (or just see www.iana.org), which discusses what are called well-known port numbers.

Virtual circuits that don't use an application with a well-known port number are assigned port numbers randomly from a specific range instead. These port numbers identify the source and destination application or process in the TCP segment.

Figure 2.5 illustrates how both TCP and UDP use port numbers.

FIGURE 2.5   Port numbers for TCP and UDP

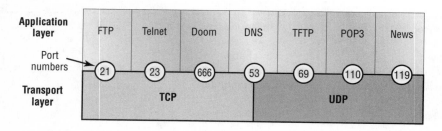

The different port numbers that can be used are explained next:

- Numbers below 1024 are considered well-known port numbers and are defined in RFC 3232.

- Numbers 1024 and above are used by the upper layers to set up sessions with other hosts and by TCP to use as source and destination addresses in the TCP segment.

In the following sections, we'll take a look at an analyzer output showing a TCP session.

TCP Session: Source Port

The following listing shows a TCP session captured with Etherpeek analyzer software:

```
TCP - Transport Control Protocol
 Source Port:       5973
 Destination Port: 23
 Sequence Number:   1456389907
```

```
Ack Number:          1242056456
Offset:              5
Reserved:            %000000
Code:                %011000
      Ack is valid
      Push Request
Window:              61320
Checksum:            0x61a6
Urgent Pointer:      0
No TCP Options
TCP Data Area:
vL.5.+.5.+.5.+.5  76 4c 19 35 11 2b 19 35 11 2b 19 35 11
  2b 19 35 +. 11 2b 19
Frame Check Sequence: 0x0d00000f
```

Notice that the source host makes up the source port and, which in this case is 5973. The destination port is 23, which is used to tell the receiving host the purpose of the intended connection (Telnet).

By looking at this session, you can see that the source host makes up the source port. But why does the source make up a port number? To differentiate between sessions with different hosts, my friend. How would a server know where information is coming from if it didn't have a different number from a sending host? TCP and the upper layers don't use hardware and logical addresses to understand the sending host's address as the Data Link and Network layer protocols do. Instead, they use port numbers. And it's easy to imagine the receiving host getting thoroughly confused if all the hosts used the same source port number to get to FTP!

TCP Session: Destination Port

You'll sometimes look at an analyzer and see that only the source port is above 1024 and the destination port is a well-known port, as shown in the following trace:

```
TCP - Transport Control Protocol
 Source Port:       1144
 Destination Port: 80 World Wide Web HTTP
 Sequence Number:  9356570
 Ack Number:       0
 Offset:           7
 Reserved:         %000000
 Code:             %000010
      Synch Sequence
 Window:           8192
 Checksum:         0x57E7
 Urgent Pointer:   0
 TCP Options:
```

```
 Option Type: 2 Maximum Segment Size
   Length:     4
   MSS:        536
 Option Type: 1 No Operation
 Option Type: 1 No Operation
 Option Type: 4
   Length:     2
   Opt Value:
 No More HTTP Data
Frame Check Sequence: 0x43697363
```

And sure enough, the source port is over 1024, but the destination port is 80, or HTTP service. The server, or receiving host, will change the destination port if it needs to.

In the preceding trace, a "syn" packet is sent to the destination device. The syn sequence is what's telling the remote destination device that it wants to create a session.

TCP Session: Syn Packet Acknowledgment

The next trace shows an acknowledgment to the syn packet:

```
TCP - Transport Control Protocol
 Source Port:      80 World Wide Web HTTP
 Destination Port: 1144
 Sequence Number:  2873580788
 Ack Number:       9356571
 Offset:           6
 Reserved:         %000000
 Code:             %010010
     Ack is valid
     Synch Sequence
 Window:           8576
 Checksum:         0x5F85
 Urgent Pointer:   0
 TCP Options:
  Option Type: 2 Maximum Segment Size
    Length:     4
    MSS:        1460
  No More HTTP Data
Frame Check Sequence: 0x6E203132
```

Notice the *Ack is valid*, which means that the source port was accepted and the device agreed to create a virtual circuit with the originating host.

And here again, you can see that the response from the server shows the source is 80 and the destination is the 1144 sent from the originating host—all's well.

Table 2.2 gives you a list of the typical applications used in the TCP/IP suite, their well-known port numbers, and the Transport layer protocols used by each application or process. It's important that you study and memorize this table.

TABLE 2.2   Key Protocols That Use TCP and UDP

TCP	UDP
Telnet 23	SNMP 161
SMTP 25	TFTP 69
HTTP 80	DNS 53
FTP 21	
DNS 53	
HTTPS 443	

Notice that DNS uses both TCP and UDP. Whether it opts for one or the other depends on what it's trying to do. Even though it's not the only application that can use both protocols, it's certainly one that you should remember in your studies.

What makes TCP reliable is sequencing, acknowledgments, and flow control (windowing). UDP does not have reliability.

The Internet Layer Protocols

In the DoD model, there are two main reasons for the Internet layer's existence: routing, and providing a single network interface to the upper layers.

None of the other upper- or lower-layer protocols have any functions relating to routing—that complex and important task belongs entirely to the Internet layer. The Internet layer's second duty is to provide a single network interface to the upper-layer protocols. Without this layer, application programmers would need to write "hooks" into every one of their applications for each different Network Access protocol. This would not only be a pain in the neck, but it would lead to different versions of each application—one for Ethernet, another one for Token Ring, and so on. To prevent this, IP provides one single network interface for the upper-layer protocols. That accomplished, it's then the job of IP and the various Network Access protocols to get along and work together.

All network roads don't lead to Rome—they lead to IP. And all the other protocols at this layer, as well as all those at the upper layers, use it. Never forget that. All paths through the DoD model go through IP. The following sections describe the protocols at the Internet layer:

- Internet Protocol (IP)
- Internet Control Message Protocol (ICMP)
- Address Resolution Protocol (ARP)
- Reverse Address Resolution Protocol (RARP)
- Proxy ARP

Internet Protocol (IP)

Internet Protocol (IP) essentially is the Internet layer. The other protocols found here merely exist to support it. IP holds the big picture and could be said to "see all," in that it's aware of all the interconnected networks. It can do this because all the machines on the network have a software, or logical, address called an IP address, which I'll cover more thoroughly later in this chapter.

IP looks at each packet's address. Then, using a routing table, it decides where a packet is to be sent next, choosing the best path. The protocols of the Network Access layer at the bottom of the DoD model don't possess IP's enlightened scope of the entire network; they deal only with physical links (local networks).

Identifying devices on networks requires answering these two questions: Which network is it on? And what is its ID on that network? The first answer is the *software address*, or *logical address* (the correct street). The second answer is the hardware address (the correct mailbox). All hosts on a network have a logical ID called an IP address. This is the software, or logical, address and contains valuable encoded information, greatly simplifying the complex task of routing. (IP is discussed in RFC 791.)

IP receives segments from the Host-to-Host layer and fragments them into datagrams (packets) if necessary. IP then reassembles datagrams back into segments on the receiving side. Each datagram is assigned the IP address of the sender and of the recipient. Each router (layer 3 device) that receives a datagram makes routing decisions based on the packet's destination IP address.

Figure 2.6 shows an IP header. This will give you an idea of what the IP protocol has to go through every time user data is sent from the upper layers and is to be sent to a remote network.

The following fields make up the IP header:

Version   IP version number.

Header length   Header length (HLEN) in 32-bit words.

Priority and Type of Service   Type of Service tells how the datagram should be handled. The first 3 bits are the priority bits.

Total length   Length of the packet including header and data.

Identification   Unique IP-packet value.

Flags   Specifies whether fragmentation should occur.

FIGURE 2.6   IP header

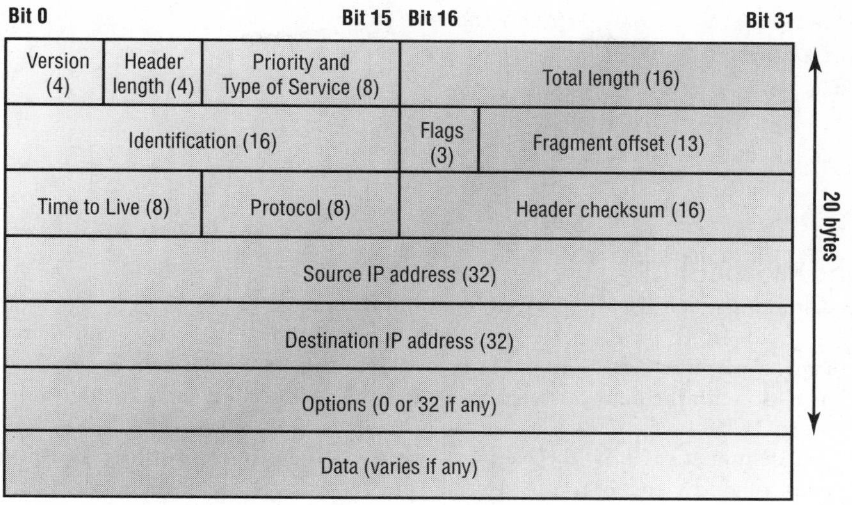

Bit 0		Bit 15	Bit 16		Bit 31

Fragment offset   Provides fragmentation and reassembly if the packet is too large to put in a frame. It also allows different maximum transmission units (MTUs) on the Internet.

Time to Live   The time to live is set into a packet when it is originally generated. If it doesn't get to where it wants to go before the TTL expires, boom—it's gone. This stops IP packets from continuously circling the network looking for a home.

Protocol   Port of upper-layer protocol (TCP is port 6 or UDP is port 17 [hex]). Also supports Network layer protocols.

Header checksum   Cyclic redundancy check (CRC) on header only.

Source IP address   32-bit IP address of sending station.

Destination IP address   32-bit IP address of the station this packet is destined for.

Options   Used for network testing, debugging, security, and more.

Data   After the IP option field will be the upper-layer data.

Here's a snapshot of an IP packet caught on a network analyzer (notice that all the header information discussed previously appears here):

```
IP Header - Internet Protocol Datagram
 Version:            4
 Header Length:      5
 Precedence:         0
 Type of Service:    %000
 Unused:             %00
```

```
Total Length:          187
Identifier:            22486
Fragmentation Flags:   %010 Do Not Fragment
Fragment Offset:       0
Time To Live:          60
IP Type:               0x06 TCP
Header Checksum:       0xd031
Source IP Address:     10.7.1.30
Dest. IP Address:      10.7.1.10
No Internet Datagram Options
```

Can you distinguish the logical, or IP, addresses in this header?

The Type field—it's typically a Protocol field, but this analyzer sees it as an IP Type field—is important. If the header didn't carry the protocol information for the next layer, IP wouldn't know what to do with the data carried in the packet. The preceding example tells IP to hand the segment to TCP.

Figure 2.7 demonstrates how the Network layer sees the protocols at the Transport layer when it needs to hand a packet to the upper-layer protocols.

FIGURE 2.7   The Protocol field in an IP header

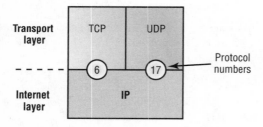

In this example, the Protocol field tells IP to send the data to either TCP port 6 or UDP port 17 (both hex addresses). But it will only be UDP or TCP if the data is part of a data stream headed for an upper-layer service or application. It could just as easily be destined for Internet Control Message Protocol (ICMP), Address Resolution Protocol (ARP), or some other type of Network layer protocol.

Table 2.3 is a list of some other popular protocols that can be specified in the Protocol field.

TABLE 2.3   Possible Protocols Found in the Protocol Field of an IP Header

Protocol	Protocol Number
ICMP	1
IGRP	9

TABLE 2.3   Possible Protocols Found in the Protocol Field of an IP Header *(continued)*

Protocol	Protocol Number
EIGRP	88
OSPF	89
IPv6	41
GRE	47
Layer 2 tunnel (L2TP)	115

Internet Control Message Protocol (ICMP)

Internet Control Message Protocol (ICMP) works at the Network layer and is used by IP for many different services. ICMP is a management protocol and messaging service provider for IP. Its messages are carried as IP datagrams. RFC 1256 is an annex to ICMP, which affords hosts' extended capability in discovering routes to gateways.

ICMP packets have the following characteristics:

- They can provide hosts with information about network problems.
- They are encapsulated within IP datagrams.

The following are some common events and messages that ICMP relates to:

Destination Unreachable   If a router can't send an IP datagram any further, it uses ICMP to send a message back to the sender, advising it of the situation. For example, take a look at Figure 2.8, which shows that interface E0 of the Lab_B router is down.

When Host A sends a packet destined for Host B, the Lab_B router will send an ICMP Destination Unreachable message back to the sending device (Host A in this example).

Buffer Full   If a router's memory buffer for receiving incoming datagrams is full, it will use ICMP to send out this message until the congestion abates.

Hops   Each IP datagram is allotted a certain number of routers, called hops, to pass through. If it reaches its limit of hops before arriving at its destination, the last router to receive that datagram deletes it. The executioner router then uses ICMP to send an obituary message, informing the sending machine of the demise of its datagram.

Ping   Packet Internet Groper (Ping) uses ICMP echo messages to check the physical and logical connectivity of machines on an internetwork.

Traceroute   Using TTL timeouts and ICMP error messages, Traceroute is used to discover the path a packet takes as it traverses an internetwork.

Both Ping and Traceroute (also just called Trace; Microsoft Windows uses tracert) allow you to verify address configurations in your internetwork.

FIGURE 2.8   ICMP error message is sent to the sending host from the remote router.

E0 of on Lab B is down. Host A is trying to communicate to Host B. What happens?

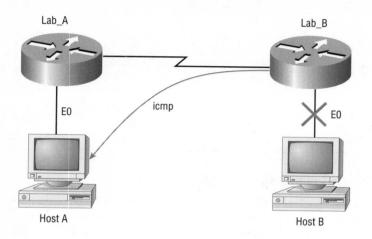

The following data is from a network analyzer catching an ICMP echo request:

```
Flags:          0x00
 Status:         0x00
 Packet Length: 78
 Timestamp:      14:04:25.967000 12/20/03
Ethernet Header
 Destination: 00:a0:24:6e:0f:a8
 Source:       00:80:c7:a8:f0:3d
 Ether-Type:   08-00 IP
IP Header - Internet Protocol Datagram
 Version:              4
 Header Length:        5
 Precedence:           0
 Type of Service:     %000
 Unused:              %00
 Total Length:         60
 Identifier:           56325
 Fragmentation Flags: %000
 Fragment Offset:      0
 Time To Live:         32
 IP Type:             0x01 ICMP
 Header Checksum:     0x2df0
```

```
Source IP Address:    100.100.100.2
Dest. IP Address:     100.100.100.1
No Internet Datagram Options
ICMP - Internet Control Messages Protocol
 ICMP Type:        8 Echo Request
 Code:             0
 Checksum:         0x395c
 Identifier:       0x0300
 Sequence Number: 4352
 ICMP Data Area:
 abcdefghijklmnop  61 62 63 64 65 66 67 68 69 6a 6b 6c 6d
 qrstuvwabcdefghi  71 72 73 74 75 76 77 61 62 63 64 65 66
Frame Check Sequence: 0x00000000
```

Notice anything unusual? Did you catch the fact that even though ICMP works at the Internet (Network) layer, it still uses IP to do the Ping request? The Type field in the IP header is 0x01, which specifies the ICMP protocol. All segments or data *must* go through IP!

The Ping program uses the alphabet in the data portion of the packet as just a payload, 100 bytes by default, unless, of course, you are pinging from a Windows device, which thinks the alphabet stops at the letter *W* and doesn't include *X*, *Y*, or *Z* and then starts at *A* again. Go figure!

If you remember reading about the Data Link layer and the different frame types in Chapter 1, you should be able to look at the preceding trace and tell what type of Ethernet frame this is. The only fields are destination hardware address, source hardware address, and Ether-Type. The only frame that uses an Ether-Type field exclusively is an Ethernet_II frame.

But before we get into the ARP protocol, let's take another look at ICMP in action. Figure 2.9 shows an internetwork (it has a router, so it's an internetwork, right?).

Here, you see that Host C telnets to 10.1.1.5 from a DOS prompt. What do you think Host C will receive as a response? Since Host C will send the Telnet data to the default gateway, which is the router, the router will drop the packet because there isn't a network 10.1.1.0 in the routing table. Because of this, Host C will receive a destination unreachable back from ICMP.

Address Resolution Protocol (ARP)

Address Resolution Protocol (ARP) finds the hardware address of a host from a known IP address. Here's how it works: When IP has a datagram to send, it must inform a Network Access protocol, such as Ethernet or Token Ring, of the destination's hardware address on the local network. (It has already been informed by upper-layer protocols of the destination's IP address.) If IP doesn't find the destination host's hardware address in the ARP cache, it uses ARP to find this information.

FIGURE 2.9 ICMP in action

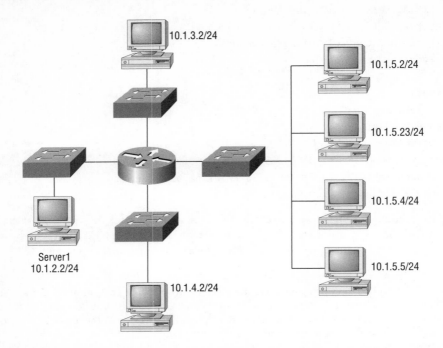

As IP's detective, ARP interrogates the local network by sending out a broadcast asking the machine with the specified IP address to reply with its hardware address. So basically, ARP translates the software (IP) address into a hardware address—for example, the destination machine's Ethernet board address—and from it, deduces its whereabouts on LAN by broadcasting for this address. Figure 2.10 shows how an ARP looks to a local network.

 NOTE   ARP resolves IP addresses to Ethernet (MAC) addresses.

The following trace shows an ARP broadcast—notice that the destination hardware address is unknown and is all *F*s in hex (all 1s in binary)—and is a hardware address broadcast:

```
Flags:          0x00
Status:         0x00
Packet Length: 64
Timestamp:      09:17:29.574000 12/06/03
Ethernet Header
Destination:    FF:FF:FF:FF:FF:FF Ethernet Broadcast
Source:         00:A0:24:48:60:A5
```

```
Protocol Type: 0x0806 IP ARP
ARP - Address Resolution Protocol
  Hardware:                  1 Ethernet (10Mb)
  Protocol:                  0x0800 IP
  Hardware Address Length: 6
  Protocol Address Length: 4
  Operation:                 1 ARP Request
  Sender Hardware Address: 00:A0:24:48:60:A5
  Sender Internet Address: 172.16.10.3
  Target Hardware Address: 00:00:00:00:00:00 (ignored)
  Target Internet Address: 172.16.10.10
Extra bytes (Padding):
  ................ 0A 0A 0A 0A 0A 0A 0A 0A 0A 0A 0A 0A 0A
  0A 0A 0A 0A 0A
Frame Check Sequence: 0x00000000
```

Reverse Address Resolution Protocol (RARP)

When an IP machine happens to be a diskless machine, it has no way of initially knowing its IP address. But it does know its MAC address. *Reverse Address Resolution Protocol (RARP)* discovers the identity of the IP address for diskless machines by sending out a packet that includes its MAC address and a request for the IP address assigned to that MAC address. A designated machine, called a *RARP server*, responds with the answer and the identity crisis is over. RARP uses the information it does know about the machine's MAC address to learn its IP address and complete the machine's ID portrait.

FIGURE 2.10   Local ARP broadcast

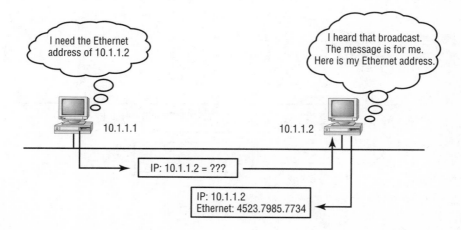

RARP resolves Ethernet (MAC) addresses to IP addresses.

Figure 2.11 shows a diskless workstation asking for its IP address with a RARP broadcast.

Proxy Address Resolution Protocol (Proxy ARP)

On a network, your hosts can't have more than one default gateway configured. Think about this…What if the default gateway (router) happens to go down? The host won't just start sending to another router automatically—you've got to reconfigure that host. But Proxy ARP can actually help machines on a subnet reach remote subnets without configuring routing or even a default gateway.

One advantage of using Proxy ARP is that is can be added to a single router on a network without disturbing the routing tables of all the other routers that live there too. But there's a serious downside to using Proxy ARP. Using Proxy ARP will definitely increase the amount of traffic on your network segment, and hosts will have a larger ARP table than usual in order to handle all the IP-to-MAC address mappings. And Proxy ARP is configured on all Cisco routers by default—you should disable it if you don't think you're going to use it.

One last thought on Proxy ARP: Proxy ARP isn't really a separate protocol. It is a service run by routers on behalf of other devices that are separated from their query by a router, although they think they share the subnet with the other device.

FIGURE 2.11 RARP broadcast example

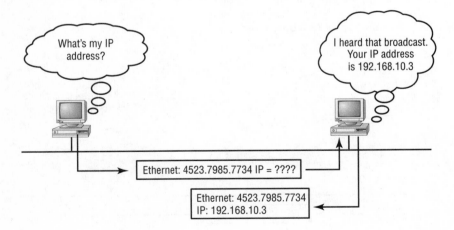

IP Addressing

One of the most important topics in any discussion of TCP/IP is IP addressing. An *IP address* is a numeric identifier assigned to each machine on an IP network. It designates the specific location of a device on the network.

An IP address is a software address, not a hardware address—the latter is hard-coded on a network interface card (NIC) and used for finding hosts on a local network. IP addressing was designed to allow hosts on one network to communicate with a host on a different network regardless of the type of LANs the hosts are participating in.

Before we get into the more complicated aspects of IP addressing, you need to understand some of the basics. First I'm going to explain some of the fundamentals of IP addressing and its terminology. Then you'll learn about the hierarchical IP addressing scheme and private IP addresses.

IP Terminology

Throughout this chapter you'll learn several important terms vital to your understanding of the Internet Protocol. Here are a few to get you started:

Bit   A *bit* is one digit, either a 1 or a 0.

Byte   A *byte* is 7 or 8 bits, depending on whether parity is used. For the rest of this chapter, always assume a byte is 8 bits.

Octet   An octet, made up of 8 bits, is just an ordinary 8-bit binary number. In this chapter, the terms *byte* and *octet* are completely interchangeable.

Network address   This is the designation used in routing to send packets to a remote network—for example, 10.0.0.0, 172.16.0.0, and 192.168.10.0.

Broadcast address   The address used by applications and hosts to send information to all nodes on a network is called the *broadcast address*. Examples include 255.255.255.255, which is all networks, all nodes; 172.16.255.255, which is all subnets and hosts on network 172.16.0.0; and 10.255.255.255, which broadcasts to all subnets and hosts on network 10.0.0.0.

The Hierarchical IP Addressing Scheme

An IP address consists of 32 bits of information. These bits are divided into four sections, referred to as *octets* or bytes, each containing 1 byte (8 bits). You can depict an IP address using one of three methods:

- Dotted-decimal, as in 172.16.30.56
- Binary, as in 10101100.00010000.00011110.00111000
- Hexadecimal, as in AC.10.1E.38

All these examples truly represent the same IP address. Hexadecimal isn't used as often as dotted-decimal or binary when IP addressing is discussed, but you still might find an IP address stored in hexadecimal in some programs. The Windows Registry is a good example of a program that stores a machine's IP address in hex.

The 32-bit IP address is a structured or hierarchical address, as opposed to a flat or nonhierarchical address. Although either type of addressing scheme could have been used, *hierarchical addressing* was chosen for a good reason. The advantage of this scheme is that it can handle a large number of addresses, namely 4.3 billion (a 32-bit address space with two possible values for each position—either 0 or 1—gives you 2^{32}, or 4,294,967,296). The disadvantage of the flat addressing scheme, and the reason it's not used for IP addressing, relates to routing. If every address were unique, all routers on the Internet would need to store the address of each and every machine on the Internet. This would make efficient routing impossible, even if only a fraction of the possible addresses were used.

The solution to this problem is to use a two- or three-level hierarchical addressing scheme that is structured by network and host or by network, subnet, and host.

This two- or three-level scheme is comparable to a telephone number. The first section, the area code, designates a very large area. The second section, the prefix, narrows the scope to a local calling area. The final segment, the customer number, zooms in on the specific connection. IP addresses use the same type of layered structure. Rather than all 32 bits being treated as a unique identifier, as in flat addressing, a part of the address is designated as the network address, and the other part is designated as either the subnet and host or just the node address.

In the following sections, I'm going to discuss IP network addressing and the different classes of address we can use to address our networks with.

Network Addressing

The *network address* (which can also be called the network number) uniquely identifies each network. Every machine on the same network shares that network address as part of its IP address. In the IP address 172.16.30.56, for example, 172.16 is the network address.

The *node address* is assigned to, and uniquely identifies, each machine on a network. This part of the address must be unique because it identifies a particular machine—an individual—as opposed to a network, which is a group. This number can also be referred to as a *host address*. In the sample IP address 172.16.30.56, the 30.56 is the node address.

The designers of the Internet decided to create classes of networks based on network size. For the small number of networks possessing a very large number of nodes, they created the rank *Class A network*. At the other extreme is the *Class C network*, which is reserved for the numerous networks with a small number of nodes. The class distinction for networks between very large and very small is predictably called the *Class B network*.

Subdividing an IP address into a network and node address is determined by the class designation of one's network. Figure 2.12 summarizes the three classes of networks—a subject I'll explain in much greater detail throughout this chapter.

FIGURE 2.12 Summary of the three classes of networks

	8 bits	8 bits	8 bits	8 bits
Class A:	Network	Host	Host	Host
Class B:	Network	Network	Host	Host
Class C:	Network	Network	Network	Host
Class D:	Multicast			
Class E:	Research			

To ensure efficient routing, Internet designers defined a mandate for the leading-bits section of the address for each different network class. For example, since a router knows that a Class A network address always starts with a 0, the router might be able to speed a packet on its way after reading only the first bit of its address. This is where the address schemes define the difference between a Class A, a Class B, and a Class C address. In the next sections, I'll discuss the differences between these three classes, followed by a discussion of the Class D and Class E addresses (Classes A, B, and C are the only ranges that are used to address hosts in our networks).

Network Address Range: Class A

The designers of the IP address scheme said that the first bit of the first byte in a Class A network address must always be off, or 0. This means a Class A address must be between 0 and 127, inclusive.

Consider the following network address:

0xxxxxxx

If we turn the other 7 bits all off and then turn them all on, we'll find the Class A range of network addresses:

00000000 = 0
01111111 = 127

So, a Class A network is defined in the first octet between 0 and 127, and it can't be less or more. (Yes, I know 0 and 127 are not valid in a Class A network. I'll talk about reserved addresses in a minute.)

Network Address Range: Class B

In a Class B network, the RFCs state that the first bit of the first byte must always be turned on but the second bit must always be turned off. If you turn the other 6 bits all off and then all on, you will find the range for a Class B network:

```
10000000 = 128
10111111 = 191
```

As you can see, a Class B network is defined when the first byte is configured from 128 to 191.

Network Address Range: Class C

For Class C networks, the RFCs define the first 2 bits of the first octet as always turned on, but the third bit can never be on. Following the same process as the previous classes, convert from binary to decimal to find the range. Here's the range for a Class C network:

```
11000000 = 192
11011111 = 223
```

So, if you see an IP address that starts at 192 and goes to 223, you'll know it is a Class C IP address.

Network Address Ranges: Classes D and E

The addresses between 224 to 255 are reserved for Class D and E networks. Class D (224–239) is used for multicast addresses and Class E (240–255) for scientific purposes, but I'm not going into these types of addresses in this book (and you don't need to know them).

Network Addresses: Special Purpose

Some IP addresses are reserved for special purposes, so network administrators can't ever assign these addresses to nodes. Table 2.4 lists the members of this exclusive little club and the reasons why they're included in it.

TABLE 2.4   Reserved IP Addresses

Address	Function
Network address of all 0s	Interpreted to mean "this network or segment."
Network address of all 1s	Interpreted to mean "all networks."
Network 127.0.0.1	Reserved for loopback tests. Designates the local node and allows that node to send a test packet to itself without generating network traffic.
Node address of all 0s	Interpreted to mean "network address" or any host on specified network.

TABLE 2.4   Reserved IP Addresses *(continued)*

Address	Function
Node address of all 1s	Interpreted to mean "all nodes" on the specified network; for example, 128.2.255.255 means "all nodes" on network 128.2 (Class B address).
Entire IP address set to all 0s	Used by Cisco routers to designate the default route. Could also mean "any network."
Entire IP address set to all 1s (same as 255.255.255.255)	Broadcast to all nodes on the current network; sometimes called an "all 1s broadcast" or limited broadcast.

Class A Addresses

In a Class A network address, the first byte is assigned to the network address and the three remaining bytes are used for the node addresses. The Class A format is as follows:

network.node.node.node

For example, in the IP address 49.22.102.70, the 49 is the network address and 22.102.70 is the node address. Every machine on this particular network would have the distinctive network address of 49.

Class A network addresses are 1 byte long, with the first bit of that byte reserved and the 7 remaining bits available for manipulation (addressing). As a result, the maximum number of Class A networks that can be created is 128. Why? Because each of the 7 bit positions can be either a 0 or a 1, thus 2^7, or 128.

To complicate matters further, the network address of all 0s (0000 0000) is reserved to designate the default route (see Table 2.4 in the previous section). Additionally, the address 127, which is reserved for diagnostics, can't be used either, which means that you can really only use the numbers 1 to 126 to designate Class A network addresses. This means the actual number of usable Class A network addresses is 128 minus 2, or 126.

The IP address 127.0.0.1 is used to test the IP stack on an individual node and cannot be used as a valid host address

Each Class A address has 3 bytes (24-bit positions) for the node address of a machine. This means there are 2^{24}—or 16,777,216—unique combinations and, therefore, precisely that many possible unique node addresses for each Class A network. Because node addresses with the two patterns of all 0s and all 1s are reserved, the actual maximum usable number of nodes for a Class A network is 2^{24} minus 2, which equals 16,777,214. Either way, that's a huge amount of hosts on a network segment!

Class A Valid Host IDs

Here's an example of how to figure out the valid host IDs in a Class A network address:

- All host bits off is the network address: 10.0.0.0.
- All host bits on is the broadcast address: 10.255.255.255.

The valid hosts are the numbers in between the network address and the broadcast address: 10.0.0.1 through 10.255.255.254. Notice that 0s and 255s can be valid host IDs. All you need to remember when trying to find valid host addresses is that the host bits can't all be turned off or all be on at the same time.

Class B Addresses

In a Class B network address, the first 2 bytes are assigned to the network address and the remaining 2 bytes are used for node addresses. The format is as follows:

network.network.node.node

For example, in the IP address 172.16.30.56, the network address is 172.16 and the node address is 30.56.

With a network address being 2 bytes (8 bits each), there would be 2^{16} unique combinations. But the Internet designers decided that all Class B network addresses should start with the binary digit 1, then 0. This leaves 14 bit positions to manipulate, therefore 16,384 (that is, 2^{14}) unique Class B network addresses.

A Class B address uses 2 bytes for node addresses. This is 2^{16} minus the two reserved patterns (all 0s and all 1s), for a total of 65,534 possible node addresses for each Class B network.

Class B Valid Host IDs

Here's an example of how to find the valid hosts in a Class B network:

- All host bits turned off is the network address: 172.16.0.0.
- All host bits turned on is the broadcast address: 172.16.255.255.

The valid hosts would be the numbers in between the network address and the broadcast address: 172.16.0.1 through 172.16.255.254.

Class C Addresses

The first 3 bytes of a Class C network address are dedicated to the network portion of the address, with only 1 measly byte remaining for the node address. Here's the format:

network.network.network.node

Using the example IP address 192.168.100.102, the network address is 192.168.100 and the node address is 102.

In a Class C network address, the first three bit positions are always the binary 110. The calculation is 3 bytes, or 24 bits, minus 3 reserved positions leaves 21 positions. Hence, there are 2^{21}, or 2,097,152, possible Class C networks.

Each unique Class C network has 1 byte to use for node addresses. This leads to 2^8 or 256, minus the two reserved patterns of all 0s and all 1s, for a total of 254 node addresses for each Class C network.

Class C Valid Host IDs

Here's an example of how to find a valid host ID in a Class C network:

- All host bits turned off is the network ID: 192.168.100.0.
- All host bits turned on is the broadcast address: 192.168.100.255.

The valid hosts would be the numbers in between the network address and the broadcast address: 192.168.100.1 through 192.168.100.254.

Private IP Addresses

The people who created the IP addressing scheme also created what we call private IP addresses. These addresses can be used on a private network, but they're not routable through the Internet. This is designed for the purpose of creating a measure of well-needed security, but it also conveniently saves valuable IP address space.

If every host on every network had to have real routable IP addresses, we would have run out of IP addresses to hand out years ago. But by using private IP addresses, ISPs, corporations, and home users only need a relatively tiny group of bona fide IP addresses to connect their networks to the Internet. This is economical because they can use private IP addresses on their inside networks and get along just fine.

To accomplish this task, the ISP and the corporation—the end user, no matter who they are—need to use something called a *Network Address Translation (NAT)*, which basically takes a private IP address and converts it for use on the Internet. Many people can use the same real IP address to transmit out onto the Internet. Doing things this way saves megatons of address space—good for us all!

The reserved private addresses are listed in Table 2.8.

TABLE 2.5   Reserved IP Address Space

Address Class	Reserved address space
Class A	10.0.0.0 through 10.255.255.255
Class B	172.16.0.0 through 172.31.255.255
Class C	192.168.0.0 through 192.168.255.255

 You must know your private address space!

🌐 Real World Scenario

So, What Private IP address Should I Use?

That's a really great question: Should you use Class A, Class B, or even Class C private addressing when setting up your network? Let's take Acme Corporation in San Francisco as an example. This company is moving into a new building and needs a whole new network (what a treat this is!). They have 14 departments, with about 70 users in each. You could probably squeeze one or two Class C addresses to use, or maybe you could use a Class B, or even a Class A just for fun.

The rule of thumb in the consulting world is, when you're setting up a corporate network—regardless of how small it is—you should use a Class A network address because it gives you the most flexibility and growth options. For example, if you used the 10.0.0.0 network address with a /24 mask, then you'd have 65,536 networks, each with 254 hosts. Lots of room for growth with that network!

But if you're setting up a home network, you'd opt for a Class C address because it is the easiest for people to understand and configure. Using the default Class C mask gives you one network with 254 hosts—plenty for a home network.

With the Acme Corporation, a nice 10.1.*x*.0 with a /24 mask (the *x* is the subnet for each department) makes this easy to design, install, and troubleshoot.

Summary

If you made it this far and understood everything the first time through, you should be proud of yourself. We really covered a lot of ground in this chapter, but understand that the information in this chapter is key to being able to navigate through the rest of this book. And even if you didn't get a complete understanding the first time around, don't stress. It really wouldn't hurt you to read this chapter more than once. There is still a lot of ground to cover, so make sure you've got it all down, and get ready for more

After you learned about the DoD model, the layers, and associated protocols, you learned about the oh-so-important IP addressing. I discussed in detail the difference between each class of address and how to find a network address, broadcast address, and valid host range, which is critical information to understand before going on to Chapter 3.

Since you've already come this far, there's no reason to stop now and waste all those brainwaves and new neurons. So don't stop—go through the written lab and review questions at the end of this chapter and make sure you understand each answer's explanation. The best is yet to come!

Exam Essentials

Remember the Process/Application layer protocols.   Telnet is a terminal emulation program that allows you to log into a remote host and run programs. File Transfer Protocol (FTP) is a connection-oriented service that allows you to transfer files. Trivial FTP (TFTP) is a connectionless file transfer program. Simple Mail Transfer Protocol (SMTP) is a send-mail program.

Remember the Host-to-Host layer protocols.   Transmission Control Protocol (TCP) is a connection-oriented protocol that provides reliable network service by using acknowledgments and flow control. User Datagram Protocol (UDP) is a connectionless protocol that provides low overhead and is considered unreliable.

Remember the Internet layer protocols.   Internet Protocol (IP) is a connectionless protocol that provides network address and routing through an internetwork. Address Resolution Protocol (ARP) finds a hardware address from a known IP address. Reverse ARP (RARP) finds an IP address from a known hardware address. Internet Control Message Protocol (ICMP) provides diagnostics and destination unreachable messages.

Remember the Class A range.   The IP range for a Class A network is 1–126. This provides 8 bits of network addressing and 24 bits of host addressing by default.

Remember the Class B range.   The IP range for a Class B network is 128–191. Class B addressing provides 16 bits of network addressing and 16 bits of host addressing by default.

Remember the Class C range.   The IP range for a Class C network is 192–223. Class C addressing provides 24 bits of network addressing and 8 bits of host addressing by default.

Remember the Private IP ranges.   Class A private address range is 10.0.0.0 through 10.255.255.255. Class B private address range is 172.16.0.0 through 172.31.255.255. Class C private address range is 192.168.0.0 through 192.168.255.255.

Written Lab 2

1. What is the Class C address range in decimal and in binary?
2. What layer of the DoD model is equivalent to the Transport layer of the OSI model?
3. What is the valid range of a Class A network address?
4. What is the 127.0.0.1 address used for?
5. How do you find the network address from a listed IP address?
6. How do you find the broadcast address from a listed IP address?
7. What is the Class A private IP address space?
8. What is the Class B private IP address space?
9. What is the Class C private IP address space?
10. What are all the available characters that you can use in hexadecimal addressing?

(The answers to Written Lab 2 can be found following the answers to the review questions for this chapter.)

Review Questions

1. What is the decimal and hexadecimal equivalent of the binary number 10011101? (Choose two.)

A. 159

B. 157

C. 185

D. 0x9D

E. 0xD9

F. 0x159

2. Which of the following allows a router to respond to an ARP request that is intended for a remote host?

A. Gateway DP

B. Reverse ARP (RARP)

C. Proxy ARP

D. Inverse ARP (IARP)

E. Address Resolution Protocol (ARP)

3. You want to implement a mechanism that automates the IP configuration, including IP address, subnet mask, default gateway, and DNS information. Which protocol will you use to accomplish this?

A. SMTP

B. SNMP

C. DHCP

D. ARP

4. What protocol is used to find the hardware address of a local device?

A. RARP

B. ARP

C. IP

D. ICMP

E. BootP

5. Which of the following are layers in the TCP/IP model? (Choose three.)

A. Application

B. Session

C. Transport

D. Internet

E. Data Link

F. Physical

6. Which class of IP address provides a maximum of only 254 host addresses per network ID?

   A. Class A

   B. Class B

   C. Class C

   D. Class D

   E. Class E

7. Which of the following describe the DHCP Discover message? (Choose two.)

   A. It uses FF:FF:FF:FF:FF:FF as a layer 2 broadcast.

   B. It uses UDP as the Transport layer protocol.

   C. It uses TCP as the Transport layer protocol.

   D. It does not use a layer 2 destination address.

8. Which layer 4 protocol is used for a Telnet connection?

   A. IP

   B. TCP

   C. TCP/IP

   D. UDP

   E. ICMP

9. Which statements are true regarding ICMP packets? (Choose two.)

   A. They acknowledge receipt of a TCP segment.

   B. They guarantee datagram delivery.

   C. They can provide hosts with information about network problems.

   D. They are encapsulated within IP datagrams.

   E. They are encapsulated within UDP datagrams.

10. Which of the following services use TCP? (Choose three.)

   A. DHCP

   B. SMTP

   C. SNMP

   D. FTP

   E. HTTP

   F. TFTP

11. Which of the following services use UDP? (Choose three.)

   A. DHCP

   B. SMTP

   C. SNMP

   D. FTP

   E. HTTP

   F. TFTP

12. Which of the following are TCP/IP protocols used at the Application layer of the OSI model? (Choose three.)

A. IP

B. TCP

C. Telnet

D. FTP

E. TFTP

13. The following illustration shows a data stricture header. What protocol is this header from?

FIGURE 2.13   Data Structure header

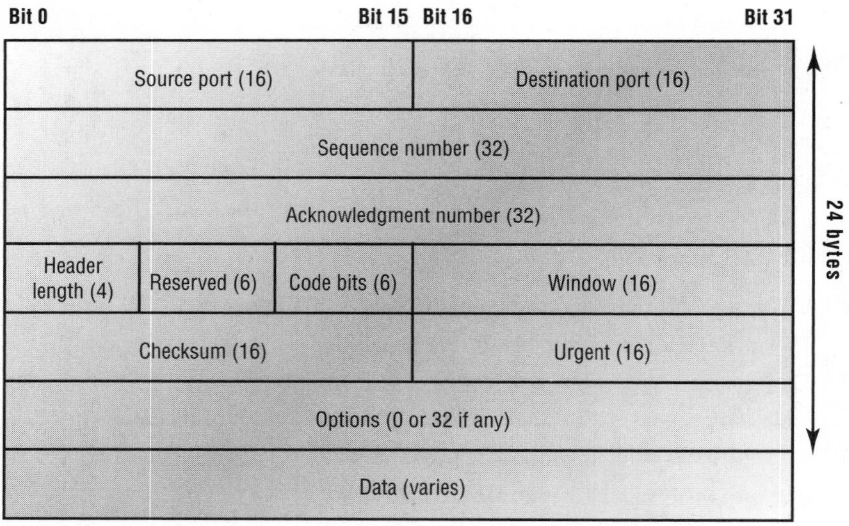

A. IP

B. ICMP

C. TCP

D. UDP

E. ARP

F. RARP

14. If you use either Telnet or FTP, which is the highest layer you are using to transmit data?

A. Application

B. Presentation

C. Session

D. Transport

15. The DoD model (also called the TCP/IP stack) has four layers. Which layer of the DoD model is equivalent to the Network layer of the OSI model?

   A. Application

   B. Host-to-Host

   C. Internet

   D. Network Access

16. Which of the following is a private IP address?

   A. 12.0.0.1

   B. 168.172.19.39

   C. 172.20.14.36

   D. 172.33.194.30

17. What layer in the TCP/IP stack is equivalent to the Transport layer of the OSI model?

   A. Application

   B. Host-to-Host

   C. Internet

   D. Network Access

18. Which statements are not true regarding ICMP packets? (choose three)

   A. UDP will send an ICMP Information request message to the source host.

   B. ICMP guarantees datagram delivery.

   C. ICMP can provide hosts with information about network problems.

   D. ICMP is encapsulated within IP datagrams.

   E. ICMP is encapsulated within UDP datagrams.

19. What is the address range of a Class B network address in binary?

   A. 01$xxxxxx$

   B. 0$xxxxxxx$

   C. 10$xxxxxx$

   D. 110$xxxxx$

20. Which of the following protocols use both TCP and UDP?

   A. FTP

   B. SMTP

   C. Telnet

   D. DNS

Answers to Review Questions

1. B, D. To turn a binary number into decimal, you just have to add the values of each bit that is a 1. The values of 10011101 are 128, 16, 8, 4, and 1. 128 + 16 + 8 + 4 + 1 = 157. Hexadecimal is a base-16 number system. The values of hexadecimal are 0, 1, 2, 3, 4, 5, 6, 7, 8, 9, A, B, C, D, E, F—16 characters total, from which to create all the numbers you'll ever need. So, if 1001 in binary is 9, then the hexadecimal equivalent is 9. Since we then have 1101, which is 13 in binary, the hexadecimal answer is D and the complete hexadecimal answer is 0x9D. Even though binary/hex numbers were discussed in Chapter 1, a good review is necessary here.

2. C. Proxy ARP can help machines on a subnet reach remote subnets without configuring routing or a default gateway.

3. C. Dynamic Host Configuration Protocol (DHCP) is used to provide IP information to hosts on your network. DHCP can provide a lot of information, but the most common is IP address, subnet mask, default gateway, and DNS information.

4. B. Address Resolution Protocol (ARP) is used to find the hardware address from a known IP address.

5. A, C, D. This seems like a hard question at first because it doesn't make sense. The listed answers are from the OSI model and the question asked about the TCP/IP protocol stack (DoD model). However, let's just look for what is wrong. First, the Session layer is not in the TCP/IP model; neither are the Data Link or Physical layers. This leaves us with the Transport layer (Host-to-Host in the DoD model), Internet layer (Network layer in the OSI), and Application layer (Application/Process in the DoD).

6. C. A Class C network address has only 8 bits for defining hosts: $2^8 - 2 = 254$.

7. A, B. A client that sends out a DHCP Discover message in order to receive an IP address sends out a broadcast at both layer 2 and layer 3. The layer 2 broadcast is all Fs in hex, or FF:FF:FF:FF:FF:FF. The layer 3 broadcast is 255.255.255.255, which means all networks and all hosts. DHCP is connectionless, which means it uses User Datagram Protocol (UDP) at the Transport layer, also called the Host-to-Host layer.

8. B. Although Telnet does use TCP and IP (TCP/IP), the question specifically asks about layer 4, and IP works at layer 3. Telnet uses TCP at layer 4.

9. C, D. Internet Control Message Protocol (ICMP) is used to send error messages through the network, but they do not work alone. Every segment or ICMP payload must be encapsulated within an IP datagram (or packet).

10. B, D, E. SMTP, FTP, and HTTP use TCP.

11. A, C, F. DHCP, SNMP, and TFTP use UDP. SMTP, FTP, and HTTP use TCP.

12. C, D, E. Telnet, File Transfer Protocol (FTP), and Trivial FTP are all Application layer protocols. IP is a Network layer protocol. Transmission Control Protocol (TCP) is a Transport layer protocol.

13. C. First, you should know easily that only TCP and UDP work at the Transport layer, so now you have a 50/50 shot. However, since the header has sequencing, acknowledgment, and window numbers, the answer can only be TCP.

14. A. Both FTP and Telnet use TCP at the Transport layer; however, they both are Application layer protocols, so the Application layer is the best answer for this question.

15. C. The four layers of the DoD model are Application/Process, Host-to-Host, Internet, and Network Access. The Internet layer is equivalent to the Network layer of the OSI model.

16. C. Class A private address range is 10.0.0.0 through 10.255.255.255. Class B private address range is 172.16.0.0 through 172.31.255.255 and Class C private address range is 192.168.0.0 through 192.168.255.255

17. B. The four layers of the TCP/IP stack (also called the DoD model) are Application/Process, Host-to-Host, Internet, and Network Access. The Host-to-Host layer is equivalent to the Transport layer of the OSI model.

18. A, B, E. ICMP is used for diagnostics and destination unreachable messages. ICMP is encapsulated within IP datagrams and because it is used for diagnostics, it will provide hosts with information about network problems.

19. C. The range of a Class B network address is 128–191. This makes our binary range 10*xxxxxx*.

20. D. DNS uses TCP for zone exchanges between server, and UDP is used when a client is trying to resolve a hostname to an IP address.

Answers to Written Lab 2

1. 192–223, 110*xxxxx*
2. Host-to-Host
3. 1–126
4. Loopback or diagnostics
5. Turn all host bits off.
6. Turn all host bits on.
7. 10.0.0.0 through 10.255.255.255
8. 172.16.0.0 through 172.31.255.255
9. 192.168.0.0 through 192.168.255.255
10. 0–9 and A, B, C, D, E, and F

Chapter

3

IP Subnetting and Variable Length Subnet Masks (VLSMs) and Troubleshooting IP

THE CCNA INTRO EXAM TOPICS COVERED IN THIS CHAPTER INCLUDE THE FOLLOWING:

✓ **Design and Support**

  ▪ Determine IP addresses

✓ **Technology**

  ▪ Describe how an IP address is associated with a device interface, and the association between physical and employ IP addressing techniques

  ▪ Employ IP addressing techniques

This chapter will pick up right where we left off in the last chapter. We will continue our discussion of IP addressing.

We'll start with subnetting an IP network. You're going to have to really apply yourself, because subnetting takes time and practice in order to nail it. So be patient. Do whatever it takes to get this stuff dialed in. This chapter truly is very important—possibly the most important chapter in this book for you to understand.

I'll thoroughly cover IP subnetting from the very beginning. I know this might sound weird to you, but I think you'll be much better off if you can try to forget everything you've learned about subnetting before reading this chapter—especially if you've been to a Microsoft class!

After our discussion of IP subnetting, I'm going to tell you all about Variable Length Subnet Masks (VLSMs) and then wrap up the chapter by going over IP address troubleshooting and take you through the steps Cisco recommends when troubleshooting an IP network.

So get psyched—you're about to go for quite a ride! This chapter will truly help you understand IP addressing and networking, so don't get discouraged or give up. If you stick with it, I promise that one day you'll look back on this and you'll be really glad you decided to hang on. It's one of those things that after you understand it, you'll wonder why you once thought it was so hard. Ready? Let's go!

Subnetting Basics

In Chapter 2, you learned how to define and find the valid host ranges used in a Class A, Class B, and Class C network address by turning the host bits all off and then all on. This is very good, but here's the catch: You were defining only one network. What happens if you wanted to take one network address and create six networks from it? You would have to do something called *subnetting*, because that's what allows you to take one larger network and break it into a bunch of smaller networks.

There are loads of reasons in favor of subnetting, including the following benefits:

Reduced network traffic   We all appreciate less traffic of any kind. Networks are no different. Without trusty routers, packet traffic could grind the entire network down to a near standstill. With routers, most traffic will stay on the local network; only packets destined for other networks will pass through the router. Routers create broadcast domains. The more broadcast domains you create, the smaller the broadcast domains and the less network traffic on each network segment.

Optimized network performance   This is a result of reduced network traffic.

Simplified management   It's easier to identify and isolate network problems in a group of smaller connected networks than within one gigantic network.

Facilitated spanning of large geographical distances   Because WAN links are considerably slower and more expensive than LAN links, a single large network that spans long distances can create problems in every area previously listed. Connecting multiple smaller networks makes the system more efficient.

In the following sections, I am going to move to subnetting a network address. This is the good part—ready?

IP Subnet-Zero

IP subnet-zero is not a new command, but in the past Cisco courseware, and Cisco exam objectives didn't cover it—but it certainly does now! This command allows you to use the first and last subnet in your network design. For example, the Class C mask of 192 provides subnets 64 and 128 (discussed thoroughly later in this chapter), but with the ip subnet-zero command, you now get to use subnets 0, 64, 128, and 192. That is two more subnets for every subnet mask we use.

Even though we don't discuss the command line interface (CLI) until the next chapter, "Introduction to the Cisco IOS," it's important for you to be familiar with this command:

```
P1R1#sh running-config
Building configuration...
Current configuration : 827 bytes
!
hostname Pod1R1
!
ip subnet-zero
!
```

This router output shows that the command `ip subnet-zero` is enabled on the router. Cisco has turned this command on by default starting with Cisco IOS version 12.*x*.

It is important to remember that when studying for your Cisco exams, make sure you read very carefully and understand if Cisco is asking you *not* to use subnet-zero. There are instances where this may happen.

How to Create Subnets

To create subnetworks, you take bits from the host portion of the IP address and reserve them to define the subnet address. This means fewer bits for hosts, so the more subnets, the fewer bits available for defining hosts.

Later in this chapter, you'll learn how to create subnets, starting with Class C addresses. But before you actually implement subnetting, you need to determine your current requirements as well as plan for future conditions.

Before we move on to designing and creating a subnet mask, you need to understand that in this first section we will be discussing classful routing, which means that all hosts (all nodes) in the network use the exact same subnet mask. When we move on to Variable Length Subnet Masks (VLSMs), I'll discuss classless routing, which means that each network segment *can* use a different subnet mask.

Follow these steps:

1. Determine the number of required network IDs:
   - One for each subnet
   - One for each wide area network connection
2. Determine the number of required host IDs per subnet:
   - One for each TCP/IP host
   - One for each router interface
3. Based on the above requirements, create the following:
   - One subnet mask for your entire network
   - A unique subnet ID for each physical segment
   - A range of host IDs for each subnet

Understanding the Powers of 2

Powers of 2 are important to understand and memorize for use with IP subnetting. To review powers of 2, remember that when you see a number with another number to its upper right (called an exponent), this means you should multiply the number by itself as many times as the upper number specifies. For example, 2^3 is $2 \times 2 \times 2$, which equals 8. Here's a list of powers of 2 that you should commit to memory:

$2^1 = 2$

$2^2 = 4$

$2^3 = 8$

$2^4 = 16$

$2^5 = 32$

$2^6 = 64$

$2^7 = 128$

$2^8 = 256$

$2^9 = 512$

$2^{10} = 1,024$

$2^{11} = 2,048$

$2^{12} = 4,096$

$2^{13} = 8,192$

$2^{14} = 16,384$

Before you get stressed out about knowing all these exponents, remember that it's helpful to know them, but it's not absolutely necessary. Here's a little trick since you're working with 2s: Each successive power of 2 is double the previous one. For example, all you have to do to remember the value of 2^9 is to first know that $2^8 = 256$. Why? Because when you double 2 to the eighth power (256), you get 2^9 (or 512). To determine the value of 2^{10}, simply start at $2^8 = 256$, and then double it twice.

You can go the other way as well. If you needed to know what 2^6 is, you just cut 256 in half two times: once to reach 2^7 and then one more time to reach 2^6.

Subnet Masks

For the subnet address scheme to work, every machine on the network must know which part of the host address will be used as the subnet address. This is accomplished by assigning a *subnet mask* to each machine. A subnet mask is a 32-bit value that allows the recipient of IP packets to distinguish the network ID portion of the IP address from the host ID portion of the IP address.

The network administrator creates a 32-bit subnet mask composed of 1s and 0s. The 1s in the subnet mask represent the positions that refer to the network or subnet addresses.

Not all networks need subnets, meaning they use the default subnet mask. This is basically the same as saying that a network doesn't have a subnet address. Table 3.1 shows the default subnet masks for Classes A, B, and C. These default masks cannot change. In other words, you can't make a Class B subnet mask read 255.0.0.0. If you try, the host will read that address as invalid and usually won't even let you type it in. For a Class A network, you can't change the first byte in a subnet mask; it must read 255.0.0.0 at a minimum. Similarly, you cannot assign 255.255.255.255, as this is all 1s—a broadcast address. A Class B address must start with 255.255.0.0, and a Class C has to start with 255.255.255.0.

TABLE 3.1   Default Subnet Mask

Class	Format	Default Subnet Mask
A	*network.node.node.node*	255.0.0.0
B	*network.network.node.node*	255.255.0.0
C	*network.network.network.node*	255.255.255.0

Classless Inter-Domain Routing (CIDR)

Another term you need to familiarize yourself with is *Classless Inter-Domain Routing (CIDR)*. It's basically the method that ISPs (Internet service providers) use to allocate an amount of addresses to a company, a home—a customer. They provide addresses in a certain block size, something I'll be going into in greater detail later in this chapter.

When you receive a block of addresses from an ISP, what you get will look something like this: 192.168.10.32/28. This is telling you what your subnet mask is. The slash notation (/) means how many bits are turned on (1s). Obviously, the maximum could only be /32 because a byte is 8 bits and there are 4 bytes in an IP address: ($4 \times 8 = 32$). But keep in mind that the largest subnet mask available (regardless of the class of address) can only be a /30 because you've got to keep at least 2 bits for host bits.

Take, for example, a Class A default subnet mask, which is 255.0.0.0. This means that the first byte of the subnet mask is all ones (1s), or 11111111. When referring to a slash notation, you need to count all the 1s bits to figure out your mask. The 255.0.0.0 is considered a /8 because it has 8 bits that are 1s—that is, 8 bits that are turned on.

A Class B default mask would be 255.255.0.0, which is a /16 because 16 bits are ones (1s): 11111111.11111111.00000000.00000000.

Table 3.2 has a listing of every available subnet mask and its equivalent CIDR slash notation.

TABLE 3.2   CIDR Values

Subnet Mask	CIDR Value
255.0.0.0	/8
255.128.0.0	/9
255.192.0.0	/10
255.224.0.0	/11
255.240.0.0	/12

TABLE 3.2   CIDR Values *(continued)*

Subnet Mask	CIDR Value
255.248.0.0	/13
255.252.0.0	/14
255.254.0.0	/15
255.255.0.0	/16
255.255.128.0	/17
255.255.192.0	/18
255.255.224.0	/19
255.255.240.0	/20
255.255.248.0	/21
255.255.252.0	/22
255.255.254.0	/23
255.255.255.0	/24
255.255.255.128	/25
255.255.255.192	/26
255.255.255.224	/27
255.255.255.240	/28
255.255.255.248	/29
255.255.255.252	/30

No, you cannot configure a Cisco router using this slash format. But wouldn't that be nice? Nevertheless, it's really important for you to know subnet masks in the slash notation (CIDR).

Subnetting Class C Addresses

There are many different ways to subnet a network. The right way is the way that works best for you. In a Class C address, only 8 bits are available for defining the hosts. Remember that subnet bits start at the left and go to the right, without skipping bits. This means that the only Class C subnet masks can be the following:

```
Binary      Decimal   CIDR
------------------------------------------------------------
10000000 = 128        /25
11000000 = 192        /26
11100000 = 224        /27
11110000 = 240        /28
11111000 = 248        /29
11111100 = 252        /30
```

We can't use a /31 or /32 because we have to have at least 2 host bits for assigning IP addresses to hosts. In the past, I never discussed the /25 in a Class C network. Cisco always had been concerned with having at least 2 subnet bits, but now, because of Cisco recognizing the `ip subnet-zero` command in its curriculum and exam objectives, we can use just 1 subnet bit.

In the following sections, I'm going to teach you an alternate method of subnetting that makes it easier to subnet larger numbers in no time.

Subnetting a Class C Address: The Fast Way!

When you've chosen a possible subnet mask for your network and need to determine the number of subnets, valid hosts, and broadcast addresses of a subnet that the mask provides, all you need to do is answer five simple questions:

- How many subnets does the chosen subnet mask produce?
- How many valid hosts per subnet are available?
- What are the valid subnets?
- What's the broadcast address of each subnet?
- What are the valid hosts in each subnet?

At this point it's important that you both understand and have memorized your powers of 2. Please refer to the sidebar "Understanding the Powers of 2" earlier in this chapter if you need some help. Here's how you get the answers to those five big questions:

- *How many subnets?* $2x$ = number of subnets. x is the number of masked bits, or the 1s. For example, in 11000000, the number of 1s gives us 2^2 subnets. In this example, there are 4 subnets.

- *How many hosts per subnet?* $2y - 2$ = number of hosts per subnet. y is the number of unmasked bits, or the 0s. For example, in 11000000, the number of 0s gives us $2^6 - 2$ hosts. In this example, there are 62 hosts per subnet. You need to subtract 2 for the subnet address and the broadcast address, which are not valid hosts.

- *What are the valid subnets?* 256 – subnet mask = block size, or increment number. An example would be 256 – 192 = 64. The block size of a 192 mask is always 64. Start counting at zero in blocks of 64 until you reach the subnet mask value and these are your subnets. 0, 64, 128, 192. Easy, huh?

- *What's the broadcast address for each subnet?* Now here's the really easy part… Since we counted our subnets in the last section as 0, 64, 128, and 192, the broadcast address is always the number right before the next subnet. For example, the 0 subnet has a broadcast address of 63 because the next subnet is 64. The 64 subnet has a broadcast address of 127 because the next subnet is 128. And so on. And remember, the broadcast of the last subnet is always 255.

- *What are the valid hosts?* Valid hosts are the numbers between the subnets, omitting the all 0s and all 1s. For example, if 64 is the subnet number and 127 is the broadcast address, then 65–126 is the valid host range—it's *always* the numbers between the subnet address and the broadcast address.

I know this can truly seem confusing. But it really isn't as hard as it seems to be at first—just hang in there! Why not try a few and see for yourself?

Subnetting Practice Examples: Class C Addresses

Here's your opportunity to practice subnetting Class C addresses using the method I just described. Exciting, isn't it! We're going to start with the first Class C subnet mask and work through every subnet that we can using a Class C address. When we're done, I'll show you how easy this is with Class A and B networks too!

Practice Example #1C: 255.255.255.128 (/25)

Since 128 is 10000000 in binary, there is only 1 bit for subnetting and 7 bits for hosts. We're going to subnet the Class C network address 192.168.10.0.

192.168.10.0 = Network address

255.255.255.128 = Subnet mask

Now, let's answer the big five:

- *How many subnets?* Since 128 is 1 bit on (10000000), the answer would be $2^1 = 2$.

- *How many hosts per subnet?* We have 7 host bits off (**10000000**), so the equation would be $2^7 - 2 = 126$ hosts.

- *What are the valid subnets?* 256 – 128 = 128. Remember, we'll start at zero and count in our block size, so our subnets are 0, 128.

- *What's the broadcast address for each subnet?* The number right before the value of the next subnet is all host bits turned on and equals the broadcast address. For the zero subnet, the next subnet is 128, so the broadcast of the 0 subnet is 127.

- *What are the valid hosts?* These are the numbers between the subnet and broadcast address. The easiest way to find the hosts is to write out the subnet address and the broadcast address. This way, the valid hosts are obvious. The following table shows the 0 and 128 subnets, the valid host ranges of each, and the broadcast address of both subnets:

Subnet	0	128
First host	1	129
Last host	126	254
Broadcast	127	255

Before moving on to the next example, take a look at Figure 3.1. Okay, looking at a Class C /25, it's pretty clear there are two subnets. But so what—why is this significant? Well actually, it's not, but that's not the right question. What you really want to know is what you would do with this information!

I know this isn't exactly everyone's favorite pastime, but it's really important, so get over it; we're going to talk about subnetting—period. You need to know that the key to understanding subnetting is to understand the very reason you need to do it. And I'm going to demonstrate this by going through the process of building a physical network— and let's add a router. (We now have an internetwork, as I truly hope you already know!) Alright, because we added that router, in order for the hosts on our internetwork to communicate, they must now have a logical network addressing scheme. We could use IPX or IPv6, but IPv4 is the most popular, and it also just happens to be what we're studying at the moment, so that's what we're going with. Okay—now take a look back to Figure 3.1. There are two physical networks, so we're going to implement a logical addressing scheme that allows for two logical networks. As always, it's a really good idea to look ahead and consider likely growth scenarios—both short and long term, but for this example, a /25 will do the trick.

FIGURE 3.1   Implementing a Class C /25 logical network

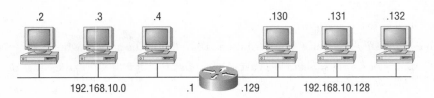

```
Router#show ip route
[output cut]
C 192.168.10.0 is directly connected to Ethernet 0.
C 192.168.10.128 is directly connected to Ethernet 1.
```

Practice Example #2C: 255.255.255.192 (/26)

In this second example, we're going to subnet the network address 192.168.10.0 using the subnet mask 255.255.255.192.

192.168.10.0 = Network address

255.255.255.192 = Subnet mask

Now, let's answer the big five:

- *How many subnets?* Since 192 is 2 bits on (**11**000000), the answer would be $2^2 = 4$ subnets.

- *How many hosts per subnet?* We have 6 host bits off (11**000000**), so the equation would be $2^6 - 2 = 62$ hosts.

- *What are the valid subnets?* $256 - 192 = 64$. Remember, we start at zero and count in our block size, so our subnets are 0, 64, 128, and 192.

- *What's the broadcast address for each subnet?* The number right before the value of the next subnet is all host bits turned on and equals the broadcast address. For the zero subnet, the next subnet is 64, so the broadcast address for the zero subnet is 63.

- *What are the valid hosts?* These are the numbers between the subnet and broadcast address. The easiest way to find the hosts is to write out the subnet address and the broadcast address. This way, the valid hosts are obvious. The following table shows the 0, 64, 128, and 192 subnets, the valid host ranges of each, and the broadcast address of each subnet:

The subnets (do this first)	0	64	128	192
Our first host (perform host addressing last)	1	65	129	193
Our last host	62	126	190	254
The broadcast address (do this second)	63	127	191	255

Okay, again, before getting into the next example, you can see that we can now subnet a /26. And what are you going to do with this fascinating information? Implement it! We'll use figure 3.2 to practice a /26 network implementation.

The /26 mask provides four subnetworks, and we need a subnet for each router interface. With this mask, we actually have room to add another router interface.

Practice Example #3C: 255.255.255.224 (/27)

This time, we'll subnet the network address 192.168.10.0 and subnet mask 255.255.255.224.

192.168.10.0 = Network address

255.255.255.224 = Subnet mask

- *How many subnets?* 224 is 11100000, so our equation would be $2^3 = 8$.

- *How many hosts?* $2^5 - 2 = 30$.

FIGURE 3.2   Implementing a Class C /26 logical network

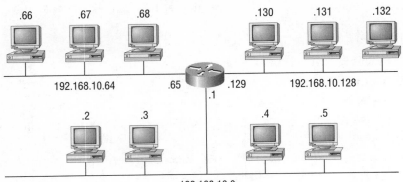

Router#show ip route
[output cut]
C 192.168.10.0 is directly connected to Ethernet 0
C 192.168.10.64 is directly connected to Ethernet 1
C 192.168.10.128 is directly connected to Ethernet 2

- *What are the valid subnets?* 256 – 224 = 32. We just start at zero and count to the subnet mask value in blocks (increments) of 32: 0, 32, 64, 96, 128, 160, 192, and 224.
- *What's the broadcast address for each subnet (always the number right before the next subnet)?*
- *What are the valid hosts (the numbers between the subnet number and the broadcast address)?*

To answer the last two questions, first just write out the subnets, then write out the broadcast addresses—the number right before the next subnet. Last, fill in the host addresses. The following table gives you all the subnets for the 255.255.255.224 Class C subnet mask:

The subnet address	0	32	64	96	128	160	192	224
The first valid host	1	33	65	97	129	161	193	225
The last valid host	30	62	94	126	158	190	222	254
The broadcast address	31	63	95	127	159	191	223	255

Practice Example #4C: 255.255.255.240 (/28)

Let's practice on another one:

192.168.10.0 = Network address

255.255.255.240 = Subnet mask

- *Subnets?* 240 is 11110000 in binary. $2^4 = 16$.
- *Hosts?* 4 host bits, or $2^4 - 2 = 14$.

- *Valid subnets?* 256 − 240 = 16. Start at 0: 0 + 16 = 16. 16 + 16 = 32. 32 + 16 = 48. 48 + 16 = 64. 64 + 16 = 80. 80 + 16 = 96. 96 + 16 = 112. 112 + 16 = 128. 128 + 16 = 144. 144 + 16 = 160. 160 + 16 = 176. 176 + 16 = 192. 192 + 16 = 208. 208 + 16 = 224. 224 + 16 = 240.

- *Broadcast address for each subnet?*

- *Valid hosts?*

To answer the last two questions, check out the following table. It gives you the subnets, valid hosts, and broadcast addresses for each subnet. First, find the address of each subnet using the block size (increment). Second, find the broadcast address of each subnet increment (it's always the number right before the next valid subnet), then just fill in the host addresses. The following table shows the available subnets, hosts, and broadcast addresses provided from a Class C 255.255.255.240 mask.

Subnet	0	16	32	48	64	80	96	112	128	144	160	176	192	208	224	240
First host	1	17	33	49	65	81	97	113	129	145	161	177	193	209	225	241
Last host	14	30	46	62	78	94	110	126	142	158	174	190	206	222	238	254
Broadcast	15	31	47	63	79	95	111	127	143	159	175	191	207	223	239	255

Cisco has figured out the most people cannot count in 16s and therefore have a hard time finding valid subnets, hosts, and broadcast addresses with the Class C 255.255.255.240 mask. You'd be wise to study this mask.

Practice Example #5C: 255.255.255.248 (/29)

Let's keep practicing:

192.168.10.0 = Network address

255.255.255.248 = Subnet mask

- *Subnets?* 248 in binary = 11111000. 2^5 = 32.

- *Hosts?* $2^3 − 2$ = 6.

- *Valid subnets?* 256 − 248 = 0, 8, 16, 24, 32, 40, 48, 56, 64, 72, 80, 88, 96, 104, 112, 120, 128, 136, 144, 152, 160, 168, 176, 184, 192, 200, 208, 216, 224, 232, 240, and 248.

- *Broadcast address for each subnet?*

- *Valid hosts?*

Take a look at the following table. It shows some of the subnets (first four and last four only), valid hosts, and broadcast addresses for the Class C 255.255.255.248 mask:

Subnet	0	8	16	24	...	224	232	240	248
First host	1	9	17	25	...	225	233	241	249
Last host	6	14	22	30	...	230	238	246	254
Broadcast	7	15	23	31	....	231	239	247	255

Practice Example #6C: 255.255.255.252 (/30)

Just one more:

192.168.10.0 = Network address

255.255.255.252 = Subnet mask

- *Subnets? 64.*
- *Hosts? 2.*
- *Valid subnets? 0, 4, 8, 12, etc., all the way to 252.*
- *Broadcast address for each subnet (always the number right before the next subnet)?*
- *Valid hosts (the numbers between the subnet number and the broadcast address)?*

 **Real World Scenario**

Should We Really Use This Mask That Provides Only Two Hosts?

You are the network administrator for Acme Corporation in San Francisco, with dozens of WAN links connecting to your corporate office. Right now your network is a classful network, which means that the same subnet mask is on each host and router interface. You've read about classless routing where you can have different size masks but don't know what to use on your point-to-point WAN links. Is the 255.255.255.252 (/30) a helpful mask in this situation?

Yes, this is a very helpful mask in wide area networks.

If you use the 255.255.255.0 mask, then each network would have 254 hosts, but you only use two addresses with a WAN link! That is a waste of 252 hosts per subnet. If you use the 255.255.255.252 mask, then each subnet has only two hosts and you don't waste precious addresses.

This is a really important subject, one that we'll address in a lot more detail in the section on VLSM network design later in this chapter.

The following table shows you the subnet, valid host, and broadcast address of the first four and last four subnets in the 255.255.255.252 Class C subnet:

Subnet	0	4	8	12	...	240	244	248	252
First host	1	5	9	13	...	241	245	249	253
Last host	2	6	10	14	...	242	246	250	254
Broadcast	3	7	11	15	...	243	247	251	255

Subnetting in Your Head: Class C Addresses

It really is possible to subnet in your head. Even if you don't believe me, I'll show you how. And it's not all that hard either—take the following example:

192.168.10.33 = Node address

255.255.255.224 = Subnet mask

First, determine the subnet and broadcast address of the above IP address. You can do this by answering question 3 of the big five questions: 256 – 224 = 32. 0, 32, 64. The address of 33 falls between the two subnets of 32 and 64 and must be part of the 192.168.10.32 subnet. The next subnet is 64, so the broadcast address of the 32 subnet is 63. (Remember that the broadcast address of a subnet is always the number right before the next subnet.) The valid host range is 33–62 (the numbers between the subnet and broadcast address). This is too easy!

Okay, let's try another one. We'll subnet another Class C address:

192.168.10.33 = Node address

255.255.255.240 = Subnet mask

What subnet and broadcast address is the above IP address a member of? 256 – 240 = 16. 0, 16, 32, 48. Bingo—the host address is between the 32 and 48 subnets. The subnet is 192.168.10.32, and the broadcast address is 47 (the next subnet is 48). The valid host range is 33–46 (the numbers between the subnet number and the broadcast address).

Okay, we need to do more, just to make sure you have this down.

You have a node address of 192.168.10.174 with a mask of 255.255.255.240. What is the valid host range?

The mask is 240, so we'd do a 256 – 240 = 16. This is our block size. Just keep adding 16 until we pass the host address of 174, starting at zero, of course: 0, 16, 32, 48, 64, 80, 96, 112, 128, 144, 160, 176. The host address of 174 is between 160 and 176, so the subnet is 160. The broadcast address is 175, so the valid host range is 161–174. That was a tough one.

One more—just for fun. This is the easiest one of all Class C subnetting:

192.168.10.17 = Node address

255.255.255.252 = Subnet mask

What subnet and broadcast address is the above IP address a member of? 256 – 252 = 0 (always start at zero unless told otherwise), 4, 8, 12, 16, 20, etc. You've got it! The host address is between the 16 and 20 subnets. The subnet is 192.168.10.16, and the broadcast address is 19. The valid host range is 17–18.

Now that you're all over Class C subnetting, let's move on to Class B Subnetting.

Subnetting Class B Addresses

Before we dive into this, let's look at all the possible Class B subnet masks first. Notice that we have a lot more possible subnet masks than we do with a Class C network address:

255.255.128.0	(/17)	255.255.255.0	(/24)
255.255.192.0	(/18)	255.255.255.128	(/25)
255.255.224.0	(/19)	255.255.255.192	(/26)
255.255.240.0	(/20)	255.255.255.224	(/27)
255.255.248.0	(/21)	255.255.255.240	(/28)
255.255.252.0	(/22)	255.255.255.248	(/29)
255.255.254.0	(/23)	255.255.255.252	(/30)

We know the Class B network address has 16 bits available for host addressing. This means we can use up to 14 bits for subnetting (because we have to leave at least 2 bits for host addressing).

By the way, do you notice anything interesting about that list of subnet values—a pattern, maybe? Ah ha! That's exactly why I had you memorize the binary-to-decimal numbers at the beginning of this section. Since subnet mask bits start on the left, move to the right, and can't skip bits, the numbers are always the same regardless of the class of address. Memorize this pattern.

The process of subnetting a Class B network is pretty much the same as it is for a Class C, except that you just have more host bits and you start in the third octet.

Use the same subnet numbers for the third octet with Class B that you used for the fourth octet with Class C, but add a zero to the network portion and a 255 to the broadcast section in the fourth octet. The following table shows you an example host range of two subnets used in a Class B 240 (/20) subnet mask:

First subnet	16.0	32.0
Second subnet	16.255	32.255

Just add the valid hosts between the numbers, and you're set!

This preceding example is true only until you get up to /24. After that, it's numerically exactly like Class C.

Subnetting Practice Examples: Class B Addresses

This section will give you an opportunity to practice subnetting Class B addresses. Again, I have to mention this is the same as subnetting with Class C, except we start in the third octet—with the exact same numbers!

Practice Example #1B: 255.255.128.0 (/17)

172.16.0.0 = Network address

255.255.128.0 = Subnet mask

- *Subnets?* $2^1 = 2$ (same as Class C).
- *Hosts?* $2^{15} - 2 = 32,766$ (7 bits in the third octet, and 8 in the fourth).
- *Valid subnets?* 256 − 128 = 128. 0, 128. Remember that subnetting is performed in the third octet, so the subnet numbers are really 0.0 and 128.0, as shown in the next table. These are the exact numbers we used with Class C; we use them in the third octet and add a 0 in the fourth octet for the network address.
- *Broadcast address for each subnet?*
- *Valid hosts?*

The following table shows the four subnets available, the valid host range, and the broadcast address of each:

Subnet	0.0	128.0
First host	0.1	128.1
Last host	127.254	255.254
Broadcast	127.255	255.255

Okay, notice that we just added the fourth octet's lowest and highest values and came up with the answers. And again, it's done exactly the same way as for a Class C subnet. We just use the same numbers in the third octet and added 0 and 255 in the fourth octet—pretty simple huh! I really can't say this enough… It's just not hard; the numbers never change; we just use them in different octets!

Practice Example #2B: 255.255.192.0 (/18)

172.16.0.0 = Network address

255.255.192.0 = Subnet mask

- *Subnets?* $2^2 = 4$.
- *Hosts?* $2^{14} - 2 = 16,382$ (6 bits in the third octet, and 8 in the fourth).
- *Valid subnets?* 256 − 192 = 64. 0, 64, 128, 192. Remember that the subnetting is performed in the third octet, so the subnet numbers are really 0.0, 64.0, 128.0, and 192.0, as shown in the next table.

- *Broadcast address for each subnet?*
- *Valid hosts?*

The following table shows the four subnets available, the valid host range, and the broadcast address of each:

Subnet	0.0	64.0	128.0	192.0
First host	0.1	64.1	128.1	192.1
Last host	63.254	127.254	191.254	255.254
Broadcast	63.255	127.255	191.255	255.255

Again, it's pretty much the same as it is for a Class C subnet—we just added 0 and 255 in the fourth octet for each subnet in the third octet.

Practice Example #3B: 255.255.240.0 (/20)

172.16.0.0 = Network address

255.255.240.0 = Subnet mask

- *Subnets?* 2^4 = 16.
- *Hosts?* $2^{12} - 2$ = 4094.
- *Valid subnets?* 256 – 240 = 0, 16, 32, 48, etc., up to 240. Notice that these are the same numbers as a Class C 240 mask—we just put them in the third octet and add a 0 and 255 in the fourth octet.
- *Broadcast address for each subnet?*
- *Valid hosts?*

The following table shows the first four subnets, valid hosts, and broadcast addresses in a Class B 255.255.240.0 mask:

Subnet	0.0	16.0	32.0	48.0
First host	0.1	16.1	32.1	48.1
Last host	15.254	31.254	47.254	63.254
Broadcast	15.255	31.255	47.255	63.255

Practice Example #4B: 255.255.254.0 (/23)

172.16.0.0 = Network address

255.255.254.0 = Subnet mask

- *Subnets?* 2^7 = 128.
- *Hosts?* $2^9 - 2$ = 510.
- *Valid subnets?* 256 – 254 = 0, 2, 4, 6, 8, etc., up to 254.

- *Broadcast address for each subnet?*
- *Valid hosts?*

The following table shows the first five subnets, valid hosts, and broadcast addresses in a Class B 255.255.254.0 mask:

Subnet	0.0	2.0	4.0	6.0	8.0
First host	0.1	2.1	4.1	6.1	8.1
Last host	1.254	3.254	5.254	7.254	9.254
Broadcast	1.255	3.255	5.255	7.255	9.255

Practice Example #5B: 255.255.255.0 (/24)

Contrary to popular belief, 255.255.255.0 used with a Class B network address is not called a Class B network with a Class C subnet mask. It's amazing how many people see this mask used in a Class B network and think it's a Class C subnet mask. This is a Class B subnet mask with 8 bits of subnetting—it's considerably different from a Class C mask. Subnetting this address is fairly simple:

172.16.0.0 = Network address

255.255.255.0 = Subnet mask

- *Subnets?* $2^8 = 256$.
- *Hosts?* $2^8 - 2 = 254$.
- *Valid subnets?* $256 - 255 = 1$. 0, 1, 2, 3, etc., all the way to 255.
- *Broadcast address for each subnet?*
- *Valid hosts?*

The following table shows the first four subnets and the last two valid hosts, and broadcast addresses in a Class B 255.255.255.0 mask:

Subnet	0.0	1.0	2.0	3.0	...	254.0	255.0
First host	0.1	1.1	2.1	3.1	...	254.1	255.1
Last host	0.254	1.254	2.254	3.254	...	254.254	255.254
Broadcast	0.255	1.255	2.255	3.255	...	254.255	255.255

Practice Example #6B: 255.255.255.128 (/25)

This is one of the hardest subnet masks you can play with, though. And worse, it actually is a really good subnet to use in production because it creates over 500 subnets with 126 hosts for each subnet—a nice mixture. So, don't skip over it!

172.16.0.0 = Network address

255.255.255.128 = Subnet mask

- *Subnets?* 2^9 = 512.
- *Hosts?* $2^7 - 2$ = 126.
- *Valid subnets?* Okay, now for the tricky part. 256 – 255 = 1. 0, 1, 2, 3, etc., for the third octet. But you can't forget the one subnet bit used in the fourth octet. Remember when I showed you how to figure one subnet bit with a Class C mask? You figure this the same way. (Now you know why I showed you the 1-bit subnet mask in the Class C section— to make this part easier.) You actually get two subnets for each third octet value, hence the 512 subnets. For example, if the third octet is showing subnet 3, the two subnets would actually be 3.0 and 3.128.
- *Broadcast address for each subnet?*
- *Valid hosts?*

The following table shows how you can create subnets, valid hosts, and broadcast addresses using the Class B 255.255.255.128 subnet mask (the first eight subnets are shown, and then the last two subnets):

Subnet	0.0	0.128	1.0	1.128	2.0	2.128	3.0	3.128	...	255.0	255.128
First host	0.1	0.129	1.1	1.129	2.1	2.129	3.1	3.129	...	255.1	255.129
Last host	0.126	0.254	1.126	1.254	2.126	2.254	3.126	3.254	...	255.126	255.254
Broadcast	0.127	0.255	1.127	1.255	2.127	2.255	3.127	3.255	...	255.127	255.255

Practice Example #7B: 255.255.255.192 (/26)

Now, this is where Class B subnetting gets easy. Since the third octet has a 255 in the mask section, whatever number is listed in the third octet is a subnet number. However, now that we have a subnet number in the fourth octet, we can subnet this octet just like we did with Class C subnetting. Let's try it out:

172.16.0.0 = Network address

255.255.255.192 = Subnet mask

- *Subnets?* 2^{10} = 1024.
- *Hosts?* $2^6 - 2$ = 62.
- *Valid subnets?* 256 – 192 = 64. The subnets are shown in the following table. Do these numbers look familiar?
- *Broadcast address for each subnet?*
- *Valid hosts?*

The following table shows the first eight subnet ranges, valid hosts, and broadcast addresses:

Subnet	0.0	0.64	0.128	0.192	1.0	1.64	1.128	1.192
First host	0.1	0.65	0.129	0.193	1.1	1.65	1.129	1.193
Last host	0.62	0.126	0.190	0.254	1.62	1.126	1.190	1.254
Broadcast	0.63	0.127	0.191	0.255	1.63	1.127	1.191	1.255

Notice that for each subnet value in the third octet, you get subnets 0, 64, 128, and 192 in the fourth octet.

Practice Example #8B: 255.255.255.224 (/27)

This is done the same way as the preceding subnet mask, except that we just have more subnets and fewer hosts per subnet available.

172.16.0.0 = Network address

255.255.255.224 = Subnet mask

- *Subnets?* 2^{11} = 2048.
- *Hosts?* $2^5 - 2$ = 30.
- *Valid subnets?* 256 − 224 = 32. 0, 32, 64, 96, 128, 160, 192, 224.
- *Broadcast address for each subnet?*
- *Valid hosts?*

The following table shows the first eight subnets:

Subnet	0.0	0.32	0.64	0.96	0.128	0.160	0.192	0.224
First host	0.1	0.33	0.65	0.97	0.129	0.161	0.193	0.225
Last host	0.30	0.62	0.94	0.126	0.158	0.190	0.222	0.254
Broadcast	0.31	0.63	0.95	0.127	0.159	0.191	0.223	0.255

This next table shows the last eight subnets:

Subnet	255.0	255.32	255.64	255.96	255.128	255.160	255.192	255.224
First host	255.1	255.33	255.65	255.97	255.129	255.161	255.193	255.225
Last host	255.30	255.62	255.94	255.126	255.158	255.190	255.222	255.254
Broadcast	255.31	255.63	255.95	255.127	255.159	255.191	255.223	255.255

Subnetting in Your Head: Class B Addresses

Are you nuts? Subnet Class B addresses in our heads? It's actually easier than writing it out—I'm not kidding! Let me show you how:

Question: What subnet and broadcast address is the IP address 172.16.10.33 255.255.255.224 (/27) a member of?

Answer: The interesting octet is the fourth octet. 256 – 224 = 32. 32 + 32 = 64. Bingo: 33 is between 32 and 64. However, remember that the third octet is considered part of the subnet, so the answer would be the 10.32 subnet. The broadcast is 10.63, since 10.64 is the next subnet. That a was a pretty easy one.

Question: What subnet and broadcast address is the IP address 172.16.66.10 255.255.192.0 (/18) a member of?

Answer: The interesting octet is the third octet instead of the fourth octet. 256 – 192 = 64. 0, 64, 128. The subnet is 172.16.64.0. The broadcast must be 172.16.127.255 since 128.0 is the next subnet.

Question: What subnet and broadcast address is the IP address 172.16.50.10 255.255.224.0 (/19) a member of?

Answer: 256 – 224 = 0, 32, 64. The subnet is 172.16.32.0, and the broadcast must be 172.16.63.25 since 64.0 is the next subnet.

Question: What subnet and broadcast address is the IP address 172.16.46.255 255.255.240.0 (/20) a member of?

Answer: 256 – 240 = 16. The third octet is interesting to us. 0, 16, 32, 48. This subnet address must be in the 172.16.32.0 subnet, and the broadcast must be 172.16.47.255 since 48.0 is the next subnet. So, yes, 172.16.46.255 is a valid host.

Question: What subnet and broadcast address is the IP address 172.16.45.14 255.255.255.252 (/30) a member of?

Answer: Where is the interesting octet? 256 – 252 = 0, 4, 8, 12, 16 (in the fourth octet). The subnet is 172.16.45.12, with a broadcast of 172.16.45.15 because the next subnet is 172.16.45.16.

Question: What is the subnet and broadcast address of the host 172.16.88.255/20?

Answer: What is a /20? If you can't answer this, you can't answer this question, can you? A /20 is 255.255.240.0, which gives us a block size of 16 in the third octet, and since no subnet bits are on in the fourth octet, the answer is always 0 and 255 in the fourth octet. 0, 16, 32, 48, 64, 80, 96…bingo. 88 is between 80 and 96, so the subnet is 80.0 and the broadcast address is 95.255.

Question: A router receives a packet on an interface with a destination address of 172.16.46.191/26. What will the router do with this packet?

Answer: Discard it. Do you know why? 172.16.46.191/26 is a 255.255.255.192 mask, which gives us a block size of 64. Our subnets are then 0, 64, 128, 192. 191 is the broadcast address of the 128 subnet, so a router, by default will discard any broadcast packets.

Subnetting Class A Addresses

Class A subnetting is not performed any differently from Classes B and C, but there are 24 bits to play with instead of the 16 in a Class B address and the 8 in a Class C address.

Let's start by listing all the Class A subnets:

255.128.0.0	(/9)	255.255.240.0	(/20)
255.192.0.0	(/10)	255.255.248.0	(/21)
255.224.0.0	(/11)	255.255.252.0	(/22)
255.240.0.0	(/12)	255.255.254.0	(/23)
255.248.0.0	(/13)	255.255.255.0	(/24)
255.252.0.0	(/14)	255.255.255.128	(/25)
255.254.0.0	(/15)	255.255.255.192	(/26)
255.255.0.0	(/16)	255.255.255.224	(/27)
255.255.128.0	(/17)	255.255.255.240	(/28)
255.255.192.0	(/18)	255.255.255.248	(/29)
255.255.224.0	(/19)	255.255.255.252	(/30)

That's it. You must leave at least 2 bits for defining hosts. And I hope you can see the pattern by now. Remember, we're going to do this the same way as a Class B or C subnet. It's just that, again, we simply have more host bits, and we just use the same subnet numbers we used with Class B and C, but we start using these numbers in the second octet.

Subnetting Practice Examples: Class A Addresses

When you look at an IP address and a subnet mask, you must be able to distinguish the bits used for subnets from the bits used for determining hosts. This is imperative. If you're still struggling with this concept, please reread the preceding "IP Addressing" section in chapter 2. It shows you how to determine the difference between the subnet and host bits and should help clear things up.

Practice Example #1A: 255.255.0.0 (/16)

Class A addresses use a default mask of 255.0.0.0, which leaves 22 bits for subnetting since you must leave 2 bits for host addressing. The 255.255.0.0 mask with a Class A address is using 8 subnet bits.

- *Subnets?* $2^8 = 256$.

- *Hosts?* $2^{16} - 2 = 65,534$.

- *Valid subnets?* What is the interesting octet? $256 - 255 = 1$. 0, 1, 2, 3, etc. (all in the second octet). The subnets would be 10.0.0.0, 10.1.0.0, 10.2.0.0, 10.3.0.0, etc., up to 10.255.0.0.

- *Broadcast address for each subnet?*

- *Valid hosts?*

The following table shows the first two and last two subnets, valid host range, and broadcast addresses for the private Class A 10.0.0.0 network:

Subnet	10.0.0.0	10.1.0.0	...	10.254.0.0	10.255.0.0
First host	10.0.0.1	10.1.0.1	...	10.254.0.1	10.255.0.1
Last host	10.0.255.254	10.1.255.254	...	10.254.255.254	10.255.255.254
Broadcast	10.0.255.255	10.1.255.255	...	10.254.255.255	10.255.255.255

Practice Example #2A: 255.255.240.0 (/20)

255.255.240.0 gives us 12 bits of subnetting and leaves us 12 bits for host addressing.

- *Subnets?* $2^{12} = 4096$.
- *Hosts?* $2^{12} - 2 = 4094$.
- *Valid subnets?* What is your interesting octet? $256 - 240 = 16$. The subnets in the second octet are a block size of 1 and the subnets in the third octet are 0, 16, 32, etc.
- *Broadcast address for each subnet?*
- *Valid hosts?*

The following table shows some examples of the host ranges—the first three and the last subnets:

Subnet	10.0.0.0	10.0.16.0	10.0.32.0	...	10.0.240.0
First host	10.0.0.1	10.0.16.1	10.0.32.1	...	10.0.240.1
Last host	10.0.15.254	10.0.31.254	10.0.47.254	...	10.0.255.254
Broadcast	10.0.15.255	10.0.31.255	10.0.47.255	...	10.0.255.255

Practice Example #3A: 255.255.255.192 (/26)

Let's do one more example using the second, third, and fourth octets for subnetting.

- *Subnets?* $2^{18} = 262,144$.
- *Hosts?* $2^6 - 2 = 62$.
- *Valid subnets?* In the second and third octet, the block size is 1, and in the fourth octet the block size is 64.
- *Broadcast address for each subnet?*
- *Valid hosts?*

The following table shows the first four subnets and their valid hosts and broadcast addresses in the Class A 255.255.255.192 mask:

Subnet	10.0.0.0	10.0.0.64	10.0.0.128	10.0.0.192
First host	10.0.0.1	10.0.0.65	10.0.0.129	10.0.0.193
Last host	10.0.0.62	10.0.0.126	10.0.0.190	10.0.0.254
Broadcast	10.0.0.63	10.0.0.127	10.0.0.191	10.0.0.255

The following table shows the last four subnets and their valid hosts and broadcast addresses:

Subnet	10.255.255.0	10.255.255.64	10.255.255.128	10.255.255.192
First host	10.255.255.1	10.255.255.65	10.255.255.129	10.255.255.193
Last host	10.255.255.62	10.255.255.126	10.255.255.190	10.255.255.254
Broadcast	10.255.255.63	10.255.255.127	10.255.255.191	10.255.255.255

Subnetting in Your Head: Class A Addresses

This sounds hard, but as with Class C and Class B, the numbers are the same; we just start in the second octet. What makes this easy? You only need to worry about the octet that has the largest block size (typically called the interesting octet; one that is something other than 0 or 255)—for example, 255.255.240.0 (/20) with a Class A network. The second octet has a block size of 1, so any number listed in that octet is a subnet. The third octet is a 240 mask, which means we have a block size of 16 in the third octet. If your host ID is 10.20.80.30, what is your subnet, broadcast address, and valid host range?

The subnet in the second octet is 20 with a block size of 1, but the third octet is in block sizes of 16, so we'll just count them out: 0, 16, 32, 48, 64, 80, 96... viola! (By the way, you can count by 16s by now, right?) This makes our subnet 10.20.80.0, with a broadcast of 10.20.95.255 because the next subnet is 10.20.96.0. The valid host range is 10.20.80.1 through 10.20.95.254. And yes, no lie! You really can do this in your head if you just get your block sizes nailed!

Okay, let's practice on one more, just for fun!

Host IP: 10.1.3.65/23

First, you can't answer this question if you don't know what a /23, is. It's 255.255.254.0. The interesting octet here is the third one— 256-254 = 2. Our subnets in the third octet are 2, 4, 6, etc. The host in this question is in subnet 2.0, and the next subnet is 4.0, so that makes the broadcast address 3.255. And any address between 10.1.2.1 and 10.1.3.254 is considered a valid host.

Variable Length Subnet Masks (VLSMs)

I could easily devote an entire chapter to *Variable Length Subnet Masks (VLSMs)*, but instead I'm going to show you a simple way to take one network and create many networks using subnet masks of different lengths on different types of network designs. This is called VLSM networking, and it does bring up another subject I mentioned at the beginning of this chapter: classful and classless networking.

Neither RIPv1 nor IGRP routing protocols have a field for subnet information, so the subnet information gets dropped. What this means is that if a router running RIP has a subnet mask of a certain value, it assumes that *all* interfaces within the classful address space have the same subnet mask. This is called classful routing, and RIP and IGRP are both considered classful routing protocols. (I'll be talking more about RIP and IGRP in Chapter 5, "IP Routing.") If you mix and match subnet mask lengths in a network running RIP or IGRP, that network just won't work!

Classless routing protocols, however, do support the advertisement of subnet information. Therefore, you can use VLSM with routing protocols such as RIPv2, EIGRP, or OSPF. (EIGRP and OSPF will be discussed in Chapter 5 as well). The benefit of this type of network is that you save a bunch of IP address space with it.

As the name suggests, with VLSMs we can have different subnet masks for different subnets. Look at Figure 3.3 to see an example of why classful network designs are inefficient.

Looking at this figure, you'll notice that we have two routers, each with two LANs and connected together with a WAN serial link. In a typical classful network design (RIP or IGRP routing protocols), you could subnet a network like this:

192.168.10.0 = Network
255.255.255.240 (/28) = Mask

FIGURE 3.3 Typical classful network

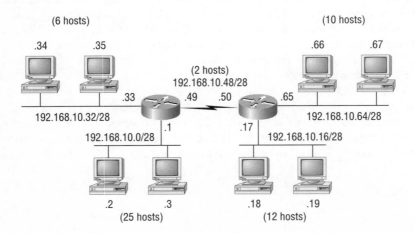

Our subnets would be (you know this part, right?) 0, 16, 32, 48, 64, 80, etc. This allows us to assign 16 subnets to our internetwork. But how many hosts would be available on each network? Well, as you probably know by now, each subnet provides only 14 hosts. This means that each LAN has 14 valid hosts available—one LAN doesn't even have enough addresses needed for all the hosts! But the point-to-point WAN link also has 14 valid hosts. It too bad we can't just nick some valid hosts from that WAN link and give them to our LANs!

All hosts and router interfaces have the same subnet mask—again, this is called classful routing. And if we want this network to be more efficient, we definitely need to add different masks to each router interface.

But there's still a problem—the link between the two routers will never use more than two valid hosts! This wastes valuable IP address space, and it's the big reason I'm going to talk to you about VLSM network design.

VLSM Design

Let's take Figure 3.3 and use a classless design…. The new network is shown in Figure 3.4! In the previous example, we wasted address space—one LAN didn't have enough addresses because every router interface and host used the same subnet mask. Not so good. What would be good is to provide only the needed amount of hosts on each router interface. To do this, we use what are referred to as Variable Length Subnet Masks (VLSMs).

Now remember that we can use different size masks on each router interface. And if we use a /30 on our WAN links and a /27, /28 and /29 on our LANs, we'll get 2 hosts per WAN interface, and 30, 14, and 8 hosts per LAN interface—nice! This makes a huge difference—not only can we get just the right amount of hosts on each LAN, we still have room to add more WANs and LANs using this same network!

FIGURE 3.4   Classless network design

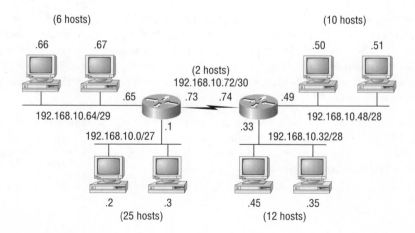

Remember, in order to implement a VLSM design on your network, you need to have a routing protocol that sends subnet mask information with the route updates. This would be RIPv2, EIGRP, and OSPF. RIPv1 and IGRP will not work in classless networks and are considered classful routing protocols.

Why Bother with VLSM Design?

You have just been hired by a new company and need to add on to the existing network. There is no problem with starting over with a new IP address scheme. Should you use a VLSM classless network or a classful network?

Let's just say you happen to have plenty of address space because you are using the Class A 10.0.0.0 private network address in your corporate environment and can't even come close to imagining that you'd ever run out of IP addresses. Why would you want to bother with the VLSM design process?

Good question. There's a good answer too!

Because by creating contiguous blocks of addresses to specific areas of your network, you can then easily summarize your network and keep route updates with a routing protocol to a minimum. Why would anyone want to advertise hundreds of networks between buildings, when you can just send one summary route between buildings and achieve the same result?

If you're confused about what summary routes are, let me explain. Summarization, also called supernetting, provides route updates in the most efficient way possible by adverting many routes in one advertisement instead of individually. This saves a ton of bandwidth and minimizes router processing. As always, you use blocks of addresses (remember that block sizes are used in all sorts of networks) to configure your summary routes and watch your network's performance hum.

But know that summarization only works if you design your network carefully. If you carelessly hand out IP subnets to any location on the network, you'll notice straight up that you no longer have any summary boundaries. And you won't get very far with creating summary routes without those, so watch your step!

Troubleshooting IP Addressing

Troubleshooting IP addressing is obviously an important skill because running in to trouble somewhere along the way is pretty much a sure thing, and it's going to happen to you. No— I'm not a pessimist; I'm just keeping it real. Because of this nasty fact, it would be a very good thing that you can save the day because you can both figure out (diagnose) the problem and fix it on an IP network whether you're at work or at home! So this is where I'm going to show you the "Cisco way" of troubleshooting IP addressing. Let's use Figure 3.5 for an example of your basic IP trouble—poor Sally can't log in to the Windows server. Do you deal with this by calling the Microsoft team to tell them their server is a pile of junk and causing all your problems? Probably not such a great idea—let's double-check our network first instead.

FIGURE 3.5   Basic IP troubleshooting

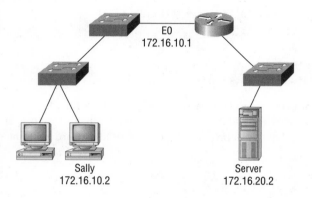

Okay let's get started by going over the troubleshooting steps that Cisco follows. They're pretty simple, but important nonetheless. Pretend you're at a customer host and they're complaining that they can't communicate to a server that just happens to be on a remote network. Here are the four troubleshooting steps Cisco recommends:

1. Open a DOS window and ping 127.0.0.1. This is the diagnostic, or loopback, address, and if you get a successful ping, your IP stack is then considered to be initialized. If it fails, then you have an IP stack failure and need to reinstall TCP/IP on the host.

   ```
   C:\>ping 127.0.0.1
   Pinging 127.0.0.1 with 32 bytes of data:
   Reply from 127.0.0.1: bytes=32 time<1ms TTL=128
   Reply from 127.0.0.1: bytes=32 time<1ms TTL=128
   Reply from 127.0.0.1: bytes=32 time<1ms TTL=128
   Reply from 127.0.0.1: bytes=32 time<1ms TTL=128
   ```

```
Ping statistics for 127.0.0.1:
    Packets: Sent = 4, Received = 4, Lost = 0 (0% loss),
Approximate round trip times in milli-seconds:
    Minimum = 0ms, Maximum = 0ms, Average = 0ms
```

2. From the DOS window, ping the IP address of the local host. If that's successful, then your network interface card (NIC) is functioning. If it fails, then there is a problem with the NIC. Success here doesn't mean that a cable is plugged into the NIC, only that the IP protocol stack on the host can communicate to the NIC (via the LAN driver).

```
C:\>ping 172.16.10.2
Pinging 172.16.10.2 with 32 bytes of data:
Reply from 172.16.10.2: bytes=32 time<1ms TTL=128
Reply from 172.16.10.2: bytes=32 time<1ms TTL=128
Reply from 172.16.10.2: bytes=32 time<1ms TTL=128
Reply from 172.16.10.2: bytes=32 time<1ms TTL=128
Ping statistics for 172.16.10.2:
    Packets: Sent = 4, Received = 4, Lost = 0 (0% loss),
Approximate round trip times in milli-seconds:
    Minimum = 0ms, Maximum = 0ms, Average = 0ms
```

3. From the DOS window, ping the default gateway (router). If the ping works, it means that the NIC is plugged into the network and can communicate on the local network. If it fails, then you have a local physical network problem that could be anywhere from the NIC to the router.

```
C:\>ping 172.16.10.1
Pinging 172.16.10.1 with 32 bytes of data:
Reply from 172.16.10.1: bytes=32 time<1ms TTL=128
Reply from 172.16.10.1: bytes=32 time<1ms TTL=128
Reply from 172.16.10.1: bytes=32 time<1ms TTL=128
Reply from 172.16.10.1: bytes=32 time<1ms TTL=128
Ping statistics for 172.16.10.1:
    Packets: Sent = 4, Received = 4, Lost = 0 (0% loss),
Approximate round trip times in milli-seconds:
    Minimum = 0ms, Maximum = 0ms, Average = 0ms
```

4. If steps 1 through 3 were successful, try to ping the remote server. If that works, then you know that you have IP communication between the local host and the remote server. You also know that the remote physical network is working.

```
C:\>ping 172.16.20.2
Pinging 172.16.20.2 with 32 bytes of data:
Reply from 172.16.20.2: bytes=32 time<1ms TTL=128
Reply from 172.16.20.2: bytes=32 time<1ms TTL=128
```

```
Reply from 172.16.20.2: bytes=32 time<1ms TTL=128
Reply from 172.16.20.2: bytes=32 time<1ms TTL=128
Ping statistics for 172.16.20.2:
    Packets: Sent = 4, Received = 4, Lost = 0 (0% loss),
Approximate round trip times in milli-seconds:
    Minimum = 0ms, Maximum = 0ms, Average = 0ms
```

If the user still can't communicate with the server after steps 1 through 4 are successful, then you probably have some type of name resolution problem and need to check your Domain Name System (DNS) settings. But if the ping to the remote server fails, then you know you have some type of remote physical network problem and need to go to the server and work through steps 1 through 3 until you find the snag.

Before we move onto determining IP address problems and how to fix them, I just want to mention some basic DOS commands that you can use to help troubleshoot your network from both a PC and a Cisco router (the commands might do the same thing, but they are implemented differently).

Packet InterNet Groper (PING): uses ICMP echo request and replies to test if a node IP stack is initialized and alive on the network

Traceroute: displays the list of routers on a path to a network destination by using TTL timeouts and ICMP error messages. This command will not work from a DOS prompt.

Tracert: same command as traceroute, but is a Microsoft Windows command and will not work on a Cisco router

Arp –a: displays IP to MAC address mappings on a Windows PC.

Show ip arp: same command as arp –a, but displays the ARP table on a Cisco router. Like traceroute and tracert, they are not interchangeable through DOS and Cisco.

Ipconfig /all: Used only from a DOS prompt, shows you the PC network configuration.

Once you've gone through all these steps, and used the appropriate DOS commands, if necessary, what do you do if you find a problem? How do you go about fixing an IP address configuration error? Let's move on and discuss how to determine the IP address problems and how to fix them.

Determining IP Address Problems

It's common for a host, router, or other network device to be configured with the wrong IP address, subnet mask, or default gateway. Because this happens way too often, I'm going to teach you how to both determine and fix IP address configuration errors.

Once you've worked through the four basic steps of troubleshooting and determined there's a problem, you obviously then need to find and fix it. It really helps to draw out the network and IP addressing scheme. If it's already done, consider yourself lucky and go buy a lottery ticket, because although it should be done, it rarely is. And if it is, it's usually outdated or inaccurate anyway. Typically it is not done, and you'll probably just have to bite the bullet and start from scratch.

NOTE I'll show you how to draw out your network using CDP in Chapter 8, "Managing a Cisco Internetwork."

Once you have your network accurately drawn out, including the IP addressing scheme, you then need to verify each host's IP address, mask, and default gateway address to determine the problem (I'm assuming you don't have a physical problem, or if you did, you've already fixed it).

Let's check out the example illustrated in Figure 3.6. A user in the sales department calls and tells you that she can't get to ServerA in the marketing department. You ask her if she can get to ServerB in the Marketing department, but she doesn't know because she doesn't have rights to log on to that server. What do you do?

You ask the client to go through the four troubleshooting steps that we learned about in the preceding section. Steps 1 through 3 work, but step 4 fails. By looking at the figure, can you determine the problem? Look for clues in the network drawing. First, the WAN link between the Lab_A router and the Lab_B router shows the mask as a /27. You should already know this mask is 255.255.255.224 and then determine that all networks are using this mask. The network address is 192.168.1.0. What are our valid subnets and hosts? 256 – 224 = 32, so this makes our subnets 32, 64, 96, 128, etc. So, by looking at the figure, you can see that subnet 32 is being used by the sales department, the WAN link is using subnet 96, and the marketing department is using subnet 64.

FIGURE 3.6   IP address problem #1

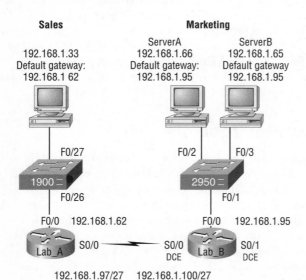

Now you've got to determine what the valid host ranges are for each subnet. From what you learned at the beginning of this chapter, you should now be able to easily determine the subnet address, broadcast addresses, and valid host ranges. The valid hosts for the Sales LAN are 33 through 62—the broadcast address is 63 because the next subnet is 64, right? For the Marketing LAN, the valid hosts are 65 through 94 (broadcast 95), and for the WAN link, 97 through 126 (broadcast 127). By looking at the figure, you can determine that the default gateway on the Lab_B router is incorrect. That address is the broadcast address of the 64 subnet, so there's no way it could be a valid host.

Did you get all that? Maybe we should try another one, just to make sure. Figure 3.7 has a network problem. A user in the Sales LAN can't get to ServerB. You have the user run through the four basic troubleshooting steps and find that the host can communicate to the local network but not to the remote network. Find and define the IP addressing problem.

If you use the same steps used to solve the last problem, you can see first that the WAN link again provides the subnet mask to use—/29 or 255.255.255.248. You need to determine what the valid subnets, broadcast addresses, and valid host ranges are to solve this problem.

The 248 mask is a block size of 8 (256 – 248 = 8), so the subnets both start and increment in multiples of 8. By looking at the figure, you see that the Sales LAN is in the 24 subnet, the WAN is in the 40 subnet, and the Marketing LAN is in the 80 subnet. Can you see the problem yet? The valid host range for the Sales LAN is 25–30, and the configuration appears correct. The valid host range for the WAN link is 41–46, and this also appears correct. The valid host range for the 80 subnet is 81–86, with a broadcast address of 87 because the next subnet is 88. ServerB has been configured with the broadcast address of the subnet.

FIGURE 3.7   IP address problem #2

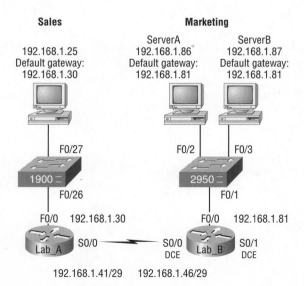

Okay, now that you can figure out misconfigured IP addresses on hosts, what do you do if a host doesn't have an IP address and you need to assign one? What you need to do is look at other hosts on the LAN and figure out the network, mask, and default gateway. Let's take a look at a couple of examples of how to find and apply valid IP addresses to hosts.

If you need to assign a server and router IP addresses on a LAN and the subnet assigned on that segment is 192.168.20.24/29 and the router needs to be assigned the first usable address and the server the last valid host ID, what are the IP address, mask, and default gateway assigned to the server?

To answer this, you must know that a /29 is a 255.255.255.248 mask, which provides a block size of 8. The subnet is known as 24, the next subnet in a block of 8 is 32, so the broadcast address of the 24 subnet is 31, which makes the valid host range 25–30.

Server IP address: 192.168.20.30

Server mask: 255.255.255.248

Default gateway: 192.168.20.25 (router's IP address)

As another example, let's take a look at Figure 3.8 and solve this problem.

Look at the router's IP address on Ethernet0. What IP address, subnet mask, and valid host range could be assigned to the host?

The IP address of the router's Ethernet0 is 192.168.10.33/27. As you already know, a /27 is a 224 mask with a block size of 32. The router's interface is in the 32 subnet. The next subnet is 64, so that makes the broadcast address of the 32 subnet 63 and the valid host range 33–62.

Host IP address: 192.168.10.34–62 (any address in the range except for 33, which is assigned to the router)

Mask: 255.255.255.224

Default gateway: 192.168.10.33

Figure 3.9 shows two routers with Ethernet configurations already assigned. What are the host addresses and subnet masks of hosts A and B?

FIGURE 3.8   Find the valid host #1

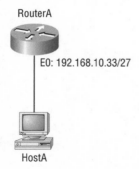

RouterA

E0: 192.168.10.33/27

HostA

FIGURE 3.9   Find the valid host #2

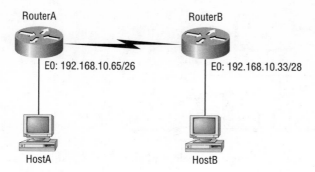

RouterA has an IP address of 192.168.10.65/26 and RouterB has an IP address of 192.168.10.33/28. What are the host configurations? RouterA Ethernet0 is in the 192.168.10.64 subnet and RouterB Ethernet0 is in the 192.168.10.32 network.

Host A IP address: 192.168.10.66–126

Host A mask: 255.255.255.192

Host A default gateway: 192.168.10.65

Host B IP address: 192.168.10.34–62

Host B mask: 255.255.255.240

Host B default gateway: 192.168.10.33

Just a couple more examples and then this chapter is history. Hang in there!

Figure 3.10 shows two routers; you need to configure the S0/0 interface on RouterA. The network assigned to the serial link is 172.16.17.0/22. What IP address can be assigned?

First, you must know that a /22 CIDR is 255.255.252.0, which makes a block size of 4 in the third octet. Since 17 is listed, the available range is 16.1 through 19.254; so, for example, the IP address S0/0 could be 172.16.18.255 since that's within the range.

Okay, last one! You have one Class C network ID and you need to provide one usable subnet per city while allowing enough usable host addresses for each city specified in Figure 3.11. What is your mask?

FIGURE 3.10   Find the valid host address #3

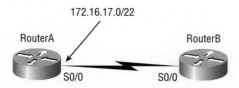

FIGURE 3.11   Find the valid subnet mask.

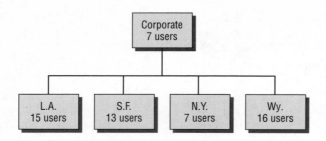

Actually, this is probably the easiest thing you've done all day! I count 5 subnets needed and the Wyoming office needs 16 users (always look for the network that needs the most hosts). What block size is needed for the Wyoming office? 32. (Remember, you cannot use a block size of 16 because you always have to subtract 2!) What mask provides you with a block size of 32? 224. Bingo! This provides 8 subnets, each with 30 hosts.

You're done, the diva has sung, the chicken has crossed the road...whew! Okay, take a good break (but skip the shot and the beer for now), then come back and go through the written and review questions.

Summary

Did you read Chapters 2 and 3 and understand everything on the first pass? If so, that is fantastic—congratulations! The thing is, you probably got lost a couple of times—and as I told you, that's what usually happens, so don't stress. Don't feel bad if you have to reread each chapter more than once, or even 10 times, before you're truly good to go.

This chapter provided you with an important understanding of IP subnetting. After reading this chapter, you should be able to subnet IP addresses in your head. You should also know how to design and implement simple VLSM networks.

You should also understand the Cisco troubleshooting methods. You must remember the four steps that Cisco recommends you take when trying to narrow down exactly where a network problem/IP addressing problem is and then know how to proceed systematically in order to fix the problem. In addition, you should be able to find valid IP addresses and subnet masks by looking at a network diagram.

Exam Essentials

Remember the steps to subnet in your head.   Understand how IP addressing and subnetting work. First, determine your block size by using the 256-subnet mask math. Then count your subnets and determine the broadcast address of each subnet—it is always the number right before the next subnet. Your valid hosts are the numbers between the subnet address and the broadcast address.

Understand the various block sizes. This is an important part of understanding IP addressing and subnetting. The valid block sizes are always 4, 8, 16, 32, 64, 128, etc. You can determine your block size by using the 256-subnet mask math.

Remember the four diagnostic steps. The four simple steps that Cisco recommends for troubleshooting are ping the loopback address, ping the NIC, ping the default gateway, and ping the remote device.

You must be able to find and fix an IP addressing problem. Once you go through the four troubleshooting steps that Cisco recommends, you must be able to determine the IP addressing problem by drawing out the network and finding the valid and invalid hosts addressed in your network.

Understand the troubleshooting tools that you can use from your host and a Cisco router *Ping 127.0.0.1* tests your local IP stack. *Tracert* is a Windows DOS command to track the path a packet takes through an internetwork to a destination. Cisco routers use the command *traceroute*, or just *trace* for short. Don't confuse the Windows and Cisco commands. Although they produce the same output, they don't work from the same prompts. *Ipconfig /all* will display your PC network configuration from a DOS prompt, and *arp –a* (again from a DOS prompt) will display IP to MAC address mapping on a Windows PC.

Written Lab 3

Write the subnet, broadcast address, and valid host range for each of the following:

1. 192.168.100.25/30
2. 192.168.100.37/28
3. 192.168.100.66/27
4. 192.168.100.17/29
5. 192.168.100.99/26
6. 192.168.100.99/25
7. You have a Class B network and need 29 subnets. What is your mask?
8. What is the broadcast address of 192.168.192.10/29?
9. How many hosts are available with a Class C /29 mask?
10. What is the subnet for host ID 10.16.3.65/23?

(The answers to Written Lab 3 can be found following the answers to the review questions for this chapter.)

Review Questions

1. What is the maximum number of IP addresses that can be assigned to hosts on a local subnet that uses the 255.255.255.224 subnet mask?

   A. 14

   B. 15

   C. 16

   D. 30

   E. 31

   F. 62

2. You have a network that needs 29 subnets while maximizing the number of host addresses available on each subnet. How many bits must you borrow from the host field to provide the correct subnet mask?

   A. 2

   B. 3

   C. 4

   D. 5

   E. 6

   F. 7

3. What is the subnetwork address for a host with the IP address 200.10.5.68/28?

   A. 200.10.5.56

   B. 200.10.5.32

   C. 200.10.5.64

   D. 200.10.5.0

4. The network address of 172.16.0.0/19 provides how many subnets and hosts?

   A. 7 subnets, 30 hosts each

   B. 7 subnets, 2,046 hosts each

   C. 7 subnets, 8,190 hosts each

   D. 8 subnets, 30 hosts each

   E. 8 subnets, 2,046 hosts each

   F. 8 subnets, 8,190 hosts each

5. Which two statements describe the IP address 10.16.3.65/23?

   A. The subnet address is 10.16.3.0 255.255.254.0.

   B. The lowest host address in the subnet is 10.16.2.1 255.255.254.0.

   C. The last valid host address in the subnet is 10.16.2.254 255.255.254.0.

   D. The broadcast address of the subnet is 10.16.3.255 255.255.254.0.

   E. The network is not subnetted.

6. If a host on a network has the address 172.16.45.14/30, what is the subnetwork this host belongs to?

    A. 172.16.45.0

    B. 172.16.45.4

    C. 172.16.45.8

    D. 172.16.45.12

    E. 172.16.45.16

7. On a VLSM network, which mask should you use on point-to-point WAN links in order to reduce the waste of IP addresses?

    A. /27

    B. /28

    C. /29

    D. /30

    E. /31

8. What is the subnetwork number of a host with an IP address of 172.16.66.0/21?

    A. 172.16.36.0

    B. 172.16.48.0

    C. 172.16.64.0

    D. 172.16.0.0

9. You have an interface on a router with the IP address of 192.168.192.10/29. Including the router interface, how many hosts can have IP addresses on the LAN attached to router interface?

    A. 6

    B. 8

    C. 30

    D. 62

    E. 126

10. You need to configure a server that is on the subnet 192.168.19.24/29. The router has the first available host address. Which of the following should you assign to the server?

    A. 192.168.19.0 255.255.255.0

    B. 192.168.19.33 255.255.255.240

    C. 192.168.19.26 255.255.255.248

    D. 192.168.19.31 255.255.255.248

    E. 192.168.19.34 255.255.255.240

11. You have an interface on a router with the IP address of 192.168.192.10/29. What is the broadcast address the hosts will use on this LAN?

    A. 192.168.192.15

    B. 192.168.192.31

    C. 192.168.192.63

    D. 192.168.192.127

    E. 192.168.192.255

12. You need to subnet a network that has five subnets, each with at least 16 hosts. Which classful subnet mask would you use?

    A. 255.255.255.192

    B. 255.255.255.224

    C. 255.255.255.240

    D. 255.255.255.248

13. A network administrator is connecting hosts A and B directly thorough their Ethernet interfaces as shown in the illustration. Ping attempts between the hosts are unsuccessful. What can be done to provide connectivity between the hosts? (choose two)

IP Address: 192.168.1.20   IP Address: 192.168.1.201
Mask 255.255.255.240   Mask 255.255.255.240

    A. A crossover cable should be used in place of the straight-through cable.

    B. A rollover cable should be used in place of the straight–through cable.

    C. The subnet masks should be set to 255.255.255.192.

    D. A default gateway needs to be set on each host.

    E. The subnet masks should be set to 255.255.255.0.

14. If an Ethernet port on a router were assigned an IP address of 172.16.112.1/25, what would be the valid subnet address of this host?

    A. 172.16.112.0

    B. 172.16.0.0

    C. 172.16.96.0

    D. 172.16.255.0

    E. 172.16.128.0

15. Using the following illustration, what would be the IP address of E0 if you were using the eighth subnet? The network ID is 192.168.10.0/28 and you need to use the last available IP address in the range. The zero subnet should not be considered valid for this question.

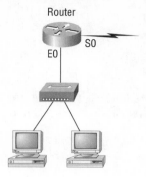

Router

S0

E0

   A. 192.168.10.142

   B. 192.168.10.66

   C. 192.168.100.254

   D. 192.168.10.143

   E. 192.168.10.126

16. Using the illustration from the previous question, what would be the IP address of S0 if you were using the first subnet? The network ID is 192.168.10.0/28 and you need to use the last available IP address in the range. Again, the zero subnet should not be considered valid for this question.

   A. 192.168.10.24

   B. 192.168.10.62

   C. 192.168.10.30

   D. 192.168.10.127

17. Which configuration command must be in effect to allow the use of 8 subnets if the Class C subnet mask is 255.255.255.224?

   A. Router(config)#ip classless

   B. Router(config)#ip version 6

   C. Router(config)#no ip classful

   D. Router(config)#ip unnumbered

   E. Router(config)#ip subnet-zero

   F. Router(config)#ip all-nets

18. You have a network with a subnet of 172.16.17.0/22. Which are valid host addresses?

    A. 172.16.17.1 255.255.255.252

    B. 172.16.0.1 255.255.240.0

    C. 172.16.20.1 255.255.254.0

    D. 172.16.16.1 255.255.255.240

    E. 172.16.18.255 255.255.252.0

    F. 172.16.0.1 255.255.255.0

19. Your router has the following IP address on Ethernet0: 172.16.2.1/23. Which of the following can be valid host ID's on the LAN interface attached to the router? (choose two)

    A. 172.16.0.5

    B. 172.16.1.100

    C. 172.16.1.198

    D. 172.16.2.255

    E. 172.16.3.0

    F. 172.16.3.255

20. To test the IP stack on your local host, which IP address would you ping?

    A. 127.0.0.0

    B. 1.0.0.127

    C. 127.0.0.1

    D. 127.0.0.255

    E. 255.255.255.255

Answers to Review Questions

1. D. A /27 (255.255.255.224) is 3 bits on and 5 bits off. This provides 8 subnets, each with 30 hosts. Does it matter if this mask is used with a Class A, B or C network address? Not at all. The amount of hosts bits would never change.

2. D. A 240 mask is 4 subnet bits and provides 16 subnets, each with 14 hosts. We need more subnets, so let's add subnet bits. One more subnet bit would be a 248 mask. This provides 5 subnet bits (32 subnets) with 3 hosts bits (6 host per subnet). This is the best answer.

3. C. This is a pretty simple question. A /28 is 255.255.255.240, which means that our block size is 16 in the fourth octet. 0, 16, 32, 48, 64, 80, etc. The host is in the 64 subnet.

4. F. A CIDR address of /19 is 255.255.224.0. This is a Class B address, so that is only 3 subnet bits but provides 13 host bits, or 8 subnets, each with 8,190 hosts.

5. B, D. The mask 255.255.254.0 (/23) used with a Class A means that there are 15 subnet bits and 9 hosts bits. The block size in the third octet is 2 (256 – 254). So this makes the subnets in the interesting octet 0, 2, 4, 6, etc., all the way to 254. The host 10.16.3.65 is in the 2.0 subnet. The next subnet is 4.0, so the broadcast address for the 2.0 subnet is 3.255. The valid host addresses are 2.1 through 3.254.

6. D. A /30, regardless of the class of address, has a 252 in the fourth octet. This means we have a block size of 4 and our subnets are 0, 4, 8, 12, 16, etc. Address 14 is obviously in the 12 subnet.

7. D. A point-to-point link uses only two hosts. A /30, or 255.255.255.252, mask provides two hosts per subnet.

8. C. A /21 is 255.255.248.0, which means we have a block size of 8 in the third octet, so we just count by 8 until we reach 66. The subnet in this question is 64.0. The next subnet is 72.0, so the broadcast address of the 64 subnet is 71.255.

9. A. A /29 (255.255.255.248), regardless of the class of address, has only three hosts bits. Six hosts is the maximum amount of hosts on this LAN, including the router interface.

10. C. A /29 is 255.255.255.248, which is a block size of 8 in the fourth octet. The subnets are 0, 8, 16, 24, 32, 40, etc. 192.168.19.24 is the 24 subnet, and since 32 is the next subnet, the broadcast address for the 24 subnet is 31. 192.168.19.26 is the only correct answer.

11. A. A /29 (255.255.255.248) has a block size of 8 in the fourth octet. This means the subnets are 0, 8, 16, 24, etc. 10 is in the 8 subnet. The next subnet is 16, so 15 is the broadcast address.

12. B. You need 5 subnets, each with at least 16 hosts. The mask 255.255.255.240 provides 16 subnets with 14 hosts—this will not work. The mask 255.255.255.224 provides 8 subnets, each with 30 hosts. This is the best answer.

13. A, E. First, if you have two hosts directly connected, as shown in the graphic, then you need a crossover cable. A straight-through cable won't work. Second, the hosts have different masks, which puts them in different subnets. The easily solution is just to set both masks to 255.255.255.0 (/24).

14. A. A /25 mask is 255.255.255.128. Used with a Class B network, the third and fourth octets are used for subnetting with a total of 9 subnet bits, 8 bits in the third octet and 1 bit in the fourth octet. Since there is only 1 bit in the fourth octet, the bit is either off or on—which is a value of 0 or 128. The host in the question is in the 0 subnet, which has a broadcast address of 127 since 128 is the next subnet.

15. A. A /28 is a 255.255.255.240 mask. We need to count to the eighth subnet, not starting at subnet-zero. 16, 32, 48, 64, 80, 96, 112, 128. The ninth subnet is 144 (we need this to help us find the 128 subnet broadcast address, which is 143).The valid host range for the eight subnet (not using subnet zero) is 129 through 142. The last available IP address available in the eighth subnet is 142.

16. C. A /28 is a 255.255.255.240 mask. The first subnet is 16 (remember that the question stated not to use subnet zero) and the next subnet is 32, so our broadcast address is 31. This makes our host range 17–30. 30 is the last valid host.

17. E. A Class C subnet mask of 255.255.255.224 is 3 bits on and 5 bits off (11100000) and provides 8 subnets, each with 30 hosts. However, if the command `ip subnet-zero` is not used, then only 6 subnets would be available for use.

18. E. A Class B network ID with a /22 mask is 255.255.252.0, with a block size of 4 in the third octet. The network address in the question is in subnet 172.16.16.0 with a broadcast address of 172.16.19.255. Only option E even has the correct subnet mask listed, and 172.16.18.255 is a valid host.

19. D, E. The routers IP address on the E0 interface is 172.16.2.1/23, which is a 255.255.254.0. This makes the third octet a block size of 2. The routers interface is in the 2.0 subnet, the broadcast address is 3.255 because the next subnet is 4.0. The valid host range is 2.1 through 3.254. The router is using the first valid host address in the range.

20. C. To test the local stack on your host, ping the loopback interface of 127.0.0.1

Answers to Written Lab 3

1. 192.168.100.25/30. A /30 is 255.255.255.252. The valid subnet is 192.168.100.24, broadcast is 192.168.100.27, and valid hosts are 192.168.100.25 and 26.

2. 192.168.100.37/28. A /28 is 255.255.255.240. The fourth octet is a block size of 16. Just count by 16s until you pass 37. 0, 16, 32, 48. The host is in the 32 subnet, with a broadcast address of 47. Valid hosts 33–46.

3. 192.168.100.66/27. A /27 is 255.255.255.224. The fourth octet is a block size of 32. Count by 32s until you pass the host address of 66. 0, 32, 64. The host is in the 32 subnet, broadcast address of 63. Valid host range of 33–62.

4. 192.168.100.17/29. A /29 is 255.255.255.248. The fourth octet is a block size of 8. 0, 8, 16, 24. The host is in the 16 subnet, broadcast of 23. Valid host 17–22.

5. 192.168.100.99/26. A /26 is 255.255.255.192. The fourth octet has a block size of 64. 0, 64, 128. The host is in the 64 subnet, broadcast of 127. Valid host 65–126.

6. 192.168.100.99/25. A /25 is 255.255.255.128. The fourth octet is a block size of 128. 0, 128. The host is in the 0 subnet, broadcast of 127. Valid host 1–126.

7. A default Class B is 255.255.0.0. A Class B 255.255.255.0 mask is 256 subnets, each with 254 hosts. We need fewer subnets. If we used 255.255.240.0, this provide 16 subnets. Let's add one more subnet bit. 255.255.248.0. This is 5 bits of subnetting, which provides 32 subnets. This is our best answer, a /21.

8. A /29 is 255.255.255.248. This is a block size of 8 in the fourth octet. 0, 8, 16. The host is in the 8 subnet, broadcast is 15.

9. A /29 is 255.255.255.248, which is 5 subnet bits and 3 hosts bits. This is only 6 hosts per subnet.

10. A /23 is 255.255.254.0. The third octet is a block size of 2. 0, 2, 4. The subnet is in the 16.2.0 subnet, the broadcast address is 16.3.255.

Chapter

4

Introduction to the Cisco IOS

THE CCNA INTRO EXAM TOPICS COVERED IN THIS CHAPTER INCLUDE THE FOLLOWING:

✓ **Implementation and Operation**

- Establish communication between a terminal device and the router IOS, and use IOS for system analysis
- Perform an initial configuration on a router and save the resultant configuration file
- Assign IP addresses

✓ **Technology**

- Describe the purpose and fundamental operation of the internetwork operating system (IOS)
- Describe how an IP address is associated with a device interface, and the association between physical and employ IP addressing techniques
- Employ IP addressing techniques

The time has come to introduce you to the Cisco Internetwork Operating System (IOS). The IOS is what runs Cisco routers as well as some Cisco switches and it's what allows you to configure the devices as well.

So that's what you're going to learn about in this chapter. I'm going to show you how to configure a Cisco IOS router using the Cisco IOS command-line interface (CLI). When you become proficient with this interface, you'll be able to configure hostnames, banners, passwords, and more. I'm also going to get you up to speed on the vital basics of router configurations and command verifications. Here's a list of the subjects we'll be covering in this chapter:

- Understanding and configuring the Cisco Internetwork Operating System (IOS)
- Connecting to a router
- Bringing up a router
- Logging into a router
- Understanding the router prompts
- Understanding the CLI prompts
- Performing editing and help features
- Gathering basic routing information
- Setting administrative functions
- Setting hostnames
- Setting banners
- Setting passwords
- Setting interface descriptions
- Performing interface configurations
- Viewing, saving, and erasing configurations
- Verifying routing configurations

And just as it was with preceding chapters, the fundamentals that you'll learn in this chapter are foundational building blocks that really need to be in place before you go on to the next chapters in the book.

The Cisco Router User Interface

The *Cisco Internetwork Operating System (IOS)* is the kernel of Cisco routers and most switches. In case you didn't know, a kernel is the basic, indispensable part of an operating system that allocates resources and manages things such as low-level hardware interfaces and security. Cisco has created something called CiscoFusion, which is supposed to make all Cisco devices run the same operating system. But they don't, because Cisco has acquired devices that they haven't designed and built themselves. Almost all Cisco routers run the same IOS, in contrast to about half of Cisco switches. The good news is that that number is growing pretty fast.

In this section, I'll show you the Cisco IOS and how to configure a Cisco router using the command-line interface (CLI).

 I'm going to save Cisco switch configurations for Chapter 7, "Layer 2 Switching."

Cisco Router IOS

The Cisco IOS was created to deliver network services and enable networked applications. It runs on most Cisco routers and, as I mentioned, on an ever-increasing number of Cisco Catalyst switches, such as the Catalyst 2950.

These are some of the important things that the Cisco router IOS software is responsible for:

- Carrying network protocols and functions
- Connecting high-speed traffic between devices
- Adding security to control access and stop unauthorized network use
- Providing scalability for ease of network growth and redundancy
- Supplying network reliability for connecting to network resources

You can access the Cisco IOS through the console port of a router, from a modem into the auxiliary (or Aux) port, or even through Telnet. Access to the IOS command line is called an *EXEC session*.

Connecting to a Cisco Router

You can connect to a Cisco router to configure it, verify its configuration, and check statistics. There are different ways to do this, but most often, the first place you would connect to is the console port. The *console port* is usually an RJ-45 (8-pin modular) connection located at the back of the router—by default, there's no password set.

 See Chapter 1, "Internetworking," for an explanation of how to configure a PC to connect to a router console port.

You can also connect to a Cisco router through an *auxiliary port*—which is really the same thing as a console port, so it follows that you can use it as one. But this auxiliary port also allows you to configure modem commands so that a modem can be connected to the router. This is a cool feature—it lets you dial up a remote router and attach to the auxiliary port if the router is down and you need to configure it "out-of-band" (meaning out of the network). "In-band" means the opposite—configuring the router through the network.

The third way to connect to a Cisco router is in-band, through the program *Telnet*. Telnet is a terminal emulation program that acts as though it's a dumb terminal. You can use Telnet to connect to any active interface on a router, such as an Ethernet or serial port.

Figure 4.1 shows an illustration of a 2501 Cisco router. Pay close attention to all the different kinds of interfaces and connections.

The 2501 router has two serial interfaces, which can be used for WAN connections, and one Attachment Unit Interface (AUI) connection for a 10Mbps Ethernet network connection. This router also has one console and one auxiliary connection via RJ-45 connectors. The 2501 router shown has two serial V.35 connections used for WAN connections like a T1, or Frame Relay. Plus, next to the console port could be another RJ45 port marked as BRI (Basic Rate Interface) that's used with ISDN. And don't stress—I'm going to cover T1, Frame Relay, ISDN, and more WAN protocols coming up in Chapter 9, "Wide Area Networks."

A Cisco 2600 series router is a cut above routers populating the 2500 series because it has a faster processor and can handle many more interfaces. Figure 4.2 shows a diagram of a Cisco 2600 modular router.

I'm mostly going to use 2600 routers throughout this book to show examples of configurations. The 2500 series machines just aren't capable of handling the demands of today's typical corporate network—you'll find 2600 or better in that kind of environment. But the 2500 series still works great for home use, and when I do use them for an example, I'll point it out.

FIGURE 4.1   A Cisco 2501 router

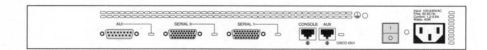

FIGURE 4.2   A Cisco 2600 router

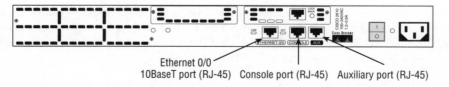

Bringing Up a Router

When you first bring up a Cisco router, it will run a power-on self-test (POST). If it passes, it will then look for and load the Cisco IOS from flash memory—if an IOS file is present. (Just in case you don't know, flash memory is electronically erasable programmable read-only memory—an EEPROM.) After that, the IOS loads and looks for a valid configuration—the startup-config—that's stored by default in nonvolatile RAM, or NVRAM.

The following messages appear when you first boot or reload a router:

```
System Bootstrap, Version 12.2(13)T, RELEASE SOFTWARE (fc1)
Copyright (c) 2000 by cisco Systems, Inc.
C2600 platform with 32768 Kbytes of main memory
```

This is the first part of the router boot process output. It's information about the bootstrap program that first runs the POST, and then it tells the router how to load, which by default is to find the IOS in flash memory.

The next part shows us that the IOS is being decompressed into RAM:

```
program load complete, entry point:0x80008000, size:0x43b7fc
Self decompressing the image :
#######################################################################
#######################################################################
#######################################################################
#######################################################################
#######################################################################
#######################################################################
#######################################################################
## [OK]
```

This step doesn't happen the same way for all routers. The output you're being shown is from my 2600. It's telling us that the IOS is being loaded into RAM. (The 2500 series router runs the IOS from flash memory—it doesn't load the IOS into RAM.)

After it is decompressed into RAM, the IOS is loaded and starts running the router, as shown below (notice that the IOS version is stated as version 12.2[13]):

```
Cisco Internetwork Operating System Software
IOS (tm) C2600 Software (C2600-I-M), Version 12.2(13),
   RELEASE SOFTWARE (fc1)
Copyright (c) 1986-2001 by cisco Systems, Inc.
Compiled Tue 17-Dec-03 04:55 by kellythw
Image text-base: 0x80008088, data-base: 0x8080853C
```

Once the IOS is loaded, the information learned from the POST will be displayed next, as shown here:

```
cisco 2621 (MPC860) processor (revision 0x101) with
  26624K/6144K bytes of memory.
Processor board ID JAD050697JB (146699779)
M860 processor: part number 0, mask 49
Bridging software.
X.25 software, Version 3.0.0.
2 FastEthernet/IEEE 802.3 interface(s)
1 Serial network interface(s)
32K bytes of non-volatile configuration memory.
8192K bytes of processor board System flash (Read/Write)
```

When the IOS is loaded and up and running, a valid configuration will be loaded from NVRAM. If there isn't a configuration in NVRAM, the router will go into what is called *setup mode*— a step-by-step process to help you configure the router. You can also enter setup mode at any time from the command line by typing the command **setup** from something called privileged mode, which I'll get to in a minute.

Setup mode covers only some global commands and is generally just unhelpful. Here is an example:

```
Would you like to enter the initial configuration dialog? [yes/no]: y

At any point you may enter a question mark '?' for help.
Use ctrl-c to abort configuration dialog at any prompt.
Default settings are in square brackets '[]'.

Basic management setup configures only enough connectivity
for management of the system, extended setup will ask you
to configure each interface on the system

Would you like to enter basic management setup? [yes/no]: y
Configuring global parameters:

  Enter host name [Router]:Ctrl-C

Configuration aborted, no changes made.
```

I highly recommend going through setup mode once, then never again. You should always use the CLI.

You can exit setup mode at any time by pressing Ctrl+C.

Command-Line Interface (CLI)

Because it's so much more flexible, the *command-line interface (CLI)* truly is the best way to configure a router. I sometimes refer to the CLI as "Cash Line Interface" because if you can create advanced configurations on Cisco routers and switches using the CLI, then you'll get the cash!

To use the CLI, just say no to entering the initial configuration dialog (setup mode). After you do that, the router will respond with messages that tell you all about the status of each and every one of the its interfaces. Here's an example:

```
Would you like to enter the initial configuration dialog?
  [yes]:n
Would you like to terminate autoinstall? [yes]:[Enter]

Press RETURN to get started!

00:00:42: %LINK-3-UPDOWN: Interface FastEthernet0/0, changed
  state to up
00:00:42: %LINK-3-UPDOWN: Interface Serial0/0, changed
  state to down
00:00:42: %LINK-3-UPDOWN: Interface Serial0/1, changed
  state to down
00:00:42: %LINEPROTO-5-UPDOWN: Line protocol on Interface
  FastEthernet0/0, changed state to up
00:00:42: %LINEPROTO-5-UPDOWN: Line protocol on Interface
  Serial0/0, changed state to down
00:00:42: %LINEPROTO-5-UPDOWN: Line protocol on Interface
  Serial0/1, changed state to down
00:01:30: %LINEPROTO-5-UPDOWN: Line protocol on Interface
  FastEthernet0/0, changed state to down
00:01:31: %LINK-5-CHANGED: Interface Serial0/0, changed
  state to administratively down
00:01:31: %LINK-5-CHANGED: Interface FastEthernet0/0, changed
  state to administratively down
00:01:31: %LINK-5-CHANGED: Interface Serial0/1, changed
  state to administratively down
00:01:32: %IP-5-WEBINST_KILL: Terminating DNS process
00:01:38: %SYS-5-RESTART: System restarted --
Cisco Internetwork Operating System Software
IOS (tm) 2600 Software (2600-BIN-M), Version 12.2(13),
  RELEASE SOFTWARE (fc1)
Copyright (c) 1986-2003 by cisco Systems, Inc.
Compiled Tue 04-Jan-03 19:23 by dschwart
```

In the following sections, I am going to show you how to log in to a router and perform some basic administrative functions.

Logging into the Router

After the interface status messages appear and you press Enter, the `Router>` prompt will appear. This is called *user exec mode* (user mode) and it's mostly used to view statistics, but it's also a stepping-stone to logging into privileged mode. You can only view and change the configuration of a Cisco router in *privileged exec mode* (privileged mode), which you get into with the `enable` command.

Here's how:

```
Router>
Router>enable
Router#
```

You now end up with a `Router#` prompt, which indicates that you're in *privileged mode*, where you can both view and change the router's configuration. You can go back from privileged mode into user mode by using the `disable` command, as seen here:

```
Router#disable
Router>
```

At this point, you can type `logout` to exit the console:

```
Router>logout

Router con0 is now available
Press RETURN to get started.
```

Or you could just type `logout` or `exit` from the privileged-mode prompt to log out:

```
Router>en
Router#logout

Router con0 is now available
Press RETURN to get started.
```

Overview of Router Modes

To configure from a CLI, you can make global changes to the router by typing `configure terminal` (or `config t` for short), which puts you in global configuration mode and changes what's known as the running-config. A global command (a command run from global config) is set only once and affects the entire router.

You can type **config** from the privileged-mode prompt and then just press Enter to take the default of `terminal`, as seen here:

```
Router#config
Configuring from terminal, memory, or network
   [terminal]? [Enter]
Enter configuration commands, one per line. End with
   CNTL/Z.
Router(config)#
```

At this point, you make changes that affect the router as a whole (globally), hence the term global configuration mode.

To change the running-config—the current configuration running in dynamic RAM (DRAM)—you use the `configure terminal`. To change the startup-config—the configuration stored in NVRAM—you use the `configure memory` command (or `config mem` for short). If you want to change a router configuration stored on a TFTP host (which is covered in Chapter 8, "Managing a Cisco Internetwork"), you use the `configure network` command (or `config net` for short).

However, you need to understand that for a router to actually make a change to a configuration, it needs to put that configuration in RAM. So, if you actually type `config mem` or `config net`, you'll append the current running-config with the config stored in NVRAM or a configuration stored on a TFTP host. Don't worry, I'll be going over all of this in much greater detail in Chapter 8.

Configure terminal, configure memory, and configure network are all considered commands that are used to configure information into RAM on a router; however, typically only the configure terminal command is used.

CLI Prompts

It's really important that you understand the different prompts you can find when configuring a router. Knowing these well will help you navigate and recognize where you are at any time within configuration mode. In this section, I'm going to demonstrate the prompts that are used on a Cisco router and discuss the various terms used. (Always check your prompts before making any changes to a router's configuration!)

I'm not going into every different command prompt offered, because doing that would be reaching beyond the scope of this exam. Instead, I'm going to describe all the different prompts you'll see throughout this chapter and the rest of the book. These command prompts really are the ones you'll use most in real life anyway; plus, they're the ones you'll need to know for the exam.

Don't Freak! It's not important that you understand what each of these command prompts accomplish yet because I'm going to completely fill you in on all of them really soon. So right now, just relax and focus on becoming familiar with the different prompts available and all will be well!

Interfaces

To make changes to an interface, you use the `interface` command from global configuration mode:

```
Router(config)#interface ?
 Async             Async interface
  BVI                Bridge-Group Virtual Interface
  CTunnel            CTunnel interface
  Dialer             Dialer interface
  FastEthernet       FastEthernet IEEE 802.3
  Group-Async        Async Group interface
  Lex                Lex interface
  Loopback           Loopback interface
  MFR                Multilink Frame Relay bundle interface
  Multilink          Multilink-group interface
  Null               Null interface
  Serial             Serial
  Tunnel             Tunnel interface
  Vif                PGM Multicast Host interface
  Virtual-Template   Virtual Template interface
  Virtual-TokenRing  Virtual TokenRing
  range              interface range command
Router(config)#interface fastethernet 0/0
Router(config-if)#
```

Did you notice that the prompt changed to Router(config-if)#? This tells you that you're in *interface configuration mode*. And wouldn't it be nice if the prompt also gave you an indication of what interface you were configuring? Well, at least for now we'll have to live without the prompt information, because it doesn't. (Could this be one of the reasons Cisco administrators make more money than Windows administrators? Or is it just that we're smarter and better looking?) One thing is for sure: You really have to pay attention when configuring a router!

Subinterfaces

Subinterfaces allow you to create logical interfaces within the router. The prompt then changes to Router(config-subif)#:

```
Router(config)#int fastethernet0/0.?
 <0-4294967295> FastEthernet interface number
Router(config)#int fastethernet0/0.1
Router(config-subif)#
```

You can read more about subinterfaces in Chapters 7, "Layer-2 Switching (VLANs)," and 9, "Wide Area Networking Protocols," but don't skip ahead just yet!

Line Commands

To configure user-mode passwords, use the `line` command. The prompt then becomes `Router(config-line)#`:

```
Router#config t
Enter configuration commands, one per line. End with
  CNTL/Z.
Router(config)#line ?
  <0-70>   First Line number
  aux      Auxiliary line
  console  Primary terminal line
  tty      Terminal controller
  vty      Virtual terminal
  x/y      Slot/Port for Modems
Router(config)#line console 0
Router(config-line)#
```

The `line console 0` command is known as a major command (also called a *global command*), and any command typed from the `(config-line)` prompt is known as a subcommand.

Routing Protocol Configurations

To configure routing protocols such as RIP and IGRP, you'll use the prompt `(config-router)#`:

```
Router#config t
Enter configuration commands, one per line. End with
  CNTL/Z.
Router(config)#router rip
Router(config-router)#
```

Defining Router Terms

Using Table 4.1, let's define some terms we've used so far.

TABLE 4.1   Router Terms

Mode	Definition
User EXEC mode	Limited to basic monitoring commands
Privileged EXEC mode	Provides access to all other router commands
Global configuration mode	Commands that affect the entire system
Specific configuration modes	Commands that affect interfaces/processes only
Setup mode	Interactive configuration dialog

Editing and Help Features

You can use the Cisco advanced editing features to help you configure your router. If you type in a question mark (**?**) at any prompt, you'll be given a list of all the commands available from that prompt:

```
Router#?
Exec commands:
 access-enable   Create a temporary Access-List entry
 access-profile  Apply user-profile to interface
 access-template Create a temporary Access-List entry
 bfe             For manual emergency modes setting
 clear           Reset functions
 clock           Manage the system clock
 configure       Enter configuration mode
 connect         Open a terminal connection
 copy            Copy configuration or image data
 debug           Debugging functions (see also 'undebug')
 disable         Turn off privileged commands
 disconnect      Disconnect an existing network connection
 enable          Turn on privileged commands
 erase           Erase flash or configuration memory
 exit            Exit from the EXEC
 help            Description of the interactive help system
 lock            Lock the terminal
 login           Log in as a particular user
 logout          Exit from the EXEC
 mrinfo          Request neighbor and version information
                 from a multicast router
 --More-
```

Plus, at this point you can press the spacebar to get another page of information, or you can press Enter to go one command at a time. You can also press Q (or any other key, for that matter) to quit and return to the prompt.

Here's a shortcut: To find commands that start with a certain letter, use the letter and the question mark with no space between them:

```
Router#c?
clear clock configure connect copy

Router#c
```

By typing **c?**, we received a response listing all the commands that start with *c*. Also notice that the Router# prompt reappears after the list of commands is displayed. This can be helpful when you have long commands and need the next possible command. It would be pretty lame if you had to retype the entire command every time you used a question mark!

To find the next command in a string, type the first command and then a question mark:

```
Router#clock ?
 set Set the time and date
Router#clock set ?
 hh:mm:ss Current Time
Router#clock set 10:30:10 ?
 <1-31> Day of the month
 MONTH  Month of the year
Router#clock set 10:30:10 28 ?
 MONTH  Month of the year
Router#clock set 10:30:10 28 august ?
 <1993-2035> Year
Router#clock set 10:30:10 28 august 2003 ?
 <cr>
Router#
```

By typing the clock ? command, you'll get a list of the next possible parameters and what they do. Notice that you should just keep typing a command, a space, and then a question mark until <cr> (carriage return) is your only option.

If you're typing commands and receive

```
Router#clock set 10:30:10
% Incomplete command.
```

you'll know that the command string isn't done yet. Just press the Up arrow key to redisplay the last command entered, then continue with the command by using your question mark.

And if you receive the error

```
Router(config)#access-list 110 permit host 1.1.1.1
                                     ^
% Invalid input detected at '^' marker.
```

you've entered a command incorrectly. See that little caret—the ^? It's a very helpful tool that marks the exact point where you blew it and entered the command wrong. Here's another example of when you'll see the caret:

```
Router#show serial 0/0
          ^
% Invalid input detected at '^' marker.
```

The above command looks right, but be careful! The problem is the full command is "show interface serial 0/0".

Now if you receive the error

```
Router#sh ru
% Ambiguous command:  "sh ru"
```

it means there are multiple commands that begin with the string you entered and it's not unique. Use the question mark to find the command you need:

```
Router#sh ru?
rudpv1  running-config
```

As you can see there are two commands that start with show ru.

Table 4.2 shows the list of the enhanced editing commands available on a Cisco router.

TABLE 4.2   Enhanced Editing Commands

Command	Meaning
Ctrl+A	Moves your cursor to the beginning of the line
Ctrl+E	Moves your cursor to the end of the line
Esc+B	Moves back one word
Ctrl+B	Moves back one character
Ctrl+F	Moves forward one character
Esc+F	Moves forward one word
Ctrl+D	Deletes a single character
Backspace	Deletes a single character
Ctrl+R	Redisplays a line

TABLE 4.2   Enhanced Editing Commands *(continued)*

Command	Meaning
Ctrl+U	Erases a line
Ctrl+W	Erases a word
Ctrl+Z	Ends configuration mode and returns to EXEC
Tab	Finishes typing a command for you

Another cool editing feature I want to show you is the automatic scrolling of long lines. In the following example, the command typed had reached the right margin and automatically moved 11 spaces to the left (the dollar sign [$] indicates that the line has been scrolled to the left):

```
Router#config t
Enter configuration commands, one per line. End with CNTL/Z.
Router(config)#$110 permit host 171.10.10.10 0.0.0.0 eq 23
```

You can review the router-command history with the commands shown in Table 4.3.

TABLE 4.3   Router-Command History

Command	Meaning
Ctrl+P or Up arrow	Shows last command entered
Ctrl+N or Down arrow	Shows previous commands entered
show history	Shows last 10 commands entered by default
show terminal	Shows terminal configurations and history buffer size
terminal history size	Changes buffer size (max 256)

The following example demonstrates the show history command and how to change the history size, as well as how to verify it with the show terminal command.

First, use the show history command to see the last 10 commands that were entered on the router:

```
Router#sh history
 en
```

```
sh history
show terminal
sh cdp neig
sh ver
sh flash
sh int fa0
sh history
sh int s0/0
sh int s0/1
```

Now use the show terminal command to verify the terminal history size:

```
Router#sh terminal
Line 0, Location: "", Type: ""
[output cut]
History is enabled, history size is 10.
Full user help is disabled
Allowed transports are lat pad v120 telnet mop rlogin
  nasi. Preferred is lat.
No output characters are padded
No special data dispatching characters
Group codes:  0
```

The terminal history size command, used from privileged mode, can change the size of the history buffer:

```
Router#terminal history size ?
 <0-256> Size of history buffer
Router#terminal history size 25
```

You verify the change with the show terminal command:

```
Router#sh terminal
Line 0, Location: "", Type: ""
[output cut]
Editing is enabled.
History is enabled, history size is 25.
Full user help is disabled
Allowed transports are lat pad v120 telnet mop rlogin
  nasi. Preferred is lat.
No output characters are padded
No special data dispatching characters
Group codes:  0
```

Real World Scenario

When Do You Use the Cisco Editing Features?

There are a couple of editing features that are used quite often and some not so much, if at all. Understand that Cisco didn't make these up; these are just old Unix commands. However, Ctrl+A is really helpful to negate a command.

For example, if you were to put in a long command and then decide you didn't want to use that command in your configuration after all, or that it didn't work, then you could just press your Up arrow key to show the last command entered, press Ctrl+A, type **no** and then a space, press Enter—and poof! The command is negated. This doesn't work on every command, but it works on a lot of them.

Gathering Basic Routing Information

The show version command will provide basic configuration for the system hardware as well as the software version, the names and sources of configuration files, and the boot images. Here's an example:

```
Router#sh version
Cisco Internetwork Operating System Software
IOS (tm) C2600 Software (C2600-BIN-M), Version 12.2(13)T1,RELEASE SOFTWARE(fc1)
TAC Support: http://www.cisco.com/tac
Copyright (c) 1986-2003 by cisco Systems, Inc.
Compiled Sat 04-Jan-03 05:58 by ccai
Image text-base: 0x80008098, data-base: 0x80C4AD94
```

The preceding section of output describes the Cisco IOS running on the router. The following section describes the read-only memory (ROM) used, which is used to boot the router:

```
ROM: System Bootstrap, Version 11.3(2)XA4, RELEASE SOFTWARE (fc1)
```

The next section shows how long the router has been running, how it was restarted (if you see a system restarted by bus error, that is a very bad thing), where the Cisco IOS was loaded from, and the IOS name. Flash is the default:

```
Router uptime is 1 week, 2 hours, 39 minutes
System returned to ROM by reload
System image file is "flash:c2600-bin-mz.122-13.T1.bin"
```

This next section displays the processor, the amount of DRAM and flash memory, and the interfaces the POST found on the router:

```
cisco 2621 (MPC860) processor (revision 0x101) with 27648K/5120K bytes of memory
Processor board ID JAB0402040J (2308906173)
```

```
M860 processor: part number 0, mask 49
Bridging software.
X.25 software, Version 3.0.0.
2 FastEthernet/IEEE 802.3 interface(s)
2 Serial network interface(s)
32K bytes of non-volatile configuration memory.
8192K bytes of processor board System flash (Read/Write)

Configuration register is 0x2102
```

The configuration register value is listed last—it's something I'll cover in Chapter 8.

In addition, the `show interfaces` command is very useful in verifying and troubleshooting a router as well as network issues. The `show interfaces` command is covered later in this chapter. Don't miss it!

Router and Switch Administrative Functions

Even though this section isn't critical to making a router or switch work on a network, it's still really important; in it, I'm going to lead you through configuring commands that will help you administer your network.

The administrative functions that you can configure on a router and switch are as follows:

- Hostnames
- Banners
- Password
- Interface descriptions

Remember, none of these will make your routers or switches work better or faster, but trust me, your life will be a whole lot better if you just take the time to set these configurations on each of your network devices. That's because doing this makes troubleshooting and maintaining your network sooooo much easier—seriously! In this next section, I'll be demonstrating commands on a Cisco router, but these commands are exactly the same on a Cisco switch.

Hostnames

You can set the identity of the router with the `hostname` command. This is only locally significant, which means that it has no bearing on how the router performs name lookups or how the router works on the internetwork. However, we'll use the hostname in Chapter 8 for authentication purposes.

Here's an example:

```
Router#config t
Enter configuration commands, one per line. End with
  CNTL/Z.
Router(config)#hostname Todd
Todd(config)#hostname Atlanta
Atlanta(config)#
```

Even though it's pretty tempting to configure the hostname after your own name, it's definitely a better idea to name the router something pertinent to the location. This is because giving it a hostname that's somehow relevant to where the device actually lives will make finding it a whole lot easier. And it also helps you confirm that you are, indeed, configuring the right device.

Banners

A *banner* is more than just a little cool—one very good reason for having a banner is to give any and all who dare attempt to telnet or dial into your internetwork a little security notice. And you can create a banner to give anyone who shows up on the router exactly the information you want them to have. Make sure you're familiar with these four available banner types: exec process creation banner, incoming terminal line banner, login banner, and message of the day banner (all illustrated in the following code):

```
Router(config)#banner ?
  LINE     c banner-text c, where 'c' is a delimiting
           character
  exec     Set EXEC process creation banner
  incoming Set incoming terminal line banner
  login    Set login banner
  motd     Set Message of the Day banner
```

Message of the day (MOTD) is the most extensively used banner. It gives a message to every person dialing into or connecting to the router via Telnet or auxiliary port, or even through a console port as seen here:

```
Router(config)#banner motd ?
LINE c banner-text c, where 'c' is a delimiting character
Router(config)#banner motd #
Enter TEXT message. End with the character '#'.
$ Acme.com network, then you must disconnect immediately.
#
Router(config)#^Z
Router#
00:25:12: %SYS-5-CONFIG_I: Configured from console by
  console
```

```
Router#exit

Router con0 is now available

Press RETURN to get started.

If you are not authorized to be in Acme.com network, then
  you must disconnect immediately.

Router>
```

The preceding MOTD banner essentially tells anyone connecting to the router that if they're not on the guest list, get lost! The part to understand is the delimiting character—the thing that's used to tell the router when the message is done. You can use any character you want for it, but (I hope this is obvious) you can't use the delimiting character in the message itself. Also, once the message is complete, press Enter, then the delimiting character, then Enter again. It'll still work if you don't do that, but if you have more than one banner, they'll be combined as one message and put on a single line.

For example, you can set a banner on one line as shown:

```
Router(config)#banner motd x Unauthorized access prohibited! x
```

This example will work just fine, but if you add another MOTD banner message, they would end up on a single line.

Here are some details of the other banners I mentioned:

Exec banner You can configure a line-activation (exec) banner to be displayed when an EXEC process (such as a line-activation or incoming connection to a VTY line) is created. By simply starting a user exec session through a console port, you'll activate the exec banner.

Incoming banner You can configure a banner to be displayed on terminals connected to reverse Telnet lines. This banner is useful for providing instructions to users who use reverse Telnet.

Login banner You can configure a login banner to be displayed on all connected terminals. This banner is displayed after the MOTD banner but before the login prompts. The login banner can't be disabled on a per-line basis, so to globally disable it, you've got to delete it with the no banner login command.

Setting Passwords

There are five passwords used to secure your Cisco routers: console, auxiliary, telnet (VTY), enable password, and enable secret. Just as you learned earlier in the chapter, the first two passwords are used to set your enable password that's used to secure privileged mode. This will prompt a user for a password when the enable command is used. The other three are used to configure a password when user mode is accessed through the console port, through the auxiliary port, or via Telnet.

Let's take a look at each of these now.

Enable Passwords

You set the enable passwords from global configuration mode like this:

```
Router(config)#enable ?
  last-resort Define enable action if no TACACS servers
              respond
  password    Assign the privileged level password
  secret      Assign the privileged level secret
  use-tacacs  Use TACACS to check enable passwords
```

The following points describe the enable password parameters:

Last-resort   Allows you to still enter the router if you set up authentication through a TACACS server and it's not available. But it isn't used if the TACACS server is working.

Password   Sets the enable password on older, pre-10.3 systems, and isn't ever used if an enable secret is set.

Secret   This is the newer, encrypted password that overrides the enable password if it's set.

Use-tacacs   This tells the router to authenticate through a TACACS server. It's convenient if you have anywhere from a dozen to multitudes of routers because, well, would you like to face the fun task of changing the password on all those routers? If you're sane, no, you wouldn't. So instead, just go through the TACACS server and you only have to change the password once—yeah!

Here's an example of setting the enable passwords:

```
Router(config)#enable secret todd
Router(config)#enable password todd
The enable password you have chosen is the same as your
  enable secret. This is not recommended. Re-enter the
  enable password.
```

If you try to set the enable secret and enable passwords the same, the router will give you a nice, polite warning to change the second password. If you don't have older legacy routers, don't even bother to use the enable password.

User-mode passwords are assigned by using the line command:

```
Router(config)#line ?
  <0-70>    First Line number
  aux       Auxiliary line
  console   Primary terminal line
  tty       Terminal controller
  vty       Virtual terminal
  x/y       Slot/Port for Modems
```

Here are the lines to be concerned with:

aux   Sets the user-mode password for the auxiliary port. It's usually used for attaching a modem to the router, but it can be used as a console as well.

console   Sets a console user-mode password.

vty   Sets a Telnet password on the router. If this password isn't set, then Telnet can't be used by default.

To configure the user-mode passwords, you configure the line you want and use either the login or no login command to tell the router to prompt for authentication. The next section will provide a line-by-line example of each line configuration.

Auxiliary Password

To configure the auxiliary password, go into global configuration mode and type **line aux ?**. You can see here that you only get a choice of 0–0 (that's because there's only one port):

```
Router#config t
Enter configuration commands, one per line. End with CNTL/Z.
Router(config)#line aux ?
 <0-0> First Line number
Router(config)#line aux 0
Router(config-line)#login
Router(config-line)#password todd
```

It's important to remember the login command, or the auxiliary port won't prompt for authentication.

Okay, now watch what happens when I try to set the Aux on the "newer" IOS that Cisco has released:

```
2600A#config t
Enter configuration commands, one per line.  End with CNTL/Z.
2600A(config)#line aux 0
2600A(config-line)#login
% Login disabled on line 65, until 'password' is set
2600A(config-line)#
```

Cisco has begun this process of not letting you set the "login" command before a password is set on a line because if you set the login command under a line, and then don't set a password, the line won't be usable. And it will prompt for a password that doesn't exist. So this is a good thing—a feature, not a hassle!

 NOTE   Definitely remember that although Cisco has this new "password feature" on its routers starting in its newer IOS (12.2 and above), it's not in all its IOSes.

Console Password

To set the console password, use the `line console 0` command. But look at what happened when I tried to type `line console 0 ?` from the aux line configuration—I received an error. You can still type `line console 0` and it will accept it, but the help screens just don't work from that prompt. Type **exit** to get back one level and you'll find that your help screens now work. This is a "feature." Really.

Here's the example:

```
Router(config-line)#line console ?
% Unrecognized command
Router(config-line)#exit
Router(config)#line console ?
 <0-0> First Line number
Router(config)#line console 0
Router(config-line)#password todd1
Router(config-line)#login
```

Since there's only one console port, I can only choose line console 0. You can set all your line passwords to the same password, but for security reasons, I'd recommend that you make them different.

There are a few other important commands to know for the console port.

For one, the `exec-timeout 0 0` command sets the time-out for the console EXEC session to zero, which basically means to never time out. The default time-out is 10 minutes. (If you're feeling mischievous, try this on people at work: Set it to 0 1. That will make the console time out in 1 second! And to fix it, you have to continually press the Down arrow key while changing the time-out time with your free hand!)

`logging synchronous` is a very cool command, and it should be a default command, but it's not. It stops annoying console messages from popping up and disrupting the input you're trying to type. The messages still pop up, but you are returned to your router prompt without your input interrupted. This makes your input messages oh-so-much easier to read.

Here's an example of how to configure both commands:

```
Router(config)#line con 0
Router(config-line)#exec-timeout ?
 <0-35791> Timeout in minutes
Router(config-line)#exec-timeout 0 ?
 <0-2147483> Timeout in seconds
 <cr>
Router(config-line)#exec-timeout 0 0
Router(config-line)#logging synchronous
```

 You can set the console to go from never timing out (0 0) to 35,791 minutes and 2,147,483 seconds. The default is 10 minutes.

Telnet Password

To set the user-mode password for Telnet access into the router, use the line vty command. Routers that aren't running the Enterprise edition of the Cisco IOS default to five VTY lines, 0 through 4. But if you have the Enterprise edition, you'll have significantly more. The best way to find out how many lines you have is to use that question mark:

```
Router(config-line)#line vty 0 ?
 <1-4> Last Line Number
 <cr>
Router(config-line)#line vty 0 4
Router(config-line)#password todd2
Router(config-line)#login
```

You may or may not have to set the login command before the password on the VTY lines—depends on the IOS version. The result is the same either way.

So what will happen if you try to telnet into a router that doesn't have a VTY password set? You'll receive an error stating that the connection is refused because, well, the password isn't set. So, if you telnet into a router and receive the message

```
Router#telnet SFRouter
Trying SFRouter (10.0.0.1)…Open

Password required, but none set
[Connection to SFRouter closed by foreign host]
Router#
```

then the remote router (SFRouter in this example) does not have the VTY (telnet) password set. But you can get around this and tell the router to allow Telnet connections without a password by using the no login command:

```
Router(config-line)#line vty 0 4
Router(config-line)#no login
```

After your routers are configured with an IP address, you can use the Telnet program to configure and check your routers instead of having to use a console cable. You can use the Telnet program by typing **telnet** from any command prompt (DOS or Cisco). Anything Telnet is covered more thoroughly in Chapter 8.

If you can ping a router but are unable to telnet into it, the likely problem is that you didn't set the password on the VTY lines.

Encrypting Your Passwords

Because only the enable secret password is encrypted by default, you'll need to manually configure the user-mode and enable passwords for encryption.

Notice that you can see all the passwords except the enable secret when performing a show running-config on a router:

```
Router#sh running-config
[output cut]
!
enable secret 5 $1$rFbM$8.aXocHg6yHrM/zzeNkAT.
enable password todd1
!
[output cut]
line con 0
 password todd1
 login
line aux 0
 password todd
 login
line vty 0 4
 password todd2
 login
!
end

Router#
```

To manually encrypt your passwords, use the service password-encryption command. Here's an example of how to do it:

```
Router#config t
Enter configuration commands, one per line. End with CNTL/Z.
Router(config)#service password-encryption
Router(config)#^Z
Router#sh run
Building configuration...
[output cut]
!
enable secret 5 $1$rFbM$8.aXocHg6yHrM/zzeNkAT.
enable password 7 0835434A0D
!
[output cut]
```

```
!
line con 0
 password 7 111D160113
 login
line aux 0
 password 7 071B2E484A
 login
line vty 0 4
 password 7 0835434A0D
 login
line vty 5 197
 password 7 09463724B
 login
!
end
```

```
Router#config t
Router(config)#no service password-encryption
Router(config)#^Z
```

There you have it! The passwords will now be encrypted. You just encrypt the passwords, perform a show run, and then turn off the command. You can see that the enable password and the line passwords are all encrypted.

Okay, before we move onto learning about setting descriptions on our routers, let's talk about Telnet and encrypting our passwords. As I mentioned, if you set your passwords and then turn on the service password-encryption command, you've got to perform a show running-config before you turn off the encryption service or your passwords will not be encrypted.

Here is an example of how you might set and encrypt your Telnet password under the CCNA INTRO objectives:

1. Enter the mode to configure Telnet access: **line vty 0 4**

2. Enable Telnet login: **login**

3. Set the password to *cisco*: **password cisco**

4. Return to global configuration mode: **exit**

5. Encrypt password in show run/start output: **service password-encryption**

This is a tad different from what I showed you in the Telnet and encryption sections earlier, but you should know this way as well. Here are the commands in order:

```
Router(config)#line vty 0 4
Router(config-line)#login
Router(config-line)#password cisco
Router(config)#exit
Router(config)#service password-encryption
```

The phrase "don't shoot the messenger" comes to mind here! Also, remember that the CCNA INTRO objectives may require that you use the login command before setting the VTY password, or they may just want you to set it after the password. Understand both ways.

Descriptions

Setting descriptions on an interface is helpful to the administrator and, like the hostname, only locally significant. The description command is a helpful one because you can, for instance, use it to keep track of circuit numbers.

Here's an example:

```
Atlanta(config)#int e0
Atlanta(config-if)#description Sales Lan
Atlanta(config-if)#int s0
Atlanta(config-if)#desc Wan to Miami circuit:6fdda4321
```

You can view the description of an interface either with the show running-config command or the show interface command:

```
Atlanta#sh run
[cut]
interface Ethernet0
 description Sales Lan
 ip address 172.16.10.30 255.255.255.0
 no ip directed-broadcast
!
interface Serial0
 description Wan to Miami circuit:6fdda4321
 no ip address
 no ip directed-broadcast
 no ip mroute-cache


Atlanta#sh int e0
Ethernet0 is up, line protocol is up
 Hardware is Lance, address is 0010.7be8.25db (bia
  0010.7be8.25db)
 Description: Sales Lan
 [output cut]


Atlanta#sh int s0
Serial0 is up, line protocol is up
 Hardware is HD64570
```

```
Description: Wan to Miami circuit:6fdda4321
[output cut]
Atlanta#
```

 Real World Scenario

description: A Helpful Command

Bob, a senior network administrator at Acme Corporation in San Francisco, has over 50 WAN links to various branches throughout the U.S. and Canada. Whenever an interface goes down, Bob spends a lot of time trying to figure out the circuit number as well as the phone number of the responsible provider of the WAN link.

The interface description command would be very helpful to Bob because he can use this command on his LAN links to discern exactly where every router interface is connected. And Bob would benefit tremendously by adding circuit numbers to each and every WAN interface, along with the phone number of the responsible provider.

So by spending the few hours it would take to add this information to each and every router interface, Bob can save a huge amount of precious time when his WAN links go down—and you know they will!

Router Interfaces

Interface configuration is one of the most important router configurations, because without interfaces, a router is pretty much a completely useless object. Plus, interface configurations must be totally precise to enable communication with other devices. Network layer addresses, media type, bandwidth, and other administrator commands are all used to configure an interface.

Different routers use different methods to choose the interfaces used on them. For instance, the following command shows a Cisco 2522 router with 10 serial interfaces, labeled 0 through 9:

```
Router(config)#int serial ?
 <0-9> Serial interface number
```

Now it's time to choose the interface you want to configure. Once you do that, you will be in interface configuration for that specific interface. The following command would be used to choose serial port 5, for example:

```
Router(config)#int serial 5
Router(config)-if)#
```

The 2522 router has one Ethernet 10BaseT port, and typing `interface ethernet 0` can configure that interface, as seen here:

```
Router(config)#int ethernet ?
 <0-0> Ethernet interface number
Router(config)#int ethernet 0
Router(config-if)#
```

The 2500 router, as previously demonstrated, is a fixed configuration router, which means that when you buy that model, you're stuck with that physical configuration.

To configure an interface, you always use the `interface type number` sequence, but the 2600, 3600, 4000, and 7000 series routers use a physical slot in the router, with a port number on the module plugged into that slot. So on a 2600 router, the configuration would be `interface type slot/port`, as seen here:

```
Router(config)#int fastethernet ?
 <0-1> FastEthernet interface number
Router(config)#int fastethernet 0
% Incomplete command.
Router(config)#int fastethernet 0?
 /
Router(config)#int fastethernet 0/?
 <0-1> FastEthernet interface number
```

And make note of the fact that you can't just type `int fastethernet 0`. You must type the full command: `type slot/port`, or `int fastethernet 0/0`, or `int fa 0/0`.

To set the type of connector used, use the `media-type` command (this is usually auto-detected):

```
Router(config)#int fa 0/0
Router(config-if)#media-type ?
 100BaseX Use RJ45 for -TX; SC FO for -FX
 MII      Use MII connector
```

I'm going to continue with our router interface discussion in the next sections, and I'll include how to bring up the interface and set an IP address on a router interface.

Bringing Up an Interface

You can turn an interface off with the interface command `shutdown`, and turn it on with the `no shutdown` command.

If an interface is shut down, it'll display administratively down when using the `show interfaces` (`sh int` for short) command:

```
Router#sh int ethernet0
Ethernet0 is administratively down, line protocol is down
[output cut]
```

Another way to check an interface's status is via the show running-config command. All interfaces are shut down by default.

You can bring up the interface with the no shutdown command (no shut for short):

```
Router#config t
Enter configuration commands, one per line. End with
  CNTL/Z.
Router(config)#int ethernet0
Router(config-if)#no shutdown
Router(config-if)#^Z
00:57:08: %LINK-3-UPDOWN: Interface Ethernet0, changed
  state to up
00:57:09: %LINEPROTO-5-UPDOWN: Line protocol on Interface
  Ethernet0, changed state to up

Router#sh int ethernet0
Ethernet0 is up, line protocol is up
[output cut]
```

Configuring an IP Address on an Interface

Even though you don't have to use IP on your routers, it's most often what people actually do use. To configure IP addresses on an interface, use the ip address command from interface configuration mode:

```
Router(config)#int e0
Router(config-if)#ip address 172.16.10.2 255.255.255.0
Router(config-if)#no shut
```

Don't forget to turn on an interface with the no shutdown command. Remember to look at the command show interface e0 to see if it's administratively shut down or not. Show running-config will also give you this information.

The ip address *address mask* command starts the IP processing on the interface.

If you want to add a second subnet address to an interface, you have to use the secondary parameter. If you type another IP address and press Enter, it will replace the existing IP address and mask. This is definitely a most excellent feature of the Cisco IOS.

So, let's try it. To add a secondary IP address, just use the secondary parameter:

```
Router(config-if)#ip address 172.16.20.2 255.255.255.0
  secondary
Router(config-if)#^Z
```

You can verify that both addresses are configured on the interface with the show running-config command (sh run for short):

```
Router#sh run
Building configuration...
Current configuration:
[output cut]
!
interface Ethernet0
 ip address 172.16.20.2 255.255.255.0 secondary
 ip address 172.16.10.2 255.255.255.0
!
```

Okay—I really wouldn't recommend having multiple IP addresses on an interface because it's ugly and inefficient, but I showed you anyway just in case you someday find yourself dealing with an MIS manager who's in love with really bad network design and makes you administer it! And who knows? Maybe someone will ask you about it someday and you'll get to seem really smart because you know this.

Summarizing Some of Our commands So Far:

Let's just use some simple terms and apply commands to them:

Enter global configuration mode: Router#**configure terminal**

Enter interface configuration mode : Router(config)#**interface s0/0**

Configure the interface IP address : Router(config-if)#**ip address 10.1.5.255 255.255.252.0**

Enable the interface: Router(config-if)#**no shutdown**

Label the interface: Router(config-if)#**description WAN to Miami**

Taking a look at the commands in order:

```
Router#config t
Router(config)#int s0/0
Router(config-if)#ip address 10.1.5.255 255.255.252.0
Router(config-if)#no shutdown
Router(config-if)#description WAN to Miami
```

Serial Interface Commands

Wait! Before you just jump in and configure a serial interface, you need some key information. Like knowing that the interface will usually be attached to a CSU/DSU type of device that provides clocking for the line to the router, as I've shown in Figure 4.3.

Okay, here you can see that the serial interface is used to connect to a DCE network via a CSU/DSU that provides the clocking to the router interface.

But if you have a back-to-back configuration, (for example, one that's used in a lab environment like I've shown you in Figure 4.4), one end—the data communication equipment (DCE) end of the cable—must provide clocking!

By default, Cisco routers are all data terminal equipment (DTE) devices, which means that you must tell an interface to provide clocking if you need it to act like a DCE device. Again, you would not provide clocking on a production T1, for example, because you would have a CSU/DSU connected to your serial interface, as Figure 4.3 shows.

FIGURE 4.3 Typical WAN connection

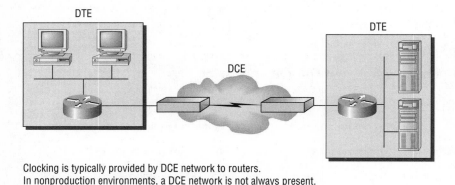

Clocking is typically provided by DCE network to routers.
In nonproduction environments, a DCE network is not always present.

FIGURE 4.4 Providing clocking on a nonproduction network

Set clock rate if needed.

Todd#config t
Todd(config)#interface serial 0
Todd(config-if)#clock rate 64000

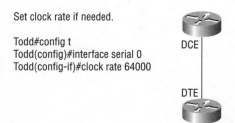

DCE side determined by cable.
Add clocking to DCE side only.

show controllers will show the cable connection type.

You configure a DCE serial interface with the `clock rate` command:

```
Router#config t
Enter configuration commands, one per line. End with CNTL/Z.
Router(config)#int s0
Router(config-if)#clock rate ?
   Speed (bits per second)
 1200
 2400
 4800
 9600
 19200
 38400
 56000
 64000
 72000
 125000
 148000
 250000
 500000
 800000
 1000000
 1300000
 2000000
 4000000

 <300-4000000>  Choose clockrate from list above

Router(config-if)#clock rate 64000
%Error: This command applies only to DCE interfaces
Router(config-if)#int s1
Router(config-if)#clock rate 64000
```

It doesn't hurt anything to try to put a clock rate on an interface. Notice that the `clock rate` command is in bits per second. You can see if a router's serial interface has a DCE cable connected with the `show controllers` *int* command:

```
Router>sh controllers s 0
HD unit 0, idb = 0x297DE8, driver structure at 0x29F3A0
buffer size 1524  HD unit 0, V.35 DCE cable
```

The next command you need to get acquainted with is the `bandwidth` command. Every Cisco router ships with a default serial link bandwidth of T1 (1.544Mbps). But this has nothing to do with how data is transferred over a link. The bandwidth of a serial link is used by routing protocols such as IGRP, EIGRP, and OSPF to calculate the best cost (path) to a remote network. So if you're using RIP routing, then the bandwidth setting of a serial link is irrelevant since RIP uses only hop count to determine that. If you're rereading this part thinking, "Huh—what? Routing protocols? Metrics?"—don't freak! I'm going over all that soon in Chapter 5, "IP Routing."

Okay—here's an example of using the bandwidth command:

```
Router(config-if)#bandwidth ?
  <1-10000000> Bandwidth in kilobits
```

```
Router(config-if)#bandwidth 64
```

Did you notice that, unlike the clock rate command, the bandwidth command is configured in kilobits?

Viewing, Saving, and Erasing Configurations

If you run through setup mode, you'll be asked if you want to use the configuration you just created. If you say yes, then it will copy the configuration running in DRAM (known as the running-config) into NVRAM and name the file startup-config.

You can manually save the file from DRAM to NVRAM by using the copy running-config startup-config command (you can use the shortcut copy run start also):

```
Atlanta#copy run start
Destination filename [startup-config]?[Enter]
Warning: Attempting to overwrite an NVRAM configuration
  previously written by a different version of the system
  image.
Overwrite the previous NVRAM configuration?[confirm][Enter]
Building configuration...
```

Notice that the message we received tells us we're trying to write over the older startup-config. The IOS had just been upgraded to version 12.2, and the last time the file was saved, 11.3 was running. Sometimes, when you see a question with an answer in [], it means that if you just press Enter, you're choosing the default answer.

Also, when the command asked for the destination filename, the default answer was startup-config. The "feature" aspect of this command output is that you can't even type anything else in or you'll get an error, as seen here:

```
Atlanta#copy run start
Destination filename [startup-config]?todd
%Error opening nvram:todd (No such file or directory)
Atlanta#
```

You're right—it's weird! Why on earth do they even ask if you can't change it at all? Well, considering that this "feature" was first introduced with the release of the 12.*x* IOS, we're all pretty sure it will turn out to be relevant and important sometime in the future.

You can view the files by typing **show running-config** or **show startup-config** from privileged mode. The sh run command, which is a shortcut for show running-config, tells us that we are viewing the current configuration:

```
Atlanta#sh run
Building configuration...

Current configuration:
!
version 12.0
service timestamps debug uptime
service timestamps log uptime
no service password-encryption
!
hostname Atlanta
ip subnet-zero
frame-relay switching
!
[output cut]
```

The sh start command—one of the shortcuts for the show startup-config command—shows us the configuration that will be used the next time the router is reloaded. It also tells us how much NVRAM is being used to store the startup-config file. Here's an example:

```
Atlanta#sh start
Using 4850 out of 32762 bytes
!
version 12.0
service timestamps debug uptime
service timestamps log uptime
no service password-encryption
!
hostname Atlanta
!
!
ip subnet-zero
```

```
frame-relay switching
!
[output cut]
```

Deleting the Configuration and Reloading the Router

You can delete the startup-config file by using the `erase startup-config` command, after which you'll receive an error if you ever try to view the startup-config file:

```
Atlanta#erase startup-config
Erasing the nvram filesystem will remove all files!
  Continue? [confirm][Enter]
[OK]
Erase of nvram: complete
Atlanta#sh start
%% Non-volatile configuration memory is not present
Atlanta#reload

System configuration has been modified. Save? [yes/no]: n
```

If you reload or power down and up the router after using the `erase startup-config` command, you'll be offered setup mode because there's no configuration saved in NVRAM. You can press Ctrl+C to exit setup mode at any time (the `reload` command can only be used from privileged mode).

At this point, you shouldn't use setup mode to configure your router. So just say no to setup mode, because it's there to help people who don't know how to use the Cash Line Interface (CLI), and this no longer applies to you. Be strong—you can do it!

Verifying Your Configuration

Obviously, `show running-config` would be the best way to verify your configuration and `show startup-config` would be the best way to verify the configuration that'll be used the next time the router is reloaded—right?

Well, once you take a look at the running-config, if all appears well, you can verify your configuration with utilities such as Ping and Telnet. Ping is Packet Internet Groper, a program that uses ICMP echo requests and replies. (ICMP is discussed in Chapter 2, "Internet Protocols.") Ping sends a packet to a remote host, and if that host responds, you know that the host is alive. But you don't know if it's alive and also *well*—just because you can ping an NT server does not mean you can log in! Even so, Ping is an awesome starting point for troubleshooting an internetwork.

Did you know that you can ping with different protocols? You can, and you can test this by typing **ping ?** at either the router user-mode or privileged-mode prompt:

```
Router#ping ?
  WORD     Ping destination address or hostname
```

```
appletalk Appletalk echo
decnet    DECnet echo
ip        IP echo
ipx       Novell/IPX echo
srb       srb echo
<cr>
```

If you want to find a neighbor's Network layer address, either you need to go to the router or switch itself or you can type **show cdp entry * protocol** to get the Network layer addresses you need for pinging.

Cisco Discovery Protocol (CDP) is covered in Chapter 8.

Traceroute uses ICMP with IP time to live (TTL) time-outs to track the path a packet takes through an internetwork, in contrast to Ping, which just finds the host and responds. And Traceroute can also be used with multiple protocols.

```
Router#traceroute ?
WORD      Trace route to destination address or hostname
appletalk AppleTalk Trace
clns      ISO CLNS Trace
ip        IP Trace
oldvines  Vines Trace (Cisco)
vines     Vines Trace (Banyan)
<cr>
```

Telnet is the really the best tool because it uses IP at the Network layer and TCP at the Transport layer to create a session with a remote host. If you can telnet into a device, your IP connectivity just has to be good. You can only telnet to devices that use IP addresses, and you can use Windows hosts or router prompts to telnet to a remote device:

```
Router#telnet ?
WORD IP address or hostname of a remote system
<cr>
```

From the router prompt, you just type a hostname or IP address and it will assume you want to telnet—you don't need to type the actual command, telnet.

In the following sections, I am going to show you how to verify the interface statistics.

Verifying with the *show interface* Command

Another way to verify your configuration is by typing show interface commands, the first of which is show interface ?. That will reveal all the available interfaces to configure.

NOTE The `show interfaces` command displays the configurable parameters and statistics of all interfaces on a router.

This command is very useful for verifying and troubleshooting router and network issues. The following output is from my 2600 routers:

```
Router#sh int ?
  Async              Async interface
  BVI                Bridge-Group Virtual Interface
  CTunnel            CTunnel interface
  Dialer             Dialer interface
  FastEthernet       FastEthernet IEEE 802.3
  Loopback           Loopback interface
  MFR                Multilink Frame Relay bundle interface
  Multilink          Multilink-group interface
  Null               Null interface
  Serial             Serial
  Tunnel             Tunnel interface
  Vif                PGM Multicast Host interface
  Virtual-Template   Virtual Template interface
  Virtual-TokenRing  Virtual TokenRing
  accounting         Show interface accounting
  crb                Show interface routing/bridging info
  dampening          Show interface dampening info
  description        Show interface description
  irb                Show interface routing/bridging info
  mac-accounting     Show interface MAC accounting info
  mpls-exp           Show interface MPLS experimental accounting info
  precedence         Show interface precedence accounting info
  rate-limit         Show interface rate-limit info
  summary            Show interface summary
  switching          Show interface switching
  |                  Output modifiers
  <cr>
```

The only "real" physical interfaces are FastEthernet, Serial, and Async; the rest are all logical interfaces.

The next command is `show interface fastethernet 0/0`. It reveals to us the hardware address, logical address, and encapsulation method, as well as statistics on collisions, as seen here:

```
Router#sh int fastethernet 0/0
FastEthernet0/0 is up, line protocol is up
```

```
Hardware is AmdFE, address is 00b0.6483.2320 (bia 00b0.6483.2320)
Description: connection to LAN 40
Internet address is 192.168.1.33/27
MTU 1500 bytes, BW 100000 Kbit, DLY 100 usec,
    reliability 255/255, txload 1/255, rxload 1/255
Encapsulation ARPA, loopback not set
Keepalive set (10 sec)
Full-duplex, 100Mb/s, 100BaseTX/FX
ARP type: ARPA, ARP Timeout 04:00:00
Last input never, output 00:00:04, output hang never
Last clearing of "show interface" counters never
Input queue: 0/75/0/0 (size/max/drops/flushes); Total output drops: 0
Queueing strategy: fifo
Output queue: 0/40 (size/max)
5 minute input rate 0 bits/sec, 0 packets/sec
5 minute output rate 0 bits/sec, 0 packets/sec
    0 packets input, 0 bytes
    Received 0 broadcasts, 0 runts, 0 giants, 0 throttles
    0 input errors, 0 CRC, 0 frame, 0 overrun, 0 ignored
    0 watchdog
    0 input packets with dribble condition detected
    84639 packets output, 8551135 bytes, 0 underruns
    0 output errors, 0 collisions, 16 interface resets
    0 babbles, 0 late collision, 0 deferred
    0 lost carrier, 0 no carrier
    0 output buffer failures, 0 output buffers swapped out
```

As you probably guessed, we're going to discuss the important statistics from this output, but first, for fun (this is all fun, right?), I've got to ask you what subnet is the FastEthernet 0/0 a member of and what's the broadcast address and valid host range? And, my friend, you really have to be able to nail these things Nascar fast! Just in case you didn't, the address is 192.168.1.33/27. And I've gotta be honest—if you don't know what a /27 is at this point, you'll need a miracle to pass the exam. (A /27 is 255.255.255.224.) The fourth octet is a block size of 32. The subnets are 0, 32, 64..., the FastEthernet interface is in the 32 subnet, the broadcast address is 63, and the valid hosts are 33–62.

NOTE If you struggled with any of this, please save yourself from certain doom and get yourself back into Chapter 3, "IP Subnetting and Variable Length Subnet Masks (VLSMs) and Troubleshooting IP," now! Read and reread it until you've got in dialed in!

The preceding interface is working and looks to be in good shape. The show interfaces command will show you if you are receiving errors on the interface, and it will show you the maximum transmission units (MTUs), bandwidth (BW), reliability (255/255 means perfect!), and load (1/255 means no load).

Continuing to use the output from above, what is the bandwidth of the interface? Well, other than the easy giveaway of the interface being called a "FastEthernet" interface, we can see the bandwidth is 10000Kbit, which is 100,000,000 (Kbit means to add three zeros), which is 100Mbits per second, or FastEthernet. Gigabit would be 1000000Kbits per second.

The most important statistic of the show interface command is the output of the line and data-link protocol status. If the output reveals that FastEthernet 0/0 is up and the line protocol is up, then the interface is up and running:

```
Router#sh int fa0/0
FastEthernet0/0 is up, line protocol is up
```

The first parameter refers to the Physical layer, and it's up when it receives carrier detect. The second parameter refers to the Data Link layer, and it looks for keepalives from the connecting end. (Keepalives are used between devices to make sure connectivity has not dropped.)

Here's an example:

```
Router#sh int s0/0
Serial0/0 is up, line protocol is down
```

If you see that the line is up but the protocol is down, as shown above, you're experiencing a clocking (keepalive) or framing problem—possibly an encapsulation mismatch. Check the keepalives on both ends to make sure that they match, that the clock rate is set, if needed, and that the encapsulation type is the same on both ends. The output above would be considered a Data Link layer problem.

If you discover that both the line interface and the protocol are down, it's a cable or interface problem. The following output would be considered a Physical layer problem:

```
Router#sh int s0/0
Serial0/0 is down, line protocol is down
```

If one end is administratively shut down (as shown next), the remote end would present as down and down:

```
Router#sh int s0/0
Serial0/0 is administratively down, line protocol is down
```

To enable the interface, use the command no shutdown from interface configuration mode.

The next show interface serial 0/0 command demonstrates the serial line and the maximum transmission unit (MTU)—1,500 bytes by default. It also shows the default bandwidth (BW) on all Cisco serial links: 1.544Kbps. This is used to determine the bandwidth of the line for routing protocols such as IGRP, EIGRP, and OSPF. Another important configuration to notice is the keepalive, which is 10 seconds by default. Each router sends a keepalive message to its neighbor every 10 seconds, and if both routers aren't configured for the same keepalive time, it won't work.

```
Router#sh int s0/0
Serial0/0 is up, line protocol is up
 Hardware is HD64570
 MTU 1500 bytes, BW 1544 Kbit, DLY 20000 usec,
   reliability 255/255, txload 1/255, rxload 1/255
 Encapsulation HDLC, loopback not set, keepalive set
  (10 sec)
 Last input never, output never, output hang never
 Last clearing of "show interface" counters never
 Queueing strategy: fifo
 Output queue 0/40, 0 drops; input queue 0/75, 0 drops
 5 minute input rate 0 bits/sec, 0 packets/sec
 5 minute output rate 0 bits/sec, 0 packets/sec
   0 packets input, 0 bytes, 0 no buffer
   Received 0 broadcasts, 0 runts, 0 giants, 0 throttles
   0 input errors, 0 CRC, 0 frame, 0 overrun, 0 ignored,
   0 abort
   0 packets output, 0 bytes, 0 underruns
   0 output errors, 0 collisions, 16 interface resets
   0 output buffer failures, 0 output buffers swapped out
   0 carrier transitions
   DCD=down DSR=down DTR=down RTS=down CTS=down
```

You can clear the counters on the interface by typing the command `clear counters`:

```
Router#clear counters ?
  Async             Async interface
  BVI               Bridge-Group Virtual Interface
  CTunnel           CTunnel interface
  Dialer            Dialer interface
  FastEthernet      FastEthernet IEEE 802.3
  Group-Async       Async Group interface
  Line              Terminal line
  Loopback          Loopback interface
  MFR               Multilink Frame Relay bundle interface
  Multilink         Multilink-group interface
  Null              Null interface
  Serial            Serial
  Tunnel            Tunnel interface
```

```
  Vif                 PGM Multicast Host interface
  Virtual-Template    Virtual Template interface
  Virtual-TokenRing   Virtual TokenRing
  <cr>
```

```
Router#clear counters s0/0
Clear "show interface" counters on this interface
  [confirm][Enter]
Router#
00:17:35: %CLEAR-5-COUNTERS: Clear counter on interface
  Serial0 by console
Router#
```

Verifying with the *show ip interface* Command

The show ip interface command will provide you with information regarding the layer 3 configurations of a router's interfaces:

```
Router#sh ip interface
FastEthernet0/0 is up, line protocol is up
  Internet address is 1.1.1.1/24
  Broadcast address is 255.255.255.255
  Address determined by setup command
  MTU is 1500 bytes
  Helper address is not set
  Directed broadcast forwarding is disabled
  Outgoing access list is not set
  Inbound  access list is not set
  Proxy ARP is enabled
  Security level is default
  Split horizon is enabled
[output cut]
```

The status of the interface, the IP address and mask, information on whether an access list is set on the interface, and basic IP information are included in this output.

Using the *show ip interface brief* Command

The show ip interface brief command is probably one of the most helpful commands that you can ever use on a Cisco router. This command provides a quick overview of the router's interfaces, including the logical address and status:

```
Router#sh ip int brief
Interface       IP-Address    OK? Method Status             Protocol
FastEthernet0/0 192.168.1.33  YES manual up                 up
```

```
FastEthernet0/1 10.3.1.88     YES manual up                       up
Serial0/0       10.1.1.1      YES manual up                       up
Serial0/1       unassigned    YES NVRAM  administratively down    down
```

Remember, the administratively down means that you need to type no shutdown under the interface.

Verifying with the *show protocols* Command

The show protocols command is a really helpful command you'd use in order to see the quick status of layers 1 and 2 of each interface as well as the IP addresses used.

Here's a look at it:

```
Router#sh protocols
Global values:
   Internet Protocol routing is enabled
Ethernet0/0 is administratively down, line protocol is down
Serial0/0 is up, line protocol is up
   Internet address is 100.30.31.5/24
Serial0/1 is administratively down, line protocol is down
Serial0/2 is up, line protocol is up
   Internet address is 100.50.31.2/24
Loopback0 is up, line protocol is up
   Internet address is 100.20.31.1/24
```

Using the *show controllers* Command

The show controllers command displays information about the physical interface itself. It'll also give you the type of serial cable plugged into a serial port. Usually, this will only be a DTE cable that plugs into a type of data service unit (DSU).

```
Router#sh controllers serial 0/0
HD unit 0, idb = 0x1229E4, driver structure at 0x127E70
buffer size 1524 HD unit 0, V.35 DTE cable
cpb = 0xE2, eda = 0x4140, cda = 0x4000

Router#sh controllers serial 0/1
HD unit 1, idb = 0x12C174, driver structure at 0x131600
buffer size 1524 HD unit 1, V.35 DCE cable
cpb = 0xE3, eda = 0x2940, cda = 0x2800
```

Notice that serial 0/0 has a DTE cable, whereas the serial 0/1 connection has a DCE cable. Serial 0/1 would have to provide clocking with the clock rate command. Serial 0/0 would get its clocking from the DSU.

Let's look at this command again. In Figure 4.5, see the DTE/DCE cable between the two routers? Know that you will not see this in production networks!

Router R1 has a DTE connection—the default for all Cisco routers. Routers R1 and R2 can't communicate. Check out the output of the show controllers s0/0 command here:

```
R1#sh controllers serial 0/0
HD unit 0, idb = 0x1229E4, driver structure at 0x127E70
buffer size 1524 HD unit 0, V.35 DCE cable
cpb = 0xE2, eda = 0x4140, cda = 0x4000
```

The show controllers s0/0 shows that the interface is a V.35 DCE cable. This means that R1 needs to provide clocking of the line to router R2. Basically, the interface has the wrong label on the cable on the R1 router's serial interface. But if you add clocking on the R1 router's serial interface, the network should come right up.

Let's check out another issue, shown in Figure 4.6, that you can solve by using the show controllers command. Again, routers R1 and R2 can't communicate. Here's the output of R1's show controllers s0/0 command and show ip interface s0/0:

```
R1#sh controllers s0/0
HD unit 0, idb = 0x1229E4, driver structure at 0x127E70
buffer size 1524 HD unit 0,
DTE V.35 clocks stopped
cpb = 0xE2, eda = 0x4140, cda = 0x4000
```

```
R1#sh ip interface s0/0
Serial0/0 is up, line protocol is down
  Internet address is 192.168.10.2/24
  Broadcast address is 255.255.255.255
```

FIGURE 4.5   The show controllers Command

FIGURE 4.6   The show controllers command used with the show ip interface command

If you use the `show controllers` command and the `show ip interface` command, you'll see that router R1 isn't receiving clocking of the line. This network is a nonproduction network, so no CSU/DSU is connected to provide clocking of the line. So the DCE end of the cable will be providing the clock rate—in this case, the R2 router. The `show ip interface` indicates that the interface is up, but the protocol is down, which means that no keepalives are being received from the far end. In this example, the likely culprit is the result of bad, or no, clocking.

Summary

This was a fun chapter! I showed you a lot about the Cisco IOS and I really hope you gained a lot of insight into the Cisco router world. This chapter started off by explaining the Cisco Internetwork Operating System (IOS) and how you can use the IOS to run and configure Cisco routers. You learned how to bring a router up and what setup mode does. Oh, and by the way, since you can now basically configure Cisco routers, you should never use setup mode, right?

After I discussed how to connect to a router with a console and LAN connection, I covered the Cisco help features and how to use the CLI to find commands and command parameters. In addition, I discussed some basic `show` commands to help you verify your configurations.

Administrative functions on a router help you administrate your network and verify that you are configuring the correct device. Setting router passwords is one of the most important configurations you can perform on your routers. I showed you the five passwords to set. In addition, I used the hostname, interface description, and banners to help you administer your router.

Well, that concludes your introduction to the Cisco Internetwork Operating System (IOS)! And, as usual, it's super-important for you to have the basics that we went over in this chapter before you move on to the following chapters.

Exam Essentials

Understand the what happens (and the sequence in which it happens) when you power on a router. When you first bring up a Cisco router, it will run a power-on self-test (POST), and if that passes, it will look for and load the Cisco IOS from flash memory, if a file is present. The IOS then proceeds to load and looks for a valid configuration in NVRAM called the startup-config. If no file is present in NVRAM, the router will go into setup mode.

Remember what setup mode provides. Setup mode is automatically started if a router boots and no startup-config is in NVRAM. You can also bring up setup mode by typing **setup** from the privileged mode. Setup provides a minimum amount of configuration in an easy format for someone who does not understand how to configure a Cisco router from the command line.

Understand the difference between user mode and privileged mode. User mode provides a command-line interface with very few available commands by default. User mode does not allow the configuration to be viewed or changed. Privileged mode allows a user to both view and change the configuration of a router. You can enter privileged mode by typing the command **enable** and entering the enable password or enable secret password, if set.

Remember what the command show version provides.   The show version command will provide basic configuration for the system hardware as well as the software version, the names and sources of configuration files, the config-register setting, and the boot images.

Remember how to set the hostname of a router.   The command sequence to set the host-name of a router is as follows:

```
enable
config t
hostname Todd
```

Remember the difference between the enable password and enable secret password.   Both of these passwords are used to gain access into privileged mode. However, the enable secret is newer and is always encrypted by default. Also, if you set the enable password and then set the enable secret, only the enable secret will be used.

Remember how to set the enable secret on a router.   To set the enable secret, you use the command enable secret. Do not use enable secret password *password* or you will set your password to *password password*. Here is an example:

```
enable
config t
enable secret todd
```

Remember how to set the console password on a router.   To set the console password, use the following sequence:

```
enable
config t
line console 0
login
password todd
```

Remember how to set the Telnet password on a router.   To set the Telnet password, the sequence is as follows:

```
enable
config t
line vty 0 4
password todd
login
```

Be able to understand how to troubleshoot a serial link problem. If you type show interface serial 0 and see down, line protocol is down, this will be considered a Physical layer problem. If you see it as up, line protocol is down, then you have a Data Link layer problem.

Be able to understand how to verify your router with the show interfaces command If you type show interfaces, you can view the statistics for the interfaces on the router, verify if the interfaces are shut down, and see the IP address of each interface.

Written Lab 4

Write out the command or commands for the following questions:

1. What command is used to set a serial interface to provide clocking to another router at 64Kb?

2. If you telnet into a router and get the response "connection refused, password not set," what would you do on the destination router to stop receiving this message and not be prompted for a password?

3. If you type **show inter et 0** and notice the port is administratively down, what would you do?

4. If you wanted to delete the configuration stored in NVRAM, what would you type?

5. If you wanted to set a user-mode password for the console port, what would you type?

6. If you wanted to set the enable secret password to *cisco*, what would you type?

7. If you wanted to see if a serial interface needed to provide clocking, what command would you use?

8. What command would you use to see the terminal history size?

9. You want to reinitialize the router and totally replace the running-config with the current startup-config. What command will you use?

10. How would you set the name of a router to *Chicago*?

(The answers to Written Lab 4 can be found following the answers to the review questions for this chapter.)

Hands-on Labs

In this section, you will perform commands on a Cisco router that will help you understand what you learned in this chapter.

You'll need at least one Cisco router—two would be better, three would be outstanding.

 The hands-on labs in this section are included for use with real Cisco routers. If you are using software from RouterSim or Sybex, please use the hands-on labs found in those programs.

The labs in this chapter include the following:

Lab 4.1: Logging into a Router

Lab 4.2: Using the Help and Editing Features

Lab 4.3: Saving a Router Configuration

Lab 4.4: Setting Your Passwords

Lab 4.5: Setting the Hostname, Descriptions, IP Address, and Clock Rate

Hands-on Lab 4.1: Logging into a Router

1. Press Enter to connect to your router. This will put you into user mode.

2. At the Router> prompt, type a question mark ?.

3. Notice the —more— at the bottom of the screen.

4. Press the Enter key to view the commands line by line.

5. Press the spacebar to view the commands a full screen at a time.

6. You can type **q** at any time to quit.

7. Type **enable** or **en** and press Enter. This will put you into privileged mode where you can change and view the router configuration.

8. At the Router# prompt, type a question mark **(?)**. Notice how many options are available to you in privileged mode.

9. Type **q** to quit.

10. Type **config** and press Enter.

11. Press Enter to configure your router using your terminal.

12. At the Router(config)# prompt, type a question mark **(?)**, then **q** to quit, or hit the spacebar to view the commands.

13. Type **interface e0** or **int e0** (or even **int fa0/0**) and press Enter. This will allow you to configure interface Ethernet 0.

14. At the Router(config-if)# prompt, type a question mark **(?)**.

15. Type **int s0** (**int s0/0**) or **interface s0** (same as the interface serial 0 command) and press Enter. This will allow you to configure interface serial 0. Notice that you can go from interface to interface easily.

16. Type **encapsulation ?**.

17. Type **exit**. Notice how this brings you back one level.

18. Press Ctrl+Z. Notice how this brings you out of configuration mode and places you back into privileged mode.

19. Type **disable**. This will put you into user mode.

20. Type **exit**, which will log you out of the router.

Hands-on Lab 4.2: Using the Help and Editing Features

1. Log into the router and go to privileged mode by typing **en** or **enable**.

2. Type a question mark (**?**).

3. Type **cl?** and then press Enter. Notice that you can see all the commands that start with *cl*.

4. Type **clock ?** and press Enter.

 Notice the difference between step 3 and 4. Step 3 has you type letters with no space and a question mark, which will give you all the commands that start with *cl*. Step 4 has you type a command, space, and question mark. By doing this, you will see the next available parameter.

5. Set the router's clock by typing **clock ?** and, following the help screens, setting the router's time and date.

6. Type **clock ?**.

7. Type **clock set ?**.

8. Type **clock set 10:30:30 ?**.

9. Type **clock set 10:30:30 14 March ?**.

10. Type **clock set 10:30:30 14 March 2002**.

11. Press Enter.

12. Type **show clock** to see the time and date.

13. From privileged mode, type **show access-list 10**. Don't press Enter.

14. Press Ctrl+A. This takes you to the beginning of the line.

15. Press Ctrl+E. This should take you back to the end of the line.

16. Press Ctrl+A, then Ctrl+F. This should move you forward one character.

17. Press Ctrl+B, which will move you back one character.

18. Press Enter, and then press Ctrl+P. This will repeat the last command.

19. Press the Up arrow on your keyboard. This will also repeat the last command.

20. Type **sh history**. This shows you the last 10 commands entered.

21. Type **terminal history size ?**. This changes the history entry size. The ? is the number of allowed lines.

22. Type **show terminal** to gather terminal statistics and history size.

23. Type **terminal no editing**. This turns off advanced editing. Repeat steps 14 through 18 to see that the shortcut editing keys have no effect until you type **terminal editing**.

24. Type **terminal editing** and press Enter to reenable advanced editing.

25. Type **sh run**, and then press your Tab key. This will finish typing the command for you.

26. Type **sh start**, and then press your Tab key. This will finish typing the command for you.

Hands-on Lab 4.3: Saving a Router Configuration

1. Log into the router and go into privileged mode by typing **en** or **enable**, and then press Enter.

2. To see the configuration stored in NVRAM, type **sh start** and press Tab and Enter, or type **show startup-config** and press Enter. However, if no configuration has been saved, you will get an error message.

3. To save a configuration to NVRAM, which is known as startup-config, you can do one of the following:
   - Type **copy run start** and press Enter.
   - Type **copy running**, press Tab, type **start**, press Tab, and press Enter.
   - Type **copy running-config startup-config** and press Enter.

4. Type **sh start**, press Tab, then press Enter.

5. Type **sh run**, press Tab, then press Enter.

6. Type **erase start**, press Tab, then press Enter.

7. Type **sh start**, press Tab, then press Enter. You should get an error message.

8. Type **reload**, and then press Enter. Acknowledge the reload by pressing Enter. Wait for the router to reload.

9. Say no to entering setup mode, or just press Ctrl+C.

Hands-on Lab 4.4: Setting Your Passwords

1. Log into the router and go into privileged mode by typing **en** or **enable**.

2. Type **config t** and press Enter.

3. Type **enable ?**.

4. Set your enable secret password by typing **enable secret *password*** (the third word should be your own personalized password) and pressing Enter. Do not add the parameter password after the parameter secret (this would make your password the word *password*). An example would be enable secret todd.

5. Now let's see what happens when you log all the way out of the router and then log in. Log out by pressing Ctrl+Z, then type **exit** and press Enter. Go to privileged mode. Before you are allowed to enter privileged mode, you will be asked for a password. If you successfully enter the secret password, you can proceed.

6. Remove the secret password. Go to privileged mode, type **config t**, and press Enter. Type **no enable secret** and press Enter. Log out and then log back in again; now you should not be asked for a password.

7. One more password used to enter privileged mode is called the enable password. It is an older, less-secure password and is not used if an enable secret password is set. Here is an example of how to set it:

```
config t
enable password todd1
```

8. Notice that the enable secret and enable passwords are different. They cannot be the same.

9. Type **config t** to be at the right level to set your console and auxiliary passwords, and then type **line ?**.

10. Notice that the parameters for the line commands are auxiliary, vty, and console. You will set all three.

11. To set the Telnet or VTY password, type **line vty 0 4** and then press Enter. The 0 4 is the range of the five available virtual lines used to connect with Telnet. If you have an enterprise IOS, the number of lines may vary. Use the question mark to determine the last line number available on your router.

12. The next command is used to set the authentication on or off. Type **login** and press Enter to prompt for a user-mode password when telnetting into the router. You will not be able to telnet into a router if the password is not set.

 You can use the no login command to disable the user-mode password prompt when using Telnet.

13. One more command you need to set for your VTY password is password. Type **password *password*** to set the password. (*password* is your password.)

14. Here is an example of how to set the VTY passwords:

```
config t
line vty 0 4
login
password todd
```

15. Set your auxiliary password by first typing **line auxiliary 0** or **line aux 0**.

16. Type **login**.

17. Type **password** *password*.

18. Set your console password by first typing **line console 0** or **line con 0**.

19. Type **login**.

20. Type **password** *password*. Here is an example of the last two commands:

```
config t
line con 0
login
password todd1
line aux 0
login
password todd
```

21. You can add the Exec-timeout 0 0 command to the console 0 line. This will stop the console from timing out and logging you out. The command will now look like this:

```
config t
line con 0
login
password todd2
exec-timeout 0 0
```

22. Set the console prompt to not overwrite the command you're typing with console messages by using the command logging synchronous.

```
config t
line con 0
logging synchronous
```

Hands-on Lab 4.5: Setting the Hostname, Descriptions, IP Address, and Clock Rate

1. Log into the router and go into privileged mode by typing **en** or **enable**.

2. Set your hostname on your router by using the hostname command. Notice that it is one word. Here is an example of setting your hostname:

```
Router#config t
Router(config)#hostname RouterA
RouterA(config)#
```

Notice that the hostname of the router changed as soon as you pressed Enter.

3. Set a banner that the network administrators will see by using the `banner` command.

4. Type **config t**, then **banner ?**.

5. Notice that you can set four different banners. For this lab we are only interested in the login and message of the day (MOTD) banners.

6. Set your MOTD banner, which will be displayed when a console, auxiliary, or Telnet connection is made to the router, by typing this:

```
config t
banner motd #
This is an motd banner
#
```

7. In the preceding example, a # sign was used as a delimiting character. This tells the router when the message is done. You cannot use the delimiting character in the message itself.

8. You can remove the MOTD banner by typing this:

```
config t
no banner motd
```

9. Set the login banner by typing the following:

```
config t
banner login #
This is a login banner
#
```

10. The login banner will display immediately after the MOTD but before the user-mode password prompt. Remember that you set your user-mode passwords by setting the console, auxiliary, and VTY line passwords.

11. You can remove the login banner by typing the following commands:

```
config t
no banner login
```

12. You can add an IP address to an interface with the `ip address` command. You need to get into interface configuration mode first; here is an example of how you do that:

```
config t
int e0 (you can use int Ethernet 0 too)
ip address 1.1.1.1 255.255.0.0
no shutdown
```

Notice that the IP address (1.1.1.1) and subnet mask (255.255.0.0) are configured on one line. The no `shutdown` (or no `shut` for short) command is used to enable the interface. All interfaces are shut down by default.

13. You can add identification to an interface by using the description command. This is useful for adding information about the connection. Only administrators see this, not users. Here is an example:

```
config t
int s0
ip address 1.1.1.2 255.255.0.0
no shut
description Wan link to Miami
```

14. You can add the bandwidth of a serial link as well as the clock rate when simulating a DCE WAN link. Here is an example:

```
config t
int s0
bandwidth 64
clock rate 64000
```

Review Questions

1. You type `show running-config` and get this output:

    ```
    [output cut]
    Line console 0
          Exec-timeout 1 44
          Password 7098C0BQR
          Login
    [output cut]
    ```

    What does the two numbers following the `exec-timeout` command mean?

    A. If no command has been typed in 44 second, the console connection will be closed.

    B. If no router activity has been detected in 1 hour and 44 minutes, the console will be locked out.

    C. If no commands have been typed in 1 minute and 44 seconds, the console connection will be closed.

    D. If you're connected to the router by a telnet connection, input must be detected within 1 minute and 44 seconds or the connection will be closed.

2. You need to find the broadcast address used on a LAN on your router. What command will you type into the router from user mode to find the broadcast address?

    A. `show running-config`

    B. `show startup-config`

    C. `show interfaces`

    D. `show protocols`

3. You want to totally reinitialize the router and replace the current running-config with the current startup-config. What command will you use?

    A. `replace run start`

    B. `copy run start`

    C. `copy start run`

    D. `reload`

4. Which command will show you whether a DTE or a DCE cable is plugged into serial 0?

    A. `sh int s0`

    B. `sh int serial 0`

    C. `sho controllers s 0`

    D. `sho serial 0 controllers`

5. What keystroke will terminate setup mode?

    A. Ctrl+Z

    B. Ctrl+^

    C. Ctrl+C

    D. Ctrl+Shift+^

6. You set the console password, but when you display the configuration, the password doesn't show up; it looks like this:

```
[output cut]
Line console 0
        Exec-timeout 1 44
        Password 7098COBQR
        Login
[output cut]
```

What cause the password to be stored like this?

A. encrypt password

B. service password-encryption

C. service-password-encryption

D. exec-timout 1 44

7. Which of the following commands will configure all the default VTY ports on a router?

A. Router#**line vty 0 4**

B. Router(config)#**line vty 0 4**

C. Router(config-if)#**line console 0**

D. Router(config)#**line vty all**

8. Which of the following commands sets the secret password to Cisco?

A. enable secret password Cisco

B. enable secret cisco

C. enable secret Cisco

D. enable password Cisco

9. If you wanted administrators to see a message when logging into the router, which command would you use?

A. message banner motd

B. banner message motd

C. banner motd

D. message motd

10. How many simultaneous Telnet sessions does a Cisco router support by default?

A. 1

B. 2

C. 3

D. 4

E. 5

F. F6

11. What command do you type to save the configuration stored in RAM to NVRAM?

A. Router(config)#**copy current to starting**

B. Router#**copy starting to running**

C. Router(config)#**copy running-config startup-config**

D. Router#**copy run startup**

12. You try to telnet into SFRouter from router Corp and receive this message:

Corp#**telnet SFRouter**
Trying SFRouter (10.0.0.1)...Open

Password required, but none set
[Connection to SFRouter closed by foreign host]
Corp#

Which of the following sequences will address this problem correctly?

A. Corp(config)#line console 0

B. Corp(config-line)#password cisco

C. SFRemote(config)#line console 0

D. SFRemote(config-line)#login

E. SFRemote(config-line)#password cisco

F. Corp(config)#line vty 0 4

G. Corp(config-line)#login

H. Corp(config-line)#password cisco

I. SFRemote(config)#line vty 0 4

J. SFRemote(config-line)#login

K. SFRemote(config-line)#password cisco

13. Which command will delete the contents of NVRAM on a router?

A. delete NVRAM

B. delete startup-config

C. erase NVRAM

D. erase start

14. What is the problem with an interface if you type show interface serial 0 and receive the following message?

Serial0 is administratively down, line protocol is down

A. The keepalives are different times.

B. The administrator has the interface shut down.

C. The administrator is pinging from the interface.

D. No cable is attached.

15. Which of the following commands displays the configurable parameters and statistics of all interfaces on a router?

   A. show running-config

   B. show startup-config

   C. show interfaces

   D. show versions

16. If you delete the contents of NVRAM and reboot the router, what mode will you be in?

   A. Privileged mode

   B. Global mode

   C. Setup mode

   D. NVRAM loaded mode

17. You type the following command into the router and receive the following output:

Router#**show serial 0/0**

                  ^

% Invalid input detected at '^' marker.

Why was this error message displayed?

   A. You need to be in privileged mode.

   B. You cannot have a space between serial and 0/0.

   C. The router does not have a serial0/0 interface.

   D. Part of the command is missing.

18. You type Router#sh ru and receive an % ambiguous command error. Why did you receive this message?

   A. The command requires additional options or parameters.

   B. There is more than one show command sthat starts with the letters *ru*.

   C. There is no show command that starts with *ru*.

   D. The command is being executed from the wrong router mode.

19. Which of the following commands will display the current IP addressing and the layer 1 and 2 status of an interface? (Choose three.)

   A. show version

   B. show protocols

   C. show interfaces

   D. show controllers

   E. show ip interface

   F. show running-config

20. What layer of the OSI model would you assume the problem is in if you type `show interface serial 1` and receive the following message?

`Serial1 is a down, line protocol is down`

    A. Physical layer

    B. Data Link layer

    C. Network layer

    D. None; it is a router problem.

Answers to Review Questions

1. C. The `exec-timeout` command is set in minutes and seconds.

2. C. The command `show ip protocols` will actually show you the broadcast address for each interface—too bad it isn't a possible answer. Your best answer is `show interfaces`, which will provide the IP address and mask for each interface. You can then determine the mask from the vast subnetting knowledge you gained in Chapter 3.

3. D. You probably picked option C, which isn't a bad answer. Remember, though, it doesn't replace the configuration, it appends it. To completely replace the running-config with the startup-config, you must reload the router.

4. C. The `show controllers serial` 0 command will show you whether either a DTE or DCE cable is connected to the interface. If it is a DCE connection, you need to add clocking with the `clock rate` command.

5. C. You can exit setup mode at any time by using the keystroke Ctrl+C.

6. B. The command `service password-encryption`, from global configuration mode, will encrypt the passwords.

7. B. From global configuration mode, use the `line vty 0 4` command to set all five default VTY lines.

8. C. The enable secret password is case sensitive, so the second option is wrong. To set the enable secret password, use the `enable secret` *password* command from global configuration mode.

9. C. The typical banner is a message of the day (MOTD) and is set by using the global configuration mode command `banner motd`.

10. E. Cisco router, if they do not have the Enterprise edition of the IOS, will default to 5 simultaneous Telnet sessions.

11. D. To copy the running-config to NVRAM so that it will be used if the router is restarted, use the `copy running-config startup-config` (copy run start, for short) command.

12. D. To allow a VTY (Telnet) session into your router, you must set the VTY password. Option C is wrong because it is setting the password on the wrong router. Notice that the answers have you set the login command before you set the password. Remember, Cisco may have you set the password before the login command.

13. D. The `erase startup-config` command erases the contents of NVRAM and will put you in setup mode if the router is restarted.

14. B. If an interface is shut down, the `show interface` command will show the interface as administratively shut down. (It is possible that no cable is attached, but you can't tell that from this message.)

15. C. With the show interfaces command, you can view the configurable parameters, get statistics for the interfaces on the router, verify if the interfaces are shut down, and see the IP address of each interface.

16. C. If you delete the startup-config and reload the router, the router will automatically enter setup mode. You can also type **setup** from privileged mode at any time.

17. D. You can view the interface statistics from user mode, but the command is `show interface serial 0/0`.

18. B. The % ambiguous command error means that there is more than one possible command that starts with *ru*. Use a question mark to find the correct command.

19. B, C, E. The commands `show protocols`, `show interfaces`, and `show ip interface` will show you the layer 1 and 2 status and the IP addresses of your router's interfaces.

20. A. If you see that a serial interface and the protocol are both down, then you have a Physical layer problem. If you see `serial1 is up, line protocol is down`, then you are not receiving (Data Link) keepalives from the remote end.

Answers to Written Lab 4

1. clock rate 64000
2. config t, line vty 0 4, no login
3. config t, int e0, no shut
4. erase startup-config
5. config t, line console 0, login, password todd
6. config t, enable secret cisco
7. show controllers *int*
8. show terminal
9. Router#reload
10. config t, hostname Chicago

Chapter

5

IP Routing

THE CCNA INTRO EXAM TOPICS COVERED IN THIS CHAPTER INCLUDE THE FOLLOWING:

✓ **Technology**

- Describe the concepts associated with routing, and the different methods and protocols used to achieve it
- Describe how an IP address is associated with a device interface, and the association between physical and employ IP addressing techniques
- Employ IP addressing techniques
- Compare and contrast collision and broadcast domains, and describe the process of network segmentation
- Describe how the protocols associated with TCP/IP allow host communication to occur
- Describe the principles and practice of packet switching utilizing the Internet Protocol (IP)

In this chapter, I'm going to discuss the IP routing process. This is an important subject to understand since it pertains to all routers and configurations that use IP. IP routing is the process of moving packets from one network to another network using routers. And as before, by routers I mean Cisco routers, of course!

But before you read this chapter, you must understand the difference between a routing protocol and a routed protocol. A *routing protocol* is used by routers to dynamically find all the networks in the internetwork and to ensure that all routers have the same routing table. Basically, a routing protocol determines the path of a packet through an internetwork. Examples of routing protocols are RIP, IGRP, EIGRP, and OSPF (all discussed in Chapter 6).

Once all routers know about all networks, a *routed protocol* can be used to send user data (packets) through the established enterprise. Routed protocols are assigned to an interface and determine the method of packet delivery. Examples of routed protocols are IP and IPX (of course, we use only IP now).

I'm pretty sure that I don't have to tell you that this is definitely important stuff to know. You most likely understand that from what I've said so far. IP routing is basically what Cisco routers do, and they do it very well. Again, this chapter is dealing with truly fundamental material—these are things you must know if you want to understand the objectives covered in this book!

In this chapter, I'm going to show you how to configure and verify IP routing with Cisco routers. I'll be covering the following:

- Routing basics
- The IP routing process
- Static routing
- Default routing

I'll be introducing you to dynamic routing protocols in Chapter 6, but first you've really got to nail down the basics of how packets actually move through an internetwork, so let's get started!

Routing Basics

Once you create an internetwork by connecting your WANs and LANs to a router, you'll need to configure logical network addresses, such as IP addresses, to all hosts on the internetwork so that they can communicate across that internetwork.

The term *routing* is used for taking a packet from one device and sending it through the network to another device on a different network. Routers don't really care about hosts—they only care about networks and the best path to each network. The logical network address of the destination host is used to get packets to a network through a routed network, and then the hardware address of the host is used to deliver the packet from a router to the correct destination host.

If your network has no routers, then it should be apparent that you are not routing. Routers route traffic to all the networks in your internetwork. To be able to route packets, a router must know, at a minimum, the following:

- Destination address
- Neighbor routers from which it can learn about remote networks
- Possible routes to all remote networks
- The best route to each remote network
- How to maintain and verify routing information

The router learns about remote networks from neighbor routers or from an administrator. The router then builds a routing table (a routing table is a map of the internetwork) that describes how to find the remote networks. If a network is directly connected, then the router already knows how to get to it.

If a network isn't directly connected to the router, the router must learn how to get to the remote network in one of two ways: by using static routing, meaning that someone must hand-type all network locations into the routing table, or through something called dynamic routing.

In *dynamic routing*, a protocol on one router communicates with the same protocol running on neighbor routers. The routers then update each other about all the networks they know about and place this information into the routing table. If a change occurs in the network, the dynamic routing protocols automatically inform all routers about the event. If *static routing* is used, the administrator is responsible for updating all changes by hand into all routers. Typically, in a large network, a combination of both dynamic and static routing is used.

Before we jump into the IP routing process, let's take a look at a simple example that demonstrates how a router uses the routing table to route packets out of an interface. We'll be going into a more detailed study of the process in the next section.

Figure 5.1 shows a simple two-router network. Lab_A has one serial interface and three LAN interfaces.

Looking at Figure 5.1, can you see which interface Lab_A will use to forward an IP datagram to a host with an IP address of 10.10.10.10?

By using the command show ip route, we can see the routing table (map of the internetwork) that Lab_A uses to make forwarding decisions:

```
Lab_A#sh ip route
[output cut]
Gateway of last resort is not set
C       10.10.10.0/24 is directly connected, FastEthernet0/0
C       10.10.20.0/24 is directly connected, FastEthernet0/1
C       10.10.30.0/24 is directly connected, FastEthernet0/2
C       10.10.40.0/24 is directly connected, Serial 0/0
```

FIGURE 5.1 A simple routing example

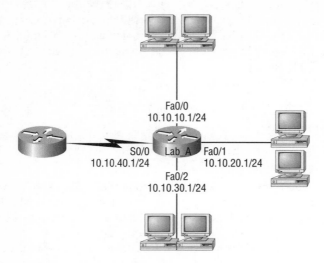

The C in the routing table output means that the networks listed are "directly connected," and until we add a routing protocol—something like RIP, IGRP, etc.—to the routers in our internetwork (or use static routes), we'll only have directly connected networks in our routing table.

So let's get back to the original question: By looking at the figure and the output of the routing table, can you tell what IP will do with a received packet that has a destination IP address of 10.10.10.10? The router will packet-switch the packet to interface FastEthernet 0/0, and this interface will frame the packet and then send it out on the network segment.

Now you're ready to get into this process in more detail.

The IP Routing Process

The IP routing process is fairly simple and doesn't change, regardless of the size network you have. For an example, we'll use Figure 5.2 to describe step-by-step what happens when Host_A wants to communicate with Host_B on a different network.

FIGURE 5.2 IP routing example using two hosts and one router

In this example, a user on Host_A pings Host_B's IP address. Routing doesn't get simpler than this, but it still involves a lot of steps. Let's work through them:

1. Internet Control Message Protocol (ICMP) creates an echo request payload (which is just the alphabet in the data field).

2. ICMP hands that payload to Internet Protocol (IP), which then creates a packet. At a minimum, this packet contains an IP source address, an IP destination address, and a Protocol field with 01h (remember that Cisco likes to use 0x in front of hex characters, so this could look like 0x01). All of that tells the receiving host whom it should hand the payload to when the destination is reached—in this example, ICMP.

3. Once the packet is created, IP determines whether the destination IP address is on the local network or a remote one.

4. Since IP determines that this is a remote request, the packet needs to be sent to the default gateway so the packet can be routed to the remote network. The Registry in Windows is parsed to find the configured default gateway.

5. The default gateway of host 172.16.10.2 (Host_A) is configured to 172.16.10.1. For this packet to be sent to the default gateway, the hardware address of the router's interface Ethernet 0 (configured with the IP address of 172.16.10.1) must be known. Why? So the packet can be handed down to the Data Link layer, framed, and sent to the router's interface that's connected to the 172.16.10.0 network. Because hosts only communicate via hardware addresses on the local LAN, it's important to recognize that for Host_A to communicate to Host_B, it has to send packets to the MAC address of the default gateway on the local network.

> **NOTE** MAC addresses are always local on the LAN and never go through and past a router!

6. Next, the ARP cache of the host is checked to see if the IP address of the default gateway has already been resolved to a hardware address:

    -   If it has, the packet is then free to be handed to the Data Link layer for framing. (The hardware destination address is also handed down with that packet.) To view the ARP cache on your host, use the following command:

```
C:\>arp -a
Interface: 172.16.10.2 --- 0x3
  Internet Address      Physical Address      Type
  172.16.10.1           00-15-05-06-31-b0     dynamic
```

    -   If the hardware address isn't already in the ARP cache of the host, an ARP broadcast is sent out onto the local network to search for the hardware address of 172.16.10.1. The router responds to the request and provides the hardware address of Ethernet 0, and the host caches this address.

7. Once the packet and destination hardware address are handed to the Data Link layer, the LAN driver is used to provide media access via the type of LAN being used (in this example, Ethernet). A frame is then generated, encapsulating the packet with control information. Within that frame are the hardware destination and source addresses plus, in this case, an Ether-Type field that describes the Network layer protocol that handed the packet to the Data Link layer—in this instance, IP. At the end of the frame is something called a Frame Check Sequence (FCS) field that houses the result of the cyclic redundancy check (CRC). The frame would look something like what I've detailed in Figure 5.3. It contains Host_A's hardware (MAC) address and the destination hardware address of the default gateway. It does not include the remote host's MAC address—remember that!

FIGURE 5.3 Frame used from Host_A to the Lab_A router when Host_B is pinged

Destination MAC (routers E0 MAC address)	Source MAC (Host_A MAC address)	Ether-Type field	Packet	FCS (CRC)

8. Once the frame is completed, it's handed down to the Physical layer to be put on the physical medium (in this example, twisted-pair wire) one bit at a time.

9. Every device in the collision domain receives these bits and builds the frame. They each run a CRC and check the answer in the FCS field. If the answers don't match, the frame is discarded.

   - If the CRC matches, then the hardware destination address is checked to see if it matches too (which, in this example, is the router's interface Ethernet 0).

   - If it's a match, then the Ether-Type field is checked to find the protocol used at the Network layer.

10. The packet is pulled from the frame, and what is left of the frame is discarded. The packet is handed to the protocol listed in the Ether-Type field—it's given to IP.

11. IP receives the packet and checks the IP destination address. Since the packet's destination address doesn't match any of the addresses configured on the receiving router itself, the router will look up the destination IP network address in its routing table.

12. The routing table must have an entry for the network 172.16.20.0 or the packet will be discarded immediately and an ICMP message will be sent back to the originating device with a "destination network unreachable" message.

13. If the router does find an entry for the destination network in its table, the packet is switched to the exit interface—in this example, interface Ethernet 1. The output below displays the Lab_A router's routing table. The C means "directly connected." No routing protocols are needed in this network since all networks (all 2 of them) are directly connected.

```
Lab_A>sh ip route
Codes:C - connected,S - static,I - IGRP,R - RIP,M - mobile,B – BGP
D - EIGRP,EX - EIGRP external,O - OSPF,IA - OSPF inter area
N1 - OSPF NSSA external type 1, N2 - OSPF NSSA external type 2
```

```
E1 - OSPF external type 1, E2 - OSPF external type 2, E - EGP
i - IS-IS, L1 - IS-IS level-1, L2 - IS-IS level-2, ia - IS-IS intearea * -
candidate default, U - per-user static route, o - ODR P - periodic downloaded
static route

Gateway of last resort is not set

     172.16.0.0/24 is subnetted, 2 subnets
C        172.16.10.0 is directly connected, Ethernet0
C        172.16.20.0 is directly connected, Ethernet1
```

14. The router packet-switches the packet to the Ethernet 1 buffer.

15. The Ethernet 1 buffer needs to know the hardware address of the destination host and first checks the ARP cache.

> If the hardware address of Host_B has already been resolved and is in the router's ARP cache, then the packet and the hardware address are handed down to the Data Link layer to be framed. Let's take a look at the ARP cache on the Lab_A router by using the show ip arp command:

> Lab_A#**sh ip arp**
> ```
> Protocol  Address        Age(min)  Hardware Addr   Type   Interface
> Internet  172.16.20.1    -         00d0.58ad.05f4  ARPA   Ethernet0
> Internet  172.16.20.2    3         0030.9492.a5dd  ARPA   Ethernet0
> Internet  172.16.10.1    -         00d0.58ad.06aa  ARPA   Ethernet0
> ```

> Internet 172.16.10.2 12 0030.9492.a4ac ARPA Ethernet0The dash (-) means that this is the physical interface on the router. From the output above, we can see that the router knows the 172.16.10.2 (Host_A and 172.16.20.2 (Host_B) hardware addresses. Cisco routers will keep an entry in the ARP table for 4 hours.

> If the hardware address has not already been resolved, the router sends an ARP request out E1 looking for the hardware address of 172.16.20.2.

> Host_B responds with its hardware address, and the packet and destination hardware address are both sent to the Data Link layer for framing.

16. The Data Link layer creates a frame with the destination and source hardware address, Ether-Type field, and FCS field at the end. The frame is handed to the Physical layer to be sent out on the physical medium one bit at a time.

17. Host_B receives the frame and immediately runs a CRC. If the result matches what's in the FCS field, the hardware destination address is then checked. If the host finds a match, the Ether-Type field is then checked to determine the protocol that the packet should be handed to at the Network layer—IP in this example.

18. At the Network layer, IP receives the packet and checks the IP destination address. Since there's finally a match made, the Protocol field is checked to find out whom the payload should be given to.

19. The payload is handed to ICMP, which understands that this is an echo request. ICMP responds to this by immediately discarding the packet and generating a new payload as an echo reply.

20. A packet is then created including the source and destination address, Protocol field, and payload. The destination device is now Host_A.

21. IP then checks to see whether the destination IP address is a device on the local LAN or on a remote network. Since the destination device is on a remote network, the packet needs to be sent to the default gateway.

22. The default gateway IP address is found in the Registry of the Windows device, and the ARP cache is checked to see if the hardware address has already been resolved from an IP address.

23. Once the hardware address of the default gateway is found, the packet and destination hardware addresses are handed down to the Data Link layer for framing.

24. The Data Link layer frames the packet of information and includes the following in the header:

    - The destination and source hardware address
    - The Ether-Type field with 0x0800 (IP) in it
    - The FCS field with the CRC result in tow

25. The frame is now handed down to the Physical layer to be sent out over the network medium one bit at a time.

26. The router's Ethernet 1 interface receives the bits and builds a frame. The CRC is run, and the FCS field is checked to make sure the answers match.

27. Once the CRC is found to be okay, the hardware destination address is checked. Since the router's interface is a match, the packet is pulled from the frame and the Ether-Type field is checked to see what protocol at the Network layer the packet should be delivered to.

28. The protocol is determined to be IP, so it gets the packet. IP runs a CRC check on the IP header first and then checks the destination IP address.

> **NOTE**   IP does not run a complete CRC as the Data Link layer does—it only checks the header for errors.

Since the IP destination address doesn't match any of the router's interfaces, the routing table is checked to see whether it has a route to 172.16.10.0. If it doesn't have a route over to the destination network, the packet will be discarded immediately. (This is the source point of confusion for a lot of administrators—when a ping fails, most people think the packet never reached the destination host. But as we see here, that's not *always* the case. All it takes is for just one of the remote routers to be lacking a route back to the originating host's network and—POOF!—the packet is dropped on the *return trip*, not on its way to the host.)

Okay, just a quick note to mention that when (if) the packet is lost on the way back to the originating host, you will typically see a "request timed out" message because it is an unknown error. If the error occurs because of a known issue, such as if a route is not in the routing table on the way to the destination device, you will see a "destination unreachable" message. This should help you determine if the problem occurred on the way to the destination or on the way back.

29. But the router does know how to get to network 172.16.10.0—the exit interface is Ethernet 0—so the packet is switched to interface Ethernet 0.

30. The router checks the ARP cache to determine whether the hardware address for 172.16.10.2 has already been resolved.

31. Since the hardware address to 172.16.10.2 is already cached from the originating trip to Host_B, the hardware address and packet are handed to the Data Link layer.

32. The Data Link layer builds a frame with the destination hardware address and source hardware address and then puts IP in the Ether-Type field. A CRC is run on the frame and the result is placed in the FCS field.

33. The frame is then handed to the Physical layer to be sent out onto the local network one bit at a time.

34. The destination host receives the frame, runs a CRC, checks the destination hardware address, and looks in the Ether-Type field to find out whom to hand the packet to.

35. IP is the designated receiver, and after the packet is handed to IP at the Network layer, it checks the protocol field for further direction. IP finds instructions to give the payload to ICMP, and ICMP determines the packet to be an ICMP echo reply.

36. ICMP acknowledges that it has received the reply by sending an exclamation point (!) to the user interface. ICMP then attempts to send four more echo requests to the destination host.

You've just experienced 36 easy steps to understanding IP routing. The key point to understand here is that if you had a much larger network, the process would be the *same*. In a really big internetwork, the packet just goes through more hops before it finds the destination host.

Okay—it's super important to remember that when Host_A sends a packet to Host_B, the destination hardware address used is the default gateway's Ethernet interface. Why? Because frames can't be placed on remote networks—only local networks. So packets destined for remote networks must go through the default gateway.

Let's take a look at Host_A's ARP cache now:

```
C:\ >arp -a
Interface: 172.16.10.2 --- 0x3
  Internet Address        Physical Address        Type
  172.16.10.1             00-15-05-06-31-b0       dynamic
  172.16.20.1             00-15-05-06-31-b0       dynamic
```

Did you notice that the hardware (MAC) address that Host_A uses to get to Host_B is the Lab_A E0 interface? Hardware addresses are *always* local, and they never pass a router's interface. Understanding this process is as important as air to you, so carve this into your memory!

Testing Your IP Routing Understanding

I really want to make sure you understand IP routing because it's super-important. So I'm going to use this section to test your understanding of the IP routing process by having you look at a couple of figures and answer some very basic IP routing questions.

Figure 5.4 shows a LAN connected to RouterA, which is, in turn, connected via a WAN link to RouterB. RouterB has a LAN connected with an HTTP server attached.

The critical information you need to glean from this figure is exactly how IP routing will occur in this example. Okay—we'll cheat a bit. I'll give you the answer, but then you should go back over the figure and see if you can answer example 2 without looking at my answers.

1. The destination address of a frame, from HostA, will be the MAC address of the F0/0 interface of the RouterA router.

2. The destination address of a packet will be the IP address of the network interface card (NIC) of the HTTP server.

3. The destination port number in the segment header will have a value of 80.

That example was a pretty simple one, and it was also very to the point. One thing to remember is that if multiple hosts are commutating to the server using HTTP, they must all use a different source port number. That is how the server keeps the data separated at the Transport layer.

Let's mix it up a little and add another internetworking device into the network and then see if you can find the answers. Figure 5.5 shows a network with only one router, but two switches.

FIGURE 5.4 IP routing example 1

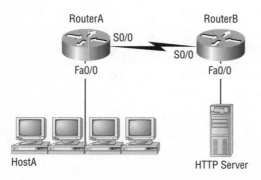

FIGURE 5.5   IP routing example 2

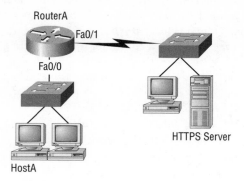

What you want to understand about the IP routing process here is what happens when HostA sends data to the HTTPS server:

1. The destination address of a frame, from HostA, will be the MAC address of the F0/0 interface of the RouterA router.

2. The destination address of a packet will be the IP address of the network interface card (NIC) of the HTTPS server.

3. The destination port number in the segment header will have a value of 443.

Notice that the switches weren't used as either a default gateway or another destination. That's because switches have nothing to do with routing. I wonder how many of you chose the switch as the default gateway (destination) MAC address for HostA? If you did, don't feel bad—just take another look with that fact in mind. It's very important to remember that the destination MAC address will always be the router's interface—if your packets are destined for outside the LAN, as they were in these last two examples.

Before we move into some of the more advanced aspects of IP routing, let's discuss ICMP in more detail, as well as how ICMP is used in an internetwork. Take a look at the network shown in Figure 5.6. Ask yourself what will happen if the LAN interface of Lab_C goes down?

FIGURE 5.6   ICMP error example

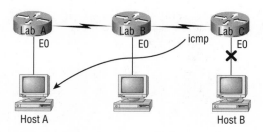

Lab_C will use ICMP to inform HostA that HostB can't be reached, and it will do this by sending an ICMP Destination Unreachable message. Lots of people think that Router Lab_A would be sending this message, but they would be wrong because the router that sends the message is the one where the interface that's down is located.

Let's look at another problem: Look at the output of a corporate router's routing table:

```
Corp#sh ip route
[output cut]
R     192.168.215.0 [120/2] via 192.168.20.2, 00:00:23, Serial0/0
R     192.168.115.0 [120/1] via 192.168.20.2, 00:00:23, Serial0/0
R     192.168.30.0 [120/1] via 192.168.20.2, 00:00:23, Serial0/0
C     192.168.20.0 is directly connected, Serial0/0
C     192.168.214.0 is directly connected, FastEthernet0/0
```

Okay—what do we see here? If I were to tell you that the corporate router received an IP packet with a source IP address of 192.168.214.20 and a destination address of 192.168.22.3, what do you think the Corp router will do with this packet?

If you said, "The packet came in on the FastEthernet 0/0 interface, but since the routing table doesn't show a route to network 192.168.22.0 (or a default route), the router will discard the packet and send an ICMP Destination Unreachable message back out interface FastEthernet 0/0," you're a genius! The reason it does this is because that's the source LAN where the packet originated from.

Now, let's check out another figure and talk about the frames and packets in detail. Really, we're not exactly chatting about anything new; I'm just making sure that you totally, completely, fully understand basic IP routing. That's because this book, and the exam objectives it's geared toward, are all about IP routing, which means you need to be all over this stuff! We'll use Figure 5.7 for the next few questions.

FIGURE 5.7   Basic IP routing using MAC and IP addresses

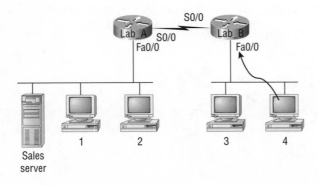

Referring to the Figure 5.7, here's a list of the all the questions you need the answers to emblazoned in your brain:

1. In order to begin communicating with the Sales server, Host 4 sends out an ARP request. How will the devices exhibited in the topology respond to this request?

2. Host 4 has received an ARP reply. Host 4 will now build a packet, then place this packet in the frame. What information will be placed in the header of the packet that leaves host 4 if host 4 is going to communicate to the Sales server?

3. At last, Router Lab_A has received the packet and will send it out Fa0/0 onto the LAN toward the server. What will the frame have in the header as the source and destination addresses?

4. Host 4 is displaying two WWW documents from the Sales server in two browser windows at the same time. How did the data find its way to the correct browser windows?

I probably should've written these in a teensy font and put them upside down and somewhere else that would make it really hard for you to cheat and peek, but since it's actually you that's going to lose out if you do that, here are your answers:

1. In order to begin communicating with the server, Host 4 sends out an ARP request. How will the devices exhibited in the topology respond to this request? Since MAC addresses must stay on the local network, the Lab_B router will respond with the MAC address of the Fa0/0 interface and Host 4 will send all frames to the MAC address of the Lab_B Fa0/0 interface when sending packets to the Sales server.

2. Host 4 has received an ARP reply. Host 4 will now build a packet, then place this packet in the frame. What information will be placed in the header of the packet that leaves host 4 if host 4 is going to communicate to the Sales server? Since we're now talking about packets, not frames, the source address will be the IP address of Host 4 and the destination address will be the IP address of the Sales server.

3. Finally, Router Lab_A has received the packet and will send it out Fa0/0 onto the LAN toward the server. What will the frame have in the header as the source and destination addresses? The source MAC address will be the Lab_A router's Fa0/0 interface, and the destination MAC address will the Sales server's MAC address (all MAC addresses must be local on the LAN).

4. Host 4 is displaying two WWW documents from the Sales server in two different browser windows at the same time. How did the data find its way to the correct browser windows? TCP port numbers are used to direct the data to the correct application window.

Great! But we're not quite done yet. I've got a few more question for you before you actually get to configure routing in a real network. Ready? Okay—Figure 5.8 shows a basic network, and Host 4 needs to get email. Which address will be placed in the destination address field of the frame when it leaves Host 4?

The answer is, Host 4 will use the destination MAC address of the Fa0/0 interface of the Lab_B router—which I'm so sure you knew, right? Look at Figure 5.8 again: Host 4 needs to communicate to Host 1. What will be the OSI layer 3 source address placed in the packet header when it reaches Host 1?

FIGURE 5.8   Testing basic routing knowledge

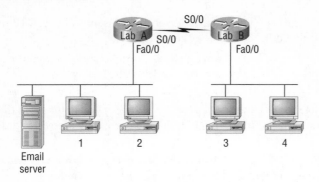

And hopefully you know this: At layer three, the source IP address will be Host 4 and the destination address in the packet will be the IP address of Host 1. Of course, the destination MAC address from Host 4 will always be the Fa0/0 address of the Lab_B router, right? And since we have more than one router, we'll need a routing protocol that communicates between both of them so that traffic can be forwarded in the right direction to reach the network in which Host 1 is attached.

Okay—one more question and you're on your way to being an IP routing genius! Again, using Figure 5.8., Host 4 is transferring a file to the email server connected to the Lab_A router. What would be the Layer 2 destination address leaving Host 4? Yes, I've asked this question more than once! But not this one: What will be the source MAC address when the frame is received at the email server?

Hopefully, you answered that the Layer 2 destination address leaving Host 4 will be the MAC address of the Fa0/0 interface of the Lab_B router and that the source layer 2 address that the email server will receive will be the Fa0/0 interface of the Lab_A router.

If you did, you're all set to get into the skinny on how IP routing is handled in a larger network.

Configuring IP Routing

Let's have some fun and configure a real network! Figure 5.9 shows three routers: Lab_A, Lab_B, and Lab_C. Remember, by default, these routers only know about networks that are directly connected to them.

FIGURE 5.9   Configuring IP routing

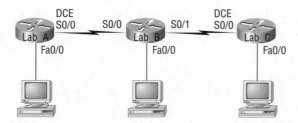

Figure 5.9 shows the three 2600 routers connected via a WAN. Each router also has an Ethernet network connected. The idea is that each router must know about all five networks.

The first step is to configure each router correctly. Table 5.1 shows the IP address scheme I'm going to use to configure the network. After we go over how the network is configured, I'll cover how to configure IP routing. Each network in the following table has a default Class C 24-bit subnet mask (255.255.255.0).

TABLE 5.1   Network Addressing for the IP Network

Router	Network Address	Interface	Address
Lab_A	192.168.10.0	Fa0/0	192.168.10.1
Lab_A	192.168.20.0	s0/0 (DCE)	192.168.20.1
Lab_B	192.168.20.0	s0/0	192.168.20.2
Lab_B	192.168.40.0	s0/1	192.168.40.1
Lab_B	192.168.30.0	Fa0/0	192.168.30.1
Lab_C	192.168.40.0	s0/0 (DCE)	192.168.40.2
Lab_C	192.168.50.0	Fa0/0	192.168.50.1

The router configuration is really a pretty straightforward process, since you just need to add IP addresses to your interfaces and then perform a no shutdown on those interfaces. It will get a tad more complex later on, but first let's configure the IP addresses in the network.

Lab_A Configuration

To configure the Lab_A router, you just need to add an IP address to interface FastEthernet 0/0 as well as the serial 0/0. Configuring the hostnames of each router will make identification easier. And why not set the interface descriptions, banner, and router passwords too? You really should get in the habit of configuring these commands on every router.

Here is how I did all that:

```
Router>en
Router#config t
Router(config)#hostname Lab_A
Lab_A(config)#enable secret todd
Lab_A(config)#interface fa0/0
Lab_A(config-if)#ip address 192.168.10.1 255.255.255.0
Lab_A(config-if)#description Lab_A LAN Connection
```

```
Lab_A(config-if)#no shut
Lab_A(config-if)#interface serial 0/0
Lab_A(config-if)#ip address 192.168.20.1 255.255.255.0
Lab_A(config-if)#description WAN Connection to Lab_B
Lab_A(config-if)#no shut
Lab_A(config-if)#exit
Lab_A(config)#line console 0
Lab_A(config-line)#password todd
Lab_A(config-line)#login
Lab_A(config-line)#line aux 0
Lab_A(config-line)#password todd
Lab_A(config-line)#login
Lab_A(config-line)#line vty 0 4
Lab_A(config-line)#password todd
Lab_A(config-line)#login
Lab_A(config-line)#exit
Lab_A(config)#banner motd #
This is the Lab_A router
#
Lab_A(config)#^z
Lab_A#copy running-config startup-config
Destination filename [startup-config]? [Enter]
Lab_A#
```

If you have a hard time understanding this configuration process, refer back to Chapter 4, "Introduction to the Cisco IOS."

To view the IP routing tables created on a Cisco router, use the command show ip route. The command output is shown as follows:

```
Lab_A#sh ip route
Codes: C - connected, S - static, I - IGRP, R - RIP,
  M - mobile, B – BGP D - EIGRP, EX - EIGRP external, O -
  OSPF, IA - OSPF inter area N1 - OSPF NSS external type
  1, N2 - OSPF NSSA external type 2 E1 - OSPF external
  type 1, E2 - OSPF external type 2, E – EGP i - IS-IS,
  L1 - IS-IS level-1, L2 - IS-IS level-2, * - candidate
  default, U - per-user static route, o - ODR, P -
  periodic downloaded static route, T - traffic
  engineered route
```

```
Gateway of last resort is not set
C       192.168.10.0/24 is directly connected, FastEthernet0/0
C       192.168.20.0/24 is directly connected, Serial 0/0
Lab_A#
```

Notice that only the configured, directly connected networks are shown in the routing table. This means that the router only knows how to get to networks 192.168.10.0 and 192.168.20.0.

Did you notice the C on the left side of the output of the routing table? When you see it there, it means that the network is directly connected. The codes for each type of connection are listed at the top of the show ip route command with their abbreviations.

The serial interface 0/0 is a DCE connection, which means that we'll have to add the clock rate command to the interface. But not yet—remember that you don't need to use the clock rate command in production. Even though this is true, it's still imperative that you know how/when you can use it and that you understand it really well when studying for your CCNA INTRO exam!

In the interest of brevity, the codes will be cut in the rest of this chapter.

Lab_B Configuration

It's now time to configure the next router. To configure Lab_B, we have three interfaces to deal with: FastEthernet 0/0, serial 0/0, and serial 0/1.

Let's make sure we don't forget to add our passwords, interface descriptions, and banner to the router configuration!

Here is the configuration I used:

```
Router>en
Router#config t
Router(config)#hostname Lab_B
Lab_B(config)#enable secret todd
Lab_B(config)#interface fa0/0
Lab_B(config-if)#ip address 192.168.30.1 255.255.255.0
Lab_B(config-if)#description Lab_B LAN Connection
Lab_B(config-if)#no shut
Lab_B(config-if)#interface serial 0/0
Lab_B(config-if)#ip address 192.168.20.2 255.255.255.0
Lab_B(config-if)#description WAN Connection to Lab_A
Lab_B(config-if)#no shut
Lab_B(config-if)#interface serial 0/1
Lab_B(config-if)#ip address 192.168.40.1 255.255.255.0
Lab_B(config-if)#description WAN Connection to Lab_C
```

```
Lab_B(config-if)#no shut
Lab_B(config-if)#exit
Lab_B(config)#line console 0
Lab_B(config-line)#password todd
Lab_B(config-line)#login
Lab_B(config-line)#line aux 0
Lab_B(config-line)#password todd
Lab_B(config-line)#login
Lab_B(config-line)#line vty 0 4
Lab_B(config-line)#password todd
Lab_B(config-line)#login
Lab_B(config-line)#exit
Lab_B(config)#banner motd #
This is the Lab_B router
#
Lab_B(config)#^z
Lab_B#copy running-config startup-config
Destination filename [startup-config]? [Enter]
Lab_B#
```

These commands configured serial 0/0 into network 192.168.20.0, serial 0/1 into network 192.168.40.0, and FastEthernet 0/0 into network 192.168.30.0. The show ip route command displays the following:

```
Lab_B#sh ip route
[output cut]
Gateway of last resort is not set
C       192.168.20.0/24 is directly connected, Serial0/0
C       192.168.40.0/24 is directly connected, Serial0/1
C       192.168.30.0 is directly connected FastEthernet 0/0
Lab_B#
```

Notice that router Lab_B knows how to get to networks 192.168.20.0, 192.168.30.0, and 172.16.40.0. Router Lab_A and Router Lab_B can now communicate because they're connected on the same WAN, but Lab_B can't get to the LAN connected to Lab_A yet.

Lab_C Configuration

The configuration of Lab_C is similar to the other two routers (make sure we remember to add passwords, interface descriptions, and a banner to the router configuration):

```
Router>en
Router#config t
Router(config)#hostname Lab_C
```

```
Lab_C(config)#enable secret todd
Lab_C(config)#interface fa0/0
Lab_C(config-if)#ip address 192.168.50.1 255.255.255.0
Lab_C(config-if)#description Lab_C LAN Connection
Lab_C(config-if)#no shut
Lab_C(config-if)#interface serial 0/0
Lab_C(config-if)#ip address 192.168.40.2 255.255.255.0
Lab_C(config-if)#description WAN Connection to Lab_B
Lab_C(config-if)#no shut
Lab_C(config-if)#exit
Lab_C(config)#line console 0
Lab_C(config-line)#password todd
Lab_C(config-line)#login
Lab_C(config-line)#line aux 0
Lab_C(config-line)#password todd
Lab_C(config-line)#login
Lab_C(config-line)#line vty 0 4
Lab_C(config-line)#password todd
Lab_C(config-line)#login
Lab_C(config-line)#exit
Lab_C(config)#banner motd #
This is the Lab_C router
#
Lab_C(config)#^z
Lab_C#copy running-config startup-config
Destination filename [startup-config]? [Enter]
Lab_C#
```

The output of the following show ip route command displays the directly connected networks of 192.168.50.0 and 192.168.40.0, as seen here:

```
Lab_C#sh ip route
[output cut]
Gateway of last resort is not set
C       192.168.50.0/24 is directly connected, FastEthernet0/0
C       192.168.40.0/24 is directly connected, Serial0/0
Lab_C#
```

Routers Lab_A and Lab_B can directly communicate because they're on the same WAN network, and Lab_B and Lab_C can directly communicate too because they're connected with a WAN link. But Router Lab_A can't communicate with the Lab_C router because it doesn't know about networks 172.16.40.0 and 192.168.50.0—yet.

The serial interface 0/0 of Lab_A and Lab_C is a DCE connection. What that means to you is that you need to add the `clock rate` command to the interface. But before adding routing to our network, let's take a closer look at the DCE/DTE interface configuration.

By using the `show controllers s0/0` and `show controllers s0/1` command on the Lab_B router, we can see that no clocking is present and the interfaces are both the DTE type, which means they're expecting clocking:

```
Lab_B#sh controllers s 0/0
Interface Serial0/0
Hardware is PowerQUICC MPC860
DTE V.35 clocks stopped.
[output cut]

Lab_B#sh controllers s 0/1
Interface Serial0/0
Hardware is PowerQUICC MPC860
DTE V.35 clocks stopped.
[output cut]
```

Here, you can see that on the Lab_A and Lab_C routers, the interfaces s0/0 are a DCE connections and so they need to provide clocking:

```
Lab_A#sh controllers s 0/0
Interface Serial0/0
Hardware is PowerQUICC MPC860
DCE V.35, no clock


Lab_C#sh controllers s 0/0
Interface Serial0/0
Hardware is PowerQUICC MPC860
DCE V.35, no clock
```

When a DTE/DCE cable is used (in nonproduction networks) and clocking isn't configured, the line protocol will be down. When the a Physical layer connection is good, the output of the `show interface` and `show ip interface` will be `Serial 0/0 is up, line protocol is down`. This means no clocking and/or no keepalives at the Data Link layer are being received. You can see that in the following output:

```
Lab_A#sh ip int s0/0
Serial0 is up, line protocol is down
Internet protocol processing disabled
```

To fix this little issue, you need to add the `clock rate` command to the DCE interfaces:

```
Lab_A#config t
Lab_A(config)#int s0/0
Lab_A(config-if)#clock rate 1000000
--------------
Lab_C#config t
Lab_C(config)#int s0/0
Lab_C(config-if)#clock rate 1000000
```

Okay—let's do some routing!

Configuring IP Routing in Our Network

Okay, our network is good to go—right? After all, it's been correctly configured with IP addressing, administrative functions, and now clocking! But how does a router send packets to remote networks when it can send them only by looking at the routing table to find out how to get to the remote networks? Our configured routers only have information about directly connected networks in each routing table. And what happens when a router receives a packet for a network that isn't listed in the routing table? It doesn't send a broadcast looking for the remote network—the router just discards it. Period.

So we're not exactly ready to rock after all. But no worries—there are several ways to configure the routing tables to include all the networks in our little internetwork so that packets will be forwarded. And what's best for one network isn't necessarily what's best for another. Understanding the different types of routing will really help you come up with the best solution for your specific environment and business requirements.

you'll learn about the following types of routing in this section:

- Static routing
- Default routing
- Dynamic routing

I'm going to start off by describing and implementing static routing on our network because if you can implement static routing *and* make it work, it means you have a solid understanding of the internetwork. So let's get started.

Static Routing

Static routing occurs when you manually add routes in each router's routing table. There are pros and cons to static routing, but that's true for all routing processes.

Static routing has the following benefits:

- There is no overhead on the router CPU, which means you could possibly buy a cheaper router than you would use if you were using dynamic routing.

- There is no bandwidth usage between routers, which means you could possibly save money on WAN links.

- It adds security, because the administrator can choose to allow routing access to certain networks only.

Static routing has the following disadvantages:

- The administrator must really understand the internetwork and how each router is connected in order to configure routes correctly.

- If a network is added to the internetwork, the administrator has to add a route to it on all routers—by hand.

- It's not feasible in large networks because maintaining it would be a full-time job in itself.

Okay—that said, here's the command syntax you use to add a static route to a routing table:

```
ip route [destination_network] [mask] [next-hop_address or
  exitinterface] [administrative_distance] [permanent]
```

This list describes each command in the string:

ip route   The command used to create the static route.

destination_network   The network you're placing in the routing table.

mask   The subnet mask being used on the network.

next-hop_address   The address of the next-hop router that will receive the packet and forward it to the remote network. This is a router interface that's on a directly connected network. You must be able to ping the router interface before you add the route. If you type in the wrong next-hop address or the interface to that router is down, the static route will show up in the router's configuration but not in the routing table.

exitinterface   Used in place of the next-hop address if you want, and shows up as a directly connected route.

administrative_distance   By default, static routes have an administrative distance of 1 (or even 0 if you use an exit interface instead of a next-hop address). You can change the default value by adding an administrative weight at the end of the command. I'll talk a lot more about this subject later in the chapter when we get to the section on dynamic routing.

permanent   If the interface is shut down or the router can't communicate to the next-hop router, the route will automatically be discarded from the routing table. Choosing the permanent option keeps the entry in the routing table no matter what happens.

Before we dive into configuring static routes, let's take a look at a sample static route and see what we can find out about it.

```
Router(config)#ip route 172.16.3.0 255.255.255.0 192.168.2.4
```

- The `ip route` command tells us simply that it is a static route.
- 172.16.3.0 is the remote network we want to send packets to.
- 255.255.255.0 is the mask of the remote network.
- 192.168.2.4 is the next hop, or router, we will send packets to.

However, suppose the static route looked like this:

```
Router(config)#ip route 172.16.3.0 255.255.255.0 192.168.2.4 150
```

The 150 at the end changes the default administrative distance (AD) of 1 to 150. No worries—I'll talk much more about AD when we get into dynamic routing. For now, just remember that the AD is the trustworthiness of a route, where 0 is best and 255 is worst.

To help you understand how static routes work, I'll demonstrate the configuration on the internetwork shown previously in Figure 5.9.

Lab_A

Each routing table automatically includes directly connected networks. To be able to route to all networks in the internetwork, the routing table must include information that describes where these other networks are located and how to get there.

The Lab_A router is connected to networks 192.168.10.0 and 192.168.20.0. For the Lab_A router to be able to route to all networks, the following networks have to be configured in its routing table:

- 192.168.30.0
- 192.168.40.0
- 192.168.50.0

The following router output shows the static routes on the Lab_A router and the routing table after the configuration. For the Lab_A router to find the remote networks, an entry is placed in the routing table describing the network, the mask, and where to send the packets. Notice that each static route sends the packets to 192.168.20.2, which is the Lab_A router's next hop:

```
Lab_A(config)#ip route 192.168.30.0 255.255.255.0 192.168.20.2
Lab_A(config)#ip route 192.168.40.0 255.255.255.0 192.168.20.2
Lab_A(config)#ip route 192.168.50.0 255.255.255.0 192.168.20.2
```

After the router is configured, you can type `show running-config` and `show ip route` to see the static routes:

```
Lab_A#sh ip route
[output cut]
S     192.168.50.0 [1/0] via 192.168.20.2
S     192.168.40.0 [1/0] via 192.168.20.2
S     192.168.30.0 [1/0] via 192.168.20.2
C     192.168.20.0 is directly connected, Serial 0/0
C     192.168.10.0 is directly connected, FastEthernet0/0
Lab_A#
```

Understand that if the routes don't appear in the routing table, it's because the router cannot communicate with the next-hop address you configured. You can use the `permanent` parameter to keep the route in the routing table even if the next-hop device can't be contacted.

The S in the preceding routing table entries means that the network is a static entry. The [1/0] is the administrative distance and metric, which I'll discuss later, to the remote network. Here the next-hop interface is 0, indicating that it's directly connected.

The Lab_A router now has all the information it needs to communicate with the other remote networks. However, if the Lab_B and Lab_C routers are not configured with all the same information, the packets will be discarded at Lab_B and at Lab_C. We need to fix this with static routes.

Lab_B

The Lab_B router is connected to the networks 192.168.20.0, 192.168.30.0, and 192.168.40.0. The following static routes must be configured on the Lab_B router:

- 192.168.10.0
- 192.168.50.0

Here's the configuration for the Lab_B router:

```
Lab_B(config)#ip route 192.168.10.0 255.255.255.0 192.168.20.1
Lab_B(config)#ip route 192.168.50.0 255.255.255.0 192.168.40.2
```

By looking at the routing table, you can see that the Lab_B router now understands how to find each network:

```
Lab_B#sh ip route
[output cut]
S     192.168.50.0 [1/0] via 192.168.40.2
C     192.168.40.0 is directly connected, Serial0/1
C     192.168.30.0 is directly connected, FastEthernet 0/0
C     192.168.20.0 is directly connected, Serial0/0
S     192.168.10.0 [1/0] via 192.168.20.1
Lab_B#
```

The Lab_B router now has a complete routing table. As soon as the other routers in the internetwork have all the networks in their routing table, Lab_B can communicate to all remote networks.

Lab_C

The Lab_C router is directly connected to networks 192.168.40.0 and 192.168.50.0. Three routes need to be added:

- 192.168.30.0
- 192.168.20.0
- 192.168.10.0

Here's the configuration for the Lab_C router:

```
Lab_C(config)#ip route 192.168.30.0 255.255.255.0 192.168.40.1
Lab_C(config)#ip route 192.168.20.0 255.255.255.0 192.168.40.1
Lab_C(config)#ip route 192.168.10.0 255.255.255.0 192.168.40.1
```

The following output shows the routing table on the Lab_C router:

```
Lab_C#sh ip route
[output cut]
C       192.168.50.0 is directly connected, FastEthernet0/0
C       192.168.40.0 is directly connected, Serial0/0
S       192.168.30.0 [1/0] via 192.168.40.1
S       192.168.20.0 [1/0] via 192.168.40.1
S       192.168.10.0 [1/0] via 192.168.40.1
Lab_C#
```

Lab_C now shows all the networks in the internetwork and can communicate with all routers and networks. All the routers have the correct routing table, and all the routers and hosts should be able to communicate without a problem—for now. But if you add even one more network or another router to the internetwork, you'll have to update all routers' routing tables by hand. As I said, this isn't a problem at all if you've got a small network, but its way too time-consuming a task if you're dealing with a large internetwork.

Verifying Your Configuration

Once all the routers' routing tables are configured, they need to be verified. The best way to do this, besides using the show ip route command, is with the Ping program. By pinging from routers Lab_A and Lab_C, the whole internetwork will be tested end to end.

Really, the best test would be to use the Telnet program from one host to another, but we'll talk about that more in Chapter 8, "Managing a Cisco Internetwork." For now, Ping is king!

Here is the output of a ping to network 192.168.50.0 from the Lab_A router:

```
Lab_A#ping 192.168.50.1
Type escape sequence to abort.
Sending 5, 100-byte ICMP Echos to 192.168.50.1, timeout is 2 seconds:
!!!!!
Success rate is 80 percent (4/5), round-trip min/avg/max = 64/66/68 ms
Lab_A#
```

From router Lab_C, a ping to 192.168.10.0 network will test for good IP connectivity. Here is the router output:

```
Lab_C#ping 192.168.10.1
Type escape sequence to abort.
Sending 5, 100-byte ICMP Echos to 192.168.10.1, timeout is 2 seconds:
!!!!!
Success rate is 100 percent (5/5), round-trip min/avg/max
  = 64/67/72 ms
```

Since we can ping from end to end without a problem, our static route configuration was a success!

Default Routing

We use *default routing* to send packets with a remote destination network not in the routing table to the next-hop router. You can only use default routing on stub networks—those with only one exit path out of the network.

In the internetworking example used in the previous section, the only routers that are considered to be in a stub network are Lab_A and Lab_C. If you tried to put a default route on router Lab_B, packets wouldn't be forwarded to the correct networks because they have more than one interface routing to other routers. And even though router Lab_C has two connections, it doesn't have another router on the 192.168.50.0 network that needs packets sent to it. Lab_C will only send packets to 192.168.40.1 (the serial 0/0 interface of Lab_B). And router Lab_A will only send packets to the 192.168.20.2 interface of Lab_A.

To configure a default route, you use wildcards in the network address and mask locations of a static route. In fact, you can just think of a default route as a static route that uses wildcards instead of network and mask information. In this section, I'll create a default route on the Lab_C router.

Router Lab_C is directly connected to networks 192.168.40.0 and 192.168.50.0. The routing table needs to know about networks 192.168.10.0, 192.168.20.0, and 192.168.30.0.

To configure the router to route to the other three networks, I placed three static routes in the routing table. By using a default route, you can just create one static route entry instead. You must first delete the existing static routes from the router and then add the default route.

```
Lab_C(config)#no ip route 192.168.10.0 255.255.255.0 192.168.40.1
Lab_C(config)#no ip route 192.168.20.0 255.255.255.0 192.168.40.1
Lab_C(config)#no ip route 192.168.30.0 255.255.255.0 192.168.40.1
Lab_C(config)#ip route 0.0.0.0 0.0.0.0 192.168.40.1
```

If you look at the routing table now, you'll see only the two directly connected networks plus an S*, which indicates that this entry is a candidate for a default route.

```
Lab_C#sh ip route
[output cut]
Gateway of last resort is 192.168.40.1 to network 0.0.0.0
C       192.168.50.0 is directly connected, FastEthernet0/0
C       192.168.40.0 is directly connected, Serial0/0
S*      0.0.0.0/0 [1/0] via 192.168.40.1
Lab_C#
```

We could have completed the default route command another way:

```
Lab_C(config)#ip route 0.0.0.0 0.0.0.0 s0/0
```

This says that if you don't have an entry for a network in the routing table, just forward it out serial 0/0. You can choose the IP address of the next-hop router or the exit interface—either way, it will work the same.

 There is one small, interesting difference when using the exit interface instead of the next-hop address: In the routing table, when you're using an exit interface with your default route, the route will show as directly connected with an administrative distance of 0 instead of the default of 1 with a next-hop configured default route.

Notice also in the routing table that the gateway of last resort is now set. Even so, there's one more command you must be aware of when using default routes: the ip classless command.

All Cisco routers are classful routers, meaning that they expect a default subnet mask on each interface of the router. When a router receives a packet for a destination subnet that's not in the routing table, it will drop the packet by default. If you're using default routing, you must use the ip classless command because it is possible that no remote subnets will be in the routing table.

Since I have version 12.x of the IOS on my routers, the ip classless command is on by default. If you're using default routing and this command isn't in your configuration, you would need to add it if you had subnetted networks on your routers (which we don't at this time). The command is shown here:

```
Lab_C(config)#ip classless
```

Notice that it's a global configuration mode command. The interesting part of the `ip classless` command is that default routing sometimes works without it but sometimes doesn't. To be on the safe side, you should always turn on the `ip classless` command when you use default routing.

Summary

This chapter covered IP routing in detail. It's extremely important that you really understand the basics we covered in this chapter because everything that's done on a Cisco router typically will have some type of IP routing configured and running.

You learned in this chapter how IP routing uses frames to transport packets between routers and to the destination host. From there, we configured static routing on our routers and discussed the administrative distance used by IP to determine the past route to a destination network. If you have a stub network, you can configure default routing, which sets the gateway of last resort on a router.

In the next chapter we will move away from static and default routing and use dynamic routing.

Exam Essentials

Understand the basic IP routing process.   You need to remember that the frame changes at each hop but that the packet is never changed or manipulated in any way until it reaches the destination device.

Understand that MAC addresses are always local.   A MAC (hardware) address will only be used on a local LAN. It will never pass a router's interface.

Understand that a frame carries a packet to only two places.   A frame uses MAC (hardware) addresses to send a packet on a LAN. The Frame will take the packet to either a host on the LAN or a router's interface if the packet is destined for a remote network

Written Lab 5

Write the answers to the following questions:

1.   Create a static route to network 172.16.10.0/24 with a next-hop gateway of 172.16.20.1 and an administrative distance of 150.

2.   What command do you type in at a router to see if serial 0/0 is a DTE or DCE connection?

3.   What command will you type to create a default route to 172.16.40.1?

4.   If you are using default routing, what command must also be used?

5. You would use a default route on which type of network?

6. To see the routing table on your router, what command will you use?

7. When creating a static or default route, you don't have to use the next-hop IP address; you can use the _____ .

8. True/False: To reach a destination host, you must know the MAC address of the remote host.

9. True/False: To reach a destination host, you must know the IP address of the remote host.

10. If you have a DCE serial interface, what command must you enter for that interface to work?

(The answers to Written Lab 5 can be found following the answers to the review questions for this chapter.)

Hands-on Labs

In the following hands-on lab, you will configure a network with three 2501 routers and one 2621 router.

The hands-on lab in this section is included for use with real Cisco routers. If you are using software from RouterSim or Sybex, please use the hands-on labs found in those programs.

This chapter includes Lab 5.1, "Creating Static Routes." Table 5.2 shows our IP addresses for each router (each interface uses a /24 mask). Figure 5.10 will be used to configure all routers.

TABLE 5.2   Our IP Addresses

Router	Interface	IP address
2621A	F0/0	172.16.10.1
2501A	E0	172.16.10.2
2501A	S0	172.16.20.1
2501B	E0	172.16.30.1
2501B	S0	172.16.20.2
2501B	S1	172.16.40.1
2501C	S0	172.16.40.2
2501C	E0	172.16.50.1

FIGURE 5.10 · Hands-on lab internetwork

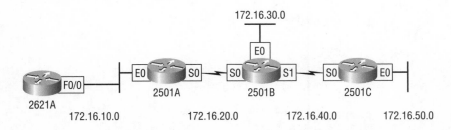

Hands-on Lab 5.1: Creating Static Routes

In this lab, you will create a static route in all four routers so that the routers see all networks. Verify with the Ping program when complete.

1. The 2621A router is connected to network 172.16.10.0/24. It does not know about networks 172.16.20.0/24, 172.16.30.0/24, 172.16.40.0/24, and 172.16.50.0/24. The 2621A router f0/0 interface has an IP address of 172.16.10.2/24, and the 2501A Ethernet 0 interface is 172.16.10.1/24. Create static routes so that the 2621A router can see all networks, as shown here:

```
2621A#config t
2621A(config)#ip route 172.16.20.0 255.255.255.0
    172.16.10.2
2621A(config)#ip route 172.16.30.0 255.255.255.0
    172.16.10.2
2621A(config)#ip route 172.16.40.0 255.255.255.0
    172.16.10.2
2621A(config)#ip route 172.16.50.0 255.255.255.0
    172.16.10.2
```

2. Save the current configuration for the 2621A router by going to the privileged mode, typing `copy run start`, and pressing Enter.

3. On Router 2501A, which is already directly connected to networks 172.16.10.0/24 and 172.16.20.0/24, create a static route to see networks 172.16.30.0/24, 172.16.40.0/24, and 172.16.50.0/24, as shown here (the 2501B serial 0 interface IP address is 172.16.20.2/24, which we will use as our next-hop address):

```
2501A#config t
2501A(config)#ip route 172.16.30.0 255.255.255.0
    172.16.20.2
2501A(config)#ip route 172.16.40.0 255.255.255.0
    172.16.20.2
2501A(config)#ip route 172.16.50.0 255.255.255.0
    172.16.20.2
```

These commands told Router 2501A to get to network 172.16.30.0/24 and use IP address 172.16.20.2, which is the closest neighbor interface connected to network 172.16.30.0/24, or Router 2501B. This is the same interface you will use to get to networks 172.16.40.0/24 and 172.16.50.0/24.

4. Save the current configuration for Router 2501A by going to the enabled mode, typing `copy run start`, and pressing Enter.

5. On Router 2501B, create a static route to see networks 172.16.10.0/24 and 172.16.50.0/24, which are not directly connected. Create static routes so that Router 2501B can see all networks, as shown here:

```
2501B#config t
2501B(config)#ip route 172.16.10.0 255.255.255.0
   172.16.20.1
2501B(config)#ip route 172.16.50.0 255.255.255.0
   172.16.40.2
```

The first command told Router 2501B that to get to network 172.16.10.0/24, it needs to use 172.16.20.1. The next command told Router 2501B to get to network 172.16.50.0/24 through 172.16.40.2, which is the 2501C serial 0 interface IP address.

Save the current configuration for Router 2501B by going to the enable mode, typing copy run start, and pressing Enter.

6. Router 2501C is connected to networks 172.16.50.0/24 and 172.16.40.0/24. It does not know about networks 172.16.30.0/24, 172.16.20.0/24, and 172.16.10.0/24. Create static routes so that Router 2501C can see all networks, as shown here (use the 2501B serial 1 interface address of 172.16.40.1):

```
2501C#config t
2501C(config)#ip route 172.16.30.0 255.255.255.0
   172.16.40.1
2501C(config)#ip route 172.16.20.0 255.255.255.0
   172.16.40.1
2501C(config)#ip route 172.16.10.0 255.255.255.0
   172.16.40.1
```

Save the current configuration for Router 2501C by going to the enable mode, typing copy run start, and pressing Enter.

7. Now ping from each router to your hosts and from each router to each router. If it is set up correctly, it will work.

Review Questions

1. Which of the following statements are true regarding the command `ip route 172.16.4.0 255.255.255.0 192.168.4.2`? (Choose two.)

   A. The command is used to establish a static route.

   B. The default administrative distance is used.

   C. The command is used to configure the default route.

   D. The subnet mask for the source address is 255.255.255.0.

   E. The command is used to establish a stub network.

2. What destination addresses will be used by HostA to send data to the HTTPS server as shown in the following illustration? (Choose two.)

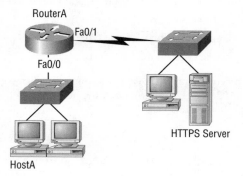

   A. The IP address of the switch

   B. The MAC address of the remote switch

   C. The IP address of the HTTPS server

   D. The MAC address of the HTTPS server

   E. The IP address of RouterA's Fa0/0 interface

   F. The MAC address of RouterA's Fa0/0 interface

3. Using the following illustration, which of the following would be true if Host A is trying to communicate to Host B and interface Fa0/0 of Router C goes down? (Choose two.)

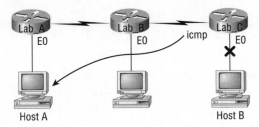

A. Lab_C will use an ICMP to inform Host A that Host B cannot be reached.

B. Lab_C will use ICMP to inform Lab B that Host B cannot be reached.

C. Lab_C will use ICMP to inform HostA, RouterA, and Lab_B that HostB cannot be reached.

D. Lab_C will send a Destination Unreachable message type.

E. Lab_C will send a Router Selection message type.

F. Lab_C will send a Source Quench message type.

4. The corporate router receives an IP packet with a source IP address of 192.168.214.20 and a destination address of 192.168.22.3. Looking at the output from the corporate router, what will the router do with this packet?

```
Corp#sh ip route
[output cut]
R    192.168.215.0 [120/2] via 192.168.20.2, 00:00:23, Serial0/0
R    192.168.115.0 [120/1] via 192.168.20.2, 00:00:23, Serial0/0
R    192.168.30.0 [120/1] via 192.168.20.2, 00:00:23, Serial0/0
C    192.168.20.0 is directly connected, Serial0/0
C    192.168.214.0 is directly connected, FastEthernet0/0
```

A. The packets will be discarded.

B. The packets will be routed out the S0/0 interface.

C. The router will broadcast looking for the destination.

D. The packets will be routed out the Fa0/0 interface.

5. For this question, refer to the following illustration. To begin communicating with the Sales server, Host 4 sends out an ARP request. How will the devices exhibited in the topology respond to this request?

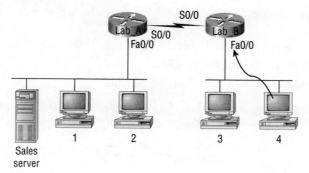

A. Host 3 will respond that the destination is not on the local LAN.

B. Router Lab_B will respond that the destination is not on the local LAN.

C. Router Lab_B will forward the ARP request to the Lab_A router.

D. Router Lab_B will respond with the MAC address of its Fa0/0 interface.

6. For this question, refer to the illustration in question 5. Host 4 has received an ARP reply. Host 4 will now build a packet and then place this packet in the frame. What information will be placed in the header of the packet that leaves Host 4 if Host 4 is going to communicate to the Sales server? (Choose two.)

A. The destination address will be the IP address of the interface Fa0/0 of the Lab_A router.

B. The destination address will be the IP Address of the Sales server.

C. The destination address will be the IP Address of the interface Fa0/0 of the Lab_B router.

D. The source address will be the IP address of Host 4.

E. The source address will be the IP address of the interface fa0/0 lf the Lab_B router.

F. The destination address will be the IP address of interface Fa0/0 of the Lab_B router.

7. For this question, refer to the illustration in question 5. Finally, Router Lab_A has received the packet and will send it out Fa0/0 onto the LAN toward the server. What will the frame have in the header as the source and destination addresses?

A. The destination address will be the MAC address of the Sales server.

B. The destination address will be the a broadcast to all hosts in the broadcast domain.

C. The source address will be the MAC address of Host F.

D. The source address will be the MAC address of interface Fa0/0 of the Lab_A router.

8. For this question, refer to the illustration in question 5. Host 4 is displaying WWW documents from the Sales server in two browser windows at the same time. How did the data find its way to the correct browser windows on Host 4?

    A. The IP source addresses of the packets will be used to direct the data to the correct browser window.

    B. TCP port numbers are used to direct the data to the correct application window.

    C. The browser tracks the data by the URL.

    D. The OSI application layer tracks the conversations.

9. Referring to the following illustration, if Host A sends an IP packet to Host B, what will be the OSI layer 3 source address in the packet when it reaches Host B?

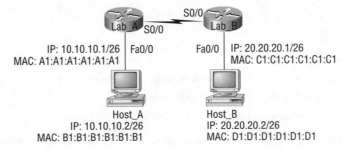

    A. 10.10.10.1

    B. 10.10.10.2

    C. 20.20.20.1

    D. 20.20.20.2

10. Referring to the illustration in question 9, if Host A sends an IP packet to Host B, what will be the OSI layer 2 source address in the frame when it reaches host B?

    A. A1:A1:A1:A1:A1:A1

    B. B1:B1:B1:B1:B1:B1

    C. C1:C1:C1:C1:C1:C1

    D. D1:D1:D1:D1:D1:D1

11. Referring again to the illustration in question 9, if Host A sends an IP packet to Host B, what will be the OSI layer 2 source address in the frame when it leaves Host A?

    A. A1:A1:A1:A1:A1:A1

    B. B1:B1:B1:B1:B1:B1

    C. C1:C1:C1:C1:C1:C1

    D. D1:D1:D1:D1:D1:D1

12. Again referring again to the illustration in question 9, if Host A sends an IP packet to Host B, what will be the OSI layer 2 destination address in the frame when it leaves Host A?

   A. A1:A1:A1:A1:A1:A1

   B. B1:B1:B1:B1:B1:B1

   C. C1:C1:C1:C1:C1:C1

   D. D1:D1:D1:D1:D1:D1

13. Which of the following statements is true regarding the command `ip route 172.16.4.0 255.255.255.0 192.168.4.2`?

   A. The command is used to establish a dynamic route.

   B. The default administrative distance is 2.

   C. The command is used to configure the default route.

   D. The subnet mask for the destination address is 255.255.255.0.

   E. The command is used to establish a stub network.

14. The corporate router receives an IP packet with a source IP address of 192.168.30.20 and a destination address of 192.168.214.3. Looking at the output from the corporate router, what will the router do with this packet?

```
Corp#sh ip route
[output cut]
R    192.168.215.0 [120/2] via 192.168.20.2, 00:00:23, Serial0/0
R    192.168.115.0 [120/1] via 192.168.20.2, 00:00:23, Serial0/0
R    192.168.30.0 [120/1] via 192.168.20.2, 00:00:23, Serial0/0
C    192.168.20.0 is directly connected, Serial0/0
C    192.168.214.0 is directly connected, FastEthernet0/0
```

   A. The packets will be discarded.

   B. The packets will be routed out the S0/0 interface.

   C. The router will broadcast looking for the destination.

   D. The packets will be routed out the Fa0/0 interface.

15. Which of the following is a valid default route?

   A. `ip route 0.0.0.0 255.255.255.0 192.168.10.1`

   B. `ip route 0.0.0.0 0.0.0.0 s0/0`

   C. `ip route 255.255.255.0 0.0.0.0 192.168.10.1`

   D. `ip route 0.0.0.0.255.255.255.0 192.168.10.1`

Answers to Review Questions

1. A, B. Although option C almost seems right, it is not; the mask is the mask used on the remote network, not the source network. Since there is no number at the end of the static route, it is using the default administrative distance of 1.

2. C, F. The switches are not used as either a default gateway or another destination. Switches have nothing to do with routing. It is very important to remember that the destination MAC address will always be the router's interface. The destination address of a frame, from HostA, will be the MAC address of the Fa0/0 interface of RouterA. The destination address of a packet will be the IP address of the network interface card (NIC) of the HTTPS server. The destination port number in the segment header will have a value of 443 (HTTPS).

3. A, D. Lab_C will use ICMP to inform Host A that Host B cannot be reached. It will perform this by sending a Destination Unreachable ICMP message type.

4. A. Since the routing table shows no route to the 192.168.22.0 network, the router will discard the packet and send an ICMP Destination Unreachable message out interface FastEthernet 0/0, which is the source LAN from which the packet originated.

5. D. Since MAC addresses must stay on the local network, the Lab_B router will respond with the MAC address of the Fa0/0 interface and Host 4 will send all frames to the MAC address of Lab_B Fa0/0 interface when sending packets to the Sales server.

6. B, D. Since we're now talking about packets, not frames, the source address will be the IP address of Host 4 and the destination address will be the IP address of the Sales server.

7. A, D. The source MAC address will be the Lab_A router's Fa0/0 interface and the destination MAC address will by the Sales server's MAC address. (All MAC addresses must be local on the LAN.)

8. B. TCP port numbers are used to direct the data to the correct application window.

9. B. The source layer 3 address will be the IP address of Host A, which is 10.10.10.2 in this question.

10. D. The source layer 2 address will be the MAC address of router Lab_B Fa0/0 interface, which is D1:D1:D1:D1:D1:D1 in this question.

11. B. The source layer 2 address will be the MAC address of Host A's interface, which is B1:B1:B1:B1:B1:B1 in this question.

12. A. The destination layer 2 address will be the MAC address of router Lab_A's Fa0/0 interface, which is A1:A1:A1:A1:A1:A1 in this question.

13. D. The mask is the used for the remote network, not the source network. Since there is no number at the end of the static route, it is using the default administrative distance of 1, not 2.

14. D. Since the routing table shows a route to network 192.168.214.0 out Fa0/0, the packet will be sent out the FastEthernet 0/0 interface.

15. B. The only valid default route is option B, which is using an exit interface. None of the other options have the correct syntax.

Answers to Written Lab 5

1. ip route 172.16.10.0 255.255.255.0 172.16.20.1
2. Router#**show controllers serial 0/0**
3. ip route 0.0.0.0 0.0.0.0 172.16.40.1
4. Router(config)#**ip classless**
5. Stub network
6. Router#**show ip route**
7. Exit interface
8. False. The MAC address would be the router interface, not the remote host.
9. True
10. Router(config-if)#**clock rate** *speed*

Chapter

6

Dynamic Routing Protocols

THE CCNA INTRO EXAM TOPICS COVERED IN THIS CHAPTER INCLUDE THE FOLLOWING:

✓ **Technology**

- Describe the concepts associated with routing, and the different methods and protocols used to achieve it

- Describe how the protocols associated with TCP/IP allow host communication to occur

- Describe the principles and practice of packet switching utilizing the Internet Protocol (IP)

Dynamic routing is when protocols are used to find networks and update routing tables on routers. True—this is easier than using static or default routing, but it'll cost you in terms of router CPU processes and bandwidth on the network links. A routing protocol defines the set of rules used by a router when it communicates routing information between neighbor routers.

The two routing protocols I'm going to talk about most in this chapter are Routing Information Protocol (RIP, including RIPv1 and RIPv2), and Interior Gateway Routing Protocol (IGRP). EIGRP and OSPF are covered in the CCNA Exam Objectives and are above the scope of this book and INTRO exam objedtives; however, I'll discuss some EIGRP and OSPF features throughout the chapter.

For more information on routing protocols, particularly EIGRP and OSPF, please see the *Sybex CCNA Study Guide*, Sixth Edition.

There are two types of routing protocols used in internetworks: interior gateway protocols (IGPs) and exterior gateway protocols (EGPs). IGPs are used to exchange routing information with routers in the same autonomous system (AS). An AS is a collection of networks under a common administrative domain, which basically means that all routers sharing the same routing table information are in the same AS. EGPs are used to communicate between ASes.

Since routing protocols are so essential to dynamic routing, I'm going to give you the basic information you need to know about them next. Later on in this chapter, we'll focus on configuration.

Routing Protocol Basics

There are some important things you should know about routing protocols before getting deeper into them. Specifically, you need to understand administrative distances, the three different kinds of routing protocols, and routing loops. We will look at each of these in more detail in the following sections.

Administrative Distances

The *administrative distance (AD)* is used to rate the trustworthiness of routing information received on a router from a neighbor router. An administrative distance is an integer from 0 to 255, where 0 is the most trusted and 255 means no traffic will be passed via this route.

If a router receives two updates listing the same remote network, the first thing the router checks is the AD. If one of the advertised routes has a lower AD than the other, then the route with the lowest AD will be placed in the routing table.

If both advertised routes to the same network have the same AD, then routing protocol metrics (such as *hop count* or bandwidth of the lines) will be used to find the best path to the remote network. The advertised route with the lowest metric will be placed in the routing table. But if both advertised routes have the same AD as well as the same metrics, then the routing protocol will load-balance to the remote network (which means that it sends packets down each link).

Table 6.1 shows the default administrative distances that a Cisco router uses to decide which route to take to a remote network.

TABLE 6.1   Default Administrative Distances

Route Source	Default AD
Connected interface	0
Static route	1
EIGRP	90
IGRP	100
OSPF	110
RIP	120
External EIGRP	170
Unknown	255 (this route will never be used)

If a network is directly connected, the router will always use the interface connected to the network. If an administrator configures a static route, the router will believe that route over any other learned routes. You can change the administrative distance of static routes, but by default, they have an AD of 1.

For example, if you have a static route, a RIP-advertised route, and an IGRP-advertised route listing the same network, then by default, the router will always use the static route unless you change the AD of the static route.

Routing Protocols

There are three classes of routing protocols:

Distance vector   The *distance-vector protocols* find the best path to a remote network by judging distance. Each time a packet goes through a router, that's called a *hop*. The route with the least number of hops to the network is determined to be the best route. The vector indicates the direction to the remote network. Both RIP and IGRP are distance-vector routing protocols. They send the entire routing table to directly connected neighbors.

Link state   In *link-state protocols*, also called *shortest-path-first protocols*, the routers each create three separate tables. One of these tables keeps track of directly attached neighbors, one determines the topology of the entire internetwork, and one is used as the routing table. Link-state routers know more about the internetwork than any distance-vector routing protocol. OSPF is an IP routing protocol that is completely link state. Link-state protocols send updates containing the state of their own links to all other routers on the network.

Hybrid   *Hybrid protocols* use aspects of both distance vector and link state—for example, EIGRP.

There's no set way of configuring routing protocols for use with every business. This is something you really have to do on a case-by-case basis. However, if you understand how the different routing protocols work, you can make good, solid decisions that truly meet the individual needs of any business.

Distance-Vector Routing Protocols

The distance-vector routing algorithm passes complete routing table contents to neighboring routers, which then combine the received routing table entries with their own routing tables to complete the router's routing table. This is called routing by rumor, because a router receiving an update from a neighbor router believes the information about remote networks without actually finding out for itself.

It's possible to have a network that has multiple links to the same remote network, and if that's the case, the administrative distance is checked first. If the AD is the same, the protocol will have to use other metrics to determine the best path to use to that remote network.

RIP uses only hop count to determine the best path to a network. If RIP finds more than one link to the same remote network with the same hop count, it will automatically perform a round-robin load balancing. RIP can perform load balancing for up to six equal-cost links (four by default).

However, a problem with this type of routing metric arises when the two links to a remote network are different bandwidths but the same hop count. Figure 6.1, for example, shows two links to remote network 172.16.10.0.

FIGURE 6.1   Pinhole congestion

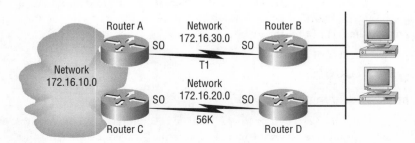

Since network 172.16.30.0 is a T1 link with a bandwidth of 1.544Mbps and network 172.16.20.0 is a 56K link, you'd want the router to choose the T1 over the 56K link, right? But because hop count is the only metric used with RIP routing, the two links would be seen as being of equal cost. This little snag is called *pinhole congestion.*

It's important to understand what a distance-vector routing protocol does when it starts up. In Figure 6.2, the four routers start off with only their directly connected networks in the routing table. After a distance-vector routing protocol is started on each router, the routing tables are updated with all route information gathered from neighbor routers. As shown in Figure 6.2, each router has only the directly connected networks in each routing table. Each router sends its complete routing table out to each active interface. The routing table of each router includes the network number, exit interface, and hop count to the network.

In Figure 6.3, the routing tables are complete because they include information about all the networks in the internetwork. They are considered *converged.* When the routers are converging, it is possible that no data will be passed. That's why fast convergence time is a serious plus. In fact, that's one of the problems with RIP—its slow convergence time.

The routing table in each router keeps information regarding the remote network number, the interface to which the router will send packets to reach that network, and the hop count or metric to the network.

Routing Information Protocol (RIP)

Routing Information Protocol (RIP) is a true distance-vector routing protocol. It sends the complete routing table out to all active interfaces every 30 seconds. RIP only uses hop count to determine the best way to a remote network, but it has a maximum allowable hop count of 15 by default, meaning that 16 is deemed unreachable. RIP works well in small networks, but it's inefficient on large networks with slow WAN links or on networks with a large number of routers installed.

FIGURE 6.2   The internetwork with distance-vector routing

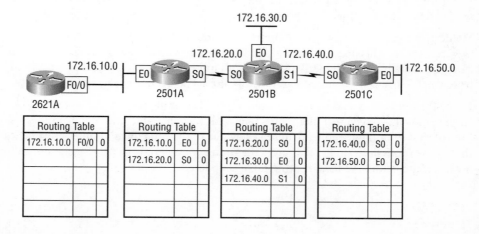

FIGURE 6.3 Converged routing tables

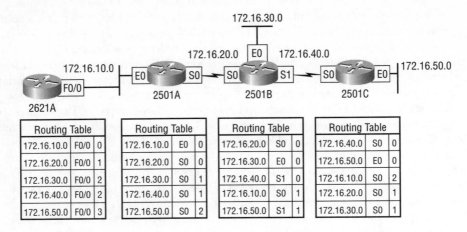

RIP version 1 uses only *classful routing*, which means that all devices in the network must use the same subnet mask. This is because RIP version 1 doesn't send updates with subnet mask information in tow. RIP version 2 provides something called *prefix routing* and does send subnet mask information with the route updates. This is called *classless routing*.

In the following sections, we will discuss the RIP timers and then RIP configuration.

RIP Timers

RIP uses four different kinds of timers to regulate its performance:

Route update timer Sets the interval (typically 30 seconds) between periodic routing updates, in which the router sends a complete copy of its routing table out to all neighbors.

Route invalid timer Determines the length of time that must elapse (180 seconds) before a router determines that a route has become invalid. It will come to this conclusion if it hasn't heard any updates about a particular route for that period. When that happens, the router will send out updates to all its neighbors letting them know that the route is invalid.

Holddown timer This sets the amount of time during which routing information is suppressed. Routes will enter into the holddown state when an update packet is received that indicates the route is unreachable. This continues until either an update packet is received with a better metric or until the holddown timer expires. The default is 180 seconds.

Route flush timer Sets the time between a route becoming invalid and its removal from the routing table (240 seconds). Before it's removed from the table, the router notifies its neighbors of that route's impending demise. The value of the route invalid timer must be less than that of the route flush timer. This gives the router enough time to tell its neighbors about the invalid route before the local routing table is updated.

Configuring RIP Routing

To configure RIP routing, just turn on the protocol with the `router rip` command and tell the RIP routing protocol which classful networks to advertise. That's it. Let's configure our three-router internetwork, shown in Figure 6.4, with RIP routing and practice that.

FIGURE 6.4   IP RIP routing example

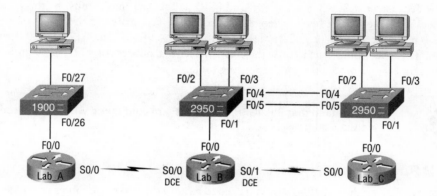

Lab_A Router

RIP has an administrative distance of 120. Static routes have an administrative distance of 1 by default, and since we currently have static routes configured (from Chapter 5), the routing tables won't be propagated with RIP information. So, the first thing we need to do is to delete the static routes off each router.

This is done with the `no ip route` command:

```
Lab_A(config)#no ip route 192.168.30.0 255.255.255.0 192.168.20.2
Lab_A(config)#no ip route 192.168.40.0 255.255.255.0 192.168.20.2
Lab_A(config)#no ip route 192.168.50.0 255.255.255.0 192.168.20.2
```

Notice that in the preceding Lab_A router output, you must type the whole `ip route` command after the keyword `no` to delete the entry.

Once the static routes are deleted from the configuration, you can add the RIP routing protocol by using the `router rip` command and the `network` command. The `network` command tells the routing protocol which network to advertise.

Look at the next router configuration:

```
Lab_A(config)#router rip
Lab_A(config-router)#network 192.168.10.0
Lab_A(config-router)#network 192.168.20.0
Lab_A(config-router)#^Z
Lab_A#
```

Note the fact that you need to type in every directly connected classful network that you want RIP to advertise. But because they're not directly connected, we're going to leave out networks 30, 40, and 50—it's RIP's job to find them and populate the routing table.

That's it. Two or three commands and you're done—sure makes your job a lot easier than when using static routes, doesn't it? However, keep in mind the extra router CPU process and bandwidth that you're consuming.

RIP (v1 and v2), IGRP, and EIGRP use the classful address when configuring the network address. Because of this, when using RIP and IGRP, all subnet masks must be the same on all devices in the network (this is called classful routing). To clarify this, let's say you're using a Class B network address of 172.16.0.0/24 with subnets 172.16.10.0, 172.16.20.0, and 172.16.30.0. You would type in only the classful network address of 172.16.0.0 and let RIP find the subnets and place them in the routing table.

Understand that RIP, IGRP, and EIGRP are configured with classful routing network addresses!

Lab_B Router

To configure RIP on the Lab_B router, you need to remove the two static routes you added from the earlier example. Once you make sure no routes are in the routing table with a better administrative distance than 120, you can add RIP. The Lab_B router has three directly connected networks and we want RIP to advertise them all, so we will add three network statements.

Again, if you don't remove the static routes, RIP routes will never be found in the routing table even though RIP will still be running in the background causing a bunch of CPU processing on the routers and gobbling up precious bandwidth!

Here is what I did to configure RIP on the Lab_B:

```
Lab_B#config t
Enter configuration commands, one per line. End with CNTL/Z.
Lab_B(config)#no ip route 192.168.10.0 255.255.255.0 192.168.20.1
Lab_B(config)#no ip route 192.168.50.0 255.255.255.0 192.168.40.2
Lab_B(config)#router rip
Lab_B(config-router)#network 192.168.20.0
Lab_B(config-router)#network 192.168.30.0
Lab_B(config-router)#network 192.168.40.0
Lab_B(config-router)#^Z
Lab_B#
```

It's important that you understand that the network numbers you use are your directly connected networks only. Since we have all Class C addresses, we type each full Class C network under RIP. However, if we were subnetting a Class C network—for example, 192.168.10.0/28—our networks would be 0, 16, 32, and so on. We would type only the classful network number of 192.168.10.0 under RIP. We let RIP find the subnets and advertise them. If you're studying the CCNA Intro objectives, you really need to understand this!

Lab_C Router

We've already removed the static routes on the Lab_C router because we placed a default route on it. So all that's needed here is to remove the default route from the Lab_C router. Once it's dust, you can turn on RIP routing for the two directly connected routes:

```
Lab_C#config t
Enter configuration commands, one per line. End with CNTL/Z.
Lab_C(config)#no ip route 0.0.0.0 0.0.0.0 192.168.40.1
Lab_C(config)#router rip
Lab_C(config-router)#network 192.168.40.0
Lab_C(config-router)#network 192.168.50.0
Lab_C(config-router)#^Z
Lab_C#
```

It's important to remember why we're doing this. Directly connected routes have an administrative distance of 0, static routes have an administrative distance of 1, and RIP has an administrative distance of 120. I call RIP the "gossip protocol" because it reminds me of junior high school, where if you hear a rumor (advertised route), it just has to be true without exception. And that pretty much sums up how RIP behaves on an internetwork—rumor mill as protocol!

Verifying the RIP Routing Tables

Each routing table should now have the routers' directly connected routes as well as RIP-injected routes received from neighboring routers. This output shows us the contents of the Lab_A routing table:

```
Lab_A#sh ip route
[output cut]

R    192.168.50.0 [120/2] via 192.168.20.2, 00:00:23, Serial0/0
R    192.168.40.0 [120/1] via 192.168.20.2, 00:00:23, Serial0/0
R    192.168.30.0 [120/1] via 192.168.20.2, 00:00:23, Serial0/0
C    192.168.20.0 is directly connected, Serial0/0
C    192.168.10.0 is directly connected, FastEthernet0/0
Lab_A#
```

Looking at this, you can see that the routing table has the same entries that they had when we were using static routes, except for that R. The R means that the networks were added dynamically using the RIP routing protocol. The [120/1] is the administrative distance of the route (120) along with the number of hops to that remote network (1).

The following output displays Lab_B's routing table:

```
Lab_B#sh ip route
[output cut]
```

```
R   192.168.50.0 [120/1] via 192.168.40.2, 00:00:11, Serial0/1
C   192.168.40.0 is directly connected, Serial0/1
C   192.168.30.0 is directly connected, FastEthernet0/0
C   192.168.20.0 is directly connected, Serial0/0
R   192.168.10.0 [120/1] via 192.168.20.1, 00:00:21, Serial0/0
Lab_B#
```

Notice that here again, the same networks are in the routing table and they weren't added manually.

Let's check out Lab_C's routing table:

```
Lab_C#sh ip route
[output cut]
Gateway of last resort is not set

C   192.168.50.0 is directly connected, FastEthernet0/0
C   192.168.40.0 is directly connected, Serial0/0
R   192.168.30.0 [120/1] via 192.168.40.1, 00:00:04, Serial0/0
R   192.168.20.0 [120/1] via 192.168.40.1, 00:00:26, Serial0/0
R   192.168.10.0 [120/2] via 192.168.40.1, 00:00:04, Serial0/0
Lab_C#
```

So while yes it's true that RIP has worked really well in our little internetwork, it's not the solution for every enterprise. That's because this technique has a maximum hop count of only 15 (16 is deemed unreachable) and it performs full routing-table updates every 30 seconds, both things that can wreak havoc in a larger internetwork.

There's one more thing I want to show you about RIP routing tables and the parameters used to advertise remote networks. Notice, as an example, that the following routing table output shows [120/15] for the 192.168.10.0 network metric:

```
Lab_C#sh ip route
[output cut]
Gateway of last resort is not set

C   192.168.50.0 is directly connected, FastEthernet0/0
C   192.168.40.0 is directly connected, Serial0/0
R   192.168.30.0 [120/1] via 192.168.40.1, 00:00:04, Serial0/0
R   192.168.20.0 [120/1] via 192.168.40.1, 00:00:26, Serial0/
R   192.168.10.0 [120/15] via 192.168.40.1, 00:00:04, Serial0/0
Lab_C#
```

This means that the administrative distance is 120, the default for RIP, but the hop count is 15. Remember that each time a router sends an update to a neighbor router, it increments the hop count by one for each route.

So this [120/15] is really bad because the next router that receives the table from router Lab_C will just discard the route to network 192.168.10.0 since the hop count would then be 16, which is invalid. I know that in this example we don't have another router connected to the right of Lab_C, but you should be able to get my point here!

Configuring RIP Routing Example 2

Before we move onto learning more about RIP as well as IGRP information and configurations, let's take another look at figure 6.4. However, in this example, we will find and implement our subnets and then add the RIP configuration to the router.

For this configuration, we are going to consider that the Lab_B and the Lab_C routers are already configured, and we just need to configure the Lab_A router. We will use the network ID of 192.168.164.0/28. The s0/0 interface will use the last available IP address in the eighth subnet and the Fa0/0 will use the last available IP address in the second subnet. Do not consider the zero subnet valid.

Before we start, you do know that /28 is a 255.255.255.240 mask, right? And that we have a block size of 16 in the fourth octet? It is very important that you do know this, and if you need another review of chapters 2 and 3, that's OK! Reviewing subnetting will never will hurt you!

Since we have a block size of 16, our subnets are 16 (remember we are not starting at zero for this example), 32, 48, 64, 80, 96, 112, 128, 144, etc. The eighth subnet (which we will use for the s0/0 interface) is subnet 128. The valid host range for the 128 subnet is 129 through 142. 143 is the broadcast address of the 128 subnet. The second subnet (which we will use for the fa0/0 interface), is the 32 subnet. The valid hosts are 33 through 46. 47 is the broadcast address of the 32 subnet.

So, here is what our configuration on the Lab_A router will look like:

```
Lab_A(config)#interface s0/0
Lab_A(config-if)#ip address 192.168.164.142 255.255.255.240
Lab_A(config-if)#no shutdown
Lab_A(config-if)#interface fa0/0
Lab_A(config-if)#ip address 192.168.164.46 255.255.255.240
Lab_A(config-if)#no shutdown
Lab_A(config-if)#router rip
Lab_A(config-router)#network 192.168.164.0
Lab_A(config-router)#^Z
Lab_A#
```

Finding the subnets and configuring the last valid host should be pretty straight forward. If not, head back to chapter 3. However, what I really want you to notice is that although we added two subnets to the Lab_A router, we only had one network statement under RIP. Sometimes it is hard to remember that you configure only the classful network statement, which means you turn all host bits off. This was the real purpose of this second RIP configuration example—to remind you of classful network addressing! And it never hurts to practice subnetting, right?

Holding Down RIP Propagations

You probably don't want your RIP network advertised everywhere on your LAN and WAN. There's not a whole lot to be gained by advertising your RIP network to the Internet, now is there?

There are a few different ways to stop unwanted RIP updates from propagating across your LANs and WANs. The easiest one is through the `passive-interface` command. This command prevents RIP update broadcasts from being sent out a defined interface, but that same interface can still receive RIP updates.

Here's an example of how to configure a `passive-interface` on a router:

```
Lab_A#config t
Lab_A(config)#router rip
Lab_A(config-router)#network 192.168.10.0
Lab_A(config-router)#passive-interface serial 0/0
```

This command will stop RIP updates from being propagated out serial interface 0, but serial interface 0 can still receive RIP updates.

 Real World Scenario

Should We Really Use RIP in an Internetwork?

You have been hired as a consultant to install a couple of Cisco routers into a growing network. There are a couple of old Unix routers that the company wants to keep in the network. These routers do not support any routing protocol except RIP. I guess these means you just have to run RIP on the entire network.

Well, yes and no. You can run RIP on a router connecting that old network, but you certainly don't need to run RIP throughout the whole internetwork!

You can do what is called *redistribution*, which is basically translating from one type of routing protocol to another. This means that you can support those old routers using RIP but use Enhanced IGRP, for example, on the rest of your network.

This will stop RIP routes from being sent all over the internetwork and eating up all that precious bandwidth.

RIP Version 2 (RIPv2)

Let's spend a couple of minutes discussing RIP version 2 (RIPv2) before we move into the distance-vector, Cisco-proprietary routing protocol IGRP.

RIPv2 is mostly the same as RIP version 1. Both RIPv1 and RIPv2 are distance-vector protocols, which means that each router running RIP sends its complete routing tables out all active interfaces at periodic time intervals. Also, the timers and loop-avoidance schemes are the same in both RIP versions. Both RIPv1 and RIPv2 are configured as classful addressing (but RIPv2 is considered classless because subnet information is sent with each route update), and both have the same administrative distance (120).

But there are some important differences that make RIPv2 more scalable than RIPv1. And I've got to add a word of advice here before we move on: I'm definitely not advocating using RIP of either version in your network. But since RIP is an open standard, you can use RIP with any brand of router. You can also use OSPF since OSPF is an open standard as well. RIP just requires too much bandwidth, making it pretty intensive to use in your network. Why go there when you have other, more elegant options?

Table 6.2 discusses the differences between RIPv1 and RIPv2.

TABLE 6.2   RIPv1 vs. RIPv2

RIPv1	RIPv2
Distance vector	Distance vector
Maximum hop count of 15	Maximum hop count of 15
Classful	Classless
No support for VLSM	Supports VLSM networks
No support for discontiguous networks	Supports discontiguous networks

RIPv2, unlike RIPv1, is a classless routing protocol (even though it is configured as classful, like RIPv1), which means that it sends subnet mask information along with the route updates. By sending the subnet mask information with the updates, RIPv2 can support Variable Length Subnet Masks (VLSMs) as well as the summarization of network boundaries. In addition, RIPv2 can support discontiguous networking.

Configuring RIPv2 is pretty straightforward. Here's an example:

```
Lab_C(config)#router rip
Lab_C(config-router)#network 192.168.40.0
Lab_C(config-router)#network 192.168.50.0
Lab_C(config-router)#version 2
```

That's it; just add the command version 2 under the (config-router)# prompt and you are now running RIPv2.

RIPv2, EIGRP and OSPF are classless, which allows them to work in VLSM and discontiguous networks.

Okay—here's one example of a situation when you may actually want to use RIPv2: Let's say you have a new corporation that's been combined with another company, and together they have four branch offices, each with its own network. They have multiple vendor routers, which are connected to the corporate office with serial links, and one Class C address that needs to use VLSM.

Hmmmm…What do we do with this? Well, personally, I'd opt for OSPF, even though Cisco says RIPv2 would be a good solution. And while it's true that if you need a network that "just" works easily, then RIPv2, which is classless and supports VLSM networking, would work in this scenario. But there really is a better way!

Interior Gateway Routing Protocol (IGRP)

Interior Gateway Routing Protocol (IGRP) is a Cisco-proprietary distance-vector routing protocol. This means that to use IGRP in your network, all your routers must be Cisco routers. Cisco created this routing protocol to overcome the problems associated with RIP.

IGRP has a maximum hop count of 255 with a default of 100. This is helpful in larger networks and solves the problem of 15 hops being the maximum possible in a RIP network.

IGRP also uses a different metric than RIP. IGRP uses bandwidth and delay of the line by default as a metric for determining the best route to an internetwork. This is called a *composite metric*. Reliability, load, and maximum transmission unit (MTU) can also be used, although they are not used by default.

The main difference between RIP and IGRP configuration is that when you configure IGRP, you supply the autonomous system number. All routers must use the same number in order to share routing table information.

Table 6.3 shows a list of IGRP characteristics that you won't find in RIP.

TABLE 6.3   IGRP vs. RIP

IGRP	RIP
Can be used in large internetworks	Works best in smaller networks
Uses an autonomous system number for activation	Does not use autonomous system numbers
Gives a full route table update every 90 seconds	Gives full route table update every 30 seconds
Has an administrative distance of 100	Has an administrative distance of 120
Uses bandwidth and delay of the line as metric (lowest composite metric), with a maximum hop count of 255	Uses only hop count to determine the best path to a remote network, with 15 hops being the maximum

In the following sections, we will discuss the IGRP timers and the configuration of IGRP.

IGRP Timers

To control performance, IGRP includes the following timers with default settings:

Update timers   These specify how frequently routing-update messages should be sent. The default is 90 seconds.

Invalid timers   These specify how long a router should wait before declaring a route invalid if it doesn't receive a specific update about it. The default is three times the update period.

Holddown timers   These specify the holddown period. The default is three times the update timer period plus 10 seconds.

Flush timers   These indicate how much time should pass before a route should be flushed from the routing table. The default is seven times the routing update period. If the update timer is 90 seconds by default, then $7 \times 90 = 630$ seconds elapse before a route will be flushed from the route table.

Configuring IGRP Routing

The command used to configure IGRP is the same as the one used to configure RIP routing with one important difference: you use an autonomous system (AS) number. All routers within an autonomous system must use the same AS number or they won't communicate with routing information. Here's how to turn on IGRP routing:

```
Lab_A#config t
Lab_A(config)#router igrp 10
Lab_A(config-router)#network 192.168.10.0
```

Notice that the configuration in the preceding router commands is as simple as in RIP routing except that IGRP uses an AS number. This number advertises only to the specific routers you want to share routing information with.

You absolutely *must* remember that you type a classful network number in when configuring IGRP!

IGRP can load-balance up to six unequal links. RIP networks must have the same hop count to load-balance, whereas IGRP uses bandwidth to determine how to load-balance. To load-balance over unequal-cost links, the `variance` command controls the load balancing between the best metric and the worst acceptable metric.

Configuring IGRP is pretty straightforward and not much different from configuring RIP. You do need to decide on an AS number before you configure your routers. Remember that all routers in your internetwork must use the same AS number if you want them to share routing information.

In the sample internetwork we've been using throughout this chapter, we'll use AS 10 to configure the routers.

Okay, let's configure our internetwork with IGRP routing.

Lab_A

The AS number, as shown in the following router output, can be any number from 1 to 65,535. A router can be a member of as many ASes as you need it to be. Here's the output:

```
Lab_A#config t
Enter configuration commands, one per line. End with CNTL/Z.
Lab_A(config)#router igrp ?
  <1-65535>  Autonomous system number

Lab_A(config)#router igrp 10
Lab_A(config-router)#network 192.168.10.0
Lab_A(config-router)#network 192.168.20.0
Lab_A(config-router)#^Z
Lab_A#
```

The `router igrp` command turns IGRP routing on in the router. As with RIP, you still need to add the network numbers you want to advertise. IGRP uses classful routing, which means that subnet mask information isn't sent along with the routing protocol updates.

Lab_B

To configure the Lab_B router, all you need to do is turn on IGRP routing using AS 10 and then add the network numbers, as shown next:

```
Lab_B#config t
Enter configuration commands, one per line. End with CNTL/Z.
Lab_B(config)#router igrp 10
Lab_B(config-router)#network 192.168.20.0
Lab_B(config-router)#network 192.168.30.0
Lab_B(config-router)#network 192.168.40.0
Lab_B(config-router)#^Z
Lab_B#
```

Lab_C

To configure Lab_C, once again you need to turn on IGRP using AS 10:

```
Lab_C#config t
Enter configuration commands, one per line. End with CNTL/Z.
Lab_C(config)#router igrp 10
```

```
Lab_C(config-router)#network 192.168.40.0
Lab_C(config-router)#network 192.168.50.0
Lab_C(config-router)#^Z
Lab_C#
```

Verifying the IGRP Routing Tables

Once the routers are configured, you need to verify the configuration with the show ip route command.

In all of the following router outputs, notice that the only routes to networks are either directly connected or IGRP-injected routes. Since we didn't turn off RIP, it's still running in the background and taking up both router CPU cycles and bandwidth. What's more, the routing tables will never use a RIP-found route because IGRP has a better administrative distance than RIP does.

The following router output is from the Lab_A router. Notice that all routes are in the routing table:

```
Lab_A#sh ip route
[output cut]
I        192.168.50.0 [100/170420] via 192.168.20.2, Serial0/0
I        192.168.40.0 [100/160260] via 192.168.20.2, Serial0/0
I        192.168.30.0 [100/158360] via 192.168.20.2, Serial0/0
C        192.168.20.0 is directly connected Serial0/0
C        192.168.10.0 is directly connected, FastEthernet0/0
```

The I means IGRP-injected routes. The 100 in [100/160360] is the administrative distance of IGRP. The 160360 is the composite metric. The lower the composite metric, the better the route.

 Remember that the composite metric is calculated by using the bandwidth and delay of the line by default. The delay of the line can also be referred to as the *cumulative interface delay*.

This is Lab_B's routing table:

```
Lab_B#sh ip route
[output cut]
I        192.168.50.0 [100/8576] via 192.168.40.2, 00:01:11, Serial0/1
C        192.168.40.0 is directly connected, Serial0/1
C        192.168.30.0 is directly connected, FastEthernet0/0
C        192.168.20.0 is directly connected, Serial0/0
I        192.168.10.0 [100/158350] via 192.168.20.1, 00:00:36, Serial0/0
Lab_B#
```

And here's Lab_C's routing table:

```
Lab_C#sh ip route
[output cut]
C       192.168.50.0 is directly connected, FastEthernet 0/0
C       192.168.40.0 is directly connected, Serial0/0
I       192.168.30.0 [100/143723] via 192.168.40.1, 00:00:42, Serial0/0
I       192.168.20.0 [100/152365] via 192.168.40.1, 00:00;52, Serial0/0
I       192.168.10.0 [100/158350] via 192.168.20.1, 00:00:36, Serial0/0
Lab_C#
```

 Real World Scenario

If RIP Isn't Good for My Network, Then I Should Use IGRP, Right?

The answer to this question is, well, no, not really. I know I said that RIP isn't exactly what anyone needs running in a large internetwork—or, actually, in any network—but that doesn't mean you should use IGRP instead.

You need to understand how RIPv1, RIPv2, and IGRP work for the CCNA Intro exam as well as for when you find yourself actually working in a production environment. By understanding information about all the various routing protocols, you can make decisions based on facts—on real knowledge of all protocols old and new—instead of just guessing about what's the best fit for the specific business requirements facing you.

But if what I'm telling you is that you really shouldn't use either RIP or IGRP on your internetwork if you can help it; then what should you use? If you have an all-Cisco router environment, the answer is that you should use Enhanced IGRP for sure. It's so much better a routing protocol than IGRP! If you've got a mixed environment of router brands, then you likely should use OSPF. And lucky you—I'm going to cover both EIGRP and OSPF in the next section. After all is said, though, I really can't recommend which protocols you should use in your network because each network truly is different. What I am recommending is that if you do have the option of using EIGRP over IGRP or RIP, use EIGRP. End of story.

Troubleshooting IGRP

Say you've connected two routers together and enabled IGRP, but for some reason they're not sharing routing information—why? See if you can figure this one out by looking at the following two outputs:

```
Lab_B#config t
Lab_B(config)#router igrp 10
```

```
Lab_B(config-router)#network 192.168.20.0
Lab_B(config-router)#network 192.168.30.0

Lab_C#config t
Lab_C(config)#router igrp 20
Lab_C(config-router)#network 192.168.40.0
Lab_C(config-router)#network 192.168.50.0
```

This should be an easy problem to spot. Router Lab_B is configured for IGRP autonomous systems 10 and router Lab_C is configured for autonomous system 20.

Using Both RIP and IGRP

If you have both RIP (either version 1 or 2) and IGRP running in your network, what you're really accomplishing is wasting a bunch of bandwidth, CPU processing, and router memory! There's absolutely no benefit to running more than one routing protocol—period!

Let's use Figure 6.5 as an example of an internetwork with both RIP and IGRP running.

Figure 6.5 shows five routers, all interconnected, and all five routers are running both RIP and IGRP routing protocols. Leaving aside the fact that this is very bad—you shouldn't do it— which path will RouterA use to send packets to RouterE?

RIP (again, remember both versions 1 and 2 perform the same calculations) will see that all links are two hops away and load-balance to routers B, C, and D. As I said, this is called pin-hole congestion, because once RIP sends a packet through the RouterB path, it will send the same amount of data through the RouterC and RouterD paths—in other words, all links are now 56Kbps circuits! RIP definitely stinks!

FIGURE 6.5   Using both RIP and IGRP

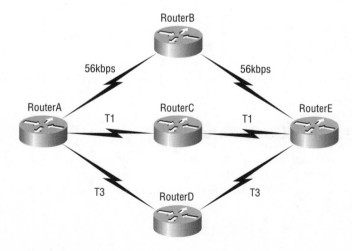

On the other hand, IGRP uses bandwidth and delay of the line, by default, to find the best path to a remote network, which means that IGRP would use only the path through RouterD to send packets to RouterE. Since IGRP can load-balance across unequal paths, you can configure IGRP (as well as EIGRP) to load-balance across the other links, but it won't load-balance by default unless all links are of equal metrics. Since IGRP has a lower administrative distance than RIP, only IGRP would be used by all the routers, and the RIP routes being broadcast across all the links (wasting bandwidth, CPU cycles, and memory) would simply be ignored by all the routers—nice!

 Both IGRP and EIGRP can load-balance across unequal-cost links by using the variance command. By default, they can load-balance across four unequal-cost links, but they can be configured to load-balance across a total of six unequal-cost links. RIP can load-balance across four equal-cost links by default (or what it thinks is equal) but can also be configured to load-balance up to six links.

Verifying Your Configurations

It's important to verify your configurations once you've completed them, or at least once you *think* you've completed them. The following list includes the commands you can use to verify the routed and routing protocols configured on your Cisco routers:

- show ip route
- show protocols
- show ip protocols
- debug ip rip
- debug ip igrp events
- debug ip igrp transactions

The first command was covered in the previous section—I'll go over the others in the following sections.

The *show protocols* Command

The show protocols command is useful because it displays all the routed protocols and the interfaces upon which each protocol is enabled.

The following output shows the IP address of the FastEthernet 0/0, serial 0/0, and serial 0/1 interfaces of the Lab_B router:

```
Lab_B#sh protocol
Global values:
  Internet Protocol routing is enabled
```

```
FastEthernet0 is up, line protocol is up
  Internet address is 192.168.30.1/24
Serial0/0 is up, line protocol is up
  Internet address is 192.168.20.2/24
Serial0/1 is up, line protocol is up
  Internet address is 192.168.40.1/24
Lab_B#
```

If IPX or AppleTalk were configured on the router, those network addresses would've appeared as well, but I don't think we need to worry about seeing those again.

The *show ip protocols* Command

The show ip protocols command shows you the routing protocols that are configured on your router. Looking at the following output, you can see that both RIP and IGRP are still running on the router but that only IGRP appears in the routing table because of its lower administrative distance (AD):

```
Lab_B#sh ip protocols
Routing Protocol is "rip"
  Sending updates every 30 seconds, next due in 6 seconds
  Invalid after 180 seconds, hold down 180, flushed after
  240
  Outgoing update filter list for all interfaces is
  Incoming update filter list for all interfaces is
  Redistributing: rip
  Default version control: send version 1, receive any
  version
    Interface        Send  Recv  Key-chain
    FastEthernet0    1     1 2
    Serial0/0        1     1 2
    Serial0/1        1     1 2
  Routing for Networks:
    192.168.10.0
    192.168.20.0
    192.168.30.0
  Routing Information Sources:
    Gateway          Distance      Last Update
    192.168.40.2         120       00:00:21
    192.168.20.1         120       00:00:23
  Distance: (default is 120)
[output continued]
```

The `show ip protocols` command also displays the timers used in the routing protocol. Notice in the preceding output that RIP is sending updates every 30 seconds, which is the default. Notice farther down that RIP is routing for all directly connected networks and the two neighbors it found are 192.168.40.2 and 192.168.20.1. The last entry is the default AD for RIP (120).

The following output shows the IGRP routing information (the default update timer is 90 seconds, and the administrative distance is 100):

```
Routing Protocol is "igrp 10"
  Sending updates every 90 seconds, next due in 42 seconds
  Invalid after 270 seconds, hold down 280, flushed after 630
  Outgoing update filter list for all interfaces is
  Incoming update filter list for all interfaces is
  Default networks flagged in outgoing updates
  Default networks accepted from incoming updates
  IGRP metric weight K1=1, K2=0, K3=1, K4=0, K5=0
  IGRP maximum hopcount 100
  IGRP maximum metric variance 1
  Redistributing: eigrp 10, igrp 10
  Routing for Networks:
    192.168.10.0
    192.168.20.0
    192.168.30.0
  Routing Information Sources:
    Gateway         Distance      Last Update
    192.168.40.2       100        00:00:47
    192.168.20.1       100        00:01:18
  Distance: (default is 100)
```

The information included in the `show ip protocols` command includes the AS, routing timers, networks being advertised, neighbors, and AD (100).

The *debug ip rip* Command

The `debug ip rip` command sends routing updates as they are sent and received on the router to the console session. If you are telnetted into the router, you'll need to use the `terminal monitor` command to be able to receive the output from the debug commands.

We can see in this output that RIP is both sent and received on serial 0/0 and serial 0/1 interfaces (the metric is the hop count):

```
Lab_B#debug ip rip
RIP protocol debugging is on
```

```
Lab_B#
07:12:56: RIP: received v1 update from 192.168.40.2 on Serial0/1
07:12:56:      192.168.50.0 in 1 hops
07:12:56: RIP: received v1 update from 192.168.20.1 on Serial0/0
07:12:56:      192.168.10.0 in 1 hops
```

In the preceding debug output, notice the route updates received on the Lab_B serial 0/0 and serial 0/1 interfaces. These are from routers Lab_A and Lab_C, respectively. In the following output, we can see that we are using RIPv1 because the update is sent as a full-on broadcast (255.255.255.255), whereas RIPv2 would have used the multicast address 224.0.0.9.

```
07:12:58: RIP: sending v1 update to 255.255.255.255 via
  FastEthernet0/0 (192.168.30.1)
07:12:58:      subnet  192.168.50.0, metric 1
07:12:58:      subnet  192.168.40.0, metric 1
07:12:58:      subnet  192.168.20.0, metric 1
07:12:58:      subnet  192.168.10.0, metric 1
07:12:58: RIP: sending v1 update to 255.255.255.255 via
  Serial0/0 (192.168.20.2)
07:12:58:      subnet  192.168,50.0, metric 1
07:12:58:      subnet  192.168.40.0, metric 1
07:12:58:      subnet  192.168.30.0, metric 1
07:12:58: RIP: sending v1 update to 255.255.255.255 via
  Serial0/1 (192.168.40.1)
07:12:58:      subnet  192.168.30.0, metric 1
07:12:58:      subnet  192.168.20.0, metric 1
07:12:58:      subnet  192.168.10.0, metric 1
```

 If the metric of a route shows 16, this is a route poison and the route being advertised is unreachable.

To turn off debugging, use the undebug all or the no debug all command. Here is an example of using the undebug all command:

```
Lab_B#undebug all
All possible debugging has been turned off
Lab_B#
```

The *debug ip igrp* Command

With the debug ip igrp command, there are two options, events and transactions, as shown in this output:

```
Lab_B#debug ip igrp ?
  events       IGRP protocol events
  transactions  IGRP protocol transactions
```

The difference between these commands is explained in the following sections.

The *debug ip igrp events* Command

The debug ip igrp events command is a summary of the IGRP routing information that is running on the network. The following router output shows the source and destination of each update as well as the number of routers in each update:

```
Lab_B#debug ip igrp events
IGRP event debugging is on
07:13:50: IGRP: received request from 192.168.40.2 on
  Serial0/1
07:13:50: IGRP: sending update to 192.168.40.2 via Serial1
  (192.168.40.1)
07:13:51: IGRP: Update contains 3 interior, 0 system, and
  0 exterior routes.
07:13:51: IGRP: Total routes in update: 3
07:13:51: IGRP: received update from 192.168.40.2 on
  Serial0/1
07:13:51: IGRP: Update contains 1 interior, 0 system, and
  0 exterior routes.
07:13:51: IGRP: Total routes in update: 1
```

Information about individual routes isn't something you'll get with this command.

You can turn the command off with the undebug ip igrp events or undebug all (or un all for short) command:

```
Lab_B#un all
All possible debugging has been turned off
```

The *debug ip igrp transactions* Command

The debug ip igrp transactions command shows message requests from neighbor routers asking for an update and the broadcasts sent from your router toward that neighbor router.

In the following output, a request was received from a neighbor router with an interface IP address of 192.168.40.2 to serial 0/1 of router Lab_B, which responded with an update packet:

```
Lab_B#debug ip igrp transactions
IGRP protocol debugging is on
07:14:05: IGRP: received request from 192.168.40.2 on
  Serial1
07:14:05: IGRP: sending update to 192.168.40.2 via Serial1
  (192.168.40.1)
07:14:05:       subnet 192.168.30.0, metric=1100
07:14:05:       subnet 192.168.20.0, metric=158250
07:14:05:       subnet 192.168.10.0, metric=158350
07:14:06: IGRP: received update from 192.168.40.2 on
  Serial1
07:14:06:       subnet 192.168.50.0, metric 8576 (neighbor
  1100)
```

You can turn off the command with the undebug all command:

```
Lab_B#un all
All possible debugging has been turned off
```

Summary

After we finished with static routing in Chapter 5, we turned our attention to dynamic routing where we discussed RIP, RIPv2 and IGRP. We even had a sentence or two regarding EIGRP and OSPF. Once we understood how dynamic routing creates and maintains routing tables, I demonstrated the configuration of RIP, IGRP and RIPv2.

After we had each routing protocol running, we discussed how to verify the routing protocols by using the show ip route, show ip protocols, and especially the debugging commands used with RIP and IGRP.

So now you've got the goods for your IP Routing studies—so eat it all up, and you're set!

Exam Essentials

Be able to configure RIP in a classful manner. By taking a look at a router's configuration, you need to be able to determine the class network address and configure the networks under RIP.

Understand the debug ip rip command The command debug ip rip displays rip updates as they are sent and received on a router

Understand the difference between classful and classless routing   Classful routing means that every node on the network has the same subnet mask. Classless routing means that you can have variable length subnet masks (VLSMs).

Remember which routing protocols are classful and which routing protocols are classless   RIPv1 and IGRP are classful. RIPv2, EIGRP and OSPF are classless routing protocols.

Written Lab 6

Answer the following questions:

1.   Which routing protocols are classless and which routing protocols are classful?

2.   What is the administrative distance of RIP?

3.   You are configuring the subnets 192.168.10.32/27, 192.168.10.64/27 and 192.168.10.128/32 using RIPv1. What will your configuration look like?

4.   What command will display the routing table used on a router?

5.   Write the commands used to turn RIP routing on in a router and advertise network 10.10.10.0/24.

6.   Write the commands to stop a router from propagating RIP information out serial 1.

7.   Write the commands to create an AS 10 with IGRP in your 172.16.0.0 network.

8.   What is the difference between RIPv1 and RIPv2?

9.   What network number do you type to configure RIP when a router is directly connected to subnets 172.16.10.0/24, 172.16.35.0/24, 192.168.10.16/28, and 192.168.10.32/28?

10.   What command is used to send RIP routing updates as the updates are sent and received on the router to the console session?

(The answers to Written Lab 6 can be found following the answers to the review questions for this chapter.)

Hands-on Labs

In the following hands-on labs, you will configure a network with three 2501 routers and one 2621 router. These labs were meant for use with real Cisco routers. If you are using Router-Sim, then please use the labs found within that software.

The following labs will be covered:

Lab 6.1: Dynamic Routing with RIP

Lab 6.2: Dynamic Routing with IGRP

Table 6.7 shows our IP addresses for each router (each interface uses a /24 mask).

TABLE 6.4 Our IP Addresses

Router	Interface	IP address
2621	F0/0	172.16.10.1
2501A	E0	172.16.10.2
2501A	S0	172.16.20.1
2501B	E0	172.16.30.1
2501B	S0	172.16.20.2
2501B	S1	172.16.40.1
2501C	S0	172.16.40.2
2501C	E0	172.16.50.1

Figure 6.8 will be used to configure all routers.

FIGURE 6.6 Hands-on lab internetwork

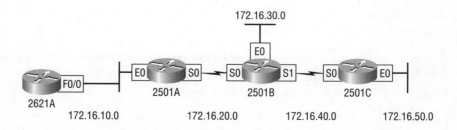

Hands-on Lab 6.1: Dynamic Routing with RIP

In this lab, we will use the dynamic routing protocol RIP instead of static and default routing.

1. Remove any static routes or default routes configured on your routers by using the no ip route command. For example, here is how you would remove the static routes on the 2501A router:

```
2501A#config t
2501A(config)#no ip route 172.16.30.0 255.255.255.0
   172.16.20.2
2501A(config)#no ip route 172.16.40.0 255.255.255.0
   172.16.20.2
2501A(config)#no ip route 172.16.50.0 255.255.255.0
   172.16.20.2
```

   Do the same thing for Routers 2501B and 2501C as well as the 2621A router. Type **sh run** and press Enter on each router to verify that all static and default routes are cleared.

2. After your static and default routes are clear, go into configuration mode on Router 2501A by typing **config t**.

3. Tell your router to use RIP routing by typing **router rip** and pressing Enter, as shown here:

```
config t
router rip
```

4. Add the network number you want to advertise by typing **network 172.16.0.0** and pressing Enter.

5. Press Ctrl+Z to get out of configuration mode.

6. Go to Routers 2501B and 2501C as well as the 2621A router and type the same commands, as shown here:

```
Config t
Router rip
network 172.16.0.0
```

7. Verify that RIP is running at each router by typing the following commands at each router:

```
show ip protocols
show ip route
show running-config or show run
```

8. Save your configurations by typing **copy run start** or **copy running-config startup-config** and pressing Enter at each router.

9. Verify the network by pinging all remote networks and hosts.

Hands-on Lab 6.2: Dynamic Routing with IGRP

In this lab, you will run the IGRP routing protocol simultaneously with RIP routing.

1. Log into your routers and go into privileged mode by typing **en** or **enable**.

2. Keep RIP running on your routers and verify that it is running on each router. If you want to remove RIP, you can use the `no router rip` global configuration command to remove it from each router. For example:

```
config t
no router rip
```

3. From the configuration mode on Router 2501A, type **router igrp ?**.

4. Notice that it asks for an autonomous system number. This is used to allow only routers with the same AS number to communicate. Type **10** and press Enter. Your router can be configured to be part of as many different AS as necessary.

5. At the config-router prompt, type **network 172.16.0.0**. Notice that we add the classful network boundary to advertise rather than the subnet numbers.

6. Press Ctrl+Z to get out of configuration mode.

7. Go to Routers 2501B and 2501C as well as the 2621A router and type the commands shown here:

```
2501B(config)#router igrp 10
2501B(config-router)#network 172.16.0.0
```

8. Verify that IGRP is running by typing the following command at each router:

```
show ip protocols
```

Notice that this shows you your RIP and IGRP routing protocols and the update timers.

Then type this command:

```
sh ip route
```

This should let you see all five subnets: 10, 20, 30, 40, and 50. Some will be directly connected, and some will be I routes, which are IGRP-injected routes. RIP is still running, but if you look at the routing table, you'll notice the network entry has the following: [100/23456]. The first number (100) is the trustworthiness rating (administrative distance). Since RIP's default trustworthiness rating is 120, the IGRP route is used before a RIP route is used. The second number is the metric, or weight, of the route that is used to determine the best path to a network.

Next, type this command:

```
show running-config
```

This lets you see that RIP and IGRP are configured.

9. To save your configurations, type **copy running-config startup-config** or **copy run start** and press Enter at each router.

10. Verify the network by pinging all routers, switches, and hosts.

Review Questions

1. What command is used to stop RIP routing updates from exiting out an interface but still receive RIP route updates?

   A. Router(config-if)#**no routing**

   B. Router(config-if)#**passive-interface**

   C. Router(config-router)#**passive-interface s0**

   D. Router(config-router)#**no routing updates**

2. Which of the following is true regarding the following output? (Choose two.)

   ```
   04:06:16: RIP: received v1 update from 192.168.40.2 on Serial0/1
   04:06:16:      192.168.50.0 in 16 hops (inaccessible)
   04:06:40: RIP: sending v1 update to 255.255.255.255 via
       FastEthernet0/0 (192.168.30.1)
   04:06:40: RIP: build update entries
   04:06:40:        network 192.168.20.0 metric 1
   04:06:40:        network 192.168.40.0 metric 1
   04:06:40:        network 192.168.50.0 metric 2
   04:06:40: RIP: sending v1 update to 255.255.255.255 via
       Serial0/1 (192.168.40.1)
   ```

   A. There are three interfaces on the router participating in this update.

   B. A ping to 192.168.50.1 will be successful.

   C. There are at least two routers exchanging information.

   D. A ping to 192.168.40.2 will be successful.

3. Which command will display the routing protocol configuration on your router?

   A. show routing

   B. show ip route

   C. sh ip protocols

   D. show protocols

4. Which command will display the routed protocol configuration on your router?

   A. show routing

   B. show ip route

   C. sh ip protocols

   D. show protocols

5. Which command displays RIP routing updates?

   A. show ip route

   B. debug ip rip

   C. show protocols

   D. debug ip route

6. A network administrator views the output from the show ip route command. A network that is advertised by both RIP and IGRP appears in the routing table flagged as an IGRP route. Why is the RIP route to this network not used in the routing table?

   A. IGRP has a faster update timer.

   B. IGRP has a lower administrative distance.

   C. RIP as a higher metric value for that route.

   D. The IGRP route has fewer hops.

   E. The RIP path has a routing loop.

7. You type **debug ip rip** on your router console and see that 172.16.10.0 is being advertised with a metric of 16. What does this mean?

   A. The route is 16 hops away.

   B. The route has a delay of 16 microseconds.

   C. The route is inaccessible.

   D. The route is queued at 16 messages a second.

8. IGRP uses which of the following as default parameters for finding the best path to a remote network? (Choose two.)

   A. Hop count

   B. MTU

   C. Cumulative interface delay

   D. STP

   E. Path bandwidth value

9. The corporate router receives an IP packet with a source IP address of 192.168.214.20 and a destination address of 192.168.22.3. By looking at the output from the Corporate router, what will the router do with this packet?

   Corp**sh ip route**

   [output cut]
   ```
   R    192.168.215.0 [120/2] via 192.168.20.2, 00:00:23, Serial0/0
   R    192.168.115.0 [120/1] via 192.168.20.2, 00:00:23, Serial0/0
   R    192.168.30.0 [120/1] via 192.168.20.2, 00:00:23, Serial0/0
   C    192.168.20.0 is directly connected, Serial0/0
   C    192.168.214.0 is directly connected, FastEthernet0/0
   ```

   A. The packets will be discarded.

   B. The packets will be routed out the S0/0 interface.

   C. The router will broadcast looking for the destination.

   D. The packets will be routed out the Fa0/0 interface.

10. If your routing table has a static, a RIP, and an IGRP route to the same network, which route will be used to route packets by default?

    A. Any available route

    B. RIP route

    C. Static route

    D. IGRP route

    E. They will all load-balance.

11. You have the following routing table. Which of the following networks will not be placed in the neighbor routing table?

    ```
    R    192.168.30.0/24 [120/1] via 192.168.40.1, 00:00:12, Serial0
    C    192.168.40.0/24 is directly connected, Serial0
         172.16.0.0/24 is subnetted, 1 subnets
    C       172.16.30.0 is directly connected, Loopback0
    R    192.168.20.0/24 [120/1] via 192.168.40.1, 00:00:12, Serial0
    R    10.0.0.0/8 [120/15] via 192.168.40.1, 00:00:07, Serial0
    C    192.168.50.0/24 is directly connected, Ethernet0
    ```

    A. 172.16.30.0

    B. 192.168.30.0

    C. 10.0.0.0

    D. All of them will be placed in the neighbors routing table.

12. Two connected routers are connected with RIP routing. What will be the result when a router receives a routing update that contains a higher-cost path to a network already in its routing table?

    A. The updated information will be added to the existing routing table.

    B. The update will be ignored and no further action will occur.

    C. The update information will replace the existing routing table entry.

    D. The existing routing table entry will be deleted from the routing table and all routers will exchange touting updates to reach convergence.

13. What is the administrative distance of RIPv2?

    A. 90

    B. 100

    C. 110

    D. 120

14. What is the administrative distance of IGRP?

    A. 90

    B. 100

    C. 110

    D. 120

15. Which of the following protocols support VLSM, summarization and discontiguous networking? (Choose three.)

   A. RIPv1

   B. IGRP

   C. EIGRP

   D. OSPF

   E. IS-IS

   F. RIPv2

16. Which command will show you the table that IP will use to forward packets to a remote network?

   A. show path

   B. show ip path

   C. show route

   D. show ip route

17. You need to configure RIP and you have the following directly connected networks: 192.168.10.0/24, 172.16.10.0/24 and 10.3.5.0/24. Which of the following would configure RIP routing on your router?

   A. router rip, network 192.168.10.0, network 172.16.10.0, network 10.3.5.0

   B. router rip, network 192.168.10.0, network 172.16.0.0, network 10.3.0.0

   C. router rip, network 192.168.10.0, network 172.16.0.0, network 10.0.0.0

   D. router rip, network 192.168.0.0, network 172.16.10.0, network 10.0.0.0

18. What is the administrative distance of RIPv1?

   A. 90

   B. 100

   C. 110

   D. 120

19. What routing protocols should you use if you have multiple vendors and need VLSM support?

   A. RIP

   B. IGRP

   C. RIPv2

   D. EIGRP

   E. OSPF

20. What is the default administrative distance of static routes?

   A. 90

   B. 100

   C. 110

   D. 120

   E. 0

   F. 1

Answers to Review Questions

1. C. The (config-router)# passive-interface command stops updates from being sent out an interface, but route updates are still received.

2. C, D. The route to 192.168.50.0 is unreachable and only interfaces s0/1 and FastEthernet 0/0 are participating in the RIP update. Since a route update was received, at least two routers are participating in the RIP routing process.

3. C. The show ip protocols command will display all configured routing protocol information on a router.

4. D. The show protocols command will display all configured routed protocols for each interface on a router.

5. B. Debug ip rip is used to show the Internet Protocol (IP) Routing Information Protocol (RIP) updates being sent and received on the router.

6. B. RIP has an administrative distance (AD) of 120, and IGRP has an administrative distance of 100, so the router will discard any route with a higher AD then 100.

7. C. You cannot have 16 hops on a RIP network by default. If you receive a route advertised with a metric of 16, this means it is inaccessible.

8. C, E. IGRP uses bandwidth and delay of the line, by default, to determine the best path to a remote network. Delay of the line can sometimes be called the cumulative interface delay.

9. A. Since the routing table shows no route to network 192.168.22.0 network, the router will discard the packet and send an ICMP Destination Unreachable message out interface FastEthernet0/0, which is the source LAN where the packet originated from.

10. C. Static routes have an administrative distance of one (1) by default. Unless you change this, a static route will always be used over any other found route. IGRP has an administrative distance of 100, and RIP has an administrative distance of 120, by default.

11. C. The network 10.0.0.0 cannot be placed in the next router's routing table because it already is at 15 hops. One more hop would make the route 16 hops, and that is not valid in RIP networking.

12. B. When a routing update is received on a router, the router first checks the administrative distance (AD) and always chooses the route with the lowest AD. However, if two routes are received and they both have the same AD, then the router will choose the one route with the lowest metrics, or in RIP's case, hop count.

13. D. The administrative distance (AD) is a very important parameter in a routing protocol. The lower the AD, the more trusted the route. If you have IGRP and OSPF running, by default IGRP routes would be placed in the routing table because it has a lower AD of 100. OSPF has an AD of 110. RIPv1 and RIPv2 both have an administrative distance of 120 and EIGRP is the lowest at 90.

14. B. The administrative distance (AD) is a very important parameter in a routing protocol. The lower the AD, the more trusted the route. If you have IGRP and OSPF running, by default IGRP routes would be placed in the routing table because it has a lower AD of 100. OSPF has an AD of 110. RIPv1 and RIPv2 both have an administrative distance of 120 and EIGRP is the lowest at 90.

15. C, D, F. RIPv1 and IGRP are true distance-vector routing protocols and can't do much, really—except build and maintain routing tables and use a lot of bandwidth! RIPv2, EIGRP, and OSPF build and maintain routing tables, but they also provide classless routing, which allows for VLSM, summarization, and discontiguous networking.

16. D. The command `show ip route` will show you the routing table the IP will use to forward packets to a destination network.

17. C. Remember that RIP is configured with classful network addressing (as well as IGRP and EIGRP). These means all hosts bits off. You would not specify a specific subnet number under a classful configuration.

18. D. The administrative distance (AD) is a very important parameter in a routing protocol. The lower the AD, the more trusted the route. If you have IGRP and OSPF running, by default IGRP routes would be placed in the routing table because it has a lower AD of 100. OSPF has an AD of 110. RIPv1 and RIPv2 both have an administrative distance of 120 and EIGRP is the lowest at 90.

19. C, E. RIP and IGRP are classful and cannot support VLSM networks. Since you have multiple vendors, you cannot use EIGRP, so the answers are RIPv2 and OSPF.

20. F. The administrative distance (AD) is a very important parameter in a routing protocol. The lower the AD, the more trusted the route. If you have IGRP and OSPF running, by default IGRP routes would be placed in the routing table because it has a lower AD of 100. OSPF has an AD of 110. RIPv1 and RIPv2 both have an administrative distance of 120 and EIGRP is the lowest at 90. Directly connected routes have an administrative distance of 0 and static routes have a default administrative distance of 1.

Answers to Written Lab 6

1. RIPv1 and IGRP are classful and RIPv2, EIGRP and OSPF are classless.

2. 120

3. `router rip, network 192.168.10.0`

4. `show ip route`

5. `router rip, network 10.0.0.0`

6. `router rip, passive-interface serial 1`

7. `router igrp 10, network 172.16.0.0`

8. RIPv1 is classful; RIPv2 is classless and uses multicasting instead of broadcasts like RIPv1.

9. `router rip, network 172.16.0.0, network 192.168.10.0`

10. `debug ip rip`

Chapter

7

Layer 2 Switching

THE CCNA INTRO EXAM TOPICS COVERED IN THIS CHAPTER INCLUDE THE FOLLOWING:

✓ **Technology**

　▪ Describe the principles and practice of switching in an Ethernet network

When Cisco discusses switching, they're talking about layer 2 switching unless they say otherwise. Layer 2 switching is the process of using the hardware address of devices on a LAN to segment a network. Since you've got the basic ideas down, I'm now going to focus on the particulars of layer 2 switching and nail down how it works.

Okay, you know that switching breaks up large collision domains into smaller ones and that a collision domain is a network segment with two or more devices sharing the same bandwidth. A hub network is a typical example of this type of technology. But since each port on a switch is actually its own collision domain, you can make a much better Ethernet LAN network just by replacing your hubs with switches!

Switches truly have changed the way networks are designed and implemented. If a pure switched design is properly implemented, it absolutely will result in a clean, cost-effective, and resilient internetwork. In this chapter, we'll survey and compare how networks were designed before and after switching technologies were introduced.

Routing protocols (such as RIP, which you learned about in Chapter 6, "Dynamic Routing Protocols") have processes for stopping network loops from occurring at the Network layer. However, if you have redundant physical links between your switches, routing protocols won't do a thing to stop loops from occurring at the Data Link layer. That's exactly the reason Spanning Tree Protocol was developed—to put a stop to loops in a layer 2 switched internetwork. The essentials of this vital protocol, as well as how it works within a switched network, are also important subjects this chapter will cover thoroughly.

When frames traverse a switched network, the LAN switch type determines how a frame is forwarded to an exit port on a switch. There are three different types of LAN switch methods, and each one handles frames differently as they are forwarded through a switch. This chapter will finish with the three LAN switch methods used by Cisco switches.

Before Layer 2 Switching

Let's go back in time a bit and take a look at the condition of networks before switches and how switches have helped segment the corporate LAN. Before LAN switching, the typical network design looked like the network in Figure 7.1.

The design in Figure 7.1 was called a collapsed backbone because all hosts would need to go to the corporate backbone to reach any network services—both LAN and mainframe.

FIGURE 7.1   Before switching

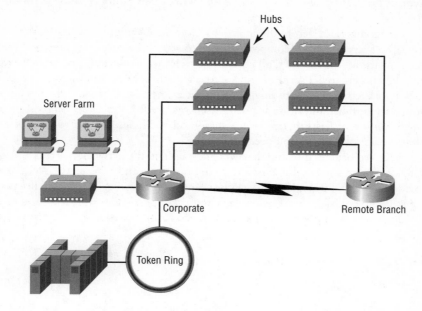

Going back even further, before networks like the one shown in Figure 7.1 had physical segmentation devices such as routers and hubs, there was the mainframe network. This network included the mainframe (IBM, Honeywell, Sperry, DEC, etc.), controllers, and dumb terminals that connected into the controller. Any remote sites were connected to the mainframe with bridges.

And then the PC began its rise to stardom and the mainframe was connected to the Ethernet or to a Token Ring LAN where the servers were installed. These servers were usually OS/2 or LAN Manager because this was "pre-NT." Each floor of a building ran either coax or twisted-pair wiring to the corporate backbone and was then connected to a router. PCs ran an emulating software program that allowed them to connect to the mainframe services, giving those PCs the ability to access services from the mainframe and LAN simultaneously. Eventually the PC became robust enough to allow application developers to port applications more effectively than they could ever before—an advance that markedly reduced networking prices and enabled businesses to grow at a much faster rate.

When Novell became more popular in the late 1980s and early 1990s, OS/2 and LAN Manager servers were by and large replaced with NetWare servers. This made the Ethernet network even more popular, because that's what Novell 3.x servers used to communicate with client/server software.

So that's the story about how the network in Figure 7.1 came into being. There was only one problem—the corporate backbone grew and grew, and as it grew, network services became slower. A big reason for this was that, at the same time this huge burst in growth was taking place, LAN services needed even faster service and the network was becoming totally saturated. Everyone was dumping the Macs and dumb terminals used for the mainframe service in favor of those slick new PCs so they could more easily connect to the corporate backbone and network services.

All this was taking place before the Internet's momentous popularity (Al Gore was still inventing it?), so everyone in the company needed to access the corporate network's services. Why? Because without the Internet, all network services were internal—exclusive to the company network. This created a screaming need to segment that one humongous and plodding corporate network, connected with sluggish old routers. At first, Cisco just created faster routers (no doubt about that), but more segmentation was needed, especially on the Ethernet LANs. The invention of FastEthernet was a very good and helpful thing, too, but it didn't address that network segmentation need at all.

But devices called bridges did, and they were first used in the network to break up collision domains. Bridges were sorely limited by the amount of ports and other network services they could provide, and that's when layer 2 switches came to the rescue. These switches saved the day by breaking up collision domains on each and every port—like a bridge—and switches could provide hundreds of ports! This early, switched LAN looked like the network pictured in Figure 7.2.

FIGURE 7.2   The first switched LAN

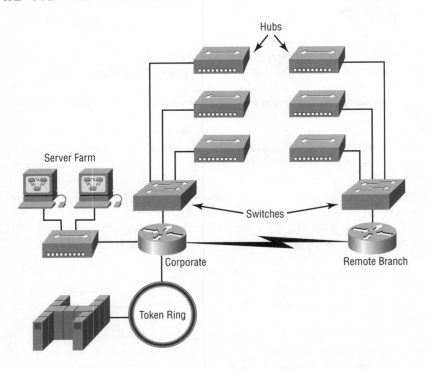

Each hub was placed into a switch port, an innovation that vastly improved the network. Now, instead of each building being crammed into the same collision domain, each hub became its own separate collision domain. But there was a catch—switch ports were still very new, hence unbelievably expensive. Because of that, simply adding a switch into each floor of the building just wasn't going to happen—at least, not yet. Thanks to whomever you choose to thank for these things, the price has dropped dramatically, so now having every one of your users plugged into a switch port is both good and feasible.

So there it is—if you're going to create a network design and implement it, including switching services is a must. A typical contemporary network design would look something like Figure 7.3, a complete switched network design and implementation.

FIGURE 7.3   The typical switched network design

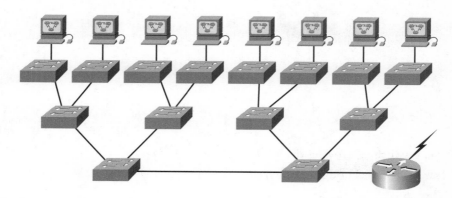

"But I still see a router in there," you say! Yes, it's not a mirage—there *is* a router in there. But its job has changed. Instead of performing physical segmentation, it now creates and handles logical segmentation. Those logical segments are called VLANs, and they are covered thoroughly in the Sybex CCNA Study Guide, but is beyond the scope of the CCNA INTRO objectives.

Switching Services

Unlike bridges that use software to create and manage a filter table, switches use application-specific integrated circuits (ASICs) to build and maintain their filter tables. But it's still okay to think of a layer 2 switch as a multiport bridge because their basic reason for being is the same: to break up collision domains.

Layer 2 switches and bridges are faster than routers because they don't take up time looking at the Network layer header information. Instead, they look at the frame's hardware addresses before deciding to either forward the frame or drop it.

Switches create private dedicated collision domains and provide independent bandwidth on each port, unlike hubs. Figure 7.4 shows five hosts connected to a switch—all running 10Mbps half-duplex to the server. Unlike a hub, each host has 10Mbps dedicated communication to the server.

FIGURE 7.4   Switches create private domains.

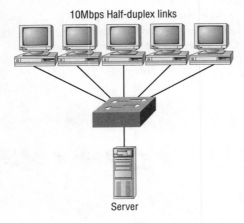

10Mbps Half-duplex links

Server

Layer 2 switching provides the following:

- Hardware-based bridging (ASIC)
- Wire speed
- Low latency
- Low cost

What makes layer 2 switching so efficient is that no modification to the data packet takes place. The device only reads the frame encapsulating the packet, which makes the switching process considerably faster and less error-prone than routing processes are.

And if you use layer 2 switching for both workgroup connectivity and network segmentation (breaking up collision domains), you can create a flatter network design with more network segments than you can with traditional routed networks.

Plus, layer 2 switching increases bandwidth for each user because, again, each connection (interface) into the switch is its own collision domain. This feature makes it possible for you to connect multiple devices to each interface.

In the following sections, I will dive deeper into the layer 2 switching technology.

Limitations of Layer 2 Switching

Since we commonly stick layer 2 switching into the same category as bridged networks, we also tend to think it has the same hang-ups and issues that bridged networks do. Keep in mind that bridges are good and helpful things if we design the network correctly, keeping their features as well as their limitations in mind. And to design well with bridges, these are the two most important considerations:

- We absolutely must break up the collision domains correctly.

- The right way to create a functional bridged network is to make sure that its users spend 80 percent of their time on the local segment.

Bridged networks break up collision domains, but remember, that network is still one large broadcast domain. Neither layer 2 switches nor bridges break up broadcast domains by default—something that not only limits your network's size and growth potential, but can also reduce its overall performance.

Broadcasts and multicasts, along with the slow convergence time of spanning trees, can give you some major grief as your network grows. These are the big reasons why layer 2 switches and bridges cannot completely replace routers (layer 3 devices) in the internetwork.

Bridging vs. LAN Switching

It's true—layer 2 switches really are pretty much just bridges that give us a lot more ports, but there are some important differences you should always keep in mind:

- Bridges are software based, while switches are hardware based because they use ASIC chips to help make filtering decisions.

- A switch can be viewed as a multiport bridge.

- Bridges can only have one spanning-tree instance per bridge, while switches can have many. (I'm going to tell you all about spanning trees in a bit.)

- Switches have a higher number of ports than most bridges.

- Both bridges and switches forward layer 2 broadcasts.

- Bridges and switches learn MAC addresses by examining the source address of each frame received.

- Both bridges and switches make forwarding decisions based on layer 2 addresses.

Three Switch Functions at Layer 2

There are three distinct functions of layer 2 switching (you need to remember these!): *address learning*, *forward/filter decisions*, and *loop avoidance*.

Address learning   Layer 2 switches and bridges remember the source hardware address of each frame received on an interface, and they enter this information into a MAC database called a forward/filter table.

Forward/filter decisions   When a frame is received on an interface, the switch looks at the destination hardware address and finds the exit interface in the MAC database. The frame is only forwarded out the specified destination port.

Loop avoidance   If multiple connections between switches are created for redundancy purposes, network loops can occur. Spanning Tree Protocol (STP) is used to stop network loops while still permitting redundancy.

I'm going to talk about address learning, forward/filtering decisions, and loop avoidance in detail in the next sections.

Address Learning

When a switch is first powered on, the MAC forward/filter table is empty, as shown in Figure 7.5.

FIGURE 7.5   Empty forward/filter table on a switch

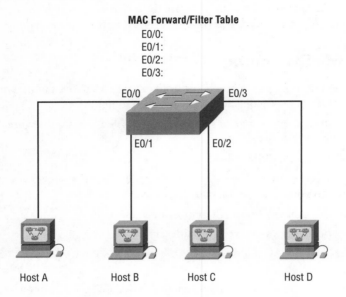

When a device transmits and an interface receives a frame, the switch places the frame's source address in the MAC forward/filter table, allowing it to remember which interface the sending device is located on. The switch then has no choice but to flood the network with this frame out of every port except the source port because it has no idea where the destination device is actually located.

If a device answers this flooded frame and sends a frame back, then the switch will take the source address from that frame and place that MAC address in its database as well, associating this address with the interface that received the frame. Since the switch now has both of the relevant MAC addresses in its filtering table, the two devices can now make a point-to-point connection. The switch doesn't need to flood the frame as it did the first time, because now the frames can and will be forwarded only between the two devices. This is exactly the thing that makes layer 2 switches better than hubs. In a hub network, all frames are forwarded out all ports every time—no matter what! Figure 7.6 shows the processes involved in building a MAC database.

FIGURE 7.6   How switches learn hosts' locations

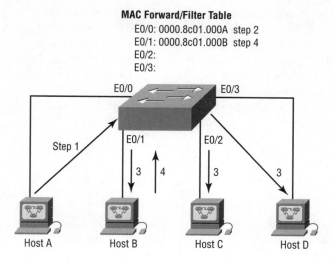

In this figure, you can see four hosts attached to a switch. When the switch is powered on, it has nothing in its MAC address forward/filter table, just as in Figure 7.5. But when the hosts start communicating, the switch places the source hardware address of each frame in the table along with the port that the frame's address corresponds to.

Let me give you an example of how a forward/filter table is populated:

1. Host A sends a frame to Host B. Host A's MAC address is 0000.8c01.000A; Host B's MAC address is 0000.8c01.000B.

2. The switch receives the frame on the E0/0 interface and places the source address in the MAC address table.

3. Since the destination address is not in the MAC database, the frame is forwarded out all interfaces—except the source port.

4. Host B receives the frame and responds to Host A. The switch receives this frame on interface E0/1 and places the source hardware address in the MAC database.

5. Host A and Host B can now make a point-to-point connection and only the two devices will receive the frames. Hosts C and D will not see the frames, nor are their MAC addresses found in the database because they haven't yet sent a frame to the switch.

If Host A and Host B don't communicate to the switch again within a certain amount of time, the switch will flush their entries from the database to keep it as current as possible.

Forward/Filter Decisions

When a frame arrives at a switch interface, the destination hardware address is compared to the forward/filter MAC database. If the destination hardware address is known and listed in the database, the frame is only sent out the correct exit interface. The switch doesn't transmit the frame out any interface except for the destination interface. This preserves bandwidth on the other network segments and is called *frame filtering*.

But if the destination hardware address is not listed in the MAC database, then the frame is flooded out all active interfaces except the interface the frame was received on. If a device answers the flooded frame, the MAC database is updated with the device's location (interface).

If a host or server sends a broadcast on the LAN, the switch will flood the frame out all active ports except the source port by default. Remember, the switch creates smaller collision domains, but it's still one large broadcast domain by default.

In Figure 7.7, Host A sends a data frame to Host D. What will the switch do when it receives the frame from Host A?

FIGURE 7.7   Forward/filter table

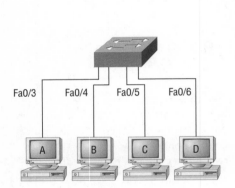

```
Switch#sh mac address-table
Vlan    Mac Address        Ports
----    -----------        -----
   1    0005.dccb.d74b     Fa0/4
   1    000a.f467.9e80     Fa0/5
   1    000a.f467.9e8b     Fa0/6
```

Since Host A's MAC address is not in the forward/filter table, the switch will add the source address and port to the MAC address table and then forward the frame to Host D. If Host D's MAC address was not in the forward/filter table, the switch would have flooded the frame out all ports except for port Fa0/3.

Now let's take a look at the output of a show mac address-table:

```
Switch#sh mac address-table
Vlan    Mac Address        Type       Ports
----    -----------        --------   -----
   1    0005.dccb.d74b     DYNAMIC    Fa0/1
   1    000a.f467.9e80     DYNAMIC    Fa0/3
   1    000a.f467.9e8b     DYNAMIC    Fa0/4
   1    000a.f467.9e8c     DYNAMIC    Fa0/3
   1    0010.7b7f.c2b0     DYNAMIC    Fa0/3
   1    0030.80dc.460b     DYNAMIC    Fa0/3
   1    0030.9492.a5dd     DYNAMIC    Fa0/1
   1    00d0.58ad.05f4     DYNAMIC    Fa0/1
```

Suppose the above switch received a frame with the following MAC addresses:

Source MAC: **0005.dccb.d74b**

Destination MAC: **000a.f467.9e8c**

How will the switch handle this frame? Answer: The destination MAC address will be found in the MAC address table and the frame will be forwarded out Fa0/3 only.

Loop Avoidance

Redundant links between switches are a good idea because they help prevent complete network failures in the event one link stops working.

Sounds great, but even though redundant links can be extremely helpful, they often cause more problems than they solve. This is because frames can be flooded down all redundant links simultaneously, creating network loops as well as other evils. Here's a list of some of the ugliest problems:

- If no loop avoidance schemes are put in place, the switches will flood broadcasts endlessly throughout the internetwork. This is sometimes referred to as a *broadcast storm*. (But most of the time it's referred to in ways we're not permitted to repeat in print!) Figure 7.8 illustrates how a broadcast can be propagated throughout the network. Observe how a frame is continually being flooded through the internetwork's physical network media.

- A device can receive multiple copies of the same frame since that frame can arrive from different segments at the same time. Figure 7.9 demonstrates how a whole bunch of frames can arrive from multiple segments simultaneously. The server in the figure sends a unicast frame to Router C. Since it's a unicast frame, Switch A forwards the frame and Switch B provides the same service—it forwards the broadcast. This is bad because it means that Router C receives that unicast frame twice, causing additional overhead on the network.

FIGURE 7.8   Broadcast storm

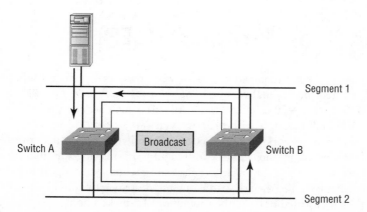

FIGURE 7.9   Multiple frame copies

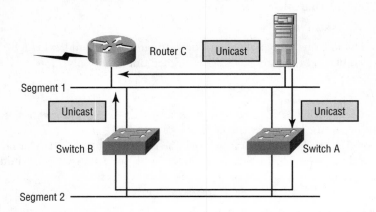

- You may have thought of this one: The MAC address filter table will be totally confused about the device's location because the switch can receive the frame from more than one link. And what's more, the bewildered switch could get so caught up in constantly updating the MAC filter table with source hardware address locations that it will fail to forward a frame! This is called thrashing the MAC table.

- One of the nastiest things that can happen is multiple loops generating throughout a network. This means that loops can occur within other loops, and if a broadcast storm were to also occur, the network wouldn't be able to perform frame switching—period!

All of these problems spell disaster (or at least close to it) and are decidedly evil situations that must be avoided, or at least fixed somehow. That's where the Spanning Tree Protocol comes into the game. It was developed to solve each and every one of the problems I just told you about.

Spanning Tree Protocol (STP)

Back before it was purchased and renamed Compaq, a company called Digital Equipment Corporation (DEC) created the original version of *Spanning Tree Protocol (STP)*. The IEEE later created its own version of STP called 802.1D. All Cisco switches run the IEEE 802.1D version of STP, which isn't compatible with the DEC version.

STP's main task is to stop network loops from occurring on your layer 2 network (bridges or switches). It vigilantly monitors the network to find all links, making sure that no loops occur by shutting down any redundant links. STP uses the spanning-tree algorithm (STA) to first create a topology database and then to search out and destroy redundant links. With STP running, frames will be forwarded only on the premium, STP-picked links.

In the following sections, I am going to hit the nitty-gritty of the Spanning Tree Protocol.

STP is a layer 2 protocol that is used to maintain a loop-free switched network

The Spanning Tree Protocol is necessary in networks such as the one shown in Figure 7.10.

FIGURE 7.10   A switched network with switching loops

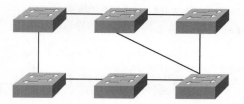

In Figure 7.10, we have a switched network with a redundant topology (switching loops). Without some type of layer 2 mechanism to stop the network loop, we would have the problems we discussed previously: broadcast storms and multiple frame copies.

Spanning Tree Terms

Before I get into describing the details of how STP works in the network, you need to understand some basic ideas and terms and how they relate within the layer 2 switched network:

Root bridge   The *root bridge* is the bridge with the best bridge ID. With STP, the key is for all the switches in the network to elect a root bridge that becomes the focal point in the network. All other decisions in the network—such as which port is to be blocked and which port is to be put in forwarding mode—are made from the perspective of this root bridge.

BPDU   All the switches exchange information to use in the selection of the root switch, as well as in subsequent configuration of the network. Each switch compares the parameters in the *Bridge Protocol Data Unit (BPDU)* that they send to one neighbor with the one that they receive from another neighbor.

Bridge ID   The bridge ID is how STP keeps track of all the switches in the network. It is determined by a combination of the bridge priority (32,768 by default on all Cisco switches) and the base MAC address. The bridge with the lowest bridge ID becomes the root bridge in the network.

Nonroot bridge   These are all bridges that are not the root bridge. Nonroot bridges exchange BPDUs with all bridges and update the STP topology database on all switches, preventing loops and providing a measure of defense against link failures.

Root port   The root port is always the link directly connected to the root bridge, or the shortest path to the root bridge. If more than one link connects to the root bridge, then a port cost is determined by checking the bandwidth of each link. The lowest-cost port becomes the root port. If multiple links have the same cost, the bridge with the lower advertising bridge ID is used. Since multiple links can be from the same device, the lowest port number will be used.

Designated port   A *designated port* is one that has been determined as having the best (lowest) cost. A designated port will be marked as a forwarding port.

Port cost   Port cost determines when multiple links are used between two switches and none are root ports. The cost of a link is determined by the bandwidth of a link.

Nondesignated port   A *nondesignated port* is one with a higher cost than the designated port. Nondesignated ports are put in blocking mode—they are not forwarding ports.

Forwarding port   A forwarding port forwards frames.

Blocked port   A blocked port is the port that, in order to prevent loops, will not forward frames. However, a blocked port will always listen to frames.

Spanning-Tree Port States

The ports on a bridge or switch running STP can transition through five different states:

Blocking   A blocked port won't forward frames; it just listens to BPDUs. The purpose of the blocking state is to prevent the use of looped paths. All ports are in blocking state by default when the switch is powered up.

Listening   The port listens to BPDUs to make sure no loops occur on the network before passing data frames. A port in listening state prepares to forward data frames without populating the MAC address table.

Learning   The switch port listens to BPDUs and learns all the paths in the switched network. A port in learning state populates the MAC address table but doesn't forward data frames.

Forwarding   The port sends and receives all data frames on the bridged port. If the port is still a designated or root port at the end of the learning state, it enters this state.

Disabled   A port in the disabled state (administratively) does not participate in the frame forwarding or STP. A port in the disabled state is virtually nonoperational.

Switch ports are most often in either the blocking or forwarding state. A forwarding port is one that has been determined to have the lowest (best) cost to the root bridge. But when and if the network experiences a topology change (because of a failed link or because someone adds in a new switch), you'll find the ports on a switch in listening and learning state.

As I mentioned, blocking ports is a strategy for preventing network loops. Once a switch determines the best path to the root bridge, then all other ports will be in blocking mode. Blocked ports can still receive BPDUs—they just don't send out any frames.

If a switch determines that a blocked port should now be the designated or root port because of a topology change, it will go into listening mode and check all BPDUs it receives to make sure that it won't create a loop once the port goes to forwarding mode.

Convergence

Convergence occurs when all ports on bridges and switches have transitioned to either the forwarding or blocking modes. No data is forwarded until convergence is complete. Before data can be forwarded again, all devices must be updated. Convergence is important to make sure all devices have the same database, but it does cost you some time. It usually takes 50 seconds to go from blocking to forwarding mode, and I don't recommend changing the default STP timers. (But you can adjust those timers if necessary.) Forward delay means the time it takes to transition a port from listening to learning mode.

LAN Switch Types

LAN switch types decide how a frame is handled when it's received on a switch port. Latency—the time it takes for a frame to be sent out an exit port once the switch receives the frame—depends on the chosen switching mode. There are three switching modes:

Cut-through (FastForward)   When in this mode, the switch only waits for the destination hardware address to be received before it looks up the destination address in the MAC filter table. Cisco sometimes calls this the FastForward method.

FragmentFree (modified cut-through)   This is the default mode for the Catalyst 1900 switch, and it's sometimes referred to as modified cut-through. In FragmentFree mode, the switch checks the first 64 bytes of a frame before forwarding it for fragmentation, thus guarding against forwarding runts, which are caused by collisions.

Store-and-forward   In this mode, the complete data frame is received on the switch's buffer, a CRC is run, and if the CRC passes, the switch looks up the destination address in the MAC filter table.

Figure 7.11 delimits the different points where the switching mode takes place in the frame. Let's now discuss these three switching modes in more detail.

FIGURE 7.11   Different switching modes within a frame

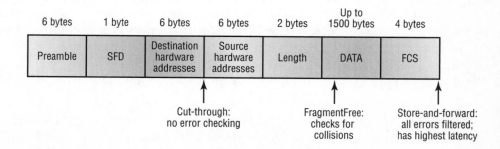

Cut-Through (Real Time)

You may see Cisco call this cut-through, FastForward, or even real time. With the *cut-through* switching method, the LAN switch reads only the destination address (the first 6 bytes following the preamble) onto its onboard buffers. That done, it then looks up the hardware destination address in the MAC switching table, determines the outgoing interface, and proceeds to forward the frame toward its destination.

A cut-through switch really helps to reduce latency because it begins to forward the frame as soon as it reads the destination address and determines the outgoing interface.

With some switches, you get an extra super-cool feature: the flexibility to perform cut-through switching on a per-port basis until a user-defined error threshold is reached. At the point that threshold is attained, the ports automatically change over to store-and-forward mode so they will stop forwarding the errors. And when the error rate on the port falls back below the threshold, the port automatically changes back to cut-through mode.

FragmentFree (Modified Cut-Through)

FragmentFree is a modified form of cut-through switching in which the switch waits for the collision window (64 bytes) to pass before forwarding. This is because if a packet has a collision error, it almost always occurs within the first 64 bytes. It means each frame will be checked into the data field to make sure no fragmentation has occurred.

FragmentFree mode provides better error checking than the cut-through mode with practically no increase in latency. It's the default switching method for the 1900 switches.

Store-and-Forward

Store-and-forward switching is Cisco's primary LAN switching method. The *store-and-forward* method provides efficient, error-free transport instead of fast transport. When in store-and-forward, the LAN switch copies the entire frame onto its onboard buffers and then computes the cyclic redundancy check (CRC). Because it copies the entire frame, latency through the switch varies with frame length.

The frame is discarded if it contains a CRC error—if it's too short (less than 64 bytes including the CRC) or if it's too long (more than 1,518 bytes including the CRC). If the frame doesn't contain any errors, the LAN switch looks up the destination hardware address in its forwarding or switching table to find the correct outgoing interface. When it does, out goes the frame toward its destination.

Summary

In this chapter, I talked about the differences between switches and bridges and how they both work at layer 2 and create a MAC address forward/filter table in order to make decisions on whether to forward or flood a frame.

I also discussed problems that can occur if you have multiple links between bridges (switches) and how to solve these problems by using the Spanning Tree Protocol (STP).

LAN switch types were also discussed in detail, as well as how each frame works through a switch.

Exam Essentials

Remember the three switch functions.   Address learning, forward/filter decisions, and loop avoidance are the functions of a switch.

Remember the command `show mac address-table`.   The command `show mac address-table` will show you the forward/filter table used on the LAN switch

Understand the main purpose of the spanning tree protocol in a switched LAN.   The main purpose of STP is to prevent switching loops in a network with redundant switched paths.

Remember the states of STP.   The purpose of the blocking state is to prevent the use of looped paths. A port in listening state prepares to forward data frames without populating the MAC address table. A port in learning state populates the MAC address table but doesn't forward data frames. The port in forwarding state sends and receives all data frames on the bridged port. Last, a port in the disabled state is virtually nonoperational.

Remember the three LAN switch methods.   The three LAN switch methods are cut-through (also called FastForward), FragmentFree (also known as modified cut-through), and store-and-forward.

Written Lab 7

Write the answers to the following questions:

1.   What command will show you the forward/filter table?

2.   If a destination MAC address is not in the forward/filter table, what will the switch do with the frame?

3.   What are the three switch functions at layer 2?

4.   If a frame is received on a switch port and the source MAC address is not in the forward/filter table, what will the switch do?

5.   What is used at layer 2 to prevent switching loops?

6.   Which LAN switch method receives the complete frame before beginning to forward it?

7.   When is STP considered to be converged?

8.   Switches break up _____ collision domains.

9.   What is used to prevent switching loops in a network with redundant switched paths?

10.   Which LAN switch method runs a CRC on every frame the switch receives?

(The answers to Written Lab 7 can be found following the review questions for this chapter.)

Review Questions

1. Which of the following is a layer 2 protocol used to maintain a loop-free network?

   A. VTP

   B. STP

   C. RIP

   D. CDP

2. What command will display the forward/filter table?

   A. `show mac filter`

   B. `show run`

   C. `show mac address-table`

   D. `show mac filter-table`

3. What is the result of segmenting a network with a bridge (switch)? (Choose two options.)

   A. It increases the number of collision domains.

   B. It decreases the number of collision domains.

   C. It increases the number of broadcast domains.

   D. It decreases the number of broadcast domains.

   E. It makes smaller collision domains.

   F. It makes larger collision domains.

4. Which statement describes a spanning-tree network that has converged?

   A. All switch and bridge ports are in the forwarding state.

   B. All switch and bridge ports are assigned as either root or designated ports.

   C. All switch and bridge ports are in either the forwarding or blocking state.

   D. All switch and bridge ports are either blocking or looping.

5. Your network design emphasizes efficient, error-free transport instead of fast transport. Which switching mode should be configured on the new switches to provide error-free transport to the network?

   A. Cut-through

   B. FragmentFree

   C. Store-and-forward

   D. FastForward

6. What are the three distinct functions of layer 2 switching that increase available bandwidth on the network?

A. Address learning

B. Routing

C. Forwarding and filtering

D. Creating network loops

E. Loop avoidance

F. IP addressing

7. What technology is used by Catalyst switches to resolve topology loops and ensure that data flows properly through a single network path?

A. RIP

B. STP

C. IGRP

D. Store-and-forward

E. Cut-through

8. Which of the following statements is true?

A. A switch creates a single collision domain and a single broadcast domain. A router creates a single collision domain.

B. A switch creates separate collision domains but one broadcast domain. A router provides a separate broadcast domain.

C. A switch creates a single collision domain and separate broadcast domains. A router provides a separate broadcast domain as well.

D. A switch creates separate collision domains and separate broadcast domains. A router provides separate collision domains.

9. Which of the following is true regarding layer 2 switches? (Choose two.)

A. A switch is a hub with more ports.

B. A switch is a multiport bridge.

C. Switches learn IP addresses from each frame and filter the network using these addresses.

D. Switches learn MAC addresses by examining the source address of each frame.

10. What does a switch do when a frame is received on an interface and the destination hardware address is unknown or not in the filter table?

A. Forwards the switch to the first available link

B. Drops the frame

C. Floods the network with the frame looking for the device

D. Sends back a message to the originating station asking for a name resolution

11. If a switch receives a frame and the source MAC address is not in the MAC address table, but the destination address is in the table, what will the switch do with the frame?

  A. Discard it and send an error message back to the originating host.

  B. Flood the network with the frame.

  C. Add the source address and port to the MAC address table and forward the frame out the destination port.

  D. Add the destination to the MAC address table and then forward the frame.

12. Which of the following are spanning-tree switch port states? (Choose three.)

  A. Learning

  B. Cut-through

  C. Listening

  D. Fragment Free

  E. Forwarding

13. What purpose in a switched LAN does STP perform?

  A. Prevents routing loops in a network with redundant paths

  B. Prevents switching loops in a network with redundant switched paths

  C. Allows VLAN information to be passed in a trunked link

  D. Creates multiple broadcast domains in a layer 2 switched network

14. Which command was used to produce the following output:

```
Vlan    Mac Address       Type        Ports
----    -----------       --------    -----
   1    0005.dccb.d74b    DYNAMIC     Fa0/1
   1    000a.f467.9e80    DYNAMIC     Fa0/3
   1    000a.f467.9e8b    DYNAMIC     Fa0/4
   1    000a.f467.9e8c    DYNAMIC     Fa0/3
   1    0010.7b7f.c2b0    DYNAMIC     Fa0/3
   1    0030.80dc.460b    DYNAMIC     Fa0/3
```

  A. `show vlan`

  B. `show ip route`

  C. `show mac address-table`

  D. `show mac address-filter`

15. Which of the following is a characteristic of having a network segment on a switch?

  A. The segment is many collision domains.

  B. The segment can translate from one media to a different media.

  C. All devices on a segment are part of a different broadcast domain.

  D. One device per segment can send frames to the switch at a time.

16. Which of the following is true in regard to bridges?

   A. Bridges do not isolate broadcast domains by default.

   B. Bridges broadcast packets into the same collision domain they were received from.

   C. Bridges use IP addresses to filter the network.

   D. Bridges can translate from one media to a different media.

17. Layer 2 switching provides which of the following? (Choose four.)

   A. Hardware-based bridging (ASIC)

   B. Wire speed

   C. Low latency

   D. Low cost

   E. Routing

   F. WAN services

18. You type show mac address-table and receive the following output:

```
Switch#sh mac address-table
Vlan    Mac Address       Type       Ports
----    -----------       --------   -----
   1    0005.dccb.d74b    DYNAMIC    Fa0/1
   1    000a.f467.9e80    DYNAMIC    Fa0/3
   1    000a.f467.9e8b    DYNAMIC    Fa0/4
   1    000a.f467.9e8c    DYNAMIC    Fa0/3
   1    0010.7b7f.c2b0    DYNAMIC    Fa0/3
   1    0030.80dc.460b    DYNAMIC    Fa0/3
```

Suppose the above switch received a frame with the following MAC addresses:

   Source MAC: 0005.dccb.d74b

   Destination MAC: 000a.f467.9e8c

   A. It will discard the frame.

   B. It will forward the frame out port Fa0/3 only.

   C. It will forward it out Fa0/1 only.

   D. It will send it out all ports except fa0/1.

19. You are working on a network design and determine that a new testing application requires multiple hosts that must be capable of sharing data between each host and server running 10Mbps. Other departments use applications that require less than 3Mbps to the server. What should you recommend?

   A. Replace the 10Mbps Ethernet hub with a 100Mbps Ethernet hub.

   B. Install a router between departments.

   C. Use a switch with a 100Mbps uplink to the server and 10Mbps to the hosts.

   D. Use a bridge to break up collision domains.

20. You have two switches connected together with two cross-over cables for redundancy, and STP is disabled. Which of the following will happen between the switches?

A. The routing tables on the switches will not update.

B. The MAC forward/filter table will not update on the switches.

C. Broadcast storms will occur on the switched network.

D. The switches will automatically load balance between the two links.

Answers to Review Questions

1. B. The Spanning Tree Protocol is used to stop switching loops in a switched network with redundant paths.

2. C. The command `show mac address-table` displays the forward/filter table on the switch.

3. A, E. Bridges break up collision domains, which would increase the number of collision domains in a network and also make smaller collision domains.

4. C. Convergence occurs when all ports on bridges and switches have transitioned to either the forwarding or blocking states. No data is forwarded until convergence is complete. Before data can be forwarded again, all devices must be updated.

5. C. Store-and-forward latency (delay) will always vary because the complete frame must be received before the frame is transmitted back out the switch. However, this will provide a more resilient, error-free network.

6. A, C, E. Layer 2 features include address learning, forwarding and filtering of the network, and loop avoidance.

7. B. Spanning Tree Protocol (STP) will make sure that no network loops occur at layer 2.

8. B. Switches break up collision domains, and routers break up broadcast domains.

9. B, D. A switch is really just a multiport bridge with more intelligence. Switches (and bridges) build their filter table by examining the source MAC address of each frame.

10. C. Switches flood all frames that have an unknown destination address. If a device answers the frame, the switch will update the MAC address table to reflect the location of the device.

11. C. Since the source MAC address is not in the MAC address table, the switch will address the source address and the port it is connected to in the MAC address table, then forward the frame to the outgoing port.

12. A, C, E. The STP states are blocking, listening, learning, forwarding, and disabled.

13. B. Spanning Tree Protocol (STP) stops loops at layer 2; in this question, the best answer is to stop loops in a switched network because switches work at layer 2. Routing protocols (RIP, IGRP, etc.) are used to stop loops at layer 3 (routing).

14. C. The command `show mac address-table` will display the forward/filter table, also called a CAM table, on a switch.

15. D. Only one device on a network segment connected to a switch can send frames to the switch at a time. A switch cannot translate from one media type to another on the same segment.

16. A. A bridge breaks up collision domains, but it is one large broadcast domain by default.

17. A, B, C, D. Switches, unlike bridges, are hardware based. Cisco says their switches are wire speed and provide low latency, and I guess they are low costs compared to their price in the 1990s.

18. C. Since the destination MAC address is in the mac address table (forward/filter table), it will send it out port fa0/3 only.

19. C. By adding a switch, you can effectively segment the network and provide 100Mbps to the server and 10Mbps to the hosts.

20. C. If spanning-tree is disabled on a switch and you have redundant links to another switch, broadcast storms will occur, among other possible problems.

Answers to Written Lab 7

1. `show mac address-table`

2. Flood the frame out all ports except the port it was received on.

3. Address learning, forward/filter decisions, loop avoidance

4. It will add the source MAC address in the forward/filter table and associate it with the port the frame was received on.

5. Spanning Tree Protocol (STP)

6. Store-and-forward

7. When all ports are in either the blocking or forwarding mode

8. Collision

9. Spanning Tree Protocol (STP)

10. Store-and-forward

Chapter

8

Managing a Cisco Internetwork

THE CCNA INTRO EXAM TOPICS COVERED IN THIS CHAPTER INCLUDE THE FOLLOWING:

✓ **Design and Support**

- Use a subset of Cisco IOS commands to analyze and report network problems

- Use embedded layer 3 through layer 7 protocols to establish, test, suspend, or disconnect connectivity to remote devices from the router console

- Determine IP addresses

✓ **Implementation and Operation**

- Establish communication between a terminal device and the router IOS, and use IOS for system analysis

- Manipulate system image and device configuration files

- Use commands incorporated within IOS to analyze and report network problems

- Use embedded data link layer functionality to perform network neighbor discovery and analysis from the router

- Use embedded layer 3 through layer 7 protocols to establish, test, suspend, or disconnect connectivity to remote devices from the router console

✓ **Technology**

- Describe the purpose and fundamental operation of the internetwork operating system (IOS)

- Identify the major internal and external components of a router, and describe the associated functionality

- Identify and describe the stages of the router boot-up sequence

- Describe how the configuration register and boot system commands modify the router boot-up sequence

As you can see from the size of the objective listing, this is very important chapter in this book. In this chapter, I'm going to show you how to manage Cisco routers on an internetwork. The Internetwork Operating System (IOS) and configuration files reside in different locations in a Cisco device, and it's important to understand where these files are located and how they work.

You'll learn about the main components of a router, the router boot sequence, and the configuration register, including how to use the configuration register for password recovery. After that, you'll find out how to manage routers by performing the following tasks:

- Backing up and restoring the Cisco IOS
- Backing up and restoring the Cisco configuration
- Gathering information about neighbor devices through CDP and Telnet
- Resolving hostnames
- Using the ping and traceroute commands to test network connectivity

The Internal Components of a Cisco Router

In order to configure and troubleshoot a Cisco internetwork, you need to know the major components of Cisco routers and understand what each one does. Table 8.1 describes the major Cisco router components.

TABLE 8.1   Cisco Router Components

Component	Description
Bootstrap	Stored in the microcode of the ROM, the bootstrap is used to bring a router up during initialization. It will boot the router and then load the IOS.
POST (power-on self-test)	Stored in the microcode of the ROM, the POST is used to check the basic functionality of the router hardware and determines which interfaces are present.

TABLE 8.1   Cisco Router Components *(continued)*

Component	Description
ROM monitor	Stored in the microcode of the ROM, the ROM monitor is used for manufacturing, testing, and troubleshooting.
Mini-IOS	Called the RXBOOT or bootloader by Cisco, the mini-IOS is a small IOS in ROM that can be used to bring up an interface and load a Cisco IOS into flash memory. The mini-IOS can also perform a few other maintenance operations.
RAM (random-access memory)	Used to hold packet buffers, ARP cache, routing tables, and also the software and data structures that allow the router to function. Running-config is stored in RAM, and the IOS can also be run from RAM in some routers.
ROM (read-only memory)	Used to start and maintain the router.
Flash memory	Used on the router to hold the Cisco IOS. Flash memory is not erased when the router is reloaded. It is EEPROM (electronically erasable programmable read-only memory) created by Intel.
NVRAM (nonvolatile RAM)	Used to hold the router and switch configuration. NVRAM is not erased when the router or switch is reloaded.
Configuration register	Used to control how the router boots up. This value can be seen with the show version command and typically is 0x2102, which tells the router to load the IOS from flash memory as well as to load the configuration from NVRAM.

The Router Boot Sequence

When a router boots up, it performs a series of steps, called the *boot sequence*, to test the hardware and load the necessary software. The boot sequence consists of the following steps:

1. The router performs a POST. The POST tests the hardware to verify that all components of the device are operational and present. For example, the POST checks for the different interfaces on the router. The POST is stored in and run from *ROM (read-only memory)*.

2. The bootstrap looks for and loads the Cisco IOS software. The bootstrap is a program in ROM that is used to execute programs. The bootstrap program is responsible for finding where each IOS program is located and then loading the file. By default, the IOS software is loaded from flash memory in all Cisco routers.

The default order of an IOS loading from a router is Flash, TFTP server, ROM.

3. The IOS software looks for a valid configuration file stored in NVRAM. This file is called startup-config and is only there if an administrator copies the running-config file into NVRAM.

4. If a startup-config file is in NVRAM, the router will load and run this file. The router is now operational. If a startup-config file is not in NVRAM, the router will start the setup-mode configuration upon bootup.

Managing Configuration Registers

All Cisco routers have a 16-bit software register that's written into NVRAM. By default, the *configuration register* is set to load the Cisco IOS from *flash memory* and to look for and load the startup-config file from NVRAM. In the following sections I am going to discuss the configuration register settings and how to use these settings to provide password recovery on your routers.

Understanding the Configuration Register Bits

The 16 bits (2 bytes) of the configuration register are read from 15 to 0, from left to right. The default configuration setting on Cisco routers is 0x2102. This means that bits 13, 8, and 1 are on, as shown in Table 8.2. Notice that each set of 4 bits is read in binary with a value of 8, 4, 2, 1.

TABLE 8.2 The Configuration Register Bit Numbers

Configuration Register		2					1			0			2		
Bit number	15	14	13	12	11	10	9	8	7	6	5	4	3	2	1	0
Binary	0	0	1	0	0	0	0	1	0	0	0	0	0	0	1	0

Add the prefix *0x* to the configuration register address. The *0x* means that the digits that follow are in hexadecimal.

Table 8.3 lists the software configuration bit meanings. Notice that bit 6 can be used to ignore the NVRAM contents. This bit is used for password recovery—something I'll go over with you soon in the section "Recovering Passwords" later in this chapter.

Remember that in hex, the scheme is 0–9 and A–F (A = 10, B = 11, C = 12, D = 13, E = 14, and F = 15). This means that a 210F setting for the configuration register is actually 210(15), or 1111 in binary.

TABLE 8.3   Software Configuration Meanings

Bit	Hex	Description
0–3	0x0000–0x000F	Boot field (see Table 8.4).
6	0x0040	Ignore NVRAM contents.
7	0x0080	OEM bit enabled.
8	0x101	Break disabled.
10	0x0400	IP broadcast with all zeros.
5, 11–12	0x0800–0x1000	Console line speed.
13	0x2000	Boot default ROM software if network boot fails.
14	0x4000	IP broadcasts do not have net numbers.
15	0x8000	Enable diagnostic messages and ignore NVRAM contents.

The boot field, which consists of bits 0–3 in the configuration register, controls the router boot sequence. Table 8.4 describes the boot field bits.

TABLE 8.4   The Boot Field (Configuration Register Bits 00–03)

Boot Field	Meaning	Use
00	ROM monitor mode	To boot to ROM monitor mode, set the configuration register to 2100. You must manually boot the router with the b command. The router will show the rommon> prompt.
01	Boot image from ROM	To boot an IOS image stored in ROM, set the configuration register to 2101. The router will show the Router(boot)> prompt.
02–F	Specifies a default boot file name	Any value from 2102 through 210F tells the router to use the boot commands specified in NVRAM.

Checking the Current Configuration Register Value

You can see the current value of the configuration register by using the `show version` command (`sh version` or `show ver` for short), as demonstrated here:

```
Router#sh version
Cisco Internetwork Operating System Software
IOS (tm) C2600 Software (C2600-I-M), Version 12.1(8)T3,
  RELEASE SOFTWARE (fc1)
[output cut]
Configuration register is 0x2102
```

The last information given from this command is the value of the configuration register. In this example, the value is 0x2102—the default setting. The configuration register setting of 0x2102 tells the router to look in NVRAM for the boot sequence.

Notice that the `show version` command also provides the IOS version, and in the preceding example, it shows the IOS version as 12.1(8)T3.

The `show version` command will display system hardware configuration information, software version, and the names and sources of configuration files and boot images on a router.

Changing the Configuration Register

You can change the configuration register value to modify how the router boots and runs. These are the main reasons you would want to change the configuration register:

- Force the system into the ROM monitor mode.
- Select a boot source and default boot filename.
- Enable or disable the `Break` function.
- Control broadcast addresses.
- Set the console terminal baud rate.
- Load operating software from ROM.
- Enable booting from a Trivial File Transfer Protocol (TFTP) server.

Before you change the configuration register, make sure you know the current configuration register value. Use the `show version` command to get this information.

You can change the configuration register by using the `config-register` command. Here's an example. The following commands tell the router to boot a small IOS from ROM and then show the current configuration register value:

```
Router(config)#config-register 0x2101
Router(config)#^Z
Router#sh ver
[output cut]
Configuration register is 0x2102 (will be 0x2101 at next
  reload)
```

Okay, notice that the `show version` command displays the current configuration register value and also what that value will be when the router reboots. Any change to the configuration register won't take effect until the router is reloaded. The 0x2101 will load the IOS from ROM the next time the router is rebooted. You may see it listed as 0x101—that's basically the same thing, and it can be written either way.

Here is our router after setting the configuration register to 0x2101 and reloading:

```
Router(boot)#sh ver
Cisco Internetwork Operating System Software
IOS (tm) 3000 Bootstrap Software (IGS-BOOT-R), Version 11.0(10c), RELEASE
SOFTWARE (fc1)
[output cut]

ROM: System Bootstrap, Version 11.0(10c), SOFTWARE

Router uptime is 1 minute
System restarted by reload
Running default software

[output cut]
Configuration register is 0x2101
```

At this point, if you typed show flash, you'd still see the IOS in flash memory ready to go. But we told our router to load from ROM, which is why the hostname shows up with (boot).

```
Router(boot)#sh flash
System flash directory:
File  Length   Name/status
  1   16466632  /c2500-jos56i-l.121-5.t17.bin
[16466696 bytes used, 310520 available, 16777216 total]
16384K bytes of processor board System flash (Read/Write)
```

So even through we have our full IOS in flash, we changed the default loading of the router's software by changing the configuration register. If you want to set the configuration register back to the default, just type this:

```
Router(boot)#config t
Router(boot)(config)#config-register 0x2102
Router(boot)(config)#^Z
Router(boot)#reload
```

In the next section, I'll show you how to load the router into ROM monitor mode so you can perform password recovery.

Recovering Passwords

If you're locked out of a router because you forgot the password, you can change the configuration register to help you get back on your feet. As I said earlier, bit 6 in the configuration register is used to tell the router whether to use the contents of NVRAM to load a router configuration.

The default configuration register value is 0x2102, meaning that bit 6 is off. With the default setting, the router will look for and load a router configuration stored in NVRAM (startup-config). To recover a password, you need to turn on bit 6. Doing this will tell the router to ignore the NVRAM contents. The configuration register value to turn on bit 6 is 0x2142.

Here are the main steps to password recovery:

1. Boot the router and interrupt the boot sequence by performing a break, which will take the router into ROM monitor mode.

2. Change the configuration register to turn on bit 6 (with the value 0x2142).

3. Reload the router.

4. Enter privileged mode.

5. Copy the startup-config file to running-config.

6. Change the password.

7. Reset the configuration register to the default value.

8. Save the router configuration.

9. Reload the router (optional).

I'm going to cover these steps in more detail in the following sections. I'll also show you the commands to restore access to 2600 and 2500 series routers.

As I said, you can enter ROM monitor mode by pressing Ctrl+Break during router bootup. But if the IOS is corrupt or missing, if there's no network connectivity available to find a TFTP host, or if the mini-IOS from ROM doesn't load (meaning the default router fallback failed), the router will enter ROM monitor mode by default.

Interrupting the Router Boot Sequence

Your first step is to boot the router and perform a break. This is usually done by pressing the Ctrl+Break key combination when using HyperTerminal and while the router first reboots.

After you've performed a break, you should see something like this:

```
System Bootstrap, Version 11.3(2)XA4, RELEASE SOFTWARE (fc1)
Copyright (c) 1999 by cisco Systems, Inc.
TAC:Home:SW:IOS:Specials for info
PC = 0xfff0a530, Vector = 0x500, SP = 0x680127b0
C2600 platform with 32768 Kbytes of main memory
PC = 0xfff0a530, Vector = 0x500, SP = 0x80004374
monitor: command "boot" aborted due to user interrupt
rommon 1 >
```

Notice the line `monitor: command "boot" aborted due to user interrupt`. At this point, you will be at the `rommon 1>` prompt, which is called ROM monitor mode.

Changing the Configuration Register

As I explained earlier, you can change the configuration register by using the `config-register` command. To turn on bit 6, use the configuration register value 0x2142.

NOTE   Remember that if you change the configuration register to 0x2142, the startup-config will be bypassed and the router will load into setup mode.

Cisco 2600 Series Commands

To change the bit value on a Cisco 2600 series router, you just enter the command at the `rommon 1>` prompt:

```
rommon 1 > confreg 0x2142
You must reset or power cycle for new config to take effect
rommon 2 > reset
```

Cisco 2500 Series Commands

To change the configuration register on a 2500 series router, type `o` after creating a break sequence on the router. This brings up a menu of configuration register option settings. To change the configuration register, enter the command `o/r`, followed by the new register value. Here's an example of turning on bit 6 on a 2501 router:

```
System Bootstrap, Version 11.0(10c), SOFTWARE
Copyright (c) 1986-1996 by cisco Systems
2500 processor with 14336 Kbytes of main memory
```

```
Abort at 0x1098FEC (PC)
>o
Configuration register = 0x2102 at last boot
Bit#    Configuration register option settings:
15      Diagnostic mode disabled
14      IP broadcasts do not have network numbers
13      Boot default ROM software if network boot fails
12-11   Console speed is 9600 baud
10      IP broadcasts with ones
08      Break disabled
07      OEM disabled
06      Ignore configuration disabled
03-00   Boot file is cisco2-2500 (or 'boot system' command)
>o/r 0x2142
```

Notice that the last entry in the router output is 03-00. This tells the router what the IOS boot file is. By default, the router will use the first file found in the flash memory, so if you want to boot a different filename, you can either change the configuration register or use the boot system *ios_name* command.

 Another way to change the configuration register on a 2500 series router is to load an IOS image from a TFTP server by using the command boot system *tftp ios_name ip_address* from global configuration mode.

Reloading the Router and Entering Privileged Mode

At this point, you need to reset the router like this:

- From the 2600 series router, type **reset**.
- From the 2500 series router, type **I** (for initialize).

The router will reload and ask if you want to use setup mode (because no startup-config is used). Answer no to entering setup mode, press Enter to go into user mode, and then type enable to go into privileged mode.

Viewing and Changing the Configuration

Now you're past the point where you would need to enter the user-mode and privileged-mode passwords in a router. Copy the startup-config file to the running-config file:

copy startup-config running-config

Or use the shortcut:

copy start run

The configuration is now running in *random access memory (RAM)*, and you're in privileged mode, meaning that you can now view and change the configuration. But you can't view the enable secret setting for the password since it is encrypted. To change the password, do this:

```
config t
enable secret todd
```

Resetting the Configuration Register and Reloading the Router

After you're finished changing passwords, set the configuration register back to the default value with the config-register command:

```
config t
config-register 0x2102
```

Finally, save the new configuration with a copy running-config startup-config and reload the router.

If you save your configuration and reload the router and it comes up in setup mode, the configuration register setting is probably incorrect.

Backing Up and Restoring the Cisco IOS

Before you upgrade or restore a Cisco IOS, you really should copy the existing file to a *TFTP host* as a backup just in case the new image crashes and burns.

And you can use any TFTP host to accomplish this. By default, the flash memory in a router is used to store the Cisco IOS. In the following sections, I'll describe how to check the amount of flash memory, how to copy the Cisco IOS from flash memory to a TFTP host, and how to copy the IOS from a TFTP host to flash memory.

But before you back up an IOS image to a network server on your intranet, you've got to do these three things:

- Make sure you can access the network server.

- Ensure that the network server has adequate space for the code image.

- Verify the file naming and path requirement.

And if you have a laptop or workstations Ethernet port directly connected to a router's Ethernet interface, as shown in Figure 8.1, you need to verify the following before attempting to copy the image to or from the router:

- TFTP server software must be running on the administrator's workstation.

- The Ethernet connection between the router and the workstation must be made with a crossover cable.

FIGURE 8.1   Copying an IOS from a workstation to a router

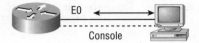

- The workstation must be on the same subnet as the router's Ethernet interface.
- The copy flash tftp command must be supplied the IP address of the workstation if you are copying from the router flash.
- And if you're copying "into" flash, you need to verify that there's enough room in flash memory to accommodate the file to be copied.

Verifying Flash Memory

Before you attempt to upgrade the Cisco IOS on your router with a new IOS file, it's a good idea to verify that your flash memory has enough room to hold the new image. You verify the amount of flash memory and the file or files being stored in flash memory by using the show flash command (sh flash for short):

```
Router#sh flash
System flash directory:
File  Length    Name/status
  1   8121000   c2500-js-1.112-18.bin
[8121064 bytes used, 8656152 available, 16777216 total]
16384K bytes of processor board System flash (Read ONLY)
Router#
```

It's important to understand that there are 16MB of flash memory on this router (16,777,216 total) and that the current IOS is using 8MB (8,121,064 bytes used).

The show flash command will display the amount of memory consumed by the current IOS image and whether there is enough room available to hold both the current and new images. If there is not enough room for both the old image and the new image you want to load, the old image will be erased.

Notice that the filename in this example is c2500-js-1.112-18.bin. The name of the file is platform specific and derived as follows:

- c2500 is the platform.
- j indicates that the file is an enterprise image.
- s indicates that the file contains extended capabilities.
- l indicates that the file can be moved from flash memory if needed and is not compressed.

- 112-18 is the revision number.
- .bin indicates that the Cisco IOS is a binary executable file.

The last line in the router output shows that the flash is 16,384KB (or 16MB). So if the new file that you want to use is, say, 10MB in size, you know that there's plenty of room for it. And once you've verified that flash memory can hold the IOS you want to copy, you're free to continue with your backup operation.

Some of the other features you may find in IOS naming conventions, which include feature capability, hardware product platform, and run location and compression status, are as follows:

- f indicates that the image runs from flash memory.
- m indicates that the image runs from RAM.
- r indicates that the image runs from ROM.
- l indicates that the image is relocatable.
- z indicates that the image is zip compressed.
- x indicates that the image is mzip compressed.

Backing Up the Cisco IOS

To back up the Cisco IOS to a TFTP server, you use the copy flash tftp command. It's a straightforward command that requires only the source filename and the IP address of the TFTP server.

The key to success in this backup routine is to make sure that you've got good, solid connectivity to the TFTP server. Check this by pinging the device from the router console prompt like this:

```
Router#ping 192.168.0.120
Type escape sequence to abort.
Sending 5, 100-byte ICMP Echos to 192.168.0.120, timeout
  is 2 seconds:
!!!!!
Success rate is 100 percent (5/5), round-trip min/avg/max
  = 4/4/8 ms
```

The *Packet Internet Groper (Ping)* utility is used to test network connectivity, and I use it in some of the examples in this chapter. I'll be talking about it in more detail in the section "Checking Network Connectivity and Troubleshooting" later in the chapter.

After you ping the TFTP server to make sure that IP is working, you can use the copy flash tftp command to copy the IOS to the TFTP server as shown next:

```
Router#copy flash tftp
System flash directory:
```

```
File   Length    Name/status
  1    8121000   c2500-js-l.112-18.bin
[8121064 bytes used, 8656152 available, 16777216 total]
Address or name of remote host [255.255.255.255]?
  192.168.0.120
Source file name?c2500-js-l.112-18.bin
Destination file name [c2500-js-l.112-18.bin]?[Enter]
Verifying checksum for 'c2500-js-l.112-18.bin')file #1)
...OK
Copy '/c2500-js-l.112-18' from Flash to server
  as '/c2500-js-l.112-18'? [yes/no]y
!!!!!!!!!!!!!!!!!!!!!!!!!!!!!!!!!!!!!!!!!!!!!!!!!!!!!!!!!!!
  !!!!!!!!!!!!!!!!!!!! [output cut]
Upload to server done
Flash copy took 00:02:30 [hh:mm:ss]
Router#
```

Look at the output—you can see that after you enter the command, the name of the file in flash memory is displayed. This is very cool because it makes things easy for you. Just copy the filename and then paste it when prompted for the source filename.

In the preceding example, the contents of flash memory were copied successfully to the TFTP server. The address of the remote host is the IP address of the TFTP server, and the source filename is the file in flash memory.

 WARNING   The copy flash tftp command won't prompt you for the location of any file or ask you where to put the file. TFTP is just a "grab it and place it" program in this situation. This means that the TFTP server must have a default directory specified or it won't work!

Restoring or Upgrading the Cisco Router IOS

What happens if you need to restore the Cisco IOS to flash memory to replace an original file that has been damaged or if you want to upgrade the IOS? You can download the file from a TFTP server to flash memory by using the copy tftp flash command. This command requires the IP address of the TFTP server and the name of the file you want to download.

But before you begin, make sure that the file you want to place in flash memory is in the default TFTP directory on your host. When you issue the command, TFTP won't ask you where the file is, so if the file you want to restore isn't in the default directory of the TFTP server, this just won't work.

After you enter the `copy tftp flash` command, you'll see a message informing you that the router must reboot and run a ROM-based IOS image to perform this operation:

```
Router#copy tftp flash
                    ****  NOTICE  ****
Flash load helper v1.0
This process will accept the copy options and then
terminate the current system image to use the ROM based
image for the copy. Routing functionality will not be
available during that time. If you are logged in via
telnet, this connection will terminate. Users with
console access can see the results of the copy operation.
                    ---- ******** ----
Proceed? [confirm][Enter]
```

After you press Enter to confirm that you truly understand that the router needs to reboot, you'll be presented with the following router output:

```
System flash directory:
File  Length   Name/status
  1   8121000  /c2500-js-1.112-18
[8121064 bytes used, 8656152 available, 16777216 total]
Address or name of remote host [192.168.0.120]?[Enter]
```

Once the router has used the TFTP server, it will remember the address, and just prompt you to press Enter.

The next prompt is for the name of the file you want to copy to flash memory (and remember—this file must be in your TFTP server's default directory):

```
Source file name?c2500-js56i-1.120-9.bin
Destination file name [c2500-js56i-1.120-9.bin]?[Enter]
Accessing file 'c2500-js56i-1.120-9.bin' on 192.168.0.120
...
Loading c2500-js56i-1.120-9.bin from 192.168.0.120
  (via Ethernet0): ! [OK]
```

After you tell the router the filename and where the file is, it will ask you to confirm that you understand that the contents of flash memory will be erased.

If you don't have enough room in flash memory to store both copies, or if the flash memory is new and no file has been written to it before, the router will ask to erase the contents of flash memory before writing the new file into flash memory.

You are prompted three times just to make sure that you really want to proceed with erasing flash memory. If you haven't issued a copy run start command, you'll be prompted to do so because the router needs to reboot:

```
Erase flash device before writing? [confirm][Enter]
Flash contains files. Are you sure you want to erase?
  [confirm][Enter]

System configuration has been modified. Save? [yes/no]: y
Building configuration...
[OK]
Copy 'c2500-js56i-1.120-9.bin' from server
  as 'c2500-js56i-1.120-9.bin' into Flash WITH erase?
  [yes/no] y
```

After you say yes three times to erasing flash memory, the router must reboot to load a small IOS from ROM memory. (You can't delete the flash file if it's in use.) This done, the contents of flash memory are erased and the file from the TFTP server is accessed and copied to flash memory:

```
%SYS-5-RELOAD: Reload requested
%FLH: c2500-js56i-1.120-9.bin from 192.168.0.120 to flash
...
System flash directory:
File  Length    Name/status
  1   8121000   /c2500-js-1.112-18
[8121064 bytes used, 8656152 available, 16777216 total]
Accessing file 'c2500-js56i-1.120-9.bin' on 192.168.0.120
...
Loading c2500-js56i-1.120-9.bin .from 192.168.0.120
  (via Ethernet0): ! [OK]

Erasing device... eeeeeeeeeeeeeeeeeeeeeeeeeeeeeeeeeeeeeeee
  eeeeeeeeeeeeeeeeeeeeeee
Loading c2500-js56i-1.120-9.bin from 192.168.0.120
  (via Ethernet0):
!!!!!!!!!!!!!!!!!!!!!!!!!!!!!!!!!!!!!!!!!!!!!!!!!!!!!!!!!!!
!!!!!!!!!!!!!!!!!!!!!!!!!!!!!!!!!!!!!! [output cut]
```

The row of e characters shows the contents of flash memory being erased. Each exclamation point (!) means that one UDP segment has been successfully transferred.

Once the copy is complete, you should receive this message:

```
[OK - 10935532/16777216 bytes]

Verifying checksum...  OK (0x2E3A)
Flash copy took 0:06:14 [hh:mm:ss]
%FLH: Re-booting system after download
```

After the file is loaded into flash memory and a checksum is performed, the router is rebooted to run the new IOS file.

 A Cisco router can become a TFTP-server host for a router system image that's run in flash memory. The global configuration command is `tftp-server flash:` *ios_name*.

Backing Up and Restoring the Cisco Configuration

Any changes that you make to the router configuration are stored in the running-config file. And if you don't enter a `copy run start` command after you make a change to running-config, that change will go poof if the router reboots or gets powered down. So, you probably want to make another backup of the configuration information just in case the router or switch completely dies on you. Even if your machine is healthy and happy, it's good to have for reference and documentation reasons.

In the following sections, I'll describe how to copy the configuration of a router and a switch to a TFTP server and how to restore that configuration.

Backing Up the Cisco Router Configuration

To copy the router's configuration from a router to a TFTP server, you can use either the `copy running-config tftp` or the `copy startup-config tftp` command. Either one will back up the router configuration that's currently running in DRAM or that's stored in NVRAM.

Verifying the Current Configuration

To verify the configuration in DRAM, use the `show running-config` command (`sh run` for short) like this:

```
Router#sh run
Building configuration...
```

```
Current configuration:
!
version 12.0
```

The current configuration information indicates that the router is now running version 12.0 of the IOS.

Verifying the Stored Configuration

Next, you should check the configuration stored in NVRAM. To see this, use the show startup-config command (sh start for short) like this:

```
Router#sh start
Using 366 out of 32762 bytes
!
version 11.2
```

The second line shows you how much room your backup configuration is using. Here, we can see that NVRAM is 32KB and that only 366 bytes of it are used. Also notice that the version of configuration in NVRAM is 11.2. That's because I haven't copied running-config to startup-config since upgrading the router.

If you're not sure that the files are the same and the running-config file is what you want to use, then use the copy running-config startup-config. This will help you verify that both files are in fact the same. I'll go through this with you in the next section.

Copying the Current Configuration to NVRAM

By copying running-config to NVRAM as a backup, as shown in the following output, you're assured that your running-config will always be reloaded if the router gets rebooted. In the new IOS version 12.0, you're prompted for the filename you want to use. And since the version of IOS was 11.2 the last time a copy run start was performed, the router will tell us that it's going to replace that file with the new 12.0 version:

```
Router#copy run start
Destination filename [startup-config]?[Enter]
Warning: Attempting to overwrite an NVRAM configuration
  previously written by a different version of the system
  image.
Overwrite the previous NVRAM configuration?
  [confirm][Enter]
Building configuration...
[OK]
```

Now when you run show startup-config, the version shows 12.0:

```
Router#sh start
Using 487 out of 32762 bytes
!
version 12.0
```

Copying the Configuration to a TFTP Server

Once the file is copied to NVRAM, you can make a second backup to a TFTP server by using the copy running-config tftp command (copy run tftp for short), like this:

```
Router#copy run tftp
Address or name of remote host []?192.168.0.120
Destination filename [router-confg]?todd1-confg
!!
487 bytes copied in 12.236 secs (40 bytes/sec)
Router#
```

Notice that this took only two exclamation points (!!)—which means that 20 packets have been transferred (10 for each exclamation point). In the preceding example, I named the file todd1-confg because I had not set a hostname for the router. If you have a hostname already configured, the command will automatically use the hostname plus the extension -confg as the name of the file.

Restoring the Cisco Router Configuration

If you've changed your router's running-config file and want to restore the configuration to the version in the startup-config file, the easiest way to do this is to use the copy startup-config running-config command (copy start run for short). You can also use the older Cisco command config mem to restore a configuration. Of course, this will work only if you first copied running-config into NVRAM before making any changes!

If you did copy the router's configuration to a TFTP server as a second backup, you can restore the configuration using the copy tftp running-config command (copy tftp run for short) or the copy tftp startup-config command (copy tftp start for short), as shown here (remember that the old command that provides this function is config net):

```
Router#copy tftp run
Address or name of remote host []?192.168.0.120
Source filename []?todd1-confg
Destination filename [running-config]?[Enter]
Accessing tftp://192.168.0.120/todd1-confg...
```

```
Loading todd1-confg from 192.168.0.120 (via Ethernet0):
!!
[OK - 487/4096 bytes]
487 bytes copied in 5.400 secs (97 bytes/sec)
Router#
00:38:31: %SYS-5-CONFIG: Configured from
  tftp://192.168.0.120/todd1-confg
Router#
```

The configuration file is an ASCII text file, meaning that before you copy the configuration stored on a TFTP server back to a router, you can make changes to the file with any text editor.

 It is important to remember that when you copy or merge a configuration from a TFTP server to a router's RAM, the interfaces are shut down by default and you must manually go and enable each interface with the no shutdown command.

Erasing the Configuration

To delete the startup-config file on a Cisco router, use the command erase startup-config, like this:

```
Router#erase startup-config
Erasing the nvram filesystem will remove all files!
  Continue? [confirm][Enter]
[OK]
Erase of nvram: complete
Router#
```

This command deletes the contents of NVRAM on the router, so the next time the router boots, it'll run the setup mode.

Using Cisco Discovery Protocol (CDP)

Cisco Discovery Protocol (CDP) is a proprietary protocol designed by Cisco to help administrators collect information about both locally attached and remote devices. By using CDP, you can gather hardware and protocol information about neighbor devices, which is useful info for troubleshooting and documenting the network!

In the following sections I am going to discuss the CDP timer and CDP commands used to verify your network.

Getting CDP Timers and Holdtime Information

The show cdp command (sh cdp for short) gives you information about two CDP global parameters that can be configured on Cisco devices:

- *CDP timer* is how often CDP packets are transmitted to all active interfaces.

- *CDP holdtime* is the amount of time that the device will hold packets received from neighbor devices.

Both Cisco routers and Cisco switches use the same parameters.

The output on a router looks like this:

```
Router#sh cdp
Global CDP information:
        Sending CDP packets every 60 seconds
        Sending a holdtime value of 180 seconds
Router#
```

Use the global commands cdp holdtime and cdp timer to configure the CDP holdtime and timer on a router:

```
Router#config t
Enter configuration commands, one per line.  End with
  CNTL/Z.
Router(config)#cdp ?
  holdtime  Specify the holdtime (in sec) to be sent in
            packets
  timer     Specify the rate at which CDP packets are
            sent (in sec)
  run

Router(config)#cdp timer 90
Router(config)#cdp holdtime 240
Router(config)#^Z
```

You can turn off CDP completely with the no cdp run command from the global configuration mode of a router. To turn CDP off or on for an interface, use the no cdp enable and cdp enable commands. Be patient—I'll work through these with you in a second.

Gathering Neighbor Information

The show cdp neighbor command (sh cdp nei for short) delivers information about directly connected devices. It's important to remember that CDP packets aren't passed through a Cisco switch and that you only see what's directly attached. So this means that if your router is connected to a switch, you won't see any of the devices hooked up to that switch.

The following output shows the show cdp neighbor command used on a 2509 router:

```
Todd2509#sh cdp nei
Capability Codes: R - Router, T - Trans Bridge,
  B - Source Route Bridge, S - Switch, H - Host,
  I - IGMP, r - Repeater
Device ID  Local Intrfce Holdtme Capability Platform Port ID
1900Switch    Eth 0        238       T S       1900     2
2500B         Ser 0        138        R        2500    Ser 0
Todd2509#
```

Okay, you are directly connected with a console cable to the 2509 router, and the 2509 router is directly connected to a switch with a hostname of 1900Switch and a 2500 router with a hostname of 2500B. Notice that no devices connected to the 1900Switch and the 2500B router show up in the CDP table on the 2509 router. All you get to see are directly connected devices.

Table 8.5 summarizes the information displayed by the show cdp neighbor command for each device.

TABLE 8.5   Output of the show cdp neighbor Command

Field	Description
Device ID	The hostname of the device directly connected.
Local Interface	The port or interface on which you are receiving the CDP packet.
Holdtime	The amount of time the router will hold the information before discarding it if no more CDP packets are received.
Capability	The capability of the neighbor, such as the router, switch, or repeater. The capability codes are listed at the top of the command output.
Platform	The type of Cisco device directly connected. In the previous output, a Cisco 2500 router and Cisco 1900 switch are attached Directly to the 2509 router. The 2509 only sees the 1900 switch and the 2500 router connected through its serial 0 interface.
Port ID	The neighbor device's port or interface on which the CDP packets are multicast.

It is imperative that you can look at the output of a show cdp neighbors command and decipher the neighbor's device (capability, i.e., router or switch), model number (platform), your port connecting to that device (local interface), and the port of the neighbor connecting to you (port ID).

Another command that'll deliver the goods on neighbor information is the show cdp neighbor detail command (show cdp nei de for short). This command can be run on both routers and switches, and it displays detailed information about each device connected to the device you're running the command on. Check out this router output for an example:

```
Todd2509#sh cdp neighbor detail
-------------------------
Device ID: 1900Switch
Entry address(es):
  IP address: 192.168.12.2
Platform: cisco 1900,  Capabilities: Trans-Bridge Switch
Interface: Ethernet0,  Port ID (outgoing port): 2
Holdtime : 166 sec
Version :
V9.00
-------------------------
Device ID: 2501B
Entry address(es):
  IP address: 172.16.10.2
Platform: cisco 2500,  Capabilities: Router
Interface: Serial0,  Port ID (outgoing port): Serial0
Holdtime : 154 sec
Version :
Cisco Internetwork Operating System Software
IOS (tm) 3000 Software (IGS-J-L), Version 11.1(5),
  RELEASE SOFTWARE (fc1)Copyright (c) 1986-1996 by cisco
  Systems, Inc.Compiled Tue 05-Aug-03 11:48 by mkamson
Todd2509#
```

What are we being shown here? First, we're given the hostname and IP address of all directly connected devices. In addition to the same information displayed by the show cdp neighbor command (see Table 8.5), the show cdp neighbor detail command also gives us the IOS version of the neighbor device.

Remember that you can only see the IP address of directly connected devices.

The show cdp entry * command displays the same information as the show cdp neighbor details command. Here's an example of the router output using the show cdp entry * command:

```
Todd2509#sh cdp entry *
-------------------------
Device ID: 1900Switch
Entry address(es):
  IP address: 192.168.12.2
Platform: cisco 1900,  Capabilities: Trans-Bridge Switch
Interface: Ethernet0,  Port ID (outgoing port): 2
Holdtime : 223 sec
Version :
V9.00

-------------------------
Device ID: 2501B
Entry address(es):
  IP address: 172.16.10.2
Platform: cisco 2500,  Capabilities: Router
Interface: Serial0,  Port ID (outgoing port): Serial0
Holdtime : 151 sec
Version :
Cisco Internetwork Operating System Software
IOS (tm) 3000 Software (IGS-J-L), Version 11.1(5),
  RELEASE SOFTWARE (fc1)Copyright (c) 1986-1996 by cisco
  Systems, Inc.Compiled Tue 05-Aug-03 11:48 by mkamson
Todd2509#
```

There isn't any difference between the show cdp neighbors detail and show cdp entry * commands. However, the sh cdp entry * command has two options that the show cdp neighbors detail command does not:

```
Todd2509#sh cdp entry * ?
  protocol  Protocol information
  version   Version information
  |         Output modifiers
  <cr>

Todd2509#sh cdp entry * protocol
Protocol information for 1900Switch :
  IP address: 192.168.12.2
Protocol information for 2501B :
  IP address: 172.16.10.2
```

The preceding output of the show cdp entry * protocols command can show you just the IP addresses of each directly connected neighbor. The show cdp entry * version will show you only the IOS version of your directly connected neighbors:

```
Todd2509#sh cdp entry * version
Version information for 1900Switch :
  Cisco Internetwork Operating System Software
Platform: cisco 1900,   Capabilities: Trans-Bridge Switch
Interface: Ethernet0,   Port ID (outgoing port): 2
Holdtime : 223 sec
Version :V9.00

Version information for 2501B :
  Cisco Internetwork Operating System Software
IOS (tm) C2600 Software (C2500-IGS-J-L), Version 11.1(5), RELEASE SOFTWARE (fc1)
Copyright (c) 1986-2004 by cisco Systems, Inc.
Compiled Wed 28-Apr-04 15:30 by kellmill
```

Although the show cdp neighbors detail and show cdp entry commands are very similar, the show cdp entry command allows you to display only one line of output for each directly connected neighbor, whereas the show cdp neighbor detail command does not. Next, let's look at the show cdp traffic command.

Gathering Interface Traffic Information

The show cdp traffic command displays information about interface traffic, including the number of CDP packets sent and received and the errors with CDP.

The following output shows the show cdp traffic command used on the 2509 router:

```
Todd2509#sh cdp traffic
CDP counters:
        Packets output: 13, Input: 8
        Hdr syntax: 0, Chksum error: 0, Encaps failed: 0
        No memory: 0, Invalid packet: 0, Fragmented: 0
Todd2509#
```

This is not really the most important information you can gather from a router, but it does show how many CDP packets are sent and received on a device.

Gathering Port and Interface Information

The show cdp interface command gives you the CDP status on router interfaces or switch ports.

As I said earlier, you can turn off CDP completely on a router by using the no cdp run command. But remember that you can also turn off CDP on a per-interface basis with the no cdp enable command. You enable a port with the cdp enable command. All ports and interfaces default to cdp enable.

On a router, the show cdp interface command displays information about each interface using CDP, including the encapsulation on the line, the timer, and the holdtime for each interface. Here's an example of this command's output on the 2509 router:

```
Todd2509#sh cdp interface
Ethernet0 is up, line protocol is up
  Encapsulation ARPA
  Sending CDP packets every 60 seconds
  Holdtime is 180 seconds
Serial0 is administratively down, line protocol is down
  Encapsulation HDLC
  Sending CDP packets every 60 seconds
  Holdtime is 180 seconds
Serial1 is administratively down, line protocol is down
  Encapsulation HDLC
  Sending CDP packets every 60 seconds
  Holdtime is 180 seconds
```

To turn off CDP on one interface on a router, use the no cdp enable command from interface configuration mode:

```
Todd2509#config t
Enter configuration commands, one per line.  End with
  CNTL/Z.
Router(config)#int s0
Router(config-if)#no cdp enable
Router(config-if)#^Z
```

Verify the change with the show cdp interface command:

```
Todd2509#sh cdp int
Ethernet0 is up, line protocol is up
  Encapsulation ARPA
  Sending CDP packets every 60 seconds
  Holdtime is 180 seconds
Serial1 is administratively down, line protocol is down
  Encapsulation HDLC
  Sending CDP packets every 60 seconds
  Holdtime is 180 seconds
Todd2509#
```

Notice that serial 0 isn't listed in the router output. To get that output, you'd have to perform a `cdp enable` on serial 0. It would then show up in the output.

Documenting a Network Topology using CDP

As the title of this section implies, I'm now going to show you how to document a current network by using CDP. You'll learn to determine the appropriate router types, interface types, and IP addresses of various interfaces using only CDP commands and the `show running-config` command. And you can only console into the Lab_A router to document the network. You'll have to assign any remote routers the next IP address in each range. Figure 8.2 is what you'll use to complete the documentation.

 **Real World Scenario**

CDP Can Save Lives!

Karen was just hired as a senior network consultant at a large hospital in Dallas, Texas. She is expected to be able to take care of any problem that comes up. No stress here—she only has to worry about people possibly not getting the right health care if the network goes down! Talk about a potential life-or-death situation!

Karen starts her job, happily. Soon, of course, the network has some problems. She asks one of the junior administrators for a network map so she can troubleshoot the network. This person tells her that the old senior administrator (who just got fired) had them with him and now no one can find them—ouch!

Doctors are calling every couple of minutes because they can't get the necessary information they need to take care of their patients. What should she do?

CDP to the rescue! Thank God this hospital has all Cisco routers and switches and that CDP is enabled by default on all Cisco devices. Also, luckily, the disgruntled administrator who just got fired didn't turn off CDP on any devices before he left.

All Karen has to do now is to use the `show cdp neighbor detail` command to find all the information she needs about each device to help draw out the hospital network and save lives!

The only snag to nailing this comes at you if you don't know the passwords of all those devices. Your only hope then is to somehow find out the access passwords or to perform password recovery on them.

So, use CDP—you never know when you may end up saving someone's life.

This is a true story.

FIGURE 8.2   Documenting a network topology using CDP

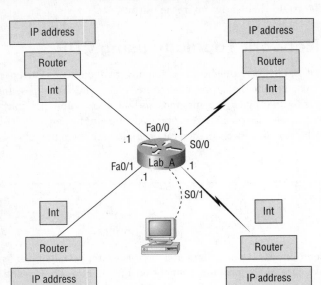

In this output, you can see that you have a router with four interfaces: two FastEthernet and two serial. First, determine the IP addresses of each interface by using the show running-config command:

```
Lab_A#sh running-config
Building configuration...

Current configuration : 960 bytes
!
version 12.2
service timestamps debug uptime
service timestamps log uptime
no service password-encryption
!
hostname Lab_A
!
ip subnet-zero
!
!
interface FastEthernet0/0
 ip address 192.168.21.1 255.255.255.0
```

```
 duplex auto
!
interface FastEthernet0/1
 ip address 192.168.18.1 255.255.255.0
 duplex auto
!
interface Serial0/0
ip address 192.168.23.1 255.255.255.0
!
interface Serial0/1
ip address 192.168.28.1 255.255.255.0
!
ip classless
!
line con 0
line aux 0
line vty 0 4
!
end
```

With this step completed, you can now write down the IP addresses of the Lab_A router's four interfaces. Next, you need to determine the type of device on the other end of each of these interfaces. It's easy to do this—just use the show cdp neighbors command:

```
Lab_A#sh cdp neighbors
Capability Codes: R - Router, T - Trans Bridge, B - Source Route Bridge
                  S - Switch, H - Host, I - IGMP, r - Repeater
  Device ID   Local Intrfce   Holdtme   Capability Platform  Port ID
  Lab_B       Fas 0/0         178          R        2501      E0
  Lab_C       Fas 0/1         137          R        2621      Fa0/0
  Lab_D       Ser 0/0         178          R        2514      S1
  Lab_E       Ser 0/1         137          R        2620      S0/1
  Lab_A#
```

You've got a good deal of information now! By using both the show running-config and show cdp neighbors commands, you know about all the IP addresses of the Lab_A router, plus the types of routers connected to each of the Lab_A router's links and all the interfaces of the remote routers.

And by using all the information gathered from show running-config and show cdp neighbors, we can now create the topology in Figure 8.3.

FIGURE 8.3 Network topology documented

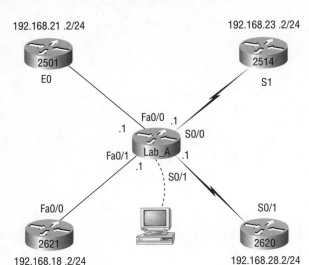

Okay—if we needed to, we could've also used the `show cdp neighbors detail` command to view the neighbor's IP addresses. But since we know the IP addresses of each link on the Lab_A router, we already know what the next available IP address is going to be.

Using Telnet

Telnet, part of the TCP/IP protocol suite, is a virtual terminal protocol that allows you to make connections to remote devices, gather information, and run programs.

After your routers and switches are configured, you can use the Telnet program to reconfigure and/or check up on your routers and switches without using a console cable. You run the Telnet program by typing `telnet` from any command prompt (DOS or Cisco). You need to have VTY passwords set on the routers for this to work.

Remember, you can't use CDP to gather information about routers and switches that aren't directly connected to your device. But you can use the Telnet application to connect to your neighbor devices and then run CDP on those remote devices to get information on them.

You can issue the `telnet` command from any router prompt like this:

```
Todd2509#telnet 172.16.10.2
Trying 172.16.10.2 ... Open

Password required, but none set

[Connection to 172.16.10.2 closed by foreign host]
Todd2509#
```

As you can see, I didn't set my passwords—how embarrassing! Remember that the VTY ports on a router are configured as login, meaning that we have to either set the VTY passwords or use the no login command. (You can review setting passwords in Chapter 4, "Introduction to the Cisco IOS," if you need to.)

 If you find you can't telnet into a device, it could be that the password on the remote device hasn't been set. It's also possible that an access control list is filtering the Telnet session.

On a Cisco router, you don't need to use the telnet command; you can just type in an IP address from a command prompt and the router will assume that you want to telnet to the device. Here's how that looks by using just the IP address:

```
Todd2509#172.16.10.2
Trying 172.16.10.2 ... Open

Password required, but none set

[Connection to 172.16.10.2 closed by foreign host]
Todd2509#
```

At this point, it would be a great idea to set those VTY passwords on the router I want to telnet into. Here's what I did on the remote router named 2501B:

```
2501B#config t
Enter configuration commands, one per line.  End with
  CNTL/Z.
2501B(config)#line vty 0 4
2501B(config-line)#password todd
2501B(config-line)#login
2501B(config-line)#^Z
2501B#
%SYS-5-CONFIG_I: Configured from console by console
```

Now let's try this again. Here I'm connecting to the router from the 2509's console:

```
Todd2509#172.16.10.2
Trying 172.16.10.2 ... Open

User Access Verification

Password:
2501B>
```

Remember that the VTY password is the user-mode password, not the enable-mode password. Watch what happens when I try to go into privileged mode after telnetting into router 2501B:

```
2501B>en
% No password set
2501B>
```

It is basically saying, "No way!" This is a really good security feature because you don't want anyone telnetting into your device and being able to just type the `enable` command to get into privileged mode. You've got to set your enable-mode password or enable secret password to use Telnet to configure remote devices!

 When you telnet into a remote device, you will not see console messages by default. For example, you will not see debugging output. To allow console messages to be sent to your Telnet session, use the `terminal monitor` command.

In the following examples, I am going to show you how to telnet into multiple devices simultaneously and then show you how to use hostnames instead of IP addresses.

Telnetting into Multiple Devices Simultaneously

If you telnet to a router or switch, you can end the connection by typing `exit` at any time. But what if you want to keep your connection to a remote device but still come back to your original router console? To do that, you can press the Ctrl+Shift+6 key combination, release it, and then press X.

Here's an example of connecting to multiple devices from my Todd2509 router console:

```
Todd2509#telnet 172.16.10.2
Trying 172.16.10.2 ... Open

User Access Verification

Password:
2501B>[Cntl+Shift+6, then X]
Todd2509#
```

In this example, I telnetted to the 2501B router and then typed the password to enter user mode. I next pressed Ctrl+Shift+6, then X (but you can't see that because it doesn't show on the screen output). Notice that my command prompt is now back at the Todd2509 router.

You can also telnet into a 1900 switch, but to get away with that you must set the enable secret password on the switch before you can gain access via the Telnet application.

In the following example, I telnetted into a 1900 switch that responded by giving me the console output of the switch:

```
Todd2509#telnet 192.168.0.148
Trying 192.168.0.148 ... Open


Catalyst 1900 Management Console
Copyright (c) Cisco Systems, Inc.  1993-1999
All rights reserved.
Enterprise Edition Software
Ethernet Address:       00-B0-64-75-6B-C0


PCA Number:             73-3122-04
PCA Serial Number:      FAB040131E2
Model Number:           WS-C1912-A
System Serial Number:   FAB0401U0JQ
Power Supply S/N:       PHI033108SD
PCB Serial Number:      FAB040131E2,73-3122-04
------------------------------------------------


1 user(s) now active on Management Console.


        User Interface Menu

     [M] Menus
     [K] Command Line


Enter Selection:
```

At this point, I pressed Ctrl+Shift+6, then X, which took me back to my Todd2509 router console:

```
Todd2509#
```

 Yes, I know the 1900 is an old switch, but it works great for home labs, testing, and explaining routing/switching concepts. I am not advocating using 1900s in production.

Checking Telnet Connections

To see the connections made from your router to a remote device, use the show sessions command.

```
Todd2509#sh sessions
Conn Host          Address         Byte Idle Conn Name
   1 172.16.10.2    172.16.10.2      0    0  172.16.10.2
*  2 192.168.0.148  192.168.0.148    0    0  192.168.0.148
Todd2509#
```

See that asterisk (*) next to connection 2? It means that session 2 was your last session. You can return to your last session by pressing Enter twice. You can also return to any session by typing the number of the connection and pressing Enter.

Checking Telnet Users

You can list all active consoles and VTY ports in use on your router with the show users command:

```
Todd2509#sh users
    Line     User    Host(s)          Idle Location
*   0 con 0          172.16.10.2      00:07:52
                     192.168.0.148    00:07:18
```

In the command's output, con represents the local console. In this example, the console is connected to two remote IP addresses, or in other words, two devices.

In the next example, I typed sh users on the 2501B router that the Todd2509 router had telnetted into:

```
2501B>sh users
    Line     User    Host(s)          Idle Location
    0 con 0          idle             9
*   2 vty 0
```

This output shows that the console is active and that VTY port 2 is being used. The asterisk represents the current terminal session from which the show user command was entered.

Closing Telnet Sessions

You can end Telnet sessions a few different ways—typing exit or disconnect is probably the easiest and quickest.

To end a session from a remote device, use the exit command:

```
Todd2509#[Enter] and again [Enter]
[Resuming connection 2 to 192.168.0.148 ... ]

1900Switch>exit
```

```
[Connection to 192.168.0.148 closed by foreign host]
Todd2509#
```

Since the 1900Switch was my last session, I just pressed Enter twice to return to that session. To end a session from a local device, use the disconnect command:

```
Todd2509#disconnect ?
  <1-2>  The number of an active network connection
  WORD   The name of an active network connection
  <cr>
```

```
Todd2509#disconnect 1
Closing connection to 172.16.10.2 [confirm] enter
Todd2509#
```

In this example, I used the session number 1 because that was the connection to the 2501B router that I wanted to end. As I said, you can use the show sessions command to see the connection number.

If you want to end a session of a device attached to your local device through Telnet, you should first check to see if any devices are attached to your router. To get that information, use the show users command like this:

```
2501B#sh users
    Line      User      Host(s)       Idle Location
*   0 con 0             idle          0
    1 aux 0             idle          0
    2 vty 0             idle          0 172.16.10.1
```

This output shows that VTY 0 has IP address 172.16.10.1 connected. That's the Todd2509 router.

To clear the connection, use the clear line # command:

```
2501B#clear line 2
[confirm]
 [OK]
```

Then verify that the user has been disconnected with the show users command:

```
2501B#sh users
    Line      User      Host(s)       Idle Location
*   0 con 0             idle          0
    1 aux 0             idle          1
```

```
2501B#
```

This output confirms that the line has been cleared.

Resolving Hostnames

In order to use a hostname rather than an IP address to connect to a remote device, the device that you are using to make the connection must be able to translate the hostname to an IP address.

There are two ways to resolve hostnames to IP addresses: building a host table on each router or building a Domain Name System (DNS) server, which is similar to a dynamic host table.

Building a Host Table

A host table provides name resolution only on the router that it was built upon. The command to build a host table on a router is as follows:

ip host *host_name tcp_port_number ip_address*

The default is TCP port number 23, but you can create a session using Telnet with a different TCP port number if you want. You can also assign up to eight IP addresses to a hostname.

Here's an example of configuring a host table with two entries to resolve the names for the 2501B router and the switch:

```
Todd2509#config t
Enter configuration commands, one per line.  End with
  CNTL/Z.
Todd2509(config)#ip host ?
  WORD  Name of host

Todd2509(config)#ip host 2501B ?
  <0-65535>  Default telnet port number
  A.B.C.D    Host IP address (maximum of 8)

Todd2509(config)#ip host 2501B 172.16.10.2 ?
  A.B.C.D  Host IP address (maximum of 8)
  <cr>
Todd2509(config)#ip host 2501B 172.16.10.2
Todd2509(config)#ip host 1900Switch 192.168.0.148
Todd2509(config)#^Z
```

And to see the newly built host table, just use the show hosts command:

```
Todd2509#sh hosts
Default domain is not set
Name/address lookup uses domain service
Name servers are 255.255.255.255

Host          Flags    Age Type   Address(es)
```

```
2501B          (perm, OK)  0    IP     172.16.10.2
1900Switch     (perm, OK)  0    IP     192.168.0.148
Todd2509#
```

You can see the two hostnames plus their associated IP addresses in the preceding router output. The `perm` in the `Flags` column means that the entry is manually configured. If it said `temp`, it would be an entry that was resolved by DNS.

 The show hosts command provides information on temporary DNS entries and permanent name-to-address mappings created using the `ip host` command.

To verify that the host table resolves names, try typing the hostnames at a router prompt. Remember that if you don't specify the command, the router assumes you want to telnet. In the following example, I used the hostnames to telnet into the remote devices, and pressed Ctrl+Shift+6, then X to return to the main console of the Todd2509 router:

```
Todd2509#2501b
Trying 2501B (172.16.10.2)... Open

User Access Verification

Password:
2501B>
Todd2509#[Ctrl+Shift+6, then X]
Todd2509#1900switch
Trying 1900switch (192.168.0.148)... Open

Catalyst 1900 Management Console
Copyright (c) Cisco Systems, Inc.  1993-1999
All rights reserved.
Enterprise Edition Software
Ethernet Address:       00-B0-64-75-6B-C0

PCA Number:             73-3122-04
PCA Serial Number:      FAB040131E2
Model Number:           WS-C1912-A
System Serial Number:   FAB0401U0JQ
Power Supply S/N:       PHI033108SD
PCB Serial Number:      FAB040131E2,73-3122-04
-------------------------------------------------

1 user(s) now active on Management Console.
```

```
      User Interface Menu

   [M] Menus
   [K] Command Line

Enter Selection:[Ctrl+Shift+6, then X]
Todd2509#
```

I successfully used entries in the host table to create a session to two devices and used the names to telnet into both devices. Notice that the entries in the following show sessions output now display the hostnames and IP addresses instead of just the IP addresses:

```
Todd2509#sh sess
Conn Host           Address          Byte  Idle Conn Name
   1 1900switch     192.168.0.148       0     0 switch
*  2 2501b          172.16.10.2         0     0 2501b
Todd2509#
```

If you want to remove a hostname from the table, just use the no ip host command like this:

```
RouterA(config)#no ip host 2501B
```

The problem with the host table method is that you would need to create a host table on each router to be able to resolve names. And if you have a whole bunch of routers and want to resolve names, using DNS is a much better choice!

Using DNS to Resolve Names

So if you have a lot of devices and don't want to create a host table in each device, you can use a DNS server to resolve hostnames.

Any time a Cisco device receives a command it doesn't understand, it will try to resolve it through DNS by default. Watch what happens when I type the special command todd at a Cisco router prompt:

```
Todd2509#todd
Translating "todd"...domain server (255.255.255.255)
% Unknown command or computer name, or unable to find
  computer address
Todd2509#
```

It doesn't know my name or what command I am trying to type, so it tries to resolve this through DNS. This is really annoying for two reasons: first, because it doesn't know my name <grin>, and second, because I need to hang out and wait for the name lookup to time out. You can get around this and prevent a time-consuming DNS lookup by using the no ip domain-lookup command on your router from global configuration mode.

If you have a DNS server on your network, you need to add a few commands to make DNS name resolution work:

- The first command is `ip domain-lookup`, which is turned on by default. It only needs to be entered if you previously turned it off (with the `no ip domain-lookup` command).

- The second command is `ip name-server`. This sets the IP address of the DNS server. You can enter the IP addresses of up to six servers.

- The last command is `ip domain-name`. Although this command is optional, it really should be set. It appends the domain name to the hostname you type in. Since DNS uses a fully qualified domain name (FQDN) system, you must have a full DNS name, in the form `domain.com`.

Here's an example of using these three commands:

```
Todd2509#config t
Enter configuration commands, one per line.  End with
  CNTL/Z.
Todd2509(config)#ip domain-lookup
Todd2509(config)#ip name-server ?
  A.B.C.D  Domain server IP address (maximum of 6)
Todd2509(config)#ip name-server 192.168.0.70
Todd2509(config)#ip domain-name lammle.com
Todd2509(config)#^Z
Todd2509#
```

After the DNS configurations are set, you can test the DNS server by using a hostname to ping or telnet a device like this:

```
Todd2509#ping 2501b
Translating "2501b"...domain server (192.168.0.70) [OK]
Type escape sequence to abort.
Sending 5, 100-byte ICMP Echos to 172.16.10.2, timeout is
  2 seconds:
!!!!!
Success rate is 100 percent (5/5), round-trip min/avg/max
  = 28/31/32 ms
```

Notice that the router uses the DNS server to resolve the name.

After a name is resolved using DNS, use the `show hosts` command to see that the device cached this information in the host table:

```
Todd2509#sh hosts
Default domain is lammle.com
Name/address lookup uses domain service
Name servers are 192.168.0.70
```

```
Host                 Flags       Age Type   Address(es)
2501b.lammle.com     (temp, OK)  0   IP     172.16.10.2
1900switch           (perm, OK)  0   IP     192.168.0.148
Todd2509#
```

 Real World Scenario

Should You Use a Host Table or DNS Server?

Karen has finally finished drawing out her network by using CDP and the doctors are much happier. However, Karen is having a difficult time administering the network because she has to look at the network drawing to find an IP address every time she needs to telnet to a remote router.

Karen was thinking about putting host tables on each router, but with literally hundreds of routers, this is a daunting task.

Most networks have a DNS server now anyway, so adding a hundred or so hostnames into it would be an easy way to go—certainly easier then adding these hostnames to each and every router! Just add the three commands on each router and blammo—you're resolving names.

Using a DNS server makes it easy to update any old entries too—remember, even one little change and off you go to each and every router to manually update its table if you're using static host tables.

Keep in mind that this has nothing to do with name resolution on the network and nothing to do with what a host on the network is trying to accomplish. This is only used when you're trying to resolve names from the router console.

The entry that was resolved is shown as `temp`, but the 1900 switch device is still `perm`, meaning that it's a static entry. Notice that the hostname is a full domain name. If I hadn't used the `ip domain-name lammle.com` command, I would have needed to type in `ping 2501b.lammle.com`, which is a pain.

Checking Network Connectivity and Troubleshooting

You can use the `ping` and `traceroute` commands to test connectivity to remote devices, and both of them can be used with many protocols, not just IP. But don't forget that the `show ip route` command is a good troubleshooting command for verifying your routing table and the `show interfaces` command will show you the status of each interface.

I'm not going to get into the show ip route and show interfaces commands here because we've already been over them in Chapter 4. But I am going to go over both the debug command and the show processes command you need to troubleshoot a router.

Using the *ping* Command

So far, you've seen many examples of pinging devices to test IP connectivity and name resolution using the DNS server. To see all the different protocols that you can use with the ping program, type ping ?:

```
Todd2509#ping ?
  WORD       Ping destination address or hostname
  apollo     Apollo echo
  appletalk  Appletalk echo
  clns       CLNS echo
  decnet     DECnet echo
  ip         IP echo
  ipx        Novell/IPX echo
  srb        srb echo
  tag        Tag encapsulated IP echo
  vines      Vines echo
  xns        XNS echo
  <cr>
```

The ping output displays the minimum, average, and maximum times it takes for a ping packet to find a specified system and return. Here's an example:

```
Todd2509#ping todd2509
Translating "todd2509"...domain server (192.168.0.70)[OK]
Type escape sequence to abort.
Sending 5, 100-byte ICMP Echos to 192.168.0.121, timeout
  is 2 seconds:
!!!!!
Success rate is 100 percent (5/5), round-trip min/avg/max
  = 32/32/32 ms
Todd2509#
```

You can see that the DNS server was used to resolve the name, and the device was pinged in 32ms (milliseconds).

The ping command can be used in user and privileged mode but not configuration mode.

Using the *traceroute* Command

Traceroute (the `traceroute` command, or `trace` for short) shows the path a packet takes to get to a remote device. It uses time to live (TTL) time-outs and ICMP error messages to outline the path a packet takes through an internetwork to arrive at remote host.

The *trace* command that can be used from either user mode or privileged mode allows you to figure out which router in the path to an unreachable network host should be examined more closely for the cause of the network's failure.

To see the protocols that you can use with the `traceroute` command, type `traceroute ?`:

```
Todd2509#traceroute ?
  WORD       Trace route to destination address or
             hostname
  appletalk  AppleTalk Trace
  clns       ISO CLNS Trace
  ip         IP Trace
  ipx        IPX Trace
  oldvines   Vines Trace (Cisco)
  vines      Vines Trace (Banyan)
  <cr>
```

The `trace` command shows the hop or hops that a packet traverses on its way to a remote device. Here's an example:

```
Todd2509#trace 2501b
Type escape sequence to abort.
Tracing the route to 2501b.lammle.com (172.16.10.2)

  1 2501b.lammle.com (172.16.10.2) 16 msec *  16 msec
Todd2509#
```

You can see that the packet went through only one hop to find the destination.

> Do not get confused! You can't use the `tracert` command—it's a Windows command. For a router, use the `traceroute` command!

Here's an example of using `tracert` from a Windows DOS prompt (notice the command `tracert`!):

```
C:\>tracert www.whitehouse.gov
Tracing route to a1289.g.akamai.net [69.8.201.74]
over a maximum of 30 hops:
  1     1 ms      1 ms     1 ms   10.0.1.1
  2     *         *        *      Request timed out.
```

```
3    46 ms    46 ms    46 ms  hlrn-dsl-gw15.hlrn.qwest.net [207.225.102.107]
4    47 ms    45 ms    52 ms  hlrn-agw1.inet.qwest.net [207.225.112.157]
5    46 ms    46 ms    46 ms  hlr-core-01.inet.qwest.net [205.171.253.45]
6    46 ms    46 ms    46 ms  hlr-core-02.inet.qwest.net [205.171.253.2]
7    46 ms    45 ms    46 ms  apa-cntr-02.inet.qwest.net [205.171.253.30]
8    46 ms    46 ms    46 ms  63.150.160.42
9    47 ms    46 ms    46 ms  69.8.201.74
Trace complete.
```

Okay, let's move on now and talk about how to troubleshoot your network using the debug command.

Debugging

Debug is a troubleshooting command that's available from the privileged exec mode (of Cisco IOS). It's used to display information about various router operations and the related traffic generated or received by the router, plus any error messages.

It's a useful and informative tool, but you really need to understand some important facts about its use. Debug is regarded as a very high-priority task because it can consume a huge amount of resources and the router is forced to process-switch the packets being debugged. So you don't just use Debug as a monitoring tool—it's meant to be used for a short period of time and only as a troubleshooting tool. By using it, you can really find out some truly significant facts about both working and faulty software and/or hardware components.

Because debugging output takes priority over other network traffic, and because the debug all command generates more output than any other debug command, it can severely diminish the router's performance—even render it unusable. So in virtually all cases, it's best to use more-specific debug commands.

As you can see from the following output, you can't enable debugging from user mode, only privileged mode:

```
Todd2509>debug ?
% Unrecognized command
Todd2509>en
Todd2509#debug ?
  aaa                 AAA Authentication, Authorization and Accounting
  access-expression   Boolean access expression
  adjacency           adjacency
  all                 Enable all debugging
[output cut]
```

If you've got the freedom to pretty much take out a router and you really want to have some fun with debugging, use the debug all command:

```
Todd2509#debug all
```

This may severely impact network performance. Continue? (yes/[no]):**yes**

All possible debugging has been turned on

```
2d20h: SNMP: HC Timer 824AE5CC fired
2d20h: SNMP: HC Timer 824AE5CC rearmed, delay = 20000
2d20h: Serial0/0: HDLC myseq 4, mineseen 0, yourseen 0, line down
2d20h:
2d20h: Rudpv1 Sent: Pkts 0,  Data Bytes 0,  Data Pkts 0
2d20h: Rudpv1 Rcvd: Pkts 0,  Data Bytes 0,  Data Pkts 0
2d20h: Rudpv1 Discarded: 0,  Retransmitted 0
2d20h:
2d20h: RIP-TIMER: periodic timer expired
2d20h: Serial0/0: HDLC myseq 5, mineseen 0, yourseen 0, line down
2d20h: Serial0/0: attempting to restart
2d20h: PowerQUICC(0/0): DCD is up.
2d20h: is_up: 0 state: 4 sub state: 1 line: 0
2d20h:
2d20h: Rudpv1 Sent: Pkts 0,  Data Bytes 0,  Data Pkts 0
2d20h: Rudpv1 Rcvd: Pkts 0,  Data Bytes 0,  Data Pkts 0
2d20h: Rudpv1 Discarded: 0,  Retransmitted 0
2d20h: un all
All possible debugging has been turned off
Todd2509#
```

To disable debugging on a router, just use the command no in front of the debug command:

```
Todd2509#no debug all
```

But I typically just use the undebug all command since it is so easy when using the shortcut:

```
Todd2509#un all
```

Remember that instead of using the debug all command, it's almost always better to use specific commands—and only for short periods of time. Here's an example of deploying debug ip rip that will show you rip updates being sent and received on a router:

```
Todd2509#debug ip rip
RIP protocol debugging is on
Todd2509#
1w4d: RIP: sending v2 update to 224.0.0.9 via Serial0/0 (192.168.12.1)
1w4d: RIP: build update entries
1w4d:    10.10.10.0/24 via 0.0.0.0, metric 2, tag 0
```

```
1w4d:    171.16.125.0/24 via 0.0.0.0, metric 3, tag 0
1w4d:    172.16.12.0/24 via 0.0.0.0, metric 1, tag 0
1w4d:    172.16.125.0/24 via 0.0.0.0, metric 3, tag 0
1w4d: RIP: sending v2 update to 224.0.0.9 via Serial0/2 (172.16.12.1)
1w4d: RIP: build update entries
1w4d:    192.168.12.0/24 via 0.0.0.0, metric 1, tag 0
1w4d:    192.168.22.0/24 via 0.0.0.0, metric 2, tag 0
1w4d: RIP: received v2 update from 192.168.12.2 on Serial0/0
1w4d:    192.168.22.0/24 via 0.0.0.0 in 1 hops
Todd2509#un all
```

Okay, I'm sure you can see that the **debug** command is one powerful command. And because of this, I'm also sure you realize that before you use any of the debugging commands, you should make sure you check the utilization of your router. This is important because in most cases, you don't want to negatively impact the device's ability to process the packets through on your internetwork. You can determine a specific router's utilization information by using the **show processes** command.

> Remember, when you telnet into a remote device, you will not see console messages by default! For example, you will not see debugging output. To allow console messages to be sent to your Telnet session, use the `terminal monitor` command.

Using the *show processes* Command

As mentioned in the previous section, you've really got to be careful when using the debug command on your devices. If your router's CPU utilization is consistently at 50 percent or more, it's probably not a good idea to type in the **debug all** command unless you want to see what a router looks like when it crashes!

So what other approaches can you use? Well, the **show processes** (or **show processes cpu**) is a good tool for determining a given router's CPU utilization. Plus, it'll give you a list of active processes along with their corresponding process ID, priority, scheduler test (status), CPU time used, number of times invoked, and so on. Lots of great stuff! And more, this command is super handy when you want to evaluate your router's performance and CPU utilization—for instance, when you find yourself otherwise tempted to reach for the debug command.

Okay—what do we see in the output below? The first line shows the CPU utilization output for the last 5 seconds, 1 minute, and 5 minutes. The output provides 2%/0% in front of the CPU utilization for the last five seconds. The first number equals the total utilization and the second one delimits the utilization due to interrupt routines:

```
Todd2509#sh processes
CPU utilization for five seconds: 2%/0%; one minute: 0%; five minutes: 0%
```

PID	QTy	PC	Runtime (ms)	Invoked	uSecs	Stacks	TTY	Process
1	Cwe	8034470C	0	1	0	5804/6000	0	Chunk Manager
2	Csp	80369A88	4	1856	2	2616/3000	0	Load Meter
3	M*	0	112	14	800010656/12000		0	Exec
5	Lst	8034FD9C	268246	52101	5148	5768/6000	0	Check heaps
6	Cwe	80355E5C	20	3	6666	5704/6000	0	Pool Manager
7	Mst	802AC3C4	0	2	0	5580/6000	0	Timers

[output cut]

So basically, the output from the show processes command shows that our router is happily able to process debugging commands without being overloaded.

Summary

In this chapter, you learned how Cisco routers are configured and how to manage those configurations.

This chapter covered the internal components of a router, which included ROM, RAM, NVRAM, and flash.

In addition, I covered what happens when a router boots and which files are loaded. The configuration register tells the router how to boot and where to find files, and you learned how to change and verify the configuration register settings for password recovery purposes.

Next, you learned how to back up and restore a Cisco IOS image, as well as how to back up and restore the configuration of a Cisco router. Then you learned how to use CDP and Telnet to gather information about remote devices. Finally, the chapter covered how to resolve hostnames and use the ping and trace commands to test network connectivity, as well as how to use the debug and show processes command.

Exam Essentials

Remember the various configuration register commands and settings. The 0x2102 setting is the default on all Cisco routers and tells the router to look in NVRAM for the boot sequence. 0x2101 tells the router to boot from ROM, and 0x2142 tells the router to not load the startup-config in NVRAM to provide password recovery.

Remember how to back up an IOS image. By using the privileged-mode command copy flash tftp, you can back up a file from flash memory to a TFTP (network) server.

Remember how to restore or upgrade an IOS image. By using the privileged-mode command copy tftp flash, you can restore or upgrade a file from a TFTP (network) server to flash memory.

Remember what you must complete before you back up an IOS image to a network server. Make sure that you can access the network server, ensure that the network server has adequate space for the code image, and verify the file naming and path requirement.

Remember how to save the configuration of a router.   There are a couple of ways to do this, but the most common, as well as most tested, method is `copy running-config startup-config`.

Remember how to erase the configuration of a router.   Type the privileged-mode command `erase startup-config` and reload the router.

Understand when to use CDP.   Cisco Discovery Protocol can be used to help you document as well as troubleshoot your network.

Remember the output from the `show cdp neighbors` command.   The `show cdp neighbors` command provides the following information: device ID, local interface, holdtime, capability, platform, and port ID (remote interface).

Understand how to telnet into a router and keep your connection but return to your originating console.   If you telnet to a router or switch, you can end the connection by typing `exit` at any time. However, if you want to keep your connection to a remote device but still come back to your original router console, you can press the Ctrl+Shift+6 key combination, release it, and then press X.

Remember the command to verify your Telnet sessions.   The command `show sessions` will provide you with all the sessions your router has with other routers.

Remember how to build a static host table on a router.   By using the global configuration command `ip host` *host_name ip_address*, you can build a static host table on your router. You can apply multiple IP addresses against the same host entry.

Remember how to verify your host table on a router.   You can verify the host table with the `show hosts` command.

Understand when to use the `ping` command.   Packet Internet Groper (Ping) uses ICMP echo request and ICMP echo replies to verify an active IP address on a network.

Remember how to ping a valid host ID.   You can ping an IP address from a router's user mode or privileged mode but not from configuration mode. You must ping a valid address, such as 1.1.1.1.

Written Lab 8

Write the answers to the following questions:

1. What is the command to copy a Cisco IOS to a TFTP server?
2. What is the command to copy a Cisco `startup-config` file to a TFTP server?
3. What is the command to copy the `startup-config` file to DRAM?

4. What is an older command that you can use to copy the startup-config file to DRAM?

5. What command can you use to see the neighbor router's IP address from your router prompt?

6. What command can you use to see the hostname, local interface, platform, and remote port of a neighbor router?

7. What keystrokes can you use to telnet into multiple devices simultaneously?

8. What command will show you your active Telnet connections to neighbor and remote devices?

9. What command can you use to upgrade a Cisco IOS?

10. What command can you use to merge a backup configuration with the configuration in RAM?

(The answers to Written Lab 8 can be found following the answers to the review questions for this chapter.)

Hands-on Labs

To complete the labs in this section, you need at least one router (three is best) and at least one PC running as a TFTP server. Remember that the labs listed here were created for use with real routers.

Here is a list of the labs in this chapter:

Lab 8.1: Backing Up Your Router IOS

Lab 8.2: Upgrading or Restoring Your Router IOS

Lab 8.3: Backing Up the Router Configuration

Lab 8.4: Using the Cisco Discovery Protocol (CDP)

Lab 8.5: Using Telnet

Lab 8.6: Resolving Hostnames

Hands-on Lab 8.1: Backing Up Your Routers IOS

1. Log into your router and go into privileged mode by typing **en** or **enable**.

2. Make sure you can connect to the TFTP server that is on your network by pinging the IP address from the router console.

3. Type **show flash** to see the contents of flash memory.

4. Type **show version** at the router privileged-mode prompt to get the name of the IOS currently running on the router. If there is only one file in flash memory, the show flash and show version commands show the same file. Remember that the show version command shows you the file that is currently running and the show flash command shows you all of the files in flash memory.

5. Once you know you have good Ethernet connectivity to the TFTP server, and you also know the IOS filename, back up your IOS by typing **copy flash tftp**. This command tells the router to copy the contents of flash memory (this is where the IOS is stored by default) to a TFTP server.

6. Enter the IP address of the TFTP server and the source IOS filename. The file is now copied and stored in the TFTP server's default directory.

Hands-on Lab 8.2: Upgrading or Restoring Your Router IOS

1. Log into your router and go into privileged mode by typing **en** or **enable**.

2. Make sure you can connect to the TFTP server by pinging the IP address of the server from the router console.

3. Once you know you have good Ethernet connectivity to the TFTP server, issue the **copy tftp flash** command.

4. Confirm that the router is not functioning during the restore or upgrade by following the prompts provided on the router console.

5. Enter the IP address of the TFTP server.

6. Enter the IOS filename you want to restore or upgrade.

7. Confirm that you understand that the contents of flash memory will be erased.

8. Watch in amazement as your IOS is deleted out of flash memory and your new IOS is copied to flash memory.

If the file that was in flash memory is deleted but the new version wasn't copied to flash memory, the router will boot from ROM monitor mode. You'll need to figure out why the copy operation did not take place.

Hands-on Lab 8.3: Backing Up the Router Configuration

1. Log into your router and go into privileged mode by typing **en** or **enable**.

2. Ping the TFTP server to make sure you have IP connectivity.

3. From RouterB, type **copy run tftp**.

4. Type the IP address of the TFTP server (for example, 172.16.30.2) and press Enter.

5. The router will prompt you for a filename. The hostname of the router is followed by the suffix -confg. You can use any name you want.

   ```
   Name of configuration file to write [RouterB-confg]?
   ```

   Press Enter to accept the default name.

   ```
   Write file RouterB-confg on host 172.16.30.2? [confirm]
   ```

   Press Enter.

Hands-on Lab 8.4: Using the Cisco Discovery Protocol CDP)

1. Log into your router and go into privileged mode by typing **en** or **enable**.

2. From the router, type **sh cdp** and press Enter. You should see that CDP packets are being sent out to all active interfaces every 60 seconds and the holdtime is 180 seconds (these are the defaults).

3. To change the CDP update frequency to 90 seconds, type **cdp timer 90** in global configuration mode.

   ```
   RouterC#config t
   Enter configuration commands, one per line.  End with
     CNTL/Z.
   RouterC(config)#cdp timer ?
     <5-900>  Rate at which CDP packets are sent (in sec)
   RouterC(config)#cdp timer 90
   ```

4. Verify that your CDP timer frequency has changed by using the command show cdp in privileged mode.

    ```
    RouterC#sh cdp
    Global CDP information:
    Sending CDP packets every 90 seconds
    Sending a holdtime value of 180 seconds
    ```

5. Now use CDP to gather information about neighbor routers. You can get the list of available commands by typing **sh cdp ?**.

    ```
    RouterC#sh cdp ?
      entry     Information for specific neighbor entry
      interface CDP interface status and configuration
      neighbors CDP neighbor entries
      traffic   CDP statistics
      <cr>
    ```

6. Type **sh cdp int** to see the interface information plus the default encapsulation used by the interface. It also shows the CDP timer information.

7. Type **sh cdp entry** * to see the CDP information received from all devices.

8. Type **show cdp neighbors** to gather information about all connected neighbors. (You should know the specific information output by this command.)

9. Type **show cdp neighbors detail**. Notice that it produces the same output as show cdp entry *.

Hands-on Lab 8.5: Using Telnet

1. Log into your router and go into privileged mode by typing **en** or **enable**.

2. From RouterA, telnet into your remote router by typing **telnet *ip_address*** from the command prompt.

3. Type in RouterB's IP address from RouterA's command prompt. Notice that the router automatically tries to telnet to the IP address you specified. You can use the telnet command or just type in the IP address.

4. From RouterB, press Ctrl+Shift+6, then X to return to RouterA's command prompt. Now telnet into your third router, RouterC. Press Ctrl+Shift+6, then X to return to RouterA.

5. From RouterA, type **show sessions**. Notice your two sessions. You can press the number displayed to the left of the session and press Enter twice to return to that session. The asterisk shows the default session. You can press Enter twice to return to that session.

6. Go to the session for your RouterB. Type **show users**. This shows the console connection and the remote connection. You can use the disconnect command to clear the session or just type **exit** from the prompt to close your session with RouterB.

7. Go to the RouterC's console port by typing **show sessions** on the first router and using the connection number to return to RouterC. Type **show user** and notice the connection to your first router, RouterA.

8. Type **clear line** to disconnect the Telnet session.

Hands-on Lab 8.6: Resolving Hostnames

1. Log into your router and go into privileged mode by typing **en** or **enable**.

2. From RouterA, type **todd** and press Enter at the command prompt. Notice the error you receive and the delay. The router is trying to resolve the hostname to an IP address by looking for a DNS server. You can turn this feature off by using the no ip domain-lookup command from global configuration mode.

3. To build a host table, you use the ip host command. From RouterA, add a host table entry for RouterB and RouterC by entering the following commands:

    ip host routerb *ip_address*
    ip host routerc *ip_address*

    Here is an example:

    ```
    ip host routerb 172.16.20.2
    ip host routerc 172.16.40.2
    ```

4. Test your host table by typing **ping routerb** from the command prompt (not the config prompt).

    ```
    RouterA#ping routerb
    Type escape sequence to abort.
    Sending 5, 100-byte ICMP Echos to 172.16.20.2, timeout
      is 2 seconds:
    !!!!!
    Success rate is 100 percent (5/5), round-trip
      min/avg/max = 4/4/4 ms
    ```

5. Test your host table by typing **ping routerc**.

    ```
    RouterA#ping routerc
    Type escape sequence to abort.
    Sending 5, 100-byte ICMP Echos to 172.16.40.2, timeout
      is 2 seconds:
    !!!!!
    Success rate is 100 percent (5/5), round-trip
      min/avg/max = 4/6/8 ms
    ```

6. Keep your session to RouterB open, and then return to RouterA by pressing Ctrl+Shift+6, then X.

7. Telnet to RouterC by typing **routerc** at the command prompt.

8. Return to RouterA and keep the session to RouterC open by pressing Ctrl+Shift+6, then X.

9. View the host table by typing **show hosts** and pressing Enter.

```
Default domain is not set
Name/address lookup uses domain service
Name servers are 255.255.255.255
Host              Flags        Age Type   Address(es)
routerb           (perm, OK)   0   IP     172.16.20.2
routerc           (perm, OK)   0   IP     172.16.40.2
```

Review Questions

1. You telnet into a router and you receive the following message:

   `Password required but none set`

   Why was this message received?

   A. No VTY password has been set.

   B. No enable password has been set.

   C. No console password has been set.

   D. No enable secret password has been set.

   E. The login command has not been set on the VTY ports.

2. Which command will copy the IOS to a backup host on your network?

   A. `transfer IOS to 172.16.10.1`

   B. `copy run start`

   C. `copy tftp flash`

   D. `copy start tftp`

   E. `copy flash tftp`

3. You are troubleshooting a connectivity problem in your corporate network and want to isolate the problem. You suspect that a router on the route to an unreachable network is at fault. What IOS user exec command should you issue?

   A. `Router>ping`

   B. `Router>trace`

   C. `Router>show ip route`

   D. `Router>show interface`

   E. `Router>show cdp neighbors`

4. During the boot sequence, a router needs to locate and load an operating system. What is the default order the router uses to find an operating system?

   A. RAM, ROM, NVRAM

   B. Flash, NVRAM, ROM

   C. Flash, TFTP server, ROM

   D. ROM, TFTP server, flash

5. A network administrator wants to upgrade the IOS of a router without removing the image currently installed. What command will display the amount of memory consumed by the current IOS image and indicate whether there is enough room available to hold both the current and new images?

    A. `show version`

    B. `show flash`

    C. `show memory`

    D. `show buffers`

    E. `show running-config`

6. You telnet into a router and type debugging commands to help you troubleshoot a problem; however, no output appears. What command should you type to view the debug output?

    A. `debug all`

    B. `debug *`

    C. `terminal monitor`

    D. `show debug`

    E. `enable debug`

7. Which command loads a new version of the Cisco IOS into a router?

    A. `copy flash ftp`

    B. `copy ftp flash`

    C. `copy flash tftp`

    D. `copy tftp flash`

8. Which command will show you the IOS version running on your router?

    A. `sh IOS`

    B. `sh flash`

    C. `sh version`

    D. `sh running-config`

9. Why is the `show processes` command used on a router before a `debug` command is entered?

    A. To verify the IOS version that is running

    B. To verify the amount of space in flash memory

    C. To view the number of timers that are currently in use

    D. To verify that the CPU utilization is low enough to handle the effects of a `debug` command

10. You save the configuration on a router with the `copy running-config startup-config` command and reboot the router. The router, however, comes up with a blank configuration. What can the problem be?

    A. You didn't boot the router with the correct command.

    B. NVRAM is corrupted.

    C. The configuration register setting is incorrect.

    D. The newly upgraded IOS is not compatible with the hardware of the router.

    E. The configuration you save is not compatible with the hardware.

11. If you want to have more than one Telnet session open at the same time, what keystroke combination would you use?

    A. Tab+spacebar

    B. Ctrl+X, then 6

    C. Ctrl+Shift+X, then 6

    D. Ctrl+Shift+6, then X

12. If NVRAM lacks boot system commands, where does the router look for the Cisco IOS by default?

    A. ROM

    B. DRAM

    C. Flash

    D. Bootstrap

13. What information is displayed by the `show hosts` command? (Choose two.)

    A. Temporary DNS entries

    B. The names of the routers created using the hostname command

    C. The IP addresses of workstations allowed to access the router

    D. Permanent name-to-address mappings created using the ip host `command`

    E. The length of time a host has been connected to the router via Telnet

14. Which three statements accurately describe CDP?

    A. CDP is an IEEE standard protocol.

    B. CDP is a Cisco proprietary protocol.

    C. CDP is a Data Link layer protocol.

    D. CDP is a Network layer protocol.

    E. CDP can discover directly connected neighboring Cisco devices.

    F. CDP can discover Cisco devices that are not directly connected.

15. You are consoled into a router and you see the following output:

```
2d20h: SNMP: HC Timer 824AE5CC fired
2d20h: SNMP: HC Timer 824AE5CC rearmed, delay = 20000
2d20h: Serial0/0: HDLC myseq 4, mineseen 0, yourseen 0, line down
2d20h:
2d20h: Rudpv1 Sent: Pkts 0,   Data Bytes 0,   Data Pkts 0
2d20h: Rudpv1 Rcvd: Pkts 0,   Data Bytes 0,   Data Pkts 0
2d20h: Rudpv1 Discarded: 0,   Retransmitted 0
```

Users are complaining about slow response. What command should you type into the console of your router to solve the problem?

A. `copy run start, then reload`

B. CTRL+C

C. `no debug all`

D. `show processses`

E. `terminal monitor`

16. Which of the following commands enables a network administrator to verify the Application layer connectivity between source and destination?

A. `ping`

B. `tracert`

C. `telnet`

D. `traceroute`

E. `trace`

17. Which command displays the configuration register setting?

A. `show ip route`

B. `show boot version`

C. `show version`

D. `show flash`

18. You need to gather the IP address of a remote switch that is located in Hawaii. What can you do to find the address?

A. Fly to Hawaii, console into the switch, then relax and have a drink with an umbrella in it.

B. Issue the `show ip route` command on the router connected to the switch.

C. Issue the `show cdp neighbor` command on the router connected to the switch.

D. Issue the `show ip arp` command on the router connected to the switch.

E. Issue the `show cdp neighbors detail` command on the router connected to the switch.

19. How will a 2600 series router respond if the conditions listed below exist during the boot process?

1. The IOS image in flash is missing.

2. No network connectivity is available.

3. The router fallback IOS image is corrupt.

   A. The router will enter setup mode.

   B. The router will enter ROM monitor mode.

   C. The router will enter global configuration mode.

   D. The boot cycle will hang until an IOS is available.

20. The default configuration register setting of 0x2102 provides what function to a router?

   A. Tells the router to boot into ROM monitor mode

   B. Provides password recovery

   C. Tells the router to look in NVRAM for the boot sequence

   D. Boots the IOS from a TFTP server

   E. Boots an IOS image stored in ROM

Answers to Review Questions

1. A. You cannot telnet into a router (or switch) by default. The login command is enabled on the VTY lines by default. If you do not configure a password or disable the login command, then you will receive the message "Password required but none set."

2. E. To copy the IOS to a backup host, which is stored in flash memory by default, use the `copy flash tftp` command.

3. B. The command `traceroute`, which can be issued from user mode or privileged mode, is used to find the path a packet takes through an internetwork and will also show you where the packet stops because of an error on a router.

4. C. Cisco routers, by default, use a fallback routine of flash, TFTP server, ROM when trying to load an IOS.

5. B. The `show flash` command will provide you with the current IOS name and size and the size of flash memory.

6. C. If you telnet into a router, console messages will not be displayed by default. Use the command `terminal monitor` to receive console messages on your VTY lines.

7. D. The command `copy tftp flash` will allow you to copy a new IOS into flash memory on your router.

8. C. The best answer is `show version`, which shows you the IOS file running currently on your router. The `show flash` shows you the contents of flash memory, not which file is running.

9. D. The `show processes` command provides the CPU cycles being used on a router. Before attempting to run the `debug` command, always check to make sure you are not going to overload your router since the `debug` command takes a lot of CPU processing to handle.

10. C. If you save a configuration and reload the router and it comes up either in setup mode or as a blank configuration, chances are you have the configuration register setting incorrect.

11. D. To keep open one or more Telnet sessions, use the Ctrl+Shift+6, then X keystroke combination.

12. C. Cisco routers, by default, use a fallback routine of flash, TFTP server, ROM when trying to load an IOS.

13. A, D. The `show hosts` command provides information on temporary DNS entries and permanent name-to-address mappings created using the `ip host` command.

14. B, C, E. CDP is a Cisco proprietary protocol that works only at the Data Link layer, and it can discover only directly connected devices.

15. C. The output is from the `debug all` command, which should rarely be used on your router. You disable the `debug all` command with the `no debug all` or `un all` command.

16. C. Traceroute (trace for short) and ping only work at the Network layer, and tracert is a Microsoft command. Telnet, FTP, TFTP, and HTTP are all examples of Application layer programs that can be used to verify application-layer-to-application-layer connectivity between two devices.

17. C. The show version command provides you with the current configuration register setting.

18. E. Although option A is certainly the "best" answer, unfortunately option E will work just fine and your boss would probably prefer you to use the show cdp neighbors detail command.

19. B. If the IOS in flash is missing or corrupted, the router will try and find a TFTP host to download an IOS from. If no network connectivity is available, then this is impossible. If it does find a TFTP host, but the backup IOS is corrupt, then the router will enter ROM monitor mode.

20. C. The default configuration setting of 0x2102 tells the router to look in NVRAM for the boot sequence.

Answers to Written Lab 8

1. `copy flash tftp`
2. `copy start tftp`
3. `copy start run`
4. `config mem`
5. `show cdp neighbor detail` or `show cdp entry *`
6. `show cdp neighbor`
7. Ctrl+Shift+6, then X
8. `show sessions`
9. `copy tftp flash`
10. Either `copy tftp run` or `copy start run`

Chapter

9

Wide Area Networking Protocols

THE CCNA INTRO EXAM TOPICS COVERED IN THIS CHAPTER INCLUDE THE FOLLOWING:

✓ **Technology**

- Identify the key characteristics of common wide area networking (WAN) configurations and technologies, and differentiate between these and common LAN technologies

- Describe the role of a router in a WAN

The Cisco IOS WAN supports many different WAN protocols that can help you extend your LANs to other LANs at remote sites. Connecting company sites together so that information can be exchanged is imperative in today's economy. But it wouldn't exactly be cost-effective to put in your own cable or connections to connect all of your company's remote locations yourself. A better way to go about it is to use service providers that will lease or share connections they already have installed and save huge amounts of money and time.

I'm not going to cover every type of Cisco WAN support in this chapter—again, this book's purpose is mainly to give you everything you need to pass the exam. For that reason, I'm going to focus on the HDLC and PPP, although we'll touch on other technologies like Frame Relay and ISDN. But first, we will look at the WAN basics, including cabling a WAN.

For more detail on WAN technologies, above and beyond the Cisco INTRO objectives, please see *CCNA: Cisco Certified Network Associate Study Guide*.

Introduction to Wide Area Networks

So what is it that makes something a *wide area network (WAN)* instead of a local area network (LAN)? Distance is the first thing that comes to mind, but these days, wireless LANs can cover some serious turf! So is it bandwidth? Here again, in many places really big pipes can be had for a price, so that's not it either. Well, what then? Perhaps one of the best ways to tell a WAN from a LAN is that you generally own a LAN infrastructure but you lease a WAN infrastructure from a service provider.

I've already talked about a data link that you usually own (Ethernet), but now we're going to take a look at the data links you most often don't own but instead lease from a service provider.

The key to understanding WAN technologies is to be familiar with the different WAN terms and connection types often used by service providers to join your networks together.

There are new WANs available today, but again, this chapter is focusing on the Cisco INTRO exam objectives only.

Defining WAN Terms

Before ordering a WAN service type, it would be a good idea to understand the following terms, which are commonly used by service providers:

Customer premises equipment (CPE)   *Customer premises equipment (CPE)* is equipment that's owned by the subscriber and located on the subscriber's premises.

Demarcation point   The *demarcation location* is the spot where the service provider's responsibility ends and the CPE begins. It's generally a device in a telecommunications closet owned and installed by the telecommunications company (telco). The customer is responsible to cable (extended demarc) from this box to the CPE, which is usually a connection to a CSU/DSU or ISDN interface.

Local loop   The *local loop* connects the demarc to the closest switching office, called a central office.

Central office (CO)   This point connects the customers to the provider's switching network. A *central office (CO)* is sometimes referred to as a *point of presence (POP)*.

Toll network   The *toll network* is a trunk line inside a WAN provider's network. This network is a collection of switches and facilities owned by the ISP.

It is important to familiarize yourself with these terms, as they are crucial to understanding WAN technologies.

WAN Connection Types

A WAN can use a number of different connection types and this section will provide you with an introduction to the various types of WAN connections you'll find on the market today. Figure 9.1 shows the different WAN connection types that can be used to connect your LANs (DTE) together over a DCE network.

The following list explains the WAN connection types:

Leased lines   Typically, these are referred to as a *point-to-point connection* or dedicated connection. A *leased line* is a pre-established WAN communications path from the CPE through the DCE switch to the CPE of the remote site, allowing DTE networks to communicate at any time with no setup procedures before transmitting data. When cost is no object, it's really the best choice. It uses synchronous serial lines up to 45Mbps. HDLC and PPP encapsulations are frequently used on leased lines, and I'll go over them with you in detail in a bit.

Circuit switching   When you hear the term *circuit switching*, think phone call. The big advantage is cost—you pay only for the time you actually use. No data can transfer before an end-to-end connection is established. *Circuit switching* uses dial-up modems or ISDN and is used for low-bandwidth data transfers.

FIGURE 9.1   WAN connection types

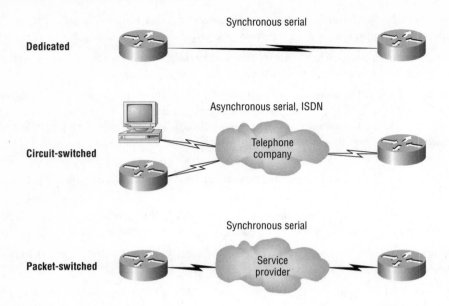

Packet switching   This is a WAN switching method that allows you to share bandwidth with other companies to save money. *Packet switching* can be thought of as a network that's designed to look like a leased line yet charges you (and costs) more like circuit switching. There is a downside: If you need to transfer data constantly, forget about this option. Just get yourself a leased line. Packet switching will work well only if your data transfers are bursty in nature. Frame Relay and X.25 are packet-switching technologies. Speeds can range from 56Kbps to T3 (45Mbps).

WAN Support

Cisco supports pretty much every WAN service available, and you can see this with the `encapsulation ?` command from any serial interface (your output may vary depending on the IOS version you are running):

```
Router#config t
Enter configuration commands, one per line.  End with CNTL/Z.
Router(config)#int s0/0
Router(config-if)#encapsulation ?
  atm-dxi        ATM-DXI encapsulation
  bstun          Block Serial tunneling (BSTUN)
  frame-relay    Frame Relay networks
  hdlc           Serial HDLC synchronous
  lapb           LAPB (X.25 Level 2)
```

```
ppp              Point-to-Point protocol
sdlc             SDLC
sdlc-primary     SDLC (primary)
sdlc-secondary   SDLC (secondary)
smds             Switched Megabit Data Service (SMDS)
stun             Serial tunneling (STUN)
x25              X.25
```

You cannot configure Ethernet or Token Ring encapsulation on a serial interface.

In this section, we will define the most prominent WAN protocols used today—Frame Relay, ISDN, LAPB, LAPD, HDLC, PPP, and ATM. Usually, though, the only WAN protocols configured on a serial interface these days (or for the exam) are HDLC, PPP, and Frame Relay.

Frame Relay   A packet-switched technology that emerged in the early 1990s, *Frame Relay* is a Data Link and Physical layer specification that provides high performance. Frame Relay is a successor to X.25, except that much of the technology in X.25 used to compensate for physical errors (noisy lines) has been eliminated. Frame Relay can be more cost-effective than point-to-point links and can typically run at speeds of 64Kbps up to 45Mbps (T3). Frame Relay provides features for dynamic bandwidth allocation and congestion control.

ISDN   *Integrated Services Digital Network (ISDN)* is a set of digital services that transmit voice and data over existing phone lines. ISDN can offer a cost-effective solution for remote users who need a higher-speed connection than analog dial-up links offer. ISDN is also a good choice as a backup link for other types of links, such as Frame Relay or a T1 connection.

LAPB   *Link Access Procedure, Balanced (LAPB)* was created to be a connection-oriented protocol at the Data Link layer for use with X.25. It can also be used as a simple data link transport. LAPB causes a tremendous amount of overhead because of its strict time-out and windowing techniques.

LAPD   *Link Access Procedure, D-Channel (LAPD)* is used with ISDN at the Data Link layer (layer 2) as a protocol for the D (signaling) channel. LAPD was derived from the Link Access Procedure, Balanced (LAPB) Protocol and is designed primarily to satisfy the signaling requirements of ISDN basic access.

HDLC   *High-Level Data Link Control (HDLC)* was derived from Synchronous Data Link Control (SDLC), which was created by IBM as a Data Link connection protocol. HDLC is a protocol at the Data Link layer, and it has very little overhead compared to LAPB. HDLC wasn't intended to encapsulate multiple Network layer protocols across the same link. The HDLC header carries no identification of the type of protocol being carried inside the HDLC encapsulation. Because of this, each vendor that uses HDLC has its own way of identifying the Network layer protocol, which means that each vendor's HDLC is proprietary for its equipment.

PPP   *Point-to-Point Protocol (PPP)* is an industry-standard protocol. Because all multi-protocol versions of HDLC are proprietary, PPP can be used to create point-to-point links between different vendors' equipment. It uses a Network Control Protocol field in the Data Link header to identify the Network layer protocol. It allows authentication and multilink connections and can be run over asynchronous and synchronous links.

ATM   Asynchronous Transfer Mode (ATM) was created for time-sensitive traffic, providing simultaneous transmission of voice, video, and data. ATM uses cells instead of packets that are a fixed 53 bytes long. It also can use isochronous clocking (external clocking) to help the data move faster.

 PPP and ATM can be configured on an asynchronous serial connection. HDLC and Frame Relay cannot.

Cabling the Wide Area Network

There are a couple of things that you need to know in order to connect your WAN. For starters, you've got to understand the WAN Physical layer implementation provided by Cisco, and you must be familiar with the various types of WAN serial connectors.

Cisco serial connections support almost any type of WAN service. The typical WAN connections are dedicated leased lines using HDLC, PPP, Integrated Services Digital Network (ISDN), and Frame Relay. Typical speeds run at anywhere from 2400bps to 45Mbps (T3).

 **Real World Scenario**

Which of the Listed WAN Services Is the best?

You are a network administrator in San Francisco for Acme Corporation and you need to install a remote connection. Which one do you use?

A leased line is almost always the choice if money is no object. But in today's economy, cost is usually a consideration. Services such as Frame Relay are hugely popular.

One of the newer WAN services that Cisco doesn't list as a WAN service in the CCNA INTRO objectives is a wireless connection. You can get from 1Mbps to over 50Mbps, depending on the service, and it actually works, too! For the speed you get, it is relatively inexpensive. If you want to connect two buildings together, then you should consider a wireless solution. Of course, Cisco handily sells everything you need to do this—and at a pretty decent price compared to a wired solution.

You can even use a wireless solution for connecting your business to the Internet. The problem with wireless ISPs (WISPs) is that they come and go—they're in business one day and gone the next. Make sure you have a backup solution in the wings if you decide on a WISP, because they just might not answer the phone tomorrow. Eventually, things will mellow out and become better as technology develops, and we'll see wireless carriers sticking around for more than a week!

HDLC, PPP, and Frame Relay can use the same Physical layer specifications, but ISDN has different pinouts and specifications at the Physical layer.

In the following sections, we'll discuss the various types of connections and then move into the nitty-gritty of the WAN protocols specified in the CCNA objectives.

Serial Transmission

WAN serial connectors use *serial transmission*, which takes place one bit at a time over a single channel.

Parallel transmission can pass at least 8 bits at a time, but all WANs use serial transmission.

Cisco routers use a proprietary 60-pin serial connector that you must get from Cisco or a provider of Cisco equipment. Cisco also has a new, smaller proprietary serial connection that is about one-tenth the size of the 60-pin basic serial cable. This is called the "smart-serial," for some reason, and you have to make sure you have the right type of interface in your router before using this cable connector. The type of connector you have on the other end of the cable depends on your service provider or end-device requirements. The different ends available are as follows:

- EIA/TIA-232
- EIA/TIA-449
- V.35 (used to connect to a CSU/DSU)
- X.21 (used in X.25)
- EIA-530

Serial links are described in frequency or cycles per second (hertz). The amount of data that can be carried within these frequencies is called *bandwidth*. Bandwidth is the amount of data in bits per second that the serial channel can carry.

Figure 9.2 shows a typical router that has both Ethernet (AUI) and serial interfaces. The serial interfaces can be used for a T1 connection, for example. The BRI is used for an ISDN connection.

In order to connect a T1 to your serial interface, you must use a CSU/DSU, which we'll discuss next.

FIGURE 9.2   Router serial interfaces

Data Terminal Equipment and Data Communication Equipment

Router interfaces are, by default, *data terminal equipment (DTE)*, and they connect into *data communication equipment (DCE)*—for example, a *channel service unit/data service unit (CSU/DSU)*. The CSU/DSU then plugs into a demarcation location (demarc) and is the service provider's last responsibility. Most of the time, the demarc is a jack that has an RJ-45 (8-pin modular) female connector located in a telecommunications closet.

You may have heard of demarcs if you've ever had the glorious experience of reporting a problem to your service provider—they'll always tell you that it tests fine up to the demarc and that the problem must be the CPE, or customer premises equipment. In other words, it's your problem, not theirs.

Figure 9.3 shows typical DTE-DCE-DTE connection and the devices used in the network.

The idea behind a WAN is to be able to connect two DTE networks together through a DCE network. The DCE network includes the area from the CSU/DSU, through the provider's wiring and switches, all the way to the CSU/DSU at the other end. The network's DCE device (CSU/DSU) provides clocking to the DTE-connected interface (the router's serial interface).

As mentioned, the DCE network provides clocking to the router; this is the CSU/DSU. If you have a non-production network and are using a WAN crossover type of cable and do not have a CSU/DSU, then you need to provide clocking on the DCE end of the cable by using the clock rate command, as I discussed in Chapters 4 and 5.

Terms such as EIA/TIA-232, V.35, X.21, and HSSI (High-Speed Serial Interface) describe the physical layer between the DTE (router) and DCE device (CSU/DSU).

FIGURE 9.3   DTE-DCE-DTE WAN Connection

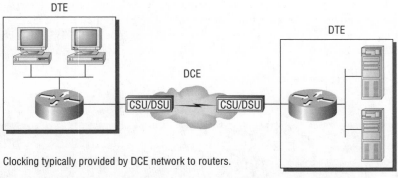

Clocking typically provided by DCE network to routers.

In non-production environments, a DCE network is not always present.

High-Level Data Link Control (HDLC) Protocol

The High-Level Data Link Control (HDLC) protocol is a popular ISO-standard, bit-oriented Data Link layer protocol. It specifies an encapsulation method for data on synchronous serial data links using frame characters and checksums. HDLC is a point-to-point protocol used on leased lines. No authentication can be used with HDLC.

In byte-oriented protocols, control information is encoded using entire bytes. On the other hand, bit-oriented protocols may use single bits to represent control information. Bit-oriented protocols include SDLC, LLC, HDLC, TCP, IP, and others.

HDLC is the default encapsulation used by Cisco routers over synchronous serial links. Cisco's HDLC is proprietary—it won't communicate with any other vendor's HDLC implementation. But don't give Cisco grief for it—*everyone's* HDLC implementation is proprietary. Figure 9.4 shows the Cisco HDLC format.

As shown in the figure, the reason that every vendor has a proprietary HDLC encapsulation method is that each vendor has a different way for the HDLC protocol to encapsulate multiple Network layer protocols. If the vendors didn't have a way for HDLC to communicate the different layer 3 protocols, then HDLC would only be able to carry one protocol. This proprietary header is placed in the data field of the HDLC encapsulation.

Let's say you only have one Cisco router and you need to connect to a different vendor's router because your other Cisco router is on order. What would you do? You couldn't use the default HDLC serial encapsulation because it wouldn't work. Instead, you would use something like PPP, an ISO-standard way of identifying the upper-layer protocols. In addition, you can check RFC 1661 for more information on the origins and standards of PPP.

FIGURE 9.4   Cisco HDLC frame format

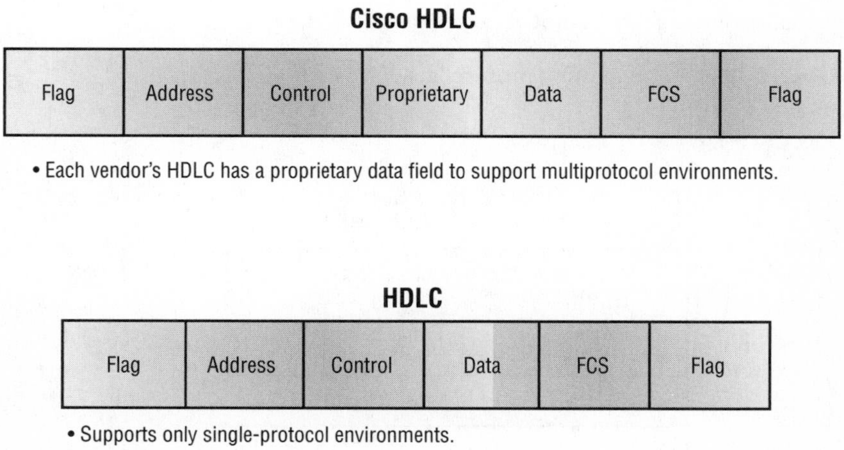

Cisco HDLC

Flag	Address	Control	Proprietary	Data	FCS	Flag

• Each vendor's HDLC has a proprietary data field to support multiprotocol environments.

HDLC

Flag	Address	Control	Data	FCS	Flag

• Supports only single-protocol environments.

Point-to-Point Protocol (PPP)

Point-to-Point Protocol (PPP) is a Data Link layer protocol that can be used over either asynchronous serial (dial-up) or synchronous serial (ISDN) media. It uses the LCP (Link Control Protocol) to build and maintain data link connections. Network Control Protocol (NCP) is used to allow multiple Network layer protocols (routed protocols) to be used on a point-to-point connection.

Since HDLC is the default serial encapsulation on Cisco serial links and it works great, when would you choose to use PPP? The basic purpose of PPP is to transport layer 3 packets across a Data Link layer point-to-point link. It is nonproprietary, which means that if you don't have all Cisco routers, PPP would be needed on your serial interfaces—the HDLC encapsulation would not work because it is Cisco proprietary. In addition, since PPP can encapsulate several layer 3 routed protocols and provide authentication, dynamic addressing, and callback, this may be the encapsulation solution of choice for you over HDLC.

Figure 9.5 shows the protocol stack compared to the OSI reference model.

PPP contains four main components:

EIA/TIA-232-C, V.24, V.35, and ISDN   A Physical layer international standard for serial communication.

HDLC   A method for encapsulating datagrams over serial links.

LCP   A method of establishing, configuring, maintaining, and terminating the point-to-point connection.

NCP   A method of establishing and configuring different Network layer protocols. NCP is designed to allow the simultaneous use of multiple Network layer protocols. Some examples of protocols here are IPCP (Internet Protocol Control Protocol) and IPXCP (Internetwork Packet Exchange Control Protocol).

It is important to understand that the PPP protocol stack is specified at the Physical and Data Link layers only. NCP is used to allow communication of multiple Network layer protocols by encapsulating the protocols across a PPP data link.

FIGURE 9.5   Point-to-point protocol stack

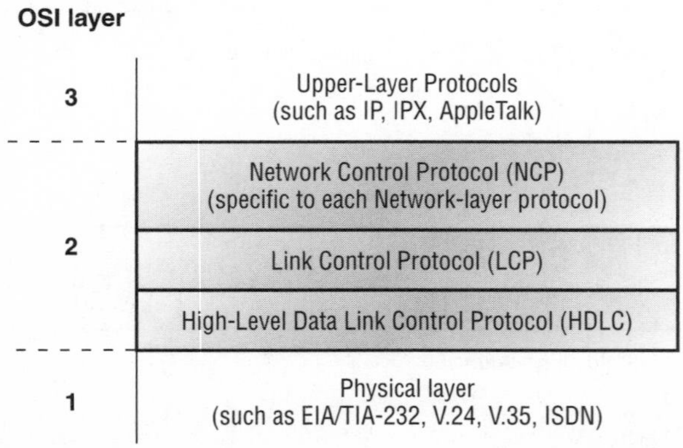

OSI layer

3	Upper-Layer Protocols (such as IP, IPX, AppleTalk)
2	Network Control Protocol (NCP) (specific to each Network-layer protocol)
	Link Control Protocol (LCP)
	High-Level Data Link Control Protocol (HDLC)
1	Physical layer (such as EIA/TIA-232, V.24, V.35, ISDN)

Remember that if you have a Cisco router and a non-Cisco router connected with a serial connection, you must configure PPP or another encapsulation method, such as Frame Relay, because the HDLC default won't work!

In the following sections, I'll discuss the options for LCP and PPP session establishment.

PPP Session Establishment

When PPP connections are started, the links go through three phases of session establishment, as shown in Figure 9.6.

Link establishment phase   LCP packets are sent by each PPP device to configure and test the link. These packets contain a field called the Configuration Option that allows each device to see the size of the data, compression, and authentication. If no Configuration Option field is present, then the default configurations are used.

Authentication phase   If required, either CHAP or PAP can be used to authenticate a link. Authentication takes place before Network layer protocol information is read. It is possible that link-quality determination may occur at this same time.

Network layer protocol phase   PPP uses the *Network Control Protocol (NCP)* to allow multiple Network layer protocols to be encapsulated and sent over a PPP data link. Each Network layer protocol (e.g., IP, IPX, AppleTalk, which are routed protocols) establishes a service with NCP.

PPP Authentication Methods

There are two methods of authentication that can be used with PPP links:

Password Authentication Protocol (PAP)   The *Password Authentication Protocol (PAP)* is the less secure of the two methods. Passwords are sent in clear text, and PAP is only performed upon the initial link establishment. When the PPP link is first established, the remote node sends back to the originating router the username and password until authentication is acknowledged. That's it.

FIGURE 9.6   PPP session establishment

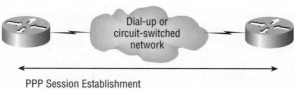

PPP Session Establishment
1. Link establishment phase
2. Authentication phase (optional)
3. Network layer protocol phase

Challenge Handshake Authentication Protocol (CHAP)   The *Challenge Handshake Authentication Protocol (CHAP)* is used at the initial startup of a link and at periodic checkups on the link to make sure the router is still communicating with the same host. After PPP finishes its initial link-establishment phase, the local router sends a challenge request to the remote device. The remote device sends a value calculated using a one-way hash function called MD5. The local router checks this hash value to make sure it matches. If the values don't match, the link is immediately terminated.

Configuring PPP on Cisco Routers

Configuring PPP encapsulation on an interface is a fairly straightforward process. To configure it, follow these router commands:

```
Router#config t
Enter configuration commands, one per line. End with CNTL/Z.
Router(config)#int s0
Router(config-if)#encapsulation ppp
Router(config-if)#^Z
Router#
```

Of course, PPP encapsulation must be enabled on both interfaces connected to a serial line to work, and there are several additional configuration options available by using the help command.

Configuring PPP Authentication

After you configure your serial interface to support PPP encapsulation, you can configure authentication using PPP between routers. First set the hostname of the router if it's not already set. Then set the username and password for the remote router connecting to your router.

Here is an example:

```
Router#config t
Enter configuration commands, one per line. End with CNTL/Z.
Router(config)#hostname RouterA
RouterA(config)#username RouterB password cisco
```

When using the hostname command, remember that the username is the hostname of the remote router connecting to your router. And it's case sensitive. Also, the password on both routers must be the same. It's a plain-text password that you can see with a show run command. And you can encrypt the password by using the command service password-encryption. You must have a username and password configured for each remote system you plan to connect to. The remote routers must also be configured with usernames and passwords.

After you set the hostname, usernames, and passwords, choose the authentication type, either CHAP or PAP:

```
RouterA#config t
Enter configuration commands, one per line. End with CNTL/Z.
RouterA(config)#int s0
RouterA(config-if)#ppp authentication chap pap
RouterA(config-if)#^Z
RouterA#
```

If both methods are configured on the same line as is shown here, then only the first method will be used during link negotiation—the second is a backup in case the first method fails.

See Hands-on Lab 9.1 for further examples of PPP authentication.

Verifying PPP Encapsulation

Now that PPP encapsulation is enabled, let's see how to verify that it's up and running.

You can verify the configuration with the show interface command:

```
Pod1R1#sh int s0/0
Serial0/0 is up, line protocol is up
  Hardware is PowerQUICC Serial
  Internet address is 10.0.1.1/24
  MTU 1500 bytes, BW 1544 Kbit, DLY 20000 usec,
     reliability 239/255, txload 1/255, rxload 1/255
  Encapsulation PPP, loopback not set Keepalive set (10 sec)
 LCP Open
  Open: IPCP, CDPCP
[output cut]
```

Notice that the sixth line lists encapsulation as PPP and the next line shows that the LCP is open, which means that it has negotiated the session establishment and is good! The eight line tells us the NCP is listening for the protocols IP and CDP.

You cannot have PPP on one side of a serial link and HDLC on the other!

Summary

This chapter covered the difference between the following WAN services: X.25/LAPB, Frame Relay, ISDN/LAPD, SDLC, HDLC, and PPP, although we only talked in depth about HDLC and PPP, the most prevalent Cisco INTRO exam objective WAN technologies.

You must understand High-Level Data Link Control (HDLC) and how to verify with the `show interface` command that HDLC is enabled. This chapter provided this important HDLC information to you as well as how the Point-to-Point Protocol (PPP) is used if you need more features than HDLC or you are using two different brands of routers. This is because HDLC is proprietary and won't work between two different vendor routers.

In the discussion of PPP, I discussed the various LCP options as well as the two types of authentication that can be used: PAP and CHAP.

Just a few more practice question and you're done with this book! Hang in there!

Exam Essentials

Remember the default serial encapsulation on Cisco routers. Cisco routers use a proprietary High-Level Data Link Control (HDLC) encapsulation on all their serial links by default.

Remember the PPP Data Link layer protocols. The three Data Link layer protocols are Network Control Protocol (NCP), which defines the Network layer protocols; Link Control Protocol (LCP), a method of establishing, configuring, maintaining, and terminating the point-to-point connection; and High-Level Data Link Control (HDLC), the MAC layer protocol that encapsulates the packets.

Remember the WAN Data Link encapsulations The most common Data Link serial encapsulations are HDLC, PPP, and Frame Relay.

Remember the ports on a router used for WANs. A serial connection would be used for a T1, and a BRI interface would be used for ISDN. AUI, or an attachment user interface, is not a WAN port but an Ethernet interface.

Written Lab 9

Write the answers to the following questions:

1. Write the command to see the encapsulation method on serial 0 of a Cisco router.
2. Write the commands to configure s0 to PPP encapsulation.
3. Write the commands to configure a username of *todd* and password of *cisco* that is used on a Cisco router.
4. What does PPP mean?

5. What are common Data Link WAN encapsulations?

6. Which type of port on a router is used for a T1?

7. If you had one serial interface on your router and needed to connect many remote locations, which Data Link encapsulation should you use?

8. What is the default serial encapsulation on a Cisco router?

9. What are the PPP Data Link protocols?

10. What is a good command to verify your serial interface on a router?

(The answers to Written Lab 9 can be found following the answers to review questions for this chapter.)

Hands-on Labs

In this section, you will configure Cisco routers in four different WAN labs using the figure supplied in each lab. (These labs are included for use with real Cisco routers.)

Lab 9.1: Configuring PPP Encapsulation and Authentication

Lab 9.2: Configuring and Monitoring HDLC

Hands-on Lab 9.1: Configuring PPP Encapsulation and Authentication

By default, Cisco routers use High-Level Data Link Control (HDLC) as a point-to-point encapsulation method on serial links. If you are connecting to non-Cisco equipment, then you can use the PPP encapsulation method to communicate.

The lab you will configure is shown in the following diagram:

1. Type **sh int s0** on RouterA and RouterB to see the encapsulation method.

2. Make sure that each router has the hostname assigned:

    RouterA#**config t**
    RouterA(config)#**hostname RouterA**

    RouterB#**config t**
    RouterB(config)#**hostname RouterB**

3. To change the default HDLC encapsulation method to PPP on both routers, use the encapsulation command at interface configuration. Both ends of the link must run the same encapsulation method.

    RouterA#**Config t**
    RouterA(config)#**int s0**
    RouterA(config-if)#**Encap ppp**

4. Now go to RouterB and set serial 0 to PPP encapsulation.

    RouterB#**config t**
    RouterB(config)#**int s0**
    RouterB(config-if)#**encap ppp**

5. Verify the configuration by typing **sh int s0** on both routers.

6. Notice the IPCP, IPXCP, and CDPCP. This is the information used to transmit the upper-layer (Network layer) information across the HDLC at the MAC sublayer.

7. Define a username and password on each router. Notice that the username is the name of the remote router. Also, the password must be the same.

```
RouterA#config t
RouterA(config)#username RouterB password todd

RouterB#config t
RouterB(config)#username RouterA password todd
```

8. Enable CHAP or PAP authentication on each interface.

```
RouterA(config)#int s0
RouterA(config-if)#ppp authentication chap

RouterB(config)#int s0
RouterB(config-if)#ppp authentication chap
```

9. Verify the PPP configuration on each router by using these two commands:

```
sh int s0
debug ppp authentication
```

Hands-on Lab 9.2: Configuring and Monitoring HDLC

There really is no configuration for HDLC, but if you completed Lab 9.1, then the PPP encapsulation would be set on both routers. This is why I put the PPP lab first. This lab allows you to actually configure HDLC encapsulation on a router.

 This second lab will use the same configuration Lab 9.1 used.

1. Set the encapsulation for each serial interface by using the `encapsulation hdlc` command.

```
RouterA#config t
RouterA(config)#int s0
RouterA(config-if)#encapsulation hdlc

RouterB#config t
RouterB(config)#int s0
RouterB(config-if)#encapsulation hdlc
```

2. Verify the HDLC encapsulation by using the `show interface s0` command on each router.

Review Questions

1. What are the two PPP authentication methods?

   A. SLARP

   B. ARP

   C. CHAP

   D. PAP

   E. SLIP

2. Which Data Link encapsulation can be used if you have one free serial interface and many remote offices to connect?

   A. HDLC

   B. PPP

   C. Frame Relay

   D. Ethernet

3. Which of the following are considered common Data Link WAN encapsulation types? (Choose three.)

   A. PPP

   B. HDLC

   C. Frame Relay

   D. ISDN

4. Which are considered WAN connection types? (Choose three.)

   A. DLCI

   B. Packet Switching

   C. Circuit Switching

   D. Inverse ARP

   E. Leased Lines

5. How do you configure a serial interface to use PPP encapsulation?

   A. ppp encapsulation

   B. encapsulation ppp

   C. no hdlc encapsulation, ppp encapsulation

   D. encapsulation frame-relay

6. Which encapsulations can be configured on a serial interface? (Choose three.)

   A. Ethernet

   B. Token Ring

   C. HDLC

   D. Frame Relay

   E. PPP

7. What is the default serial encapsulation used on Cisco routers?

   A. HDLC

   B. PPP

   C. SLIP

   D. Frame Relay

8. When a router is connected to a Frame Relay WAN link using a serial DTE interface, how is the clock rate determined?

   A. Supplied by the CSU/DSU

   B. By the far end router

   C. By the `clock rate` command

   D. By the physical layer bit stream timing

9. HDLC stands for what?

   A. High-Data Low Control

   B. High-Level Data Link Control

   C. Hands-on Data Link Configuration

   D. High Definition Link Configuration

10. When PPP connections are started, the links go through three phases of session establishment. What are the three phases?

   A. Link establishment

   B. High Definition Link Control

   C. Authentication phases (optional)

   D. Network layer protocol phase

   E. Physical layer bit streaming timing

11. Which of the following protocols are used with ISDN as an out-of-band protocol?

   A. LAPB

   B. LAPD

   C. BRI

   D. PRI

12. The Acme Corporation is implementing dial-up services to enable remote-office employees to connect to the local network. The company uses multiple routed protocols, needs authentication of users connecting to the network, and, since some calls will be long distance, will need callback support. Which of the following protocols is the best choice for these remote services?

   A. 802.1

   B. Frame Relay

   C. HDLC

   D. PPP

   E. PAP

13. Which of that following is a packet-switching encapsulation?

- **A.** PPP
- **B.** Frame Relay
- **C.** HDLC
- **D.** ISDN

14. Which of the following encapsulations was considered an upgrade from x.25?

- **A.** DSL
- **B.** ISDN
- **C.** Frame Relay
- **D.** Dedicated T1
- **E.** Wireless
- **F.** POTS

15. What is the reason why the serial link between the Corp router and the Remote router will not come up?

```
Corp#sh int s0/0
Serial0/0 is up, line protocol is down
  Hardware is PowerQUICC Serial
  Internet address is 10.0.1.1/24
  MTU 1500 bytes, BW 1544 Kbit, DLY 20000 usec,
    reliability 254/255, txload 1/255, rxload 1/255
  Encapsulation PPP, loopback not set

Remote#sh int s0/0
Serial0/0 is up, line protocol is down
  Hardware is PowerQUICC Serial
  Internet address is 10.0.1.2/24
  MTU 1500 bytes, BW 1544 Kbit, DLY 20000 usec,
    reliability 254/255, txload 1/255, rxload 1/255
  Encapsulation HDLC, loopback not set
```

- **A.** The serial cable is faulty.
- **B.** The IP addresses are not in the same subnet.
- **C.** The subnet masks are not correct.
- **D.** The keepalive settings are not correct.
- **E.** The layer 2 frame types are not compatible.

16. WAN stands for?

   A. "Wish" I had "A Network"

   B. "Waaa"...my "Network" doesn't work

   C. Wide area network

   D. Width of a Network

17. If you have a T1, what must you connect from your router to a demarc?

   A. Ethernet switches

   B. CSU/DSU

   C. Air conditioning to keep the line cool

   D. A T2 to connect the DTE to the DCE

18. Which is true regarding HDLC?

   A. It is an IEEE nonproprietary protocol.

   B. It is Cisco proprietary.

   C. It can be used with PPP on the same data link.

   D. It can be used with Frame Relay on the same data link.

19. Which PPP protocol provides link establishment?

   A. HDLC

   B. LAPD

   C. LCP

   D. NCP

20. Which protocol in PPP is used to identify the routed protocols?

   A. HDLC

   B. LAPD

   C. LCP

   D. NCP

Answers to Review Questions

1. C, D. The two authentication methods are CHAP and PAP.

2. C. If you have only one free serial interface on your router, you can use Frame Relay to connect multiple remote sites.

3. A, B, C. ISDN is considered a layer 3 WAN technology. Cisco considers PPP, HDLC, and Frame Relay the most command WAN technologies.

4. B, C, E. Leased lines, circuit switching, and packet switching are the typical WAN connection types.

5. B. You cannot use the no encapsulation command on a serial interface. To enable a certain encapsulation, use encapsulation ppp, for example.

6. C, D, E. Ethernet and Token Ring are LAN technologies and cannot be configured on a serial interface. PPP, HDLC, and Frame Relay are layer 2 WAN technologies that are typically configured on a serial interface.

7. A. Cisco, as do most router vendors, uses HDLC as the default serial encapsulation.

8. A. Clocking on a serial interface is always provided by the CSU/DSU (DCE device). However, if you do not have a CSU/DSU in your nonproduction test environment, then you need to supply clocking with the clock rate command on the serial interface of the router with the DCE cable attached.

9. B. High-Level Data Link Control (HDLC) was derived from Synchronous Data Link Control (SDLC), which was created by IBM as a Data Link connection protocol.

10. A, C, E. When PPP connections are started, the links go through three phases of session establishment: link-establishment, authentication phases, network layer protocol phase.

11. B. Link Access Procedure, D-Channel (LAPD) is used with ISDN at the Data Link layer (layer 2) as a protocol for the D (signaling) channel.

12. D. PPP is your only option, as HDLC and Frame Relay do not support these types of business requirements. PPP provides dynamic addressing, authentication using PAP or CHAP, and callback services.

13. B. A packet-switched technology that emerged in the early 1990s, Frame Relay is a Data Link and Physical layer specification that provides high performance.

14. C. Frame Relay is a successor to X.25, except that much of the technology in X.25 used to compensate for physical errors (noisy lines) has been eliminated. Frame Relay can be more cost-effective than point-to-point links and can typically run at speeds of 64Kbps up to 45Mbps (T3).

15. E. This is an easy question because the Remote router is using the default HDLC serial encapsulation and the Corp router is using the PPP serial encapsulation. You should go to the Remote router and set that encapsulation to PPP, or change the Corp router back to the default of HDLC.

16. C. WAN means wide area network. Although it seems as though the other answers might be correct at times, WANs are typically DCE networks that we lease to connect our DTE networks together.

17. B. Router interfaces are, by default, data terminal equipment (DTE), and they connect into data communication equipment (DCE)—for example, a channel service unit/data service unit (CSU/DSU). The CSU/DSU then plugs into a demarcation location (demarc) and is the service provider's last responsibility. Most of the time, the demarc is a jack that has an RJ-45 (8-pin modular) female connector located in a telecommunications closet.

18. B. HDLC is Cisco proprietary, and you cannot have HDLC on one side of a link and PPP or Frame Relay on the other side.

19. C. LCP provides a method of establishing, configuring, maintaining, and terminating the point-to-point connection. At startup, LCP provides link establishment.

20. D. Network Control Protocol works at the Logical Link Layer of the Data Link layer and identifies the Network layer (routed) protocols.

Answers to Written Lab 9

1. show interface serial 0
2. Config t, interface serial 0, encapsulation ppp
3. username todd password cisco
4. Point-to-Point Protocol
5. HDLC, PPP, and Frame Relay
6. Serial
7. Frame Relay
8. HDLC
9. HDLC, LCP, NCP
10. show interface

Glossary

10BaseT   Part of the original IEEE 802.3 standard, 10BaseT is the Ethernet specification of 10Mbps baseband that uses two pairs of twisted-pair, category 3, 4, or 5 cabling—using one pair to send data and the other to receive. 10BaseT has a distance limit of about 100 meters per segment. *See also Ethernet* and *IEEE 802.3.*

100BaseT   Based on the IEEE 802.3u standard, 100BaseT is the Fast Ethernet specification of 100Mbps baseband that uses UTP wiring. 100BaseT sends link pulses (containing more information than those used in 10BaseT) over the network when no traffic is present. *See also 10BaseT, Fast Ethernet,* and *IEEE 802.3.*

100BaseTX   Based on the IEEE 802.3u standard, 100BaseTX is the 100Mbps baseband Fast Ethernet specification that uses two pairs of UTP or STP wiring. The first pair of wires receives data; the second pair sends data. To ensure correct signal timing, a 100BaseTX segment cannot be longer than 100 meters.

A&B bit signaling   Used in T1 transmission facilities and sometimes called "24th channel signaling." Each of the 24 T1 subchannels in this procedure uses one bit of every sixth frame to send supervisory signaling information.

AAA   Authentication, Authorization, and Accounting: A system developed by Cisco to provide network security. *See also authentication, authorization,* and *accounting.*

AAL   ATM Adaptation Layer: A service-dependent sublayer of the Data Link layer that accepts data from other applications and brings it to the ATM layer in 48-byte ATM payload segments. CS and SAR are the two sublayers that form AALs. Currently, the four types of AAL recommended by the ITU-T are AAL1, AAL2, AAL3/4, and AAL5. AALs are differentiated by the source-destination timing they use, whether they are CBR or VBR, and whether they are used for connection-oriented or connectionless mode data transmission. *See also AAL1, AAL2, AAL3/4, AAL5, ATM,* and *ATM layer.*

AAL1   ATM Adaptation Layer 1: One of four AALs recommended by the ITU-T, it is used for connection-oriented, time-sensitive services that need constant bit rates, such as isochronous traffic and uncompressed video. *See also AAL.*

AAL2   ATM Adaptation Layer 2: One of four AALs recommended by the ITU-T, it is used for connection-oriented services that support a variable bit rate, such as compressed voice traffic. *See also AAL.*

AAL3/4   ATM Adaptation Layer 3/4: One of four AALs (a product of two initially distinct layers) recommended by the ITU-T, supporting both connectionless and connection-oriented links. Its primary use is in sending SMDS packets over ATM networks. *See also AAL.*

AAL5   ATM Adaptation Layer 5: One of four AALs recommended by the ITU-T, it is used to support connection-oriented VBR services primarily to transfer classical IP over ATM and LANE traffic. This least complex of the AAL recommendations uses SEAL, offering lower bandwidth costs and simpler processing requirements but also providing reduced bandwidth and error-recovery capacities. *See also AAL.*

AARP   AppleTalk Address Resolution Protocol: The protocol in an AppleTalk stack that maps data-link addresses to network addresses.

AARP probe packets   Packets sent by the AARP to determine whether a given node ID is being used by another node in a nonextended AppleTalk network. If the node ID is not in use, the sending node appropriates that node's ID. If the node ID is in use, the sending node will select a different ID and then send out more AARP probe packets. *See also AARP.*

ABM   Asynchronous Balanced Mode: When two stations can initiate a transmission, ABM is an HDLC (or one of its derived protocols) communication technology that supports peer-oriented, point-to-point communications between both stations.

ABR   Area Border Router: An OSPF router that is located on the border of one or more OSPF areas. ABRs are used to connect OSPF areas to the OSPF backbone area.

access layer   One of the layers in Cisco's three-layer hierarchical model. The access layer provides users with access to the internetwork.

access link   A link that is used with switches and is part of only one virtual LAN (VLAN). Trunk links carry information from multiple VLANs.

access list   A set of test conditions kept by routers that determines "interesting traffic" to and from the router for various services on the network.

access method   The manner in which network devices approach gaining access to the network itself.

access rate   Defines the bandwidth rate of the circuit. For example, the access rate of a T1 circuit is 1.544Mbps. In Frame Relay and other technologies, there may be a fractional T1 connection—256Kbps, for example—however, the access rate and clock rate are still 1.544Mbps.

access server   Also known as a network access server, it is a communications process connecting asynchronous devices to a LAN or WAN through network and terminal emulation software, providing synchronous or asynchronous routing of supported protocols.

accounting   One of the three components in AAA. Accounting provides auditing and logging functionalities to the security model.

acknowledgment   Verification sent from one network device to another signifying that an event has occurred. May be abbreviated as ACK. *Contrast with NAK.*

ACR   allowed cell rate: A designation defined by the ATM Forum for managing ATM traffic. Dynamically controlled using congestion control measures, the ACR varies between the minimum cell rate (MCR) and the peak cell rate (PCR). *See also MCR and PCR.*

active monitor   The mechanism used to manage a token ring. The network node with the highest MAC address on the ring becomes the active monitor and is responsible for management tasks such as preventing loops and ensuring that tokens are not lost.

active state   In regard to an EIGRP routing table, a route will be in active state when a router is undergoing a route convergence.

address learning   Used with transparent bridges to learn the hardware addresses of all devices on a network. The switch then filters the network with the known hardware (MAC) addresses.

address mapping   By translating network addresses from one format to another, this methodology permits different protocols to operate interchangeably.

address mask   A bit combination descriptor identifying which portion of an address refers to the network or subnet and which part refers to the host. Sometimes simply called the mask. *See also subnet mask.*

address resolution   The process used for resolving differences between computer addressing schemes. Address resolution typically defines a method for tracing Network layer (layer 3) addresses to Data Link layer (layer 2) addresses. *See also address mapping.*

adjacency   The relationship made between defined neighboring routers and end nodes, using a common media segment, to exchange routing information.

administrative distance (AD)   A number from 0 to 255 that expresses the level of trustworthiness of a routing information source. The lower the number, the higher the integrity rating.

administrative weight   A value designated by a network administrator to rate the preference given to a network link. It is one of four link metrics exchanged by PTSPs to test ATM network resource availability.

ADSU   ATM Data Service Unit: The terminal adapter used to connect to an ATM network through an HSSI-compatible mechanism. *See also DSU.*

advertising   The process whereby routing or service updates are transmitted at given intervals, allowing other routers on the network to maintain a record of viable routes.

AEP   AppleTalk Echo Protocol: A test for connectivity between two AppleTalk nodes in which one node sends a packet to another and receives an echo, or copy, in response.

AFI   Authority and Format Identifier: The part of an NSAP ATM address that delineates the type and format of the IDI section of an ATM address.

AFP   AppleTalk Filing Protocol: A Presentation layer protocol that supports AppleShare and Mac OS File Sharing and permits users to share files and applications on a server.

AIP   ATM Interface Processor: Supporting AAL3/4 and AAL5, this interface for Cisco 7000 series routers minimizes performance bottlenecks at the UNI. *See also AAL3/4 and AAL5.*

algorithm   A set of rules or processes used to solve a problem. In networking, algorithms are typically used for finding the best route for traffic from a source to its destination.

alignment error   In Ethernet networks, an error in which a received frame has extra bits— that is, a number not divisible by eight. Alignment errors are generally the result of frame damage caused by collisions.

all-routes explorer packet   An explorer packet that can move across an entire SRB network, tracing all possible paths to a given destination. Also known as an all-rings explorer packet. *See also explorer packet, local explorer packet,* and *spanning explorer packet.*

AM   amplitude modulation: A modulation method that represents information by varying the amplitude of the carrier signal. *See also modulation.*

AMI Alternate Mark Inversion: A line-code type on T1 and E1 circuits that shows 0s as 01 during each bit cell and 1s as 11 or 00, alternately, during each bit cell. The sending device must maintain ones density in AMI but not independently of the data stream. Also known as binary-coded, alternate mark inversion. *Contrast with B8ZS. See also ones density.*

amplitude An analog or digital waveform's highest value.

analog transmission Signal messaging whereby information is represented by various combinations of signal amplitude, frequency, and phase.

ANSI American National Standards Institute: The organization of corporate, government, and other volunteer members that coordinates standards-related activities, approves U.S. national standards, and develops U.S. positions in international standards organizations. ANSI assists in the creation of international and U.S. standards in disciplines such as communications, networking, and a variety of technical fields. It publishes over 13,000 standards for engineered products and technologies ranging from screw threads to networking protocols. ANSI is a member of the International Electrotechnical Commission (IEC) and International Organization for Standardization (ISO).

anycast An ATM address that can be shared by more than one end system, allowing requests to be routed to a node that provides a particular service.

AppleTalk Currently in two versions, the group of communication protocols designed by Apple Computer for use in Macintosh environments. The earlier Phase 1 protocols support one physical network with only one network number that resides in one zone. The later Phase 2 protocols support more than one logical network on a single physical network, allowing networks to exist in more than one zone. *See also zone.*

Application layer Layer 7 of the OSI reference network model, supplying services to application procedures (such as electronic mail or file transfer) that are outside the OSI model. This layer chooses and determines the availability of communicating partners along with the resources necessary to make the connection, coordinates partnering applications, and forms a consensus on procedures for controlling data integrity and error recovery. *See also Data Link layer, Network layer, Physical layer, Presentation layer, Session layer, and Transport layer.*

ARA AppleTalk Remote Access: A protocol for Macintosh users establishing their access to resources and data from a remote AppleTalk location.

area A logical, rather than physical, set of segments (based on either CLNS, DECnet, or OSPF) along with their attached devices. Areas are commonly connected to others using routers to create a single autonomous system. .

ARM Asynchronous Response Mode: An HDLC communication mode using one primary station and at least one additional station and allowing transmission to be initiated from either the primary or one of the secondary units.

ARP Address Resolution Protocol: Defined in RFC 826, the protocol that traces IP addresses to MAC addresses. *See also RARP.*

AS   autonomous system: A group of networks under mutual administration that share the same routing methodology. Autonomous systems are subdivided by areas and must be assigned an individual 16-bit number by the IANA. *See also area.*

AS path prepending   The use of route maps in BGP to lengthen the autonomous system path by adding false ASNs.

ASBR   Autonomous System Boundary Router: An area border router placed between an OSPF autonomous system and a non-OSPF network that operates both OSPF and an additional routing protocol, such as RIP. ASBRs must be located in a non-stub OSPF area. *See also ABR, non-stub area,* and *OSPF.*

ASCII   American Standard Code for Information Interchange: An 8-bit code for representing characters, it consists of 7 data bits plus 1 parity bit.

ASICs   application-specific integrated circuits: Used in layer 2 switches to make filtering decisions. The ASIC looks in the filter table of MAC addresses and determines which port the destination hardware address of a received hardware address is destined for. The frame will be allowed to traverse only that one segment. If the hardware address is unknown, the frame is forwarded out all ports.

ASN.1   Abstract Syntax Notation One: An OSI language used to describe types of data that are independent of computer structures and depicting methods. Described by ISO International Standard 8824.

ASP   AppleTalk Session Protocol: A protocol employing ATP to establish, maintain, and tear down sessions as well as sequence requests. *See also ATP.*

AST   Automatic Spanning Tree: A function that supplies one path for spanning explorer frames traveling from one node in the network to another, supporting the automatic resolution of spanning trees in SRB networks. AST is based on the IEEE 802.1d standard. *See also IEEE 802.1* and *SRB.*

asynchronous transmission   Digital signals sent without precise timing, usually with different frequencies and phase relationships. Asynchronous transmissions generally enclose individual characters in control bits (called start and stop bits) that show the beginning and end of each character. *Contrast with isochronous transmission* and *synchronous transmission.*

ATCP   AppleTalk Control Program: The protocol for establishing and configuring Apple-Talk over PPP, defined in RFC 1378. *See also PPP.*

ATDM   Asynchronous Time-Division Multiplexing: A technique for sending information, it differs from normal TDM in that the time slots are assigned when necessary rather than pre-assigned to certain transmitters. *Contrast with FDM, statistical multiplexing,* and *TDM.*

ATG   Address Translation Gateway: The mechanism within Cisco DECnet routing software that enables routers to route multiple, independent DECnet networks and to establish a user-designated address translation for chosen nodes between networks.

ATM   Asynchronous Transfer Mode: The international standard, identified by fixed-length 53-byte cells, for transmitting cells in multiple service systems, such as voice, video, or data. Transit delays are reduced because the fixed-length cells permit processing to occur in the hardware. ATM is designed to maximize the benefits of high-speed transmission media, such as SONET, E3, and T3.

ATM ARP server   A device that supplies logical subnets running classical IP over ATM with address-resolution services.

ATM endpoint   The initiating or terminating connection in an ATM network. ATM endpoints include servers, workstations, ATM-to-LAN switches, and ATM routers.

ATM Forum   The international organization founded jointly by Northern Telecom, Sprint, Cisco Systems, and NET/ADAPTIVE in 1991 to develop and promote standards-based implementation agreements for ATM technology. The ATM Forum broadens official standards developed by ANSI and ITU-T and creates implementation agreements before official standards are published.

ATM layer   A sublayer of the Data Link layer in an ATM network that is service independent. To create standard 53-byte ATM cells, the ATM layer receives 48-byte segments from the AAL and attaches a 5-byte header to each. These cells are then sent to the physical layer for transmission across the physical medium. *See also AAL.*

ATMM   ATM Management: A procedure that runs on ATM switches, managing rate enforcement and VCI translation. *See also ATM.*

ATM user-user connection   A connection made by the ATM layer to supply communication between at least two ATM service users, such as ATMM processes. These communications can be uni- or bidirectional, using one or two VCs, respectively. *See also ATM layer and ATMM.*

ATP   AppleTalk Transaction Protocol: A transport-level protocol that enables reliable transactions between two sockets, where one requests the other to perform a given task and to report the results. ATP fastens the request and response together, assuring a loss-free exchange of request-response pairs.

attenuation   In communication, weakening or loss of signal energy, typically caused by distance.

AURP   AppleTalk Update-based Routing Protocol: A technique for encapsulating AppleTalk traffic in the header of a foreign protocol that allows the connection of at least two noncontiguous AppleTalk internetworks through a foreign network (such as TCP/IP) to create an AppleTalk WAN. The connection made is called an AURP tunnel. By exchanging routing information between exterior routers, the AURP maintains routing tables for the complete AppleTalk WAN. *See also AURP tunnel.*

AURP tunnel   A connection made in an AURP WAN that acts as a single, virtual link between AppleTalk internetworks separated physically by a foreign network such as a TCP/IP network. *See also AURP.*

authentication   The first component in the AAA model. Users are typically authenticated via a username and password, which are used to uniquely identify them.

authority zone   A portion of the domain-name tree associated with DNS for which one name server is the authority. *See also DNS.*

authorization   The act of permitting access to a resource based on authentication information in the AAA model.

auto-detect mechanism   Used in Ethernet switch, hub, and interface cards to determine the duplex and speed that can be used.

auto duplex   A setting on layer 1 and layer 2 devices that sets the duplex of a switch or hub port automatically.

automatic call reconnect   A function that enables automatic call rerouting away from a failed trunk line.

autonomous confederation   A collection of self-governed systems that depend more on their own network accessibility and routing information than on information received from other systems or groups.

autonomous switching   The ability of Cisco routers to process packets more quickly by using the ciscoBus to switch packets independently of the system processor.

autonomous system   *See AS.*

autoreconfiguration   A procedure executed by nodes within the failure domain of a token ring, wherein nodes automatically perform diagnostics, trying to reconfigure the network around failed areas.

auxiliary port   The console port on the back of Cisco routers that allows you to connect a modem and dial the router and make console configuration settings.

B8ZS   Binary 8-Zero Substitution: A line-code type, interpreted at the remote end of the connection, that uses a special code substitution whenever eight consecutive 0s are transmitted over the link on T1 and E1 circuits. This technique assures ones density independent of the data stream. Also known as bipolar 8-zero substitution. *Contrast with AMI. See also ones density.*

backbone   The basic portion of the network that provides the primary path for traffic sent to and initiated from other networks.

back end   A node or software program supplying services to a front end. *See also server.*

bandwidth   The gap between the highest and lowest frequencies employed by network signals. More commonly, it refers to the rated throughput capacity of a network protocol or medium.

bandwidth on demand (BoD)   This function allows an additional B channel to be used to increase the amount of bandwidth available for a particular connection.

baseband   A feature of a network technology that uses only one carrier frequency. Ethernet is an example. Also named narrowband. *Compare with broadband.*

baseline   Baseline information includes historical data about the network and routine utilization information. This information can be used to determine whether there were recent changes made to the network that may contribute to the problem at hand.

Basic Management Setup   Used with Cisco routers when in setup mode. Only provides enough management and configuration to get the router working so someone can telnet into the router and configure it.

baud   Synonymous with bits per second (bps) if each signal element represents 1 bit. It is a unit of signaling speed equivalent to the number of separate signal elements transmitted per second.

B channel   bearer channel: A full-duplex, 64Kbps channel in ISDN that transmits user data. *Compare with D channel, E channel, and H channel.*

BDR   backup designated router: This is used in an OSPF network to back up the designated router in case of failure.

beacon   An FDDI frame or Token Ring frame that points to a serious problem with the ring, such as a broken cable. The beacon frame carries the address of the station thought to be down. *See also failure domain.*

BECN   Backward Explicit Congestion Notification: BECN is the bit set by a Frame Relay network in frames moving away from frames headed into a congested path. A DTE that receives frames with the BECN may ask higher-level protocols to take necessary flow control measures. *Compare with FECN.*

BGP4   BGP version 4: Version 4 of the interdomain routing protocol most commonly used on the Internet. BGP4 supports CIDR and uses route-counting mechanisms to decrease the size of routing tables. *See also CIDR.*

BGP Identifier   This field contains a value that identifies the BGP speaker. This is a random value chosen by the BGP router when sending an OPEN message.

BGP neighbors   Two routers running BGP that begin a communication process to exchange dynamic routing information; they use a TCP port at layer 4 of the OSI reference model. Specifically, TCP port 179 is used. Also known as BGP peers.

BGP peers   *See BGP neighbors.*

BGP speaker   A router that advertises its prefixes or routes.

bidirectional shared tree   A method of shared tree multicast forwarding. This method allows group members to receive data from the source or the RP, whichever is closer. *See also RP (routes processort).*

binary   A two-character numbering method that uses 1s and 0s. The binary numbering system underlies all digital representation of information.

binding   Configuring a Network layer protocol to use a certain frame type on a LAN.

BIP Bit Interleaved Parity: A method used in ATM to monitor errors on a link, sending a check bit or word in the link overhead for the previous block or frame. This allows bit errors in transmissions to be found and delivered as maintenance information.

BISDN Broadband ISDN: ITU-T standards created to manage high-bandwidth technologies such as video. BISDN presently employs ATM technology along SONET-based transmission circuits, supplying data rates typically between 155Mbps and 622Mbps and now even into the gigabyte range (if you have the big bucks). *See also BRI, ISDN, and PRI.*

bit One binary digit; either a 1 or a 0. Eight bits make a byte.

bit-oriented protocol Regardless of frame content, the class of Data Link layer communication protocols that transmits frames. Bit-oriented protocols, as compared with byte-oriented, supply more efficient and trustworthy full-duplex operation. *Compare with byte-oriented protocol.*

block size Number of hosts that can be used in a subnet. Block sizes typically can be used in increments of 4, 8, 16, 32, 64, and 128.

Boot ROM Used in routers to put the router into bootstrap mode. Bootstrap mode then boots the device with an operating system. The ROM can also hold a small Cisco IOS.

boot sequence Defines how a router boots. The configuration register tells the router where to boot the IOS from as well as how to load the configuration.

bootstrap protocol (BootP) A protocol used to dynamically assign IP addresses and gateways to requesting clients.

border gateway A router that facilitates communication with routers in different autonomous systems.

border peer The device in charge of a peer group; it exists at the edge of a hierarchical design. When any member of the peer group wants to locate a resource, it sends a single explorer to the border peer. The border peer then forwards this request on behalf of the requesting router, thus eliminating duplicate traffic.

border router Typically defined within Open Shortest Path First (OSPF) as a router that connects an area to the backbone area. However, a border router can be a router that connects a company to the Internet as well. *See also OSPF.*

BPDU Bridge Protocol Data Unit: A Spanning Tree Protocol initializing packet that is sent at definable intervals for the purpose of exchanging information among bridges in networks.

BRI Basic Rate Interface: The ISDN interface that facilitates circuit-switched communication between video, data, and voice; it is made up of two B channels (64Kbps each) and one D channel (16Kbps). *Compare with PRI. See also BISDN.*

bridge A device for connecting two segments of a network and transmitting packets between them. Both segments must use identical protocols to communicate. Bridges function at the Data Link layer, layer 2 of the OSI reference model. The purpose of a bridge is to filter, send, or flood any incoming frame based on the MAC address of that particular frame.

bridge group   Used in the router configuration of bridging, bridge groups are defined by a unique number. Network traffic is bridged between all interfaces that are a member of the same bridge group.

bridge identifier   Used to elect the root bridge in a layer 2 switched internetwork. The bridge ID is a combination of the bridge priority and base MAC address.

bridge priority   Sets the STP priority of the bridge. All bridge priorities are set to 32,768 by default.

bridging loop   Loops occur in a bridged network if more than one link to a network exists and the STP protocol is not turned on.

broadband   A transmission methodology for multiplexing several independent signals onto one cable. In telecommunications, broadband is classified as any channel with bandwidth greater than 4kHz (typical voice grade In LAN terminology, it is classified as a coaxial cable on which analog signaling is employed. Also known as wideband).

broadcast   A data frame or packet that is transmitted to every node on the local network segment (as defined by the broadcast domain). Broadcasts are known by their broadcast address, which is a destination network and host address with all the bits turned on. Also called local broadcast. *Compare with directed broadcast.*

broadcast address   Used in both logical addressing and hardware addressing. In logical addressing, the host addresses will be all 1s. With hardware addressing, the hardware address will be all 1s in binary (all *F*s in hex).

broadcast domain   A group of devices receiving broadcast frames initiating from any device within the group. Because routers do not forward broadcast frames, broadcast domains are not forwarded from one broadcast to another.

Broadcast (multiaccess) networks   Broadcast (multiaccess) networks such as Ethernet allow multiple devices to connect to (or access) the same network as well as provide a broadcast ability in which a single packet is delivered to all nodes on the network

broadcast storm   An undesired event on the network caused by the simultaneous transmission of any number of broadcasts across the network segment. Such an occurrence can overwhelm network bandwidth, resulting in time-outs.

buffer   A storage area dedicated to handling data while in transit. Buffers are used to receive/store sporadic deliveries of data bursts (usually received from faster devices), compensating for the variations in processing speed. Incoming information is stored until everything is received prior to sending data on. Also known as an information buffer.

bursting   Some technologies, including ATM and Frame Relay, are considered burstable. This means that user data can exceed the bandwidth normally reserved for the connection; however, it cannot exceed the port speed. An example of this would be a 128Kbps Frame Relay CIR on a T1—depending on the vendor, it may be possible to send more than 128Kbps for a short time.

bus   Any common physical path, typically wires or copper, through which a digital signal can be used to send data from one part of a computer to another.

BUS   broadcast and unknown servers: In LAN emulation, the hardware or software responsible for resolving all broadcasts and packets with unknown (unregistered) addresses into the point-to-point virtual circuits required by ATM. *See also LANE, LEC, LECS,* and *LES.*

bus topology   A linear LAN architecture in which transmissions from various stations on the network are reproduced over the length of the medium and are accepted by all other stations. *Compare with ring topology* and *star topology.*

BX.25   AT&T's use of X.25. *See also X.25.*

bypass mode   An FDDI and Token Ring network operation that deletes an interface.

bypass relay   A device that enables a particular interface in the token ring to be closed down and effectively taken off the ring.

byte   Eight bits. *See also octet.*

byte-oriented protocol   Any type of data-link communication protocol that, in order to mark the boundaries of frames, uses a specific character from the user character set. These protocols have generally been superseded by bit-oriented protocols. *Compare with bit-oriented protocol.*

cable range   In an extended AppleTalk network, the range of numbers allotted for use by existing nodes on the network. The value of the cable range can be anywhere from a single to a sequence of several touching network numbers. Node addresses are determined by their cable range value.

CAC   Connection Admission Control: The sequence of actions executed by every ATM switch while connection setup is performed in order to determine if a request for connection is violating the guarantees of QoS for established connections. Also, CAC is used to route a connection request through an ATM network.

call admission control   A device for managing traffic in ATM networks, determining the possibility of a path containing adequate bandwidth for a requested VCC.

call establishment   Used to reference an ISDN call setup scheme when the call is working.

call priority   In circuit-switched systems, the defining priority given to each originating port; it specifies in which order calls will be reconnected. Additionally, call priority identifies which calls are allowed during a bandwidth reservation.

call setup   Handshaking scheme that defines how a source and destination device will establish a call to each other.

call setup time   The length of time necessary to effect a switched call between DTE devices.

CBR   constant bit rate: An ATM Forum QoS class created for use in ATM networks. CBR is used for connections that rely on precision clocking to guarantee trustworthy delivery. *Compare with ABR* and *VBR.*

CD   carrier detect: A signal indicating that an interface is active or that a connection generated by a modem has been established.

CDP   Cisco Discovery Protocol: Cisco's proprietary protocol that is used to tell a neighbor Cisco device about the type of hardware, software version, and active interfaces that the Cisco device is using. It uses a SNAP frame between devices and is not routable.

CDP holdtime   The amount of time a router will hold Cisco Discovery Protocol information received from a neighbor router before discarding it if the information is not updated by the neighbor. This timer is set to 180 seconds by default.

CDP timer   The amount of time between when Cisco Discovery Protocol advertisements are transmitted out of all router interfaces by default. The CDP timer is 90 seconds by default.

CDVT   Cell Delay Variation Tolerance: A QoS parameter for traffic management in ATM networks specified when a connection is established. The allowable fluctuation levels for data samples taken by the PCR in CBR transmissions are determined by the CDVT. *See also CBR and PCR.*

cell   In ATM networking, the basic unit of data for switching and multiplexing. Cells have a defined length of 53 bytes, including a 5-byte header that identifies the cell's data stream and 48 bytes of payload. *See also cell relay.*

cell payload scrambling   The method by which an ATM switch maintains framing on some medium-speed edge and trunk interfaces (T3 or E3 circuits). Cell payload scrambling rearranges the data portion of a cell to maintain the line synchronization with certain common bit patterns.

cell relay   A technology that uses small packets of fixed size, known as cells. Their fixed length enables them to be processed and switched in hardware at high speeds, making this technology the foundation for ATM and other high-speed network protocols. *See also cell.*

Centrex   A local exchange carrier service that provides local switching that resembles that of an on-site PBX. Centrex has no on-site switching capability. Therefore, all customer connections return to the central office (CO). *See also CO.*

CER   cell error ratio: The ratio in ATM of transmitted cells having errors to the total number of cells transmitted within a certain span of time.

CGMP   Cisco Group Management Protocol: A proprietary protocol developed by Cisco. The router uses CGMP to send multicast membership commands to Catalyst switches.

channelized E1   Operating at 2.048Mpbs, an access link that is sectioned into 29 B channels and one D channel and supports DDR, Frame Relay, and X.25. *Compare with channelized T1.*

channelized T1   Operating at 1.544Mbps, an access link that is sectioned into 23 B channels and 1 D channel of 64Kbps each, where individual channels or groups of channels connect to various destinations, Channelized T1 supports DDR, Frame Relay, and X.25. *Compare with channelized E1.*

CHAP   Challenge Handshake Authentication Protocol: Supported on lines using PPP encapsulation, it is a security feature that identifies the remote end, helping keep out unauthorized users. After CHAP is performed, the router or access server determines whether a given user is permitted access. It is a newer, more secure protocol than PAP. *Compare with PAP.*

checksum   A test for ensuring the integrity of sent data. It is a number calculated from a series of values taken through a sequence of mathematical functions, typically placed at the end of the data from which it is calculated, and then recalculated at the receiving end for verification. *Compare with CRC.*

choke packet   When congestion exists, it is a packet sent to inform a transmitter that it should decrease its sending rate.

CIDR   Classless Inter-Domain Routing (CIDR): allows a group of IP networks to appear to other networks as a unified, larger entity. In CIDR, IP addresses and their subnet masks are written as four dotted octets followed by a forward slash and the number of masking bits (a form of subnet notation shorthand). *See also BGP4.*

CIP   Channel Interface Processor: A channel attachment interface for use in Cisco 7000 series routers that connects a host mainframe to a control unit. This device eliminates the need for an FBP to attach channels.

CIR   committed information rate: Averaged over a minimum span of time and measured in bps, a Frame Relay network's agreed-upon minimum rate of transferring information.

circuit switching   Used with dial-up networks such as PPP and ISDN. Passes data but needs to set up the connection first—just like making a phone call.

Cisco FRAD   Cisco Frame Relay Access Device: A Cisco product that supports Cisco IPS Frame Relay SNA services, connecting SDLC devices to Frame Relay without requiring an existing LAN. May be upgraded to a fully functioning multiprotocol router. Can activate conversion from SDLC to Ethernet and Token Ring, but does not support attached LANs. *See also FRAD.*

CiscoFusion   Cisco's name for the internetworking architecture under which its Cisco IOS operates. It is designed to "fuse" together the capabilities of its disparate collection of acquired routers and switches.

Cisco IOS   Cisco Internetwork Operating System software. The kernel of the Cisco line of routers and switches that supplies shared functionality, scalability, and security for all products under its CiscoFusion architecture. *See also CiscoFusion.*

CiscoView   GUI-based management software for Cisco networking devices, enabling dynamic status, statistics, and comprehensive configuration information. Displays a physical view of the Cisco device chassis and provides device-monitoring functions and fundamental troubleshooting capabilities. May be integrated with a number of SNMP-based network management platforms.

Class A network   Part of the Internet Protocol hierarchical addressing scheme. Class A networks have only 8 bits for defining networks and 24 bits for defining hosts and subnets on each network.

Class B network   Part of the Internet Protocol hierarchical addressing scheme. Class B networks have 16 bits for defining networks and 16 bits for defining hosts and subnets on each network.

Class C network   Part of the Internet Protocol hierarchical addressing scheme. Class C networks have 24 bits for defining networks and only 8 bits for defining hosts and subnets on each network.

classful routing   Routing protocols that do not send subnet mask information when a route update is sent out.

classical IP over ATM   Defined in RFC 1577, the specification for running IP over ATM that maximizes ATM features. Also known as CIA.

classless routing   Routing that sends subnet mask information in the routing updates. Classless routing allows Variable Length Subnet Masks (VLSM) and supernetting. Routing protocols that support classless routing are RIP version 2, EIGRP, and OSPF.

CLI   command-line interface: Allows you to configure Cisco routers and switches with maximum flexibility.

CLP   Cell Loss Priority: The area in the ATM cell header that determines the likelihood of a cell being dropped during network congestion. Cells with CLP = 0 are considered insured traffic and are not apt to be dropped. Cells with CLP = 1 are considered best-effort traffic that may be dropped during congested episodes, delivering more resources to handle insured traffic.

CLR   Cell Loss Ratio: The ratio of discarded cells to successfully delivered cells in ATM. CLR can be designated a QoS parameter when establishing a connection.

CO   central office: The local telephone company office where all loops in a certain area connect and where circuit switching of subscriber lines occurs.

collapsed backbone   A nondistributed backbone where all network segments are connected to each other through an internetworking device. A collapsed backbone can be a virtual network segment at work in a device such as a router, hub, or switch.

collision   The effect of two nodes sending transmissions simultaneously in Ethernet. When they meet on the physical media, the frames from each node collide and are damaged. *See also collision domain.*

collision domain   The network area in Ethernet over which frames that have collided will be detected. Collisions are propagated by hubs and repeaters but not by LAN switches, routers, or bridges. *See also collision.*

composite metric   Used with routing protocols, such as IGRP and EIGRP, that use more than one metric to find the best path to a remote network. IGRP and EIGRP both use bandwidth and delay of the line by default. However, maximum transmission unit (MTU), load, and reliability of a link can be used as well.

compression   A technique to send across a link more data than would be normally permitted by representing repetitious strings of data with a single marker.

configuration register   A 16-bit configurable value stored in hardware or software that determines how Cisco routers function during initialization. In hardware, the bit position is set using a jumper. In software, it is set by specifying specific bit patterns used to set startup options, configured using a hexadecimal value with configuration commands.

congestion   Traffic that exceeds the network's ability to handle it.

congestion avoidance   To minimize delays, the method a network uses to control traffic entering the system. Lower-priority traffic is discarded at the edge of the network when indicators signal it cannot be delivered, thus using resources efficiently.

congestion collapse   The situation that results from the retransmission of packets in ATM networks where little or no traffic successfully arrives at destination points. It usually happens in networks made of switches with ineffective or inadequate buffering capabilities combined with poor packet discard or ABR congestion feedback mechanisms.

connection ID   Identifications given to each Telnet session into a router. The show sessions command will give you the connections a local router will have to a remote router. The show users command will show the connection IDs of users telnetted into your local router.

connectionless   Data transfer that occurs without the creation of a virtual circuit. It has low overhead, uses best-effort delivery, and is not reliable. *Contrast with connection-oriented. See also virtual circuit.*

Connectionless Network Service (CLNS)   See *connectionless.*

connection-oriented   Data transfer method that sets up a virtual circuit before any data is transferred. Uses acknowledgments and flow control for reliable data transfer. *Contrast with connectionless. See also virtual circuit.*

console port   Typically an RJ-45 (8-pin modular) port on a Cisco router and switch that allows command-line interface capability.

control direct VCC   One of two control connections defined by Phase I LAN emulation; a bidirectional virtual control connection (VCC) established in ATM by an LEC to an LES. *See also control distribute VCC.*

control distribute VCC   One of two control connections defined by Phase 1 LAN emulation; a unidirectional virtual control connection (VCC) set up in ATM from an LES to an LEC. Usually, the VCC is a point-to-multipoint connection. *See also control direct VCC.*

convergence   The process required for all routers in an internetwork to update their routing tables and create a consistent view of the network using the best possible paths. No user data is passed during an STP convergence time.

core layer   Top layer in the Cisco three-layer hierarchical model, which helps you design, build, and maintain Cisco hierarchical networks. The core layer passes packets quickly to distribution layer devices only. No packet filtering should take place at this layer.

cost   Also known as path cost, an arbitrary value, based on hop count, bandwidth, or other calculation, that is typically assigned by a network administrator and used by the routing protocol to compare different routes through an internetwork. Routing protocols use cost values to select the best path to a certain destination: the lowest cost identifies the best path. Also known as path cost. *See also routing metric.*

count to infinity   A problem occurring in routing algorithms that are slow to converge where routers keep increasing the hop count to particular networks. To avoid this problem, various solutions have been implemented into each of the different routing protocols. Some of those solutions include defining a maximum hop count (defining infinity), route poising, poison reverse, and split horizon.

CPCS   Common Part Convergence Sublayer: One of two AAL sublayers that is service dependent, it is further segmented into the CS and SAR sublayers. The CPCS prepares data for transmission across the ATM network; it creates the 48-byte payload cells that are sent to the ATM layer. *See also AAL* and *ATM layer.*

CPE   customer premises equipment: Items such as telephones, modems, and terminals installed at customer locations and connected to the service provider network.

crankback   In ATM, a correction technique used when a node somewhere on a chosen path cannot accept a connection setup request, blocking the request. The path is rolled back to an intermediate node, which then uses GCAC to attempt to find an alternate path to the final destination.

CRC   cyclic redundancy check: A methodology that detects errors, whereby the frame recipient makes a calculation by dividing frame contents with a prime binary divisor and compares the remainder to a value stored in the frame by the sending node. *Contrast with checksum.*

crossover cable   Type of Ethernet cable that connects a switch to switch, host to host, hub to hub, or switch to hub.

CSMA/CD   Carrier Sense Multiple Access with Collision Detection: A technology defined by the Ethernet IEEE 802.3 committee. Each device senses the cable for a digital signal before transmitting. Also, CSMA/CD allows all devices on the network to share the same cable, but one at a time. If two devices transmit at the same time, a frame collision will occur and a jamming pattern will be sent; the devices will stop transmitting, wait a predetermined as well as a self-imposed random amount of time, and then try to transmit again.

CSU   channel service unit: A digital mechanism that connects end-user equipment to the local digital telephone loop. Frequently referred to along with the data service unit as CSU/DSU. *See also DSU.*

CSU/DSU   channel service unit/data service unit: Physical layer device used in wide area networks to convert the CPE digital signals to what is understood by the provider's switch. A CSU/DSU is typically one device that plugs into a RJ-45 (8-pin modular) jack, known as the demarcation point.

CTD   Cell Transfer Delay: For a given connection in ATM, the time period between a cell exit event at the source user-network interface (UNI) and the corresponding cell entry event at the destination. The CTD between these points is the sum of the total inter-ATM transmission delay and the total ATM processing delay.

cumulative interface delay   This is a Cisco term for delay of the line. The composite metric in IGRP and EIGRP is calculated by using the bandwidth and delay of the line by default.

cut-through frame switching   A frame-switching technique that flows data through a switch so that the leading edge exits the switch at the output port before the packet finishes entering the input port. Frames will be read, processed, and forwarded by devices that use cut-through switching as soon as the destination address of the frame is confirmed and the outgoing port is identified.

data compression   *See compression*

data direct VCC   A bidirectional point-to-point virtual control connection (VCC) set up between two LECs in ATM and one of three data connections defined by Phase 1 LAN emulation. Because data direct VCCs do not guarantee QoS, they are generally reserved for UBR and ABR connections. *Compare with control distribute VCC and control direct VCC.*

data encapsulation   The process in which the information in a protocol is wrapped, or contained, in the data section of another protocol. In the OSI reference model, each layer encapsulates the layer immediately above it as the data flows down the protocol stack.

data frame   Protocol Data Unit encapsulation at the Data Link layer of the OSI reference model. Encapsulates packets from the Network layer and prepares the data for transmission on a network medium.

datagram   A logical collection of information transmitted as a Network layer unit over a medium without a previously established virtual circuit. IP datagrams have become the primary information unit of the Internet. At various layers of the OSI reference model, the terms *cell, frame, message, packet,* and *segment* also define these logical information groupings.

Data Link Control layer   Layer 2 of the SNA architectural model, it is responsible for the transmission of data over a given physical link and compares somewhat to the Data Link layer of the OSI model.

Data Link layer   Layer 2 of the OSI reference model, it ensures the trustworthy transmission of data across a physical link and is primarily concerned with physical addressing, line discipline, network topology, error notification, ordered delivery of frames, and flow control. The IEEE has further segmented this layer into the MAC sublayer and the LLC sublayer. Also known as the link layer. Can be compared somewhat to the Data Link Control Layer of the SNA model. *See also Application layer, LLC, MAC, Network layer, Physical layer, Presentation layer, Session layer,* and *Transport layer.*

data terminal equipment   *See DTE.*

DCC   Data Country Code: Developed by the ATM Forum, one of two ATM address formats designed for use by private networks. *Compare with ICD.*

DCE   data communication equipment (as defined by the EIA) or data circuit-terminating equipment (as defined by the ITU-T): The mechanisms and links of a communications network that make up the network portion of the user-to-network interface, such as modems. The DCE supplies the physical connection to the network, forwards traffic, and provides a clocking signal to synchronize data transmission between DTE and DCE devices. *Compare with DTE.*

D channel   (1) data channel: A full-duplex, 16Kbps (BRI) or 64Kbps (PRI) ISDN channel. *Compare with B channel, E channel,* and *H channel.* (2) In SNA, anything that provides a connection between the processor and main storage with any peripherals.

DDP   Datagram Delivery Protocol: Used in the AppleTalk suite of protocols as a connectionless protocol that is responsible for sending datagrams through an internetwork.

DDR   dial-on-demand routing: A technique that allows a router to automatically initiate and end a circuit-switched session per the requirements of the sending station. By mimicking keep-alives, the router fools the end station into treating the session as active. DDR permits routing over ISDN or telephone lines via a modem or external ISDN terminal adapter.

DE   Discard Eligibility: Used in Frame Relay networks to tell a switch that a frame can be preferentially discarded if the switch is too busy. The DE is a field in the frame that is turned on by transmitting routers if the committed information rate (CIR) is oversubscribed or set to 0.

dedicated line   Point-to-point connection that does not share any bandwidth.

de-encapsulation   The technique used by layered protocols in which a layer removes header information from the Protocol Data Unit (PDU) from the layer below. *See also encapsulation.*

default route   The static routing table entry used to direct frames whose next hop is not otherwise spelled out in the routing table.

delay   The time elapsed between a sender's initiation of a transaction and the first response they receive. Also, the time needed to move a packet from its source to its destination over a path. *See also latency.*

demarc   The demarcation point between the customer premises equipment (CPE) and the telco's carrier equipment.

demodulation   A series of steps that return a modulated signal to its original form. When receiving, a modem demodulates an analog signal to its original digital form (and, conversely, modulates the digital data it sends into an analog signal). *See also modulation.*

demultiplexing   The process of converting a multiplexed signal, comprising more than one input stream, back into separate output streams. *See also multiplexing.*

designated bridge   In the process of forwarding a frame from a segment to the root bridge, the bridge with the lowest root path cost.

designated port   Used with the Spanning Tree Protocol (STP) to designate forwarding ports. If there are multiple links to the same network, STP will shut a port down to stop network loops.

designated router (DR)   An OSPF router that creates LSAs for a multiaccess network and is required to perform other special tasks in OSPF operations. Multiaccess OSPF networks that maintain a minimum of two attached routers identify one router that is chosen by the OSPF Hello protocol, which makes possible a decrease in the number of adjacencies necessary on a multiaccess network. This in turn reduces the quantity of routing protocol traffic and the physical size of the database.

desktop layer   The access layer of the Cisco hierarchical model is sometimes referred to as the desktop layer. The access layer controls user and workgroup access to internetwork resources.

destination address   The address for the network device(s) that will receive a packet.

DHCP   Dynamic Host Configuration Protocol: DHCP is a superset of the BootP protocol. This means that it uses the same protocol structure as BootP but it has enhancements added. Both of these protocols use servers that dynamically configure clients when requested. The two major enhancements are address pools and lease times.

dial backup   Dial backup connections are typically used to provide redundancy to Frame Relay connections. The backup link is activated over an analog modem or ISDN.

directed broadcast   A data frame or packet that is transmitted to a specific group of nodes on a remote network segment. Directed broadcasts are known by their broadcast address, which is a destination subnet address with all the host bits turned on.

discovery mode   Also known as dynamic configuration, this technique is used by an Apple-Talk interface to gain information from a working node about an attached network. The information is subsequently used by the interface for self-configuration.

distance-vector protocols   The distance-vector protocols find the best path to a remote network by judging distance. Each time a packet goes through a router, that's called a hop. The route with the least number of hops to the network is determined to be the best route. However, Cisco's IGRP is considered Distance Vector and uses a composite metric of bandwidth and delay of the line to determine the best path to a remote network.

distance-vector routing algorithm   In order to find the shortest path, this group of routing algorithms reports on the number of hops in a given route, requiring each router to send its complete routing table with each update, but only to its neighbors. Routing algorithms of this type tend to generate loops, but they are fundamentally simpler than their link-state counterparts. *See also link-state routing algorithm* and *SPF.*

distribution layer   Middle layer of the Cisco three-layer hierarchical model, which helps you design, install, and maintain Cisco hierarchical networks. The distribution layer is the point where Access layer devices connect. Routing is performed at this layer.

DLCI   Data-Link Connection Identifier: Used to identify virtual circuits in a Frame Relay network.

DLSw   Data Link Switching: IBM developed DLSw in 1992 to provide support for SNA (Systems Network Architecture) and NetBIOS protocols in router-based networks. SNA and Net-BIOS are nonroutable protocols that do not contain any logical layer 3 network information. DLSw encapsulates these protocols into TCP/IP messages that can be routed and is an alternative to Remote Source-Route Bridging (RSRB).

DLSw+ Cisco's implementation of DLSw. In addition to support for the RFC standards, Cisco added enhancements intended to increase scalability and to improve performance and availability.

DNS Domain Name System: Used to resolve hostnames to IP addresses.

DSAP Destination Service Access Point: The service access point of a network node, specified in the destination field of a packet. *See also SSAP and SAP.*

DSR Data Set Ready: When a DCE is powered up and ready to run, this EIA/TIA-232 interface circuit is also engaged.

DSU data service unit: This device is used to adapt the physical interface on a data terminal equipment (DTE) mechanism to a transmission facility such as T1 or E1 and is also responsible for signal timing. It is commonly grouped with the channel service unit and referred to as the CSU/DSU. *See also CSU.*

DTE data terminal equipment: Any device located at the user end of a user-network interface serving as a destination, a source, or both. DTE includes devices such as multiplexers, routers, protocol translators, and computers. The connection to a data network is made through data communication equipment (DCE) such as a modem using the clocking signals generated by that device. *See also DCE.*

DTR Data Terminal Ready: An activated EIA/TIA-232 circuit communicating to the DCE the state of preparedness of the DTE to transmit or receive data.

DUAL Diffusing Update Algorithm: Used in Enhanced IGRP, this convergence algorithm provides loop-free operation throughout an entire route's computation. DUAL grants routers involved in a topology revision the ability to synchronize simultaneously, while routers unaffected by this change are not involved. *See also EIGRP.*

DVMRP Distance Vector Multicast Routing Protocol: Based primarily on the Routing Information Protocol (RIP), this Internet gateway protocol implements a common, condensed-mode IP multicast scheme, using IGMP to transfer routing datagrams between its neighbors. *See also IGMP.*

DXI Data Exchange Interface: DXI defines the effectiveness of a network device such as a router, bridge, or hub to act as an FEP to an ATM network by using a special DSU that accomplishes packet encapsulation.

dynamic entries Used in layer 2 and layer 3 devices to dynamically create a table of either hardware addresses or logical addresses dynamically.

dynamic routing Also known as adaptive routing, this technique automatically adapts to traffic or physical network revisions.

dynamic VLAN An administrator will create an entry in a special server with the hardware addresses of all devices on the internetwork. The server will then report the associated VLAN to a switch that requests it, based on the new device's hardware address.

E1   Generally used in Europe, a wide-area digital transmission scheme carrying data at 2.048Mbps. E1 transmission lines are available for lease from common carriers for private use.

E.164   (1) Evolved from standard telephone numbering system, the standard recommended by ITU-T for international telecommunication numbering, particularly in ISDN, SMDS, and BISDN. (2) Label of field in an ATM address containing numbers in E.164 format.

eBGP   External Border Gateway Protocol: Used to exchange route information between different autonomous systems.

E channel   echo channel: A 64Kbps ISDN control channel used for circuit switching. Specific description of this channel can be found in the 1984 ITU-T ISDN specification but was dropped from the 1988 version. *See also B channel, D channel, and H channel.*

edge device   A device that enables packets to be forwarded between legacy interfaces (such as Ethernet and Token Ring) and ATM interfaces based on information in the Data Link and Network layers. An edge device does not take part in the running of any Network layer routing protocol; it merely uses the route description protocol in order to get the forwarding information required.

EEPROM   electronically erasable programmable read-only memory: Programmed after their manufacture, these nonvolatile memory chips can be erased if necessary using electric power and reprogrammed. *See also EPROM and PROM.*

EFCI   Explicit Forward Congestion Indication: A congestion feedback mode permitted by ABR service in an ATM network. The EFCI may be set by any network element that is in a state of immediate or certain congestion. The destination end system is able to carry out a protocol that adjusts and lowers the cell rate of the connection based on value of the EFCI. *See also ABR.*

EIGRP   Enhanced Interior Gateway Routing Protocol: An advanced routing protocol created by Cisco and combining the advantages of link-state and distance-vector protocols. Enhanced IGRP has superior convergence attributes, including high operating efficiency. *See also IGP, OSPF, and RIP.*

EIP   Ethernet Interface Processor: A Cisco 7000 series router interface processor card supplying 10Mbps AUI ports to support Ethernet Version 1 and Ethernet Version 2 or IEEE 802.3 interfaces with a high-speed data path to other interface processors.

ELAN   emulated LAN: An ATM network configured using a client/server model in order to emulate either an Ethernet or Token Ring LAN. Multiple ELANs can exist at the same time on a single ATM network and are made up of a LAN emulation client (LEC), a LAN emulation server (LES), a broadcast and unknown server (BUS), and a LAN emulation configuration server (LECS). ELANs are defined by the LANE specification. *See also LANE, LEC, LECS, and LES.*

ELAP   EtherTalk Link Access Protocol: In an EtherTalk network, the link-access protocol constructed above the standard Ethernet Data Link layer.

encapsulation   The technique used by layered protocols in which a layer adds header information to the Protocol Data Unit (PDU) from the layer above. As an example, in Internet terminology, a packet would contain a header from the Data Link layer, followed by a header from the Network layer (IP), followed by a header from the Transport layer (TCP), followed by the application protocol data.

encryption   The conversion of information into a scrambled form that effectively disguises it to prevent unauthorized access. Every encryption scheme uses some well-defined algorithm, which is reversed at the receiving end by an opposite algorithm in a process known as decryption.

end-to-end VLANs   VLANs that span the switch-fabric from end to end; all switches in end-to-end VLANs understand about all configured VLANs. End-to-end VLANs are configured to allow membership based on function, project, department, and so on.

enterprise network   A privately owned and operated network that joins most major locations in a large company or organization.

EPROM   erasable programmable read-only memory: Programmed after their manufacture, these nonvolatile memory chips can be erased if necessary using high-power light and reprogrammed. *See also EEPROM and PROM.*

ESF   Extended Superframe: Made up of 24 frames with 192 bits each, with the 193rd bit providing other functions, including timing. This is an enhanced version of SF. *See also SF.*

Ethernet   A baseband LAN specification created by the Xerox Corporation and then improved through joint efforts of Xerox, Digital Equipment Corporation, and Intel. Ethernet is similar to the IEEE 802.3 series standard and, using CSMA/CD, operates over various types of cables at 10Mbps. Also called DIX (Digital/Intel/Xerox) Ethernet. *See also 10BaseT, Fast Ethernet, and IEEE.*

EtherTalk   A data-link product from Apple Computer that permits AppleTalk networks to be connected by Ethernet.

excess burst size   The amount of traffic by which the user may exceed the committed burst size.

excess rate   In ATM networking, traffic exceeding a connection's insured rate. The excess rate is the maximum rate less the insured rate. Depending on the availability of network resources, excess traffic can be discarded during congestion episodes. *Compare with maximum rate.*

EXEC session   Cisco term used to describe the command-line interface. The EXEC session exists in user mode and privileged mode.

expansion   The procedure of directing compressed data through an algorithm, restoring information to its original size.

expedited delivery   An option that can be specified by one protocol layer, communicating either with other layers or with the identical protocol layer in a different network device, requiring that identified data be processed faster.

explorer frame   Used with Source Route bridging to find the route to the remote bridged network before a frame is transmitted.

explorer packet   An SNA packet transmitted by a source Token Ring device to find the path through a source-route-bridged network.

extended IP access list   IP access list that filters the network by logical address, protocol field in the Network layer header, and even the port field in the Transport layer header.

extended IPX access list   IPX access list that filters the network by logical IPX address, protocol field in the Network layer header, or even socket number in the Transport layer header.

extended setup   Used in setup mode to configure the router with more detail than basic setup mode. Allows multiple-protocol support and interface configuration.

external EIGRP route   Normally, the administrative distance of an EIGRP route is 90, but this is true only for what is known as an internal EIGRP route. These are routes originated within a specific autonomous system by EIGRP routers that are members of the same autonomous system. The other type of route is called an external EIGRP route and has an administrative distance of 170, which is not so good. These routes appear within EIGRP route tables courtesy of either manual or automatic redistribution, and they represent networks that originated outside of the EIGRP autonomous system.

failure domain   The region in which a failure has occurred in a token ring. When a station gains information that a serious problem, such as a cable break, has occurred with the network, it sends a beacon frame that includes the station reporting the failure, its NAUN, and everything between. This defines the failure domain. Beaconing then initiates the procedure known as autoreconfiguration. *See also autoreconfiguration* and *beacon.*

fallback   In ATM networks, this mechanism is used for scouting a path if it isn't possible to locate one using customary methods. The device relaxes requirements for certain characteristics, such as delay, in an attempt to find a path that meets a certain set of the most important requirements.

Fast Ethernet   Any Ethernet specification with a speed of 100Mbps. Fast Ethernet is 10 times faster than 10BaseT, while retaining qualities such as MAC mechanisms, MTU, and frame format. These similarities make it possible for existing 10BaseT applications and management tools to be used on Fast Ethernet networks. Fast Ethernet is based on an extension of IEEE 802.3 specification (IEEE 802.3u). *Compare with Ethernet. See also 100BaseT, 100BaseTX,* and *IEEE.*

fast switching   A Cisco feature that uses a route cache to speed packet switching through a router. *Contrast with process switching.*

fault tolerance   The extent to which a network device or a communication link can fail without communication being interrupted. Fault tolerance can be provided by adding secondary routes to a remote network.

FDDI   Fiber Distributed Data Interface: A LAN standard, defined by ANSI X3T9.5, that can run at speeds up to 200Mbps and uses token-passing media access on fiber-optic cable. For redundancy, FDDI can use a dual-ring architecture.

FDM Frequency-Division Multiplexing: A technique that permits information from several channels to be assigned bandwidth on one wire based on frequency. *See also TDM, ATDM, and statistical multiplexing.*

FECN Forward Explicit Congestion Notification: A bit set by a Frame Relay network that informs the DTE receptor that congestion was encountered along the path from source to destination. A device receiving frames with the FECN bit set can ask higher-priority protocols to take flow-control action as needed. *See also BECN.*

FEIP Fast Ethernet Interface Processor: An interface processor employed on Cisco 7000 series routers, supporting up to two 100Mbps 100BaseT ports.

filtering Used to provide security on the network with access lists. LAN switches filter the network by MAC (hardware) address.

firewall A barrier that is purposefully erected between any connected public networks and a private network, is made up of a router or access server or several routers or access servers, and uses access lists and other methods to ensure the security of the private network.

fixed configuration router A router that cannot be upgraded with any new interfaces.

flapping Term used to describe a serial interface that is going up and down.

Flash Electronically erasable programmable read-only memory (EEPROM). Used to hold the Cisco IOS in a router by default.

flash memory Developed by Intel and licensed to other semiconductor manufacturers, it is nonvolatile storage, physically located on an EEPROM chip, that can be erased electronically and reprogrammed. Flash memory permits software images to be stored, booted, and rewritten as needed. Cisco routers and switches use flash memory to hold the IOS by default. *See also EPROM and EEPROM.*

flat network Network that is one large collision domain and one large broadcast domain.

floating routes Used with dynamic routing to provide backup routes (static routes) in case of failure.

flooding When traffic is received on an interface, it is then transmitted to every other interface connected to that device except from the interface from which the traffic originated. This technique can be used for traffic transfer by bridges and switches throughout the network.

flow control A methodology used to ensure that receiving units are not overwhelmed with data from sending devices. Pacing, as it is called in IBM networks, means that when buffers at a receiving unit are full, a message is transmitted to the sending unit to temporarily halt transmissions until all the data in the receiving buffer has been processed and the buffer is again ready for action.

forward/filter decisions When a frame is received on an interface, the switch looks at the destination hardware address and finds the exit interface in the MAC database. The frame is only forwarded out the specified destination port.

FQDN fully qualified domain name: Used within the DNS domain structure to provide name-to-IP-address resolution on the Internet. An example of an FQDN is bob.acme.com.

FRAD Frame Relay access device: Any device affording a connection between a LAN and a Frame Relay WAN. *See also Cisco FRAD and FRAS.*

fragment Any portion of a larger packet that has been intentionally segmented into smaller pieces. A packet fragment does not necessarily indicate an error and can be intentional. *See also fragmentation.*

fragmentation The process of intentionally segmenting a packet into smaller pieces when sending data over an intermediate network medium that cannot support the larger packet size.

FragmentFree LAN switch type that reads into the data section of a frame to make sure fragmentation did not occur. Sometimes called modified cut-through.

frame A logical unit of information sent by the Data Link layer over a transmission medium. The term often refers to the header and trailer, employed for synchronization and error control, that surround the data contained in the unit.

frame filtering Frame filtering is used on a layer 2 switch to provide more bandwidth. A switch reads the destination hardware address of a frame and then looks for this address in the filter table built by the switch. It then sends the frame out only the port where the hardware address is located, and the other ports do not see the frame.

frame identification (frame tagging) VLANs can span multiple connected switches, which Cisco calls a switch-fabric. Switches within this switch-fabric must keep track of frames as they are received on the switch ports, and they must keep track of the VLAN they belong to as the frames traverse this switch-fabric. Frame tagging performs this function. Switches can then direct frames to the appropriate port.

Frame Relay A more efficient replacement of the X.25 protocol (an unrelated packet relay technology that guarantees data delivery). Frame Relay is an industry-standard, shared-access, best-effort, switched Data Link layer encapsulation that services multiple virtual circuits and protocols between connected mechanisms.

Frame Relay bridging Defined in RFC 1490, this bridging method uses the identical spanning-tree algorithm other bridging operations use but permits packets to be encapsulated for transmission across a Frame Relay network.

Frame Relay switching Packet switching for Frame Relay packets that is provided by a service provider.

frame tagging *See frame identification.*

frame types Used in LANs to determine how a packet is put on the local network. Ethernet provides four different frame types. These are not compatible with each other, so for two hosts to communicate, they must use the same frame type.

framing Encapsulation at the Data Link layer of the OSI model. It is called framing because the packet is encapsulated with both a header and a trailer.

FRAS   Frame Relay Access Support: A feature of Cisco IOS software that enables SDLC, Ethernet, Token Ring, and Frame Relay-attached IBM devices to be linked with other IBM mechanisms on a Frame Relay network. *See also FRAD.*

frequency   The number of cycles of an alternating current signal per time unit, measured in hertz (cycles per second).

FSIP   Fast Serial Interface Processor: The Cisco 7000 routers' default serial interface processor, it provides four or eight high-speed serial ports.

FTP   File Transfer Protocol: The TCP/IP protocol used for transmitting files between network nodes, it supports a broad range of file types and is defined in RFC 959. *See also TFTP.*

full duplex   The capacity to transmit information between a sending station and a receiving unit at the same time. *See also half duplex.*

full mesh   A type of network topology where every node has either a physical or a virtual circuit linking it to every other network node. A full mesh supplies a great deal of redundancy but is typically reserved for network backbones because of its expense. *See also partial mesh.*

global command   Cisco term used to define commands that are used to change the router configuration and that affect the whole router. In contrast, an interface command only affects an interface.

GMII   Gigabit MII: Media Independent Interface that provides 8 bits at a time of data transfer.

GNS   Get Nearest Server: On an IPX network, a request packet sent by a customer for determining the location of the nearest active server of a given type. An IPX network client launches a GNS request to get either a direct answer from a connected server or a response from a router disclosing the location of the service on the internetwork to the GNS. GNS is part of IPX and SAP. *See also IPX and SAP.*

grafting   A process that activates an interface that has been deactivated by the pruning process. It is initiated by an IGMP membership report sent to the router.

GRE   Generic Routing Encapsulation: A tunneling protocol created by Cisco with the capacity for encapsulating a wide variety of protocol packet types inside IP tunnels, thereby generating a virtual point-to-point connection to Cisco routers across an IP network at remote points. IP tunneling using GRE permits network expansion across a single-protocol backbone environment by linking multiprotocol subnetworks in a single-protocol backbone environment.

guardband   The unused frequency area found between two communications channels, furnishing the space necessary to avoid interference between the two.

half duplex   The capacity to transfer data in only one direction at a time between a sending unit and receiving unit. *See also full duplex.*

handshake   Any series of transmissions exchanged between two or more devices on a network to ensure synchronized operations.

H channel   high-speed channel: A full-duplex, ISDN primary rate channel operating at a speed of 384Kbps. *See also B channel, D channel, and E channel.*

HDLC   High-Level Data-Link Control: Using frame characters, including checksums, HDLC designates a method for data encapsulation on synchronous serial links and is the default encapsulation for Cisco routers. HDLC is a bit-oriented synchronous Data Link layer protocol created by ISO and derived from SDLC. However, most HDLC vendor implementations (including Cisco's) are proprietary. *See also SDLC.*

helper address   The unicast address specified, which configures the Cisco router to change the client's local broadcast request for a service into a directed unicast to the server.

hierarchical addressing   Any addressing plan employing a logical chain of commands to determine location. IP addresses are made up of a hierarchy of network numbers, subnet numbers, and host numbers to direct packets to the appropriate destination.

hierarchy   Term used in defining IP addressing; in hierarchical addressing, some bits are used for networking and some bits for host addressing. Also used in the DNS structure and the Cisco design model.

HIP   HSSI Interface Processor: An interface processor used on Cisco 7000 series routers, providing one HSSI port that supports connections to ATM, SMDS, Frame Relay, or private lines at speeds up to T3 or E3.

holddown   The state a route is placed in so that routers can neither advertise the route nor accept advertisements about it for a defined time period. Holddowns are used to avoid accepting bad information. The actual information might be good, but it is not trusted. A route is generally placed in holddown when one of its links fails.

hop   The movement of a packet between any two network nodes. *See also hop count.*

hop count   A routing metric that calculates the distance between a source and a destination based on the number of routers in the path. RIP employs hop count as its sole metric. *See also hop and RIP.*

host address   Logical address configured by an administrator or server on a device. Logically identifies this device on an internetwork.

Host-to-Host layer   Layer in the Internet Protocol suite that is equal to the Transport layer of the OSI model.

HSCI   High-Speed Communication Interface: Developed by Cisco, a single-port interface that provides full-duplex synchronous serial communications capability at speeds up to 52Mbps.

HSRP   Hot Standby Router Protocol: A protocol that provides high network availability and provides nearly instantaneous hardware fail-over without administrator intervention. It generates a Hot Standby router group, including a lead router that lends its services to any packet being transferred to the Hot Standby address. If the lead router fails, it will be replaced by any of the other routers—the standby routers—that monitor it.

HSSI   High-Speed Serial Interface: A network standard physical connector for high-speed serial linking over a WAN at speeds of up to 52Mbps.

hubs   Physical layer devices that are really just multiple port repeaters. When an electronic digital signal is received on a port, the signal is reamplified or regenerated and forwarded out all segments except the segment from which it was received.

hybrid routing protocol   Routing protocol that uses the attributes of both distance-vector and link-state. Enhanced Interior Gateway Routing Protocol (Enhanced IGRP) is a hybrid routing protocol.

ICD   International Code Designator: Adapted from the subnetwork model of addressing, this assigns the mapping of Network layer addresses to ATM addresses. ICD is one of two ATM formats for addressing created by the ATM Forum to be utilized with private networks. *See also DCC.*

ICMP   Internet Control Message Protocol: Documented in RFC 792, it is a Network layer Internet protocol for the purpose of reporting errors and providing information pertinent to IP packet procedures.

IEEE   Institute of Electrical and Electronics Engineers: A professional organization that, among other activities, defines standards in a number of fields within computing and electronics, including networking and communications. IEEE standards are the predominant LAN standards used today throughout the industry. Many protocols are commonly known by the reference number of the corresponding IEEE standard.

IEEE 802.1   The IEEE committee specification that defines the bridging group. The specification for STP (Spanning Tree Protocol) is IEEE 802.1D. The STP uses STA (spanning-tree algorithm) to find and prevent network loops in bridged networks. The specification for VLAN trunking is IEEE 802.1Q.

IEEE 802.3   The IEEE committee specification that defines the Ethernet group, specifically the original 10Mbps standard. Ethernet is a LAN protocol that specifies physical layer and MAC sublayer media access. IEEE 802.3 uses CSMA/CD to provide access for many devices on the same network. Fast Ethernet is defined as 802.3U, and Gigabit Ethernet is defined as 802.3Q. *See also CSMA/CD.*

IEEE 802.5   IEEE committee that defines Token Ring media access.

IGMP   Internet Group Management Protocol: Employed by IP hosts, the protocol that reports their multicast group memberships to an adjacent multicast router.

IGP   interior gateway protocol: Any protocol used by an internetwork to exchange routing data within an independent system. Examples include RIP, IGRP, and OSPF.

IGRP   Interior Gateway Routing Protocol: Cisco proprietary distance-vector routing algorithm. Upgrade from the RIP protocol.

ILMI   Integrated (or Interim) Local Management Interface. A specification created by the ATM Forum and designated for the incorporation of network-management capability into the ATM UNI. Integrated Local Management Interface cells provide for automatic configuration between ATM systems. In LAN emulation, ILMI can provide sufficient information for the ATM end station to find an LECS. In addition, ILMI provides the ATM NSAP (Network Service Access Point) prefix information to the end station.

in-band management   In-band management is the management of a network device "through" the network. Examples include using Simple Network Management Protocol (SNMP) or Telnet directly via the local LAN. *Compare with out-of-band management.*

in-band signaling   In-band signaling is the use of the bearer channel to deliver signaling, such as call waiting in analog POTS lines. This is as opposed to out-of-band signaling, as in the case of the D channel being used to present a second active call in an ISDN circuit.

inside network   In NAT terminology, the inside network is the set of networks that are subject to translation. The outside network refers to all other addresses—usually those located on the Internet

insured burst   In an ATM network, it is the largest, temporarily permitted data burst exceeding the insured rate on a PVC and not tagged by the traffic policing function for being dropped if network congestion occurs. This insured burst is designated in bytes or cells.

interarea routing   Routing between two or more logical areas. *Contrast with intra-area routing. See also area.*

interface configuration mode   Mode that allows you to configure a Cisco router or switch port with specific information, such as an IP address and mask.

interface processor   Any of several processor modules used with Cisco 7000 series routers. *See also AIP, CIP, EIP, FEIP, HIP, MIP, and TRIP.*

internal EIGRP route   These are routes originated within a specific autonomous system by EIGRP routers that are members of the same autonomous system.

Internet   The global "network of networks," whose popularity has exploded in the last few years. Originally a tool for collaborative academic research, it has become a medium for exchanging and distributing information of all kinds. The Internet's need to link disparate computer platforms and technologies has led to the development of uniform protocols and standards that have also found widespread use within corporate LANs. *See also TCP/IP and MBONE.*

internet   Before the rise of the Internet, this lowercase form was shorthand for "internetwork" in the generic sense. Now rarely used. *See also internetwork.*

internet layer   Layer in the Internet Protocol suite of protocols that provides network addressing and routing through an internetwork.

Internet Protocol (IP)   Any protocol belonging to the TCP/IP protocol stack. *See also TCP/IP.*

internetwork   Any group of networks interconnected by routers and other mechanisms, typically operating as a single entity.

internetworking   Broadly, anything associated with the general task of linking networks to each other. The term encompasses technologies, procedures, and products. When you connect networks to a router, you are creating an internetwork.

intra-area routing   Routing that occurs within a logical area. *Contrast with interarea routing.*

Inverse ARP   Inverse Address Resolution Protocol: A technique by which dynamic mappings are constructed in a network, allowing a device such as a router to locate the logical network address and associate it with a permanent virtual circuit (PVC). Commonly used in Frame Relay to determine the far-end node's TCP/IP address by sending the Inverse ARP request across the local DLCI.

IP   Internet Protocol: Defined in RFC 791, it is a Network layer protocol that is part of the TCP/IP stack and offers connectionless service. IP furnishes an array of features for addressing, type-of-service specification, fragmentation and reassembly, and security.

IP address   Often called an Internet address, this is an address uniquely identifying any device (host) on the Internet (or any TCP/IP network). Each address consists of four octets (32 bits), represented as decimal numbers separated by periods (a format known as dotted-decimal). Every address is made up of a network number, an optional subnetwork number, and a host number. The network and subnetwork numbers together are used for routing, while the host number addresses an individual host within the network or subnetwork. The network and subnetwork information is extracted from the IP address using the subnet mask. There are five classes of IP addresses (A–E), in which classes A through C allocate different numbers of bits to the network, subnetwork, and host portions of the address. *See also CIDR, IP,* and *subnet mask.*

IPCP   IP Control Program: The protocol used to establish and configure IP over PPP. *See also IP* and *PPP.*

IP multicast   A technique for routing that enables IP traffic to be reproduced from one source to several endpoints or from multiple sources to many destinations. Instead of one packet being transmitted to each individual point of destination, one packet is sent to a multicast group specified by only one IP endpoint address for the group.

IPX   Internetwork Packet Exchange: Network layer protocol (layer 3) used in Novell NetWare networks for transferring information from servers to workstations. Similar to IP and XNS.

IPXCP   IPX Control Protocol: The protocol used to establish and configure IPX over PPP. *See also IPX* and *PPP.*

IPXWAN   Protocol used for new WAN links to provide and negotiate line options on the link using IPX. After the link is up and the options have been agreed upon by the two end-to-end links, normal IPX transmission begins.

ISDN   Integrated Services Digital Network: Offered as a service by telephone companies, a communication protocol that allows telephone networks to carry data, voice, and other digital traffic. *See also BISDN, BRI,* and *PRI.*

IS-IS   Intermediate System-to-Intermediate System: An OSI link-state hierarchical routing protocol.

ISL routing   Inter-Switch Link routing: A Cisco proprietary method of frame tagging in a switched internetwork. Frame tagging is a way to identify the VLAN membership of a frame as it traverses a switched internetwork.

isochronous transmission   Asynchronous data transfer over a synchronous data link, requiring a constant bit rate for reliable transport. *Compare with asynchronous transmission* and *synchronous transmission.*

ITU-T   International Telecommunication Union-Telecommunication Standardization Sector: This is a group of engineers that develops worldwide standards for telecommunications technologies.

Kerberos   An authentication and encryption method that can be used by Cisco routers to ensure that data cannot be "sniffed" off of the network. Kerberos was developed at MIT and was designed to provide strong security using the Data Encryption Standard (DES) cryptographic algorithm.

LAN   local area network: Broadly, any network linking two or more computers and related devices within a limited geographical area (up to a few kilometers). LANs are typically high-speed, low-error networks within a company. Cabling and signaling at the Physical and Data Link layers of the OSI are dictated by LAN standards. Ethernet, FDDI, and Token Ring are among the most popular LAN technologies. *Compare with MAN.*

LANE   LAN emulation: The technology that allows an ATM network to operate as a LAN backbone. To do so, the ATM network is required to provide multicast and broadcast support, address mapping (MAC-to-ATM), and SVC management, in addition to an operable packet format. Additionally, LANE defines Ethernet and Token Ring ELANs. *See also ELAN.*

LAN switch   A high-speed, multiple-interface transparent bridging mechanism that transmits packets between segments of data links, usually referred to specifically as an Ethernet switch. LAN switches transfer traffic based on MAC addresses. *See also multilayer switch* and *store-and-forward packet switching.*

LAPB   Link Accessed Procedure, Balanced: A bit-oriented Data Link layer protocol that is part of the X.25 stack and has its origin in SDLC. *See also SDLC and X.25.*

LAPD   Link Access Procedure, D-Channel: The ISDN Data Link layer protocol used specifically for the D channel and defined by ITU-T Recommendations Q.920 and Q.921. LAPD evolved from LAPB and is created to comply with the signaling requirements of ISDN basic access.

latency   Broadly, the time it takes a data packet to get from one location to another. In specific networking contexts, it can mean either (1) the time elapsed (delay) between the execution of a request for access to a network by a device and the time the mechanism actually is permitted transmission, or (2) the time elapsed between when a mechanism receives a frame and the time that frame is forwarded out of the destination port.

layer Term used in networking to define how the OSI model works to encapsulate data for transmission on the network.

layer 3 switch *See multilayer switch.*

layered architecture Industry standard way of creating applications to work on a network. Layered architecture allows the application developer to make changes in only one layer instead of the whole program.

LCP Link Control Protocol: The protocol designed to establish, configure, and test data-link connections for use by PPP. *See also PPP.*

leaky bucket An analogy for the generic cell rate algorithm (GCRA) used in ATM networks for checking the conformance of cell flows from a user or network. The bucket's "hole" is understood to be the prolonged rate at which cells can be accommodated, and the "depth" is the tolerance for cell bursts over a certain time period.

learning bridge A bridge that transparently builds a dynamic database of MAC addresses and the interfaces associated with each address. Transparent bridges help to reduce traffic congestion on the network.

LE ARP LAN Emulation Address Resolution Protocol: The protocol providing the ATM address that corresponds to a MAC address.

leased line Permanent connection between two points leased from the telephone companies.

LEC LAN emulation client: Software providing the emulation of the link layer interface that allows the operation and communication of all higher-level protocols and applications to continue. The LEC runs in all ATM devices, which include hosts, servers, bridges, and routers. *See also ELAN* and *LES.*

LECS LAN emulation configuration server: An important part of emulated LAN services, providing the configuration data that is furnished upon request from the LES. These services include address registration for Integrated Local Management Interface (ILMI) support, configuration support for the LES addresses and their corresponding emulated LAN identifiers, and an interface to the emulated LAN. *See also LES* and *ELAN.*

LES LAN emulation server: The central LANE component that provides the initial configuration data for each connecting LEC. The LES typically is located on either an ATM-integrated router or a switch. Responsibilities of the LES include configuration and support for the LEC, address registration for the LEC, database storage and response concerning ATM addresses, and interfacing to the emulated LAN. *See also ELAN, LEC,* and *LECS.*

link A link is a network or router interface assigned to any given network. When an interface is added to the OSPF process, it's considered by OSPF to be a link. This link, or interface, will have state information associated with it (up or down) as well as one or more IP addresses.

link-state protocols In link-state protocols, also called shortest-path-first protocols, the routers each create three separate tables. One of these tables keeps track of directly attached neighbors, one determines the topology of the entire internetwork, and one is used as the routing table. Link-state routers know more about the internetwork than any distance-vector routing protocol

link-state routing algorithm   A routing algorithm that allows each router to broadcast or multicast information regarding the cost of reaching all its neighbors to every node in the internetwork. Link-state algorithms provide a consistent view of the network and are therefore not vulnerable to routing loops. However, this loop-free network is achieved at the cost of somewhat greater difficulty in computation and more widespread traffic (compared with distance-vector routing algorithms). *See also distance-vector routing algorithm.*

LLAP   LocalTalk Link Access Protocol: In a LocalTalk environment, the data link–level protocol that manages node-to-node delivery of data. This protocol provides node addressing and management of bus access, and it also controls data sending and receiving to ensure packet length and integrity.

LLC   Logical Link Control: Defined by the IEEE, the higher of two Data Link layer sublayers. LLC is responsible for error detection (but not correction), flow control, framing, and software-sublayer addressing. The predominant LLC protocol, IEEE 802.2, defines both connectionless and connection-oriented operations. *See also Data Link layer* and *MAC*.

LMI   Local Management Interface: An enhancement to the original Frame Relay specification. Among the features it provides are a keepalive mechanism, a multicast mechanism, global addressing, and a status mechanism.

LNNI   LAN Emulation Network-to-Network Interface: In the Phase 2 LANE specification, an interface that supports communication between the server components within one ELAN.

load   The amount of data on a link. Like IGRP, EIGRP uses only bandwidth and delay of the line to determine the best path to a remote network by default. However, EIGRP can use a combination of bandwidth, delay, load, and reliability in its quest to find the best path to a remote network.

load balancing   The act of balancing packet load over multiple links to the same remote network.

local explorer packet   In a Token Ring SRB network, a packet generated by an end system to find a host linked to the local ring. If no local host can be found, the end system will produce one of two solutions: a spanning explorer packet or an all-routes explorer packet.

local loop   Connection from a demarcation point to the closest switching office.

LocalTalk   Utilizing CSMA/CD, in addition to supporting data transmission at speeds of 230.4Kbps, LocalTalk is Apple Computer's proprietary baseband protocol, operating at the Data Link and Physical layers of the OSI reference model.

logical address   Network layer address that defines how data is sent from one network to another. Examples of logical addresses are IP and IPX.

loop avoidance   Where multiple connections between switches are created for redundancy purposes, using Spanning Tree Protocol (STP) to stop network loops while still permitting redundancy.

loopback address   The IP address 127.0.0.1 is called the diagnostic or loopback address, and if you get a successful ping to this address, your IP stack is then considered to be initialized. If it fails, then you have an IP stack failure and need to reinstall TCP/IP on the host.

loopback interface   Loopback interfaces are logical interfaces, which means they are not real router interfaces. They can be used for diagnostic purposes as well as OSPF configuration.

LPD   Line Printer Daemon: Used in the Unix world to allow printing to an IP address.

LSA   Link-State Advertisement: Contained inside of link-state packets (LSPs), these advertisements are usually multicast packets that contain information about neighbors and path costs and are employed by link-state protocols. Receiving routers use LSAs to maintain their link-state databases and, ultimately, routing tables.

LUNI   LAN Emulation User-to-Network Interface: Defining the interface between the LAN emulation client (LEC) and the LAN emulation server (LES), LUNI is the ATM Forum's standard for LAN emulation on ATM networks. *See also LES and LECS.*

MAC   Media Access Control: The lower sublayer in the Data Link layer, it is responsible for hardware addressing, media access, and error detection of frames. *See also Data Link layer and LLC.*

MAC address   A Data Link layer hardware address that every port or device needs in order to connect to a LAN segment. These addresses are used by various devices in the network for accurate location of logical addresses. MAC addresses are defined by the IEEE standard and their length is six characters, typically using the burned-in address (BIA) of the local LAN interface. Variously called hardware address, physical address, burned-in address, or MAC layer address.

MacIP   In AppleTalk, the Network layer protocol encapsulating IP packets in Datagram Delivery Protocol (DDP) packets. MacIP also supplies substitute ARP services.

MAN   metropolitan area network: Any network that encompasses a metropolitan area; that is, an area typically larger than a LAN but smaller than a WAN. *See also LAN.*

Manchester encoding   A method for digital coding in which a mid-bit-time transition is employed for clocking and a 1 (one) is denoted by a high voltage level during the first half of the bit time. This scheme is used by Ethernet and IEEE 802.3.

maximum burst   Specified in bytes or cells, the largest burst of information exceeding the insured rate that will be permitted on an ATM permanent virtual connection for a short time and will not be dropped even if it goes over the specified maximum rate. *Compare with insured burst. See also maximum rate.*

maximum hop count   Number of routers a packet is allowed to pass before it is terminated. This is created to prevent a packet from circling a network forever.

maximum rate   The maximum permitted data throughput on a particular virtual circuit, equal to the total of insured and uninsured traffic from the traffic source. Should traffic congestion occur, uninsured information may be deleted from the path. Measured in bits or cells per second, the maximum rate represents the highest throughput of data the virtual circuit is ever able to deliver and cannot exceed the media rate. *Compare with excess rate. See also maximum burst.*

MBONE   The multicast backbone of the Internet, it is a virtual multicast network made up of multicast LANs, including point-to-point tunnels interconnecting them.

MBS   Maximum Burst Size: In an ATM signaling message, this metric, coded as a number of cells, is used to convey the burst tolerance.

MCDV   Maximum Cell Delay Variation: The maximum two-point CDV objective across a link or node for the identified service category in an ATM network.

MCLR   Maximum Cell Loss Ratio: The maximum ratio of cells in an ATM network that fail to transit a link or node compared with the total number of cells that arrive at the link or node. MCLR is one of four link metrics that are exchanged using PTSPs to verify the available resources of an ATM network. The MCLR applies to cells in VBR and CBR traffic classes whose CLP bit is set to zero. *See also CBR, CLP,* and *VBR.*

MCR   minimum cell rate: A parameter determined by the ATM Forum for traffic management of the ATM networks. MCR is specifically defined for ABR transmissions and specifies the minimum value for the allowed cell rate (ACR). *See also ACR* and *PCR.*

MCTD   Maximum Cell Transfer Delay: In an ATM network, the total of the maximum cell delay variation and the fixed delay across the link or node. MCTD is one of four link metrics that are exchanged using PNNI topology state packets to verify the available resources of an ATM network. There is one MCTD value assigned to each traffic class. *See also MCDV.*

media translation   A router property that allows two different types of LAN to communicate—for example, Ethernet to Token Ring.

MIB   Management Information Base: Used with SNMP management software to gather information from remote devices. The management station can poll the remote device for information, or the MIB running on the remote station can be programmed to send information on a regular basis.

MII   Media Independent Interface: Used in Fast Ethernet and Gigabit Ethernet to provide faster bit transfer rates of 4 and 8 bits at a time. Contrast to AUI interface, which is 1 bit at a time.

MIP   Multichannel Interface Processor: The resident interface processor on Cisco 7000 series routers, providing up to two channelized T1 or E1 connections by serial cables connected to a CSU. The two controllers are capable of providing 24 T1 or 30 E1 channel groups, with each group being introduced to the system as a serial interface that can be configured individually.

mips   millions of instructions per second: A measure of processor speed.

MLP   Multilink PPP: A technique used to split, recombine, and sequence datagrams across numerous logical data links.

MMP   Multichassis Multilink PPP: A protocol that supplies MLP support across multiple routers and access servers. MMP enables several routers and access servers to work as a single, large dial-up pool with one network address and ISDN access number. MMP successfully supports packet fragmenting and reassembly when the user connection is split between two physical access devices.

modem   modulator-demodulator: A device that converts digital signals to analog and vice versa so that digital information can be transmitted over analog communication facilities, such as voice-grade telephone lines. This is achieved by converting digital signals at the source to analog for transmission and reconverting the analog signals back into digital form at the destination. *See also modulation* and *demodulation.*

modem eliminator   A mechanism that makes possible a connection between two DTE devices without modems by simulating the commands and physical signaling required.

modulation   The process of modifying some characteristic of an electrical signal, such as amplitude (AM) or frequency (FM), in order to represent digital or analog information. *See also AM.*

MOSPF   Multicast OSPF: An extension of the OSPF unicast protocol that enables IP multicast routing within the domain. *See also OSPF.*

MPOA   Multiprotocol over ATM: An effort by the ATM Forum to standardize how existing and future Network layer protocols such as IP, IPv6, AppleTalk, and IPX run over an ATM network with directly attached hosts, routers, and multilayer LAN switches.

MTU   maximum transmission unit: The largest packet size, measured in bytes, that an interface can handle.

multicast   Broadly, any communication between a single sender and multiple receivers. Unlike broadcast messages, which are sent to all addresses on a network, multicast messages are sent to a defined subset of the network addresses; this subset has a group multicast address, which is specified in the packet's destination address field. *See also broadcast* and *directed broadcast.*

multicast address   A single address that points to more than one device on the network by specifying a special nonexistent MAC address transmitted in that particular multicast protocol. Identical to group address. *See also multicast.*

multicast group   Multicast works by sending messages or data to IP multicast group addresses. This group is a defined set of users or hosts that are allowed to read or view the data sent via multicast.

multicast send VCC   A two-directional point-to-point virtual control connection (VCC) arranged by an LEC to a BUS, it is one of the three types of informational links specified by phase 1 LANE. *See also control distribute VCC* and *control direct VCC.*

multilayer switch   A highly specialized, high-speed, hardware-based type of LAN router, the device filters and forwards packets based on their layer 2 MAC addresses and layer 3 network addresses. It's possible that even layer 4 can be read. Sometimes called a layer 3 switch. *See also LAN switch.*

multilink   Used to combine multiple async or ISDN links to provide combined bandwidth.

multiplexing   The process of converting several logical signals into a single physical signal for transmission across one physical channel. *Contrast with demultiplexing.*

NAK   negative acknowledgment: A response sent from a receiver telling the sender that the information was not received or contained errors. *Compare with acknowledgment.*

named access list   Used in both standard and extended lists to help with administration of access lists by allowing you to name the lists instead of using numbers. This also allows you to change a single line of an access list, which isn't possible in regular, numbered access lists.

NAT   Network Address Translation: An algorithm instrumental in minimizing the requirement for globally unique IP addresses, permitting an organization whose addresses are not all globally unique to connect to the Internet nevertheless by translating those addresses into globally routable address space.

native VLAN   Cisco switches all have a native VLAN called VLAN 1. This cannot be deleted or changed in any way. All switch ports are in VLAN 1 by default.

NBP   Name Binding Protocol: In AppleTalk, the transport-level protocol that interprets a socket client's name, entered as a character string, into the corresponding DDP address. NBP gives AppleTalk protocols the capacity to discern user-defined zones and names of mechanisms by showing and keeping translation tables that map names to their corresponding socket addresses.

neighbors   EIGRP and OSPF routers become neighbors when each router sees the other's Hello packets.

neighboring routers   Two routers in OSPF that have interfaces to a common network. On networks with multiaccess, these neighboring routers are dynamically discovered using the Hello protocol of OSPF.

neighborship table   In OSPF and EIGRP routing protocols, each router keeps state information about adjacent neighbors. When newly discovered neighbors are learned, the address and interface of the neighbor is recorded. This information is stored in the neighbor data structure and the neighbor table holds these entries. Neighborship table can also be referred to as neighbor table or neighborship database.

NetBEUI   NetBIOS Extended User Interface: An improved version of the NetBIOS protocol used in a number of network operating systems (including LAN Manager, Windows NT, LAN Server, and Windows for Workgroups) and implementing the OSI LLC2 protocol. NetBEUI formalizes the transport frame not standardized in NetBIOS and adds more functions. *See also OSI.*

NetBIOS   Network Basic Input Output System: The API employed by applications residing on an IBM LAN to ask for services, such as session termination or information transfer, from lower-level network processes.

NetView   A mainframe network product from IBM used for monitoring SNA (Systems Network Architecture) networks. It runs as a VTAM (Virtual Telecommunications Access Method) application.

NetWare   A widely used NOS created by Novell that provides a number of distributed network services and remote file access.

Network Access layer   Bottom layer in the Internet Protocol suite that provides media access to packets.

network address   Used with the logical network addresses to identify the network segment in an internetwork. Logical addresses are hierarchical in nature and have at least two parts: network and host. An example of a hierarchical address is 172.16.10.5, where 172.16 is the network and 10.5 is the host address.

Network Control Protocol (NCP)   A method of establishing and configuring different Network layer protocols. NCP is designed to allow the simultaneous use of multiple Network layer protocols. Some examples of protocols here are IPCP (Internet Protocol Control Protocol) and IPXCP (Internetwork Packet Exchange Control Protocol).

Network layer   In the OSI reference model, it is layer 3—the layer in which routing is implemented, enabling connections and path selection between two end systems. *See also Application layer, Data Link layer, Physical layer, Presentation layer, Session layer,* and *Transport layer.*

network segmentation   Breaking up a large network into smaller networks. Routers, switches, and bridges are used to create network segmentation.

NFS   Network File System: One of the protocols in Sun Microsystems's widely used file system protocol suite, allowing remote file access across a network. The name is loosely used to refer to the entire Sun protocol suite, which also includes RPC, XDR (External Data Representation), and other protocols.

NHRP   Next Hop Resolution Protocol: In a nonbroadcast multiaccess (NBMA) network, the protocol employed by routers in order to dynamically locate MAC addresses of various hosts and routers. It enables systems to communicate directly without requiring an intermediate hop, thus facilitating increased performance in ATM, Frame Relay, X.25, and SMDS systems.

NHS   Next Hop Server: Defined by the NHRP protocol, this server maintains the next-hop resolution cache tables, listing IP-to-ATM address maps of related nodes and nodes that can be reached through routers served by the NHS.

nibble   Four bits.

NIC   network interface card: An electronic circuit board placed in a computer. The NIC provides network communication to a LAN.

NLSP NetWare Link Services Protocol: Novell's link-state routing protocol, based on the IS-IS model.

NMP Network Management Processor: A Catalyst 5000 switch processor module used to control and monitor the switch.

node address Used to identify a specific device in an internetwork. Can be a hardware address, which is burned into the network interface card, or a logical network address, which an administrator or server assigns to the node.

nonbroadcast multiaccess (NBMA) networks Nonbroadcast multiaccess (NBMA) networks are types such as Frame Relay, X.25, and Asynchronous Transfer Mode (ATM). These networks allow for multiple access but have no broadcast ability like Ethernet. NBMA networks require special OSPF configuration to function properly and neighbor relationships must be defined.

nondesignated port A switch port that will not forward frames in order to prevent a switching loop. Spanning Tree Protocol (STP) is responsible for deciding whether a port is designated (forwarding) or nondesignated (blocking).

non-stub area In OSPF, a resource-consuming area carrying a default route, intra-area routes, interarea routes, static routes, and external routes. Non-stub areas are the only areas that can have virtual links configured across them and exclusively contain an autonomous system boundary router (ASBR). *Compare with stub area. See also ASBR and OSPF.*

NRZ nonreturn to zero: One of several encoding schemes for transmitting digital data. NRZ signals sustain constant levels of voltage with no signal shifting (no return to zero-voltage level) during a bit interval. If there is a series of bits with the same value (1 or 0), there will be no state change. The signal is not self-clocking. *See also NRZI.*

NRZI nonreturn to zero inverted: One of several encoding schemes for transmitting digital data. A transition in voltage level (either from high to low or vice versa) at the beginning of a bit interval is interpreted as a value of 1; the absence of a transition is interpreted as a 0. Thus, the voltage assigned to each value is continually inverted. NRZI signals are not self-clocking. *See also NRZ.*

NT network termination: A point in an ISDN network. *See also NT1 and NT2.*

NT1 NT1 is the device that converts the two-wire U interface to the four-wire S/T.

NT2 NT2 is an ISDN-compliant switching device, like a PBX, that splits the S/T bus into two separate but electrically equivalent interfaces. The T interface connects to the NT1, while the S interface connects to TE1 devices.

NVRAM nonvolatile RAM: Random-access memory that keeps its contents intact while power is turned off.

OC Optical Carrier: A series of physical protocols, designated as OC-1, OC-2, OC-3, and so on, for SONET optical signal transmissions. OC signal levels place STS frames on a multimode fiber-optic line at various speeds, of which 51.84Mbps is the lowest (OC-1). Each subsequent protocol runs at a speed divisible by 51.84. *See also SONET.*

octet   Base-8 numbering system used to identify a section of a dotted-decimal IP address. Also referred to as a byte.

ones density   Also known as pulse density, this is a method of signal clocking. The CSU/DSU retrieves the clocking information from data that passes through it. For this scheme to work, the data needs to be encoded to contain at least one binary 1 for each 8 bits transmitted. *See also CSU* and *DSU.*

OSI   Open Systems Interconnection: International standardization program designed by ISO and ITU-T for the development of data networking standards that make multivendor equipment interoperability a reality.

OSI reference model   Open Systems Interconnection reference model: A conceptual model defined by the International Organization for Standardization (ISO), describing how any combination of devices can be connected for the purpose of communication. The OSI model divides the task into seven functional layers, forming a hierarchy with the applications at the top and the physical medium at the bottom, and it defines the functions each layer must provide. *See also Application layer, Data Link layer, Network layer, Physical layer, Presentation layer, Session layer,* and *Transport layer.*

OSPF   Open Shortest Path First: A link-state, hierarchical routing algorithm that is derived from an earlier version of the IS-IS protocol and whose features include multipath routing, load balancing, and least-cost routing. OSPF is the suggested successor to RIP in the Internet environment. *See also Enhanced IGRP, IGP,* and *IP.*

OSPF area   An OSPF area is a grouping of contiguous networks and routers. All routers in the same area share a common Area ID. Because a router can be a member of more than one area at a time, the Area ID is associated with specific interfaces on the router. This would allow some interfaces to belong to area 1 while the remaining interfaces can belong to area 0. All of the routers within the same area have the same topology table.

OUI   organizationally unique identifier: Code assigned by the IEEE to an organization that makes network interface cards. The organization then puts this OUI on each and every card it manufactures. The OUI is 3 bytes (24 bits) long. The manufacturer then adds a 3-byte identifier to uniquely identify the host. The address is 48 bits (6 bytes) in length and is called a hardware address or MAC address.

out-of-band management   Management "outside" of the network's physical channels—for example, using a console connection not directly interfaced through the local LAN or WAN or a dial-in modem. *Compare to in-band management.*

out-of-band signaling   Within a network, any transmission that uses physical channels or frequencies separate from those ordinarily used for data transfer.

outside network   In NAT terminology, the inside network is the set of networks that are subject to translation. The outside network refers to all other addresses—usually those located on the Internet.

packet   In data communications, the basic logical unit of information transferred. A packet consists of a certain number of data bytes wrapped or encapsulated in headers and/or trailers that contain information about where the packet came from, where it's going, and so on. The various protocols involved in sending a transmission add their own layers of header information, which the corresponding protocols in receiving devices then interpret.

packet switch   A physical device that makes it possible for a communication channel to share several connections; its functions include finding the most efficient transmission path for packets.

packet switching   A networking technology based on the transmission of data in packets. Dividing a continuous stream of data into small units—packets—enables data from multiple devices on a network to share the same communication channel simultaneously but also requires the use of precise routing information.

PAP   Password Authentication Protocol: In Point-to-Point Protocol (PPP) networks, a method of validating connection requests. The requesting (remote) device must send an authentication request containing a password and ID to the local router when attempting to connect. Unlike the more secure CHAP (Challenge Handshake Authentication Protocol), PAP sends the password unencrypted and does not attempt to verify whether the user is authorized to access the requested resource; it merely identifies the remote end. *See also CHAP.*

parity checking   A method of error checking in data transmissions. An extra bit (the parity bit) is added to each character or data word so that the sum of the bits will be either an odd number (in odd parity) or an even number (even parity).

partial mesh   A type of network topology in which some network nodes form a full mesh (where every node has either a physical or a virtual circuit linking it to every other network node) but others are attached to only one or two nodes in the network. A typical use of partial-mesh topology is in peripheral networks linked to a fully meshed backbone. *See also full mesh.*

passive state   Regarding an EIGRP routing table, a route is considered to be in the passive state when a router is not performing a route convergence.

PAT   Port Address Translation: This process allows a single IP address to represent multiple resources by altering the source TCP or UDP port number.

PCM   pulse code modulation: Process by which an analog signal is converted into digital information.

PCR   peak cell rate: As defined by the ATM Forum, the parameter specifying, in cells per second, the maximum rate at which a source may transmit.

PDN   public data network: Generally for a fee, a PDN offers the public access to a computer communication network operated by private concerns or government agencies. Small organizations can take advantage of PDNs, aiding them to create WANs without investing in long-distance equipment and circuitry.

PDU   Protocol Data Unit: The processes at each layer of the OSI model. PDUs at the Transport layer are called segments; PDUs at the Network layer are called packets or datagrams; and PDUs at the Data Link layer are called frames. The Physical layer uses bits.

PGP   Pretty Good Privacy: A popular public-key/private-key encryption application offering protected transfer of files and messages.

phantom router   Used in a Hot Standby Router Protocol (HSRP) network to provide an IP default gateway address to hosts.

Physical layer   The lowest layer—layer 1—in the OSI reference model, it is responsible for converting data frames from the Data Link layer (layer 2) into electrical signals. Physical layer protocols and standards define, for example, the type of cable and connectors to be used, including their pin assignments and the encoding scheme for signaling 0 and 1 values. *See also Application layer, Data Link layer, Network layer, Presentation layer, Session layer,* and *Transport layer.*

PIM   Protocol Independent Multicast: A multicast protocol that handles the IGMP requests as well as requests for multicast data forwarding.

PIM-DM   Protocol Independent Multicast Dense Mode: PIM-DM utilizes the unicast route table and relies on the source root distribution architecture for multicast data forwarding.

PIM-SM   Protocol Independent Multicast Sparse Mode: PIM-SM utilizes the unicast route table and relies on the shared root distribution architecture for multicast data forwarding.

Ping   Packet Internet Groper: A Unix-based Internet diagnostic tool consisting of a message sent to test the accessibility of a particular device on the IP network. The term's acronym reflects the underlying metaphor of submarine sonar. Just as the sonar operator sends out a signal and waits to hear it echo ("ping") back from a submerged object, the network user can ping another node on the network and wait to see if it responds.

pinhole congestion   A problem associated with distance-vector routing protocols if more than one connection to a remote network is known but they are different bandwidths.

plesiochronous   Nearly synchronous, except that clocking comes from an outside source instead of being embedded within the signal as in synchronous transmissions.

PLP   Packet Level Protocol: Occasionally called X.25 level 3 or X.25 Protocol, a Network layer protocol that is part of the X.25 stack.

PNNI   Private Network-Network Interface: An ATM Forum specification for offering topology data used for the calculation of paths through the network and among switches and groups of switches. It is based on well-known link-state routing procedures and allows for automatic configuration in networks whose addressing scheme is determined by the topology.

point-to-multipoint connection   In ATM, a communication path going only one way, connecting a single system at the starting point (called the root node) to systems at multiple points of destination (called leaves). *See also point-to-point connection.*

point-to-point connection   In ATM, a channel of communication that can be directed either one way or two ways between two ATM end systems. Also refers to a point-to-point WAN serial connection. *See also point-to-multipoint connection.*

poison reverse updates   These update messages are transmitted by a router back to the originator (thus ignoring the split-horizon rule) after route poisoning has occurred. Typically used with DV routing protocols in order to overcome large routing loops and offer explicit information when a subnet or network is not accessible (instead of merely suggesting that the network is unreachable by not including it in updates). *See also route poisoning.*

polling   The procedure of orderly inquiry used by a primary network mechanism to determine if secondary devices have data to transmit. A message is sent to each secondary, granting the secondary the right to transmit.

POP   (1) point of presence: The physical location where an interexchange carrier has placed equipment to interconnect with a local exchange carrier. (2) Post Office Protocol (currently at version 3): A protocol used by client e-mail applications for recovery of mail from a mail server.

port security   Used with layer 2 switches to provide some security. Not typically used in production because it is difficult to manage. Allows only certain frames to traverse administrator-assigned segments.

port numbers   Used at the transport layer with TCP and UDP to keep track of host-to-host virtual circuits.

positive acknowledgment with retransmission   A connection-oriented session that provides acknowledgment and retransmission of the data if it is not acknowledged by the receiving host within a certain time frame.

POTS   plain old telephone service: This refers to the traditional analog phone service that is found in most installations.

PPP   Point-to-Point Protocol: The protocol most commonly used for dial-up Internet access, superseding the earlier SLIP. Its features include address notification, authentication via CHAP or PAP, support for multiple protocols, and link monitoring. PPP has two layers: the Link Control Protocol (LCP) establishes, configures, and tests a link, and then any of various Network Control Protocols (NCPs) transport traffic for a specific protocol suite, such as IPX. *See also CHAP, PAP,* and *SLIP.*

prefix routing   Method of defining how many bits are used in a subnet and how this information is sent in a routing update. For example, RIP version 1 does not send subnet mask information in the route updates. However, RIP version 2 does. This means that RIP v2 updates will send /24, /25, /26, etc., with a route update, which RIP v1 will not.

Presentation layer   Layer 6 of the OSI reference model, it defines how data is formatted, presented, encoded, and converted for use by software at the Application layer. *See also Application layer, Data Link layer, Network layer, Physical layer, Session layer,* and *Transport layer.*

PRI   Primary Rate Interface: A type of ISDN connection between a PBX and a long-distance carrier; made up of a single 64Kbps D channel in addition to 23 (T1) or 30 (E1) B channels. *See also ISDN.*

priority queuing   A routing function in which frames temporarily placed in an interface output queue are assigned priorities based on traits such as packet size or type of interface.

privileged mode   Command-line EXEC mode used in Cisco routers and switches that provides both viewing and changing of configurations.

Process/Application layer   Upper layer in the Internet Protocol stack. Responsible for network services.

process switching   As a packet arrives on a router to be forwarded, it's copied to the router's process buffer and the router performs a lookup on the layer 3 address. Using the route table, an exit interface is associated with the destination address. The processor forwards the packet with the added new information to the exit interface, while the router initializes the fast-switching cache. Subsequent packets bound for the same destination address follow the same path as the first packet.

PROM   programmable read-only memory: ROM that is programmable only once, using special equipment. *Compare with EPROM.*

propagation delay   The time it takes data to traverse a network from its source to its destination.

protocol   In networking, the specification of a set of rules for a particular type of communication. The term is also used to refer to the software that implements a protocol.

protocol-dependent modules   The protocol-dependent modules used in the EIGRP routing protocol are responsible for network layer, protocol-specific requirements that allow multiple protocol support for IP, IPX and AppleTalk.

protocol stack   A collection of related protocols.

Proxy ARP   Proxy Address Resolution Protocol: Used to allow redundancy in case of a failure with the configured default gateway on a host. Proxy ARP is a variation of the ARP protocol in which an intermediate device, such as a router, sends an ARP response on behalf of an end node to the requesting host.

pruning   The act of trimming down the shortest-path tree. This deactivates interfaces that do not have group participants.

PSE   packet switching exchange: The X.25 term for a switch.

PSN   packet-switched network: Any network that uses packet-switching technology. Also known as packet-switched data network (PSDN). *See also packet switching.*

PSTN   public switched telephone network: Colloquially referred to as plain old telephone service (POTS). A term that describes the assortment of telephone networks and services available globally.

PVC   permanent virtual circuit: In a Frame Relay or ATM network, a logical connection, defined in software, that is maintained permanently. *Compare with SVC. See also virtual circuit.*

PVP   permanent virtual path: A virtual path made up of PVCs. *See also PVC.*

PVP tunneling   permanent virtual path tunneling: A technique that links two private ATM networks across a public network using a virtual path, wherein the public network transparently trunks the complete collection of virtual channels in the virtual path between the two private networks.

QoS   quality of service: A set of metrics used to measure the quality of transmission and service availability of any given transmission system.

queue   Broadly, any list of elements arranged in an orderly fashion and ready for processing, such as a line of people waiting to enter a movie theater. In routing, it refers to a backlog of information packets waiting in line to be transmitted over a router interface.

R reference point   Used with ISDN networks to identify the connection between an NT1 and an S/T device. The S/T device converts the four-wire network to the two-wire ISDN standard network.

RADIUS   Remote Authentication Dial-In User Service: A protocol that is used to communicate between the remote access device and an authentication server. Sometimes an authentication server running RADIUS will be called a RADIUS server.

RAM   random-access memory: Used by all computers to store information. Cisco routers use RAM to store packet buffers and routing tables along with the hardware addresses cache.

RARP   Reverse Address Resolution Protocol: The protocol within the TCP/IP stack that maps MAC addresses to IP addresses. *See also ARP.*

RARP server   A Reverse Address Resolution Protocol server is used to provide an IP address from a known MAC address.

rate queue   A value, assigned to one or more virtual circuits, that specifies the speed at which an individual virtual circuit will transmit data to the remote end. Every rate queue identifies a segment of the total bandwidth available on an ATM link. The sum of all rate queues should not exceed the total available bandwidth.

RCP   Remote Copy Protocol: A protocol for copying files to or from a file system that resides on a remote server on a network; uses TCP to guarantee reliable data delivery.

redundancy   In internetworking, the duplication of connections, devices, or services that can be used as a backup in the event that the primary connections, devices, or services fail.

reference model   Used by application developers to create applications that work on any type of network. The most popular reference model is the Open Systems Interconnection (OSI) model.

reliability   Refers to the reliability of a link to each remote network. Like IGRP, EIGRP uses only bandwidth and delay of the line to determine the best path to a remote network by default. However, EIGRP can use a combination of bandwidth, delay, load and reliability in its quest to find the best path to a remote network.

reliable multicast   When EIGRP sends multicast traffic, it uses the Class D address 224.0.0.10. Each EIGRP router is aware of who its neighbors are, and for each multicast it sends out, it maintains a list of the neighbors who have replied. If EIGRP doesn't get a reply from a neighbor, it will switch to using unicasts to resend the same data. If it still doesn't get a reply after 16 unicast attempts, the neighbor is declared dead. People often refer to this process as reliable multicast.

Reliable Transport Protocol (RTP)   The reliable transport protocol, used in the EIGRP routing protocol, is responsible for guaranteed, ordered delivery of EIGRP packets to all neighbors

reload   An event or command that causes Cisco routers to reboot.

RIF   Routing Information Field: In Source-Route bridging, a header field that defines the path direction of the frame or token. If the Route Information Indicator (RII) bit is not set, the RIF is read from source to destination (left to right). If the RII bit is set, the RIF is read from the destination back to the source, so the RIF is read right to left. It is defined as part of the token ring frame header for source-routed frames, which contains path information.

ring   Two or more stations connected in a logical circular topology. In this topology, which is the basis for Token Ring, FDDI, and CDDI, information is transferred from station to station in sequence.

ring topology   A network logical topology comprising a series of repeaters that form one closed loop by connecting unidirectional transmission links. Individual stations on the network are connected to the network at a repeater. Physically, ring topologies are generally organized in a closed-loop star. *Compare with bus topology* and *star topology.*

RIP   Routing Information Protocol: The most commonly used interior gateway protocol in the Internet. RIP employs hop count as a routing metric. *See also EIGRP, IGP, OSPF,* and *hop count.*

RJ connector   registered jack connector: Used with twisted-pair wiring to connect the copper wire to network interface cards, switches, and hubs.

rolled cable   Type of wiring cable that is used to connect a PC's COM port to a router or switch console port.

ROM   read-only memory: Chip used in computers to help boot the device. Cisco routers use a ROM chip to load the bootstrap, which runs a power-on self-test, and then find and load the IOS in flash memory by default.

root bridge   Used with Spanning Tree Protocol to stop network loops from occurring. The root bridge is elected by having the lowest bridge ID. The bridge ID is determined by the priority (32,768 by default on all bridges and switches) and the main hardware address of the device.

routed protocol   Routed protocols (such as IP and IPX) are used to transmit user data through an internetwork. By contrast, routing protocols (such as RIP, IGRP, and OSPF) are used to update routing tables between routers.

route flap   A route that is being announced in an up/down fashion.

route poisoning   Used by various DV routing protocols in order to overcome large routing loops and offer explicit information about when a subnet or network is not accessible (instead of merely suggesting that the network is unreachable by not including it in updates). Typically, this is accomplished by setting the hop count to one more than maximum. *See also poison reverse updates.*

route summarization   In various routing protocols, such as OSPF, EIGRP, and IS-IS, the consolidation of publicized subnetwork addresses so that a single summary route is advertised to other areas by an area border router.

router   A Network layer mechanism, either software or hardware, using one or more metrics to decide on the best path to use for transmission of network traffic. Sending packets between networks by routers is based on the information provided on Network layers. Historically, this device has sometimes been called a gateway.

Router ID (RID)   The Router ID (RID) is an IP address used to identify the router. Cisco chooses the Router ID by using the highest IP address of all configured loopback interfaces. If no loopback interfaces are configured with addresses, OSPF will choose the highest IP address of all active physical interfaces.

routing   The process of forwarding logically addressed packets from their local subnetwork toward their ultimate destination. In large networks, the numerous intermediary destinations a packet might travel before reaching its destination can make routing very complex.

routing domain   Any collection of end systems and intermediate systems that operate under an identical set of administrative rules. Every routing domain contains one or several areas, all individually given a certain area address.

routing metric   Any value that is used by routing algorithms to determine whether one route is superior to another. Metrics include such information as bandwidth, delay, hop count, path cost, load, MTU, reliability, and communication cost. Only the best possible routes are stored in the routing table, while all other information may be stored in link-state or topological databases. *See also cost.*

routing protocol   Any protocol that defines algorithms to be used for updating routing tables between routers. Examples include IGRP, RIP, and OSPF.

routing table   A table kept in a router or other internetworking mechanism that maintains a record of only the best possible routes to certain network destinations and the metrics associated with those routes.

RP   Route Processor: Also known as a supervisory processor; a module on Cisco 7000 series routers that holds the CPU, system software, and most of the memory components used in the router.

RSP   Route/Switch Processor: A processor module combining the functions of RP and SP used in Cisco 7500 series routers. *See also RP and SP.*

RTS Request To Send: An EIA/TIA-232 control signal requesting permission to transmit data on a communication line.

S reference point ISDN reference point that works with a T reference point to convert a four-wire ISDN network to the two-wire ISDN network needed to communicate with the ISDN switches at the network provider.

sampling rate The rate at which samples of a specific waveform amplitude are collected within a specified period of time.

SAP (1) Service Access Point: A field specified by IEEE 802.2 that is part of an address specification. (2) Service Advertising Protocol: The Novell NetWare protocol that supplies a way, using routers and servers, to inform network clients of resources and services availability on a network. *See also IPX.*

SCR sustainable cell rate: An ATM Forum parameter used for traffic management, it is the long-term average cell rate for VBR connections that can be transmitted.

SDH Synchronous Digital Hierarchy: One of the standards developed for Fiber Optics Transmission Systems (FOTS).

SDLC Synchronous Data Link Control: A protocol used in SNA Data Link layer communications. SDLC is a bit-oriented, full-duplex serial protocol that is the basis for several similar protocols, including HDLC and LAPB. *See also HDLC and LAPB.*

seed router In an AppleTalk network, the router that is equipped with the network number or cable range in its port descriptor. The seed router specifies the network number or cable range for other routers in that network section and answers to configuration requests from nonseed routers on its connected AppleTalk network, permitting those routers to affirm or modify their configurations accordingly. Every AppleTalk network needs at least one seed router physically connected to each network segment.

sequencing Used in virtual circuits and segmentation to number segments so they can be put back together again in the correct order.

serial transmission WAN serial connectors use serial transmission, which takes place one bit at a time, over a single channel.

server Hardware and software that provide network services to clients.

Session layer Layer 5 of the OSI reference model, responsible for creating, managing, and terminating sessions between applications and overseeing data exchange between Presentation layer entities. *See also Application layer, Data Link layer, Network layer, Physical layer, Presentation layer,* and *Transport layer.*

set-based Set-based routers and switches use the `set` command to configure devices. Cisco is moving away from set-based commands and is using the command-line interface (CLI) on all new devices.

setup mode   Mode that a router will enter if no configuration is found in nonvolatile RAM when the router boots. Allows the administrator to configure a router step-by-step. Not as robust or flexible as the command-line interface.

SF   super frame (also called a D4 frame): Consists of 12 frames with 192 bits each, the 193rd bit providing other functions including error checking. SF is frequently used on T1 circuits. A newer version of the technology is Extended Superframe (ESF), which uses 24 frames. *See also ESF.*

shared tree   A method of multicast data forwarding. Shared trees use an architecture in which multiple sources share a common rendezvous point.

signaling packet   An informational packet created by an ATM-connected mechanism that wants to establish connection with another such mechanism. The packet contains the QoS parameters needed for connection and the ATM NSAP address of the endpoint. The endpoint responds with a message of acceptance if it is able to support the desired QoS, and the connection is established. *See also QoS.*

silicon switching   A type of high-speed switching used in Cisco 7000 series routers, based on the use of a separate processor (the Silicon Switch Processor, or SSP). *See also SSE.*

simplex   A mode at which data or a digital signal is transmitted. Simplex is a way of transmitting in only one direction. Half duplex transmits in two directions but only one direction at a time. Full duplex transmits both directions simultaneously.

sliding window   The method of flow control used by TCP, as well as several Data Link layer protocols. This method places a buffer between the receiving application and the network data flow. The "window" available for accepting data is the size of the buffer minus the amount of data already there. This window increases in size as the application reads data from it and decreases as new data is sent. The receiver sends the transmitter announcements of the current window size, and it may stop accepting data until the window increases above a certain threshold.

SLIP   Serial Line Internet Protocol: An industry standard serial encapsulation for point-to-point connections that supports only a single routed protocol, TCP/IP. SLIP is the predecessor to PPP. *See also PPP.*

SMDS   Switched Multimegabit Data Service: A packet-switched, datagram-based WAN networking technology offered by telephone companies that provides high speed.

SMTP   Simple Mail Transfer Protocol: A protocol used on the Internet to provide electronic mail services.

SNA   Systems Network Architecture: A complex, feature-rich, network architecture similar to the OSI reference model but with several variations; created by IBM in the 1970s and essentially composed of seven layers.

SNAP   Subnetwork Access Protocol: SNAP is a frame used in Ethernet, Token Ring, and FDDI LANs. Data transfer, connection management, and QoS selection are three primary functions executed by the SNAP frame.

snapshot routing   Snapshot routing takes a point-in-time capture of a dynamic routing table and maintains it even when the remote connection goes down. This allows the use of a dynamic routing protocol without requiring the link to remain active, which might incur per-minute usage charges.

SNMP   Simple Network Management Protocol: This protocol polls SNMP agents or devices for statistical and environmental data. This data can include device temperature, name, performance statistics, and much more. SNMP works with MIB objects that are present on the SNMP agent. This information is queried, then sent to the SNMP server.

socket   (1) A software structure that operates within a network device as a destination point for communications. (2) In AppleTalk networks, an entity at a specific location within a node; AppleTalk sockets are conceptually similar to TCP/IP ports.

software address   Also called a logical address. This is typically an IP address, but it can also be an IPX address.

SOHO   small office, home office: A contemporary term for remote users.

SONET   Synchronous Optical Network: The ANSI standard for synchronous transmission on fiber-optic media, developed at Bell Labs. It specifies a base signal rate of 51.84Mbps and a set of multiples of that rate, known as Optical Carrier levels, up to 2.5Gbps.

source tree   A method of multicast data forwarding. Source trees use the architecture of the source of the multicast traffic as the root of the tree.

SP   Switch Processor: Also known as a ciscoBus controller, it is a Cisco 7000 series processor module acting as governing agent for all CxBus activities.

SPF   Shortest Path First: A type of routing algorithm. The only true SPF protocol is Open Shortest Path First (OSPF).

span   A full-duplex digital transmission line connecting two facilities.

SPAN   Switched Port Analyzer: A feature of the Catalyst 5000 switch that offers freedom to manipulate within a switched Ethernet environment by extending the monitoring ability of the existing network analyzers into the environment. At one switched segment, the SPAN mirrors traffic onto a predetermined SPAN port, while a network analyzer connected to the SPAN port is able to monitor traffic from any other Catalyst switched port.

spanning explorer packet   Sometimes called limited-route or single-route explorer packet, it pursues a statically configured spanning tree when searching for paths in a Source-Route bridging network. *See also all-routes explorer packet, explorer packet,* and *local explorer packet.*

spanning tree   A subset of a network topology within which no loops exist. When bridges are interconnected into a loop, the bridge, or switch, cannot identify a frame that has been forwarded previously, so there is no mechanism for removing a frame as it passes the interface numerous times. Without a method of removing these frames, the bridges continuously forward them—consuming bandwidth and adding overhead to the network. Spanning trees prune the network to provide only one path for any packet. *See also STP* and *STA.*

SPF Shortest Path First algorithm: A routing algorithm used to decide on the shortest-path. Sometimes called Dijkstra's algorithm and frequently used in link-state routing algorithms. *See also link-state routing algorithm.*

SPID Service Profile Identifier: A number assigned by service providers or local telephone companies and configured by administrators to a BRI port. SPIDs are used to determine subscription services of a device connected via ISDN. ISDN devices use SPID when accessing the telephone company switch that initializes the link to a service provider.

split horizon Useful for preventing routing loops, a type of distance-vector routing rule where information about routes is prevented from leaving the router interface through which that information was received.

spoofing (1) In dial-on-demand routing (DDR), where a circuit-switched link is taken down to save toll charges when there is no traffic to be sent, spoofing is a scheme used by routers that causes a host to treat an interface as if it were functioning and supporting a session. The router pretends to send "spoof" replies to keepalive messages from the host in an effort to convince the host that the session is up and running. *See also DDR.* (2) The illegal act of sending a packet labeled with a false address in order to deceive network security mechanisms such as filters and access lists.

spooler A management application that processes requests submitted to it for execution in a sequential fashion from a queue. A good example is a print spooler.

SPX Sequenced Packet Exchange: A Novell NetWare transport protocol that augments the datagram service provided by Network layer (layer 3) protocols, it was derived from the Switch-to-Switch Protocol of the XNS protocol suite.

SQE Signal Quality Error: In an Ethernet network, a message sent from a transceiver to an attached machine that the collision-detection circuitry is working.

SRB Source-Route bridging: Created by IBM, the bridging method used in Token Ring networks. The source determines the entire route to a destination before sending the data and includes that information in Routing Information Fields (RIFs) within each packet. *Contrast with transparent bridging.*

SRT Source-Route Transparent bridging: A bridging scheme developed by IBM that merges Source-Route and Transparent bridging. SRT takes advantage of both technologies in one device, fulfilling the needs of all end nodes. Translation between bridging protocols is not necessary. *Compare with SR/TLB.*

SR/TLB Source-Route Translational bridging: A bridging method that allows source-route stations to communicate with transparent bridge stations aided by an intermediate bridge that translates between the two bridge protocols. Used for bridging between Token Ring and Ethernet. *Compare with SRT.*

SSAP Source Service Access Point: The SAP of the network node identified in the Source field of the packet identifying the Network layer protocol. *See also DSAP and SAP.*

SSE   Silicon Switching Engine: The software component of Cisco's silicon switching technology, hard-coded into the Silicon Switch Processor (SSP). Silicon switching is available only on the Cisco 7000 with an SSP. Silicon-switched packets are compared to the silicon-switching cache on the SSE. The SSP is a dedicated switch processor that offloads the switching process from the route processor, providing a fast-switching solution, but packets must still traverse the backplane of the router to get to the SSP and then back to the exit interface.

STA   spanning-tree algorithm: An algorithm that creates a spanning tree using the Spanning Tree Protocol (STP). *See also spanning tree* and *STP.*

standard IP access list   IP access list that uses only the source IP addresses to filter a network.

standard IPX access list   IPX access list that uses only the source and destination IPX address to filter a network.

star topology   A LAN physical topology with endpoints on the network converging at a common central device (known as a hub) using point-to-point links. A logical ring topology can be configured as a physical star topology using a unidirectional closed-loop star rather than point-to-point links. That is, connections within the hub are arranged in an internal ring. *See also bus topology* and *ring topology.*

startup range   If an AppleTalk node does not have a number saved from the last time it was booted, then the node selects from the range of values from 65,280 to 65,534.

state transitions   Digital signaling scheme that reads the "state" of the digital signal in the middle of the bit cell. If it is five volts, the cell is read as a one. If the state of the digital signal is zero volts, the bit cell is read as a zero.

static route   A route whose information is purposefully entered into the routing table by an administrator and takes priority over those chosen by dynamic routing protocols.

static VLAN   A VLAN that is manually configured port by port. This is the method typically used in production networks.

statistical multiplexing   Multiplexing in general is a technique that allows data from multiple logical channels to be sent across a single physical channel. Statistical multiplexing dynamically assigns bandwidth only to input channels that are active, optimizing available bandwidth so that more devices can be connected than with other multiplexing techniques. Also known as statistical time-division multiplexing or stat mux.

STM-1   Synchronous Transport Module Level 1. In the European SDH standard, one of many formats identifying the frame structure for the 155.52Mbps lines that are used to carry ATM cells.

store-and-forward packet switching   A technique in which the switch first copies each packet into its buffer and performs a cyclic redundancy check (CRC). If the packet is error free, the switch then looks up the destination address in its filter table, determines the appropriate exit port, and sends the packet.

STP   (1) shielded twisted-pair: A wiring scheme, used in many network implementations, that has a layer of shielded insulation to reduce EMI. (2) Spanning Tree Protocol. The bridge protocol (IEEE 802.1D) that enables a learning bridge to dynamically avoid loops in the network topology by creating a spanning tree using the spanning-tree algorithm. Spanning-tree frames called Bridge Protocol Data Units (BPDUs) are sent and received by all switches in the network at regular intervals. The switches participating in the spanning tree don't forward the frames; instead, they're processed to determine the spanning-tree topology itself. Cisco Catalyst series switches use STP 802.1D to perform this function. *See also BPDU, learning bridge, MAC address, spanning tree,* and *STA.*

straight-through cable   Type of Ethernet cable that connects a host to a switch, host to a hub, or router to a switch or hub.

stub area   An OSPF area carrying a default route, intra-area routes, and interarea routes but no external routes. Configuration of virtual links cannot be achieved across a stub area, and stub areas are not allowed to contain an ASBR. *See also non-stub area, ASBR,* and *OSPF.*

stub network   A network having only one connection to a router.

STUN   Serial Tunnel: A technology used to connect an HDLC link to an SDLC link over a serial link.

subarea   A portion of an SNA network made up of a subarea node and its attached links and peripheral nodes.

subarea node   An SNA communications host or controller that handles entire network addresses.

subchannel   A frequency-based subdivision that creates a separate broadband communications channel.

subinterface   One of many virtual interfaces available on a single physical interface.

subnet   *See subnetwork.*

subnet address   The portion of an IP address that is specifically identified by the subnet mask as the subnetwork. *See also IP address, subnetwork,* and *subnet mask.*

subnet mask   Also simply known as mask, a 32-bit address mask used in IP to identify the bits of an IP address that are used for the subnet address. Using a mask, the router does not need to examine all 32 bits, only those indicated by the mask. *See also address mask* and *IP address.*

subnetting   Used in IP networks to break up larger networks into smaller subnetworks.

subnetwork   (1) Any network that is part of a larger IP network and is identified by a subnet address. A network administrator segments a network into subnetworks in order to provide a hierarchical, multilevel routing structure and at the same time protect the subnetwork from the addressing complexity of networks that are attached. Also known as a subnet. *See also IP address, subnet mask,* and *subnet address.* (2) In OSI networks, the term specifically refers to a collection of ESs and ISs controlled by only one administrative domain using a solitary network connection protocol.

summarization   Term used to describe the process of summarizing multiple routing table entries into one entry.

supernetting   *See summarization.*

SVC   switched virtual circuit: A dynamically established virtual circuit created on demand and dissolved as soon as transmission is over and the circuit is no longer needed. In ATM terminology, it is referred to as a switched virtual connection. *See also PVC.*

switch   (1) In networking, a device responsible for multiple functions such as filtering, flooding, and sending frames. It works using the destination address of individual frames. Switches operate at the Data Link layer of the OSI model. (2) Broadly, any electronic/mechanical device allowing connections to be established as needed and terminated if no longer necessary.

switch block   A combination of layer 2 switches and layer 3 routers. The layer 2 switches connect users in the wiring closet into the access layer and provide 10 or 100Mbps dedicated connections. 1900/2820 and 2900 Catalyst switches can be used in the switch block.

switch fabric   Term used to identify a layer 2 switched internetwork with many switches. More commonly, it is a term used to identify the inner workings of a switch itself. Thus, it is the matrix of pathways that any frame or cell might be able to traverse as it is switched from input port to output port.

switched LAN   Any LAN implemented using LAN switches. *See also LAN switch.*

synchronous transmission   Signals transmitted digitally with precision clocking. These signals have identical frequencies and contain individual characters encapsulated in control bits (called start/stop bits) that designate the beginning and ending of each character. *See also asynchronous transmission* and *isochronous transmission.*

syslog   A protocol used to monitor system log messages by a remote device.

T reference point   Used with an S reference point to change a four-wire ISDN network to a two-wire ISDN network.

T1   Digital WAN that uses 24 DS0s at 64Kbps each to create a bandwidth of 1.536Mbps, minus clocking overhead, providing 1.544Mbps of usable bandwidth.

T3   Digital WAN that can provide bandwidth of 44.763Mbps.

TACACS+   Terminal Access Controller Access Control System Plus: An enhanced version of TACACS, this protocol is similar to RADIUS. *See also RADIUS.*

tagged traffic   ATM cells with their Cell Loss Priority (CLP) bit set to 1. Also referred to as Discard Eligible (DE) traffic in Frame Relay networks. Tagged traffic can be eliminated in order to ensure trouble-free delivery of higher priority traffic if the network is congested. *See also CLP.*

TCP   Transmission Control Protocol: A connection-oriented protocol that is defined at the Transport layer of the OSI reference model. Provides reliable delivery of data.

TCP/IP Transmission Control Protocol/Internet Protocol. The suite of protocols underlying the Internet. TCP and IP are the most widely known protocols in that suite. *See also IP* and *TCP.*

TDM Time Division Multiplexing: A technique for assigning bandwidth on a single wire, based on preassigned time slots, to data from several channels. Bandwidth is allotted to each channel regardless of a station's intent to send data. *See also ATDM, FDM,* and *multiplexing.*

TE terminal equipment: Any peripheral device that is ISDN compatible and attached to a network, such as a telephone or computer. TE1s are devices that are ISDN-ready and understand ISDN signaling techniques. TE2s are devices that are not ISDN-ready and do not understand ISDN signaling techniques. A terminal adapter must be used with a TE2.

TE1 Terminal Equipment Type 1. A device with a four-wire, twisted-pair digital interface is referred to as Terminal Equipment Type 1. Most modern ISDN devices are of this type.

TE2 Terminal Equipment Type 2. Devices known as Terminal Equipment Type 2 do not understand ISDN signaling techniques, and a terminal adapter must be used to convert the signaling.

telco A common abbreviation for the telephone company.

Telnet The standard terminal emulation protocol within the TCP/IP protocol stack. Method of remote terminal connection, enabling users to log in on remote networks and use those resources as if they were locally connected. Telnet is defined in RFC 854.

terminal adapter (TA) A hardware interface between a computer without a native ISDN interface and an ISDN line. In effect, a device to connect a standard async interface to a nonnative ISDN device, emulating a modem.

terminal emulation The use of software, installed on a PC or LAN server, that allows the PC to function as if it were a "dumb" terminal directly attached to a particular type of mainframe.

TFTP Trivial File Transfer Protocol: Conceptually, a stripped-down version of FTP; it's the protocol of choice if you know exactly what you want and where it's to be found. TFTP doesn't provide the abundance of functions that FTP does. In particular, it has no directory browsing abilities; it can do nothing but send and receive files.

TFTP host/server Trivial File Transfer Protocol is used to send files using IP at the Network layer and UDP at the Transport layer, which makes it unreliable.

thicknet Also called 10Base5. Bus network that uses a thick coaxial cable and runs Ethernet up to 500 meters.

thinnet Also called 10Base2. Bus network that uses a thin coax cable and runs Ethernet media access up to 185 meters.

three-way handshake Term used in a TCP session to define how a virtual circuit is set up. It is called a "three-way" handshake because it uses three data segments.

token A frame containing only control information. Possessing this control information gives a network device permission to transmit data onto the network. *See also token passing.*

token bus   LAN architecture that is the basis for the IEEE 802.4 LAN specification and employs token-passing access over a bus topology. *See also IEEE.*

token passing   A method used by network devices to access the physical medium in a systematic way based on possession of a small frame called a token. *See also token.*

Token Ring   IBM's token-passing LAN technology. It runs at 4Mbps or 16Mbps over a ring topology. Defined formally by IEEE 802.5. *See also ring topology* and *token passing.*

toll network   WAN network that uses the public switched telephone network (PSTN) to send packets.

topology database   A topology database (also called a topology table) contains all destinations advertised by neighboring routers. Associated with each entry is the destination address and a list of neighbors that have advertised the destination.

Traceroute (also Trace)   IP command used to trace the path a packet takes through an internetwork.

transparent bridging   The bridging scheme used in Ethernet and IEEE 802.3 networks, it passes frames along one hop at a time, using bridging information stored in tables that associate end-node MAC addresses with bridge ports. This type of bridging is considered transparent because the source node does not know it has been bridged because the destination frames are addressed directly to the end node. *Contrast with SRB.*

Transport layer   Layer 4 of the OSI reference model, used for reliable communication between end nodes over the network. The Transport layer provides mechanisms used for establishing, maintaining, and terminating virtual circuits; transport fault detection and recovery; and controlling the flow of information. *See also Application layer, Data Link layer, Network layer, Physical layer, Presentation layer,* and *Session layer.*

trap   Used to send SNMP messages to SNMP managers.

TRIP   Token Ring Interface Processor: A high-speed interface processor used on Cisco 7000 series routers. The TRIP provides two or four ports for interconnection with IEEE 802.5 and IBM media with ports set to speeds of either 4Mbps or 16Mbps set independently of each other.

trunk link   Link used between switches and from some servers to the switches. Trunk links carry traffic for many VLANs. Access links are used to connect host devices to a switch and carry only VLAN information that the device is a member of.

TTL   time to live: A field in an IP header, indicating the length of time a packet is valid.

TUD   Trunk Up-Down: A protocol used in ATM networks for the monitoring of trunks. Should a trunk miss a given number of test messages being sent by ATM switches to ensure trunk line quality, TUD declares the trunk down. When a trunk reverses state and comes back up, TUD recognizes that the trunk is up and returns the trunk to service.

tunneling   A method of avoiding protocol restrictions by wrapping packets from one protocol in another protocol's frame and transmitting this encapsulated packet over a network that supports the wrapper protocol. *See also encapsulation.*

U reference point   Reference point between a TE1 and an ISDN network. The U reference point understands ISDN signaling techniques and uses a two-wire connection.

UDP   User Datagram Protocol: A connectionless Transport layer protocol in the TCP/IP protocol stack that simply allows datagrams to be exchanged without acknowledgments or delivery guarantees, requiring other protocols to handle error processing and retransmission. UDP is defined in RFC 768.

unicast   Used for direct host-to-host communication. Communication is directed to only one destination and is originated only from one source.

unidirectional shared tree   A method of shared tree multicast forwarding. This method allows only multicast data to be forwarded from the RP.

unnumbered frames   HDLC frames used for control-management purposes, such as link startup and shutdown or mode specification.

user mode   Cisco IOS EXEC mode that allows an administrator to perform very few commands. You can only verify statistics in user mode; you cannot see or change the router or switch configuration.

UTP   unshielded twisted-pair: Copper wiring used in small-to-large networks to connect host devices to hubs and switches. Also used to connect switch to switch or hub to hub.

VBR   variable bit rate: A QoS class, as defined by the ATM Forum, for use in ATM networks that is subdivided into real time (RT) class and non–real time (NRT) class. RT is employed when connections have a fixed-time relationship between samples. Conversely, NRT is employed when connections do not have a fixed-time relationship between samples but still need an assured QoS.

VCC   virtual channel connection: A logical circuit that is created by VCLs (virtual channel links). VCCs carry data between two endpoints in an ATM network. Sometimes called a virtual circuit connection.

VIP   (1) Versatile Interface Processor: An interface card for Cisco 7000 and 7500 series routers, providing multilayer switching and running the Cisco IOS software. The most recent version of VIP is VIP2. (2) Virtual IP: A function making it possible for logically separated switched IP workgroups to run Virtual Networking Services across the switch port.

virtual circuit (VC)   A logical circuit devised to assure reliable communication between two devices on a network. Defined by a virtual path identifier/virtual channel (really the only time "channel" is used) identifier (VPI/VCI) pair, a virtual circuit can be permanent (PVC) or switched (SVC). Virtual circuits are used in Frame Relay and X.25. Known as virtual channel in ATM. *See also PVC and SVC.*

virtual ring   In an SRB network, a logical connection between physical rings, either local or remote.

VLAN   virtual LAN: A group of devices on one or more logically segmented LANs (configured by use of management software), enabling devices to communicate as if attached to the same physical medium when they are actually located on numerous different LAN segments. VLANs are based on logical instead of physical connections and thus are tremendously flexible.

VLAN ID   Sometimes referred to as VLAN color, the VLAN ID is tagged onto a frame to tell a receiving switch which VLAN the frame is a member of.

VLSM   Variable Length Subnet Mask: Helps optimize available address space and specify a different subnet mask for the same network number on various subnets. Also commonly referred to as "subnetting a subnet."

VMPS   VLAN Management Policy Server: Used to dynamically assign VLANs to a switch port.

VPN   virtual private network: A method of encrypting point-to-point logical connections across a public network, such as the Internet. This allows secure communications across a public network.

VTP   VLAN Trunking Protocol: Used to update switches in a switch fabric about VLANs configured on a VTP server. VTP devices can be a VTP server, client, or transparent device. Servers update clients. Transparent devices are only local devices and do not share information with VTP clients. VTP devices send VLAN information down trunked links only.

VTP transparent mode   Switch mode that receives VLAN Trunking Protocol VLAN information and passes it on but doesn't read the information.

WAN   wide area network: A designation used to connect LANs together across a DCE (data communications equipment) network. Typically, a WAN is a leased line or dial-up connection across a PSTN network. Examples of WAN protocols include Frame Relay, PPP, ISDN, and HDLC.

wildcard   Used with access lists and OSPF configurations. Wildcards are designations used to identify a range of subnets.

windowing   Flow-control method used with TCP at the Transport layer of the OSI model.

WINS   Windows Internet Name Service: Name resolution database for NetBIOS names to TCP/IP address.

WinSock   Windows Socket Interface: A software interface that makes it possible for an assortment of applications to use and share an Internet connection. The WinSock software consists of a dynamic link library (DLL) with supporting programs such as a dialer program that initiates the connection.

workgroup layer   The distribution layer is sometimes referred to as the workgroup layer and is the communication point between the access layer and the core. The primary functions of the distribution layer are to provide routing, filtering, and WAN access and to determine how packets can access the core, if needed.

workgroup switching   A switching method that supplies high-speed (100Mbps) transparent bridging between Ethernet networks as well as high-speed translational bridging between Ethernet and CDDI or FDDI.

X Window   A distributed multitasking windowing and graphics system originally developed by MIT for communication between X terminals and Unix workstations.

X.25   An ITU-T packet-relay standard that defines communication between DTE and DCE network devices. X.25 uses a reliable Data Link layer protocol called LAPB. X.25 also uses PLP at the Network layer. X.25 has mostly been replaced by Frame Relay.

ZIP   Zone Information Protocol: A Session layer protocol used by AppleTalk to map network numbers to zone names. NBP uses ZIP in the determination of networks containing nodes that belong to a zone. *See also ZIP storm* and *zone.*

ZIP storm   A broadcast storm occurring when a router running AppleTalk reproduces or transmits a route for which there is no corresponding zone name at the time of execution. The route is then forwarded by other routers downstream, thus causing a ZIP storm. *See also broadcast storm* and *ZIP.*

zone   A logical grouping of network devices in AppleTalk. Also used in DNS. *See also ZIP.*

Index

Note to the reader: Throughout this index **boldfaced** page numbers indicate primary discussions of a topic. *Italicized* page numbers indicate illustrations.

D

E

Wiley Publishing, Inc. End-User License Agreement

READ THIS. You should carefully read these terms and conditions before opening the software packet(s) included with this book "Book". This is a license agreement "Agreement" between you and Wiley Publishing, Inc. "WPI". By opening the accompanying software packet(s), you acknowledge that you have read and accept the following terms and conditions. If you do not agree and do not want to be bound by such terms and conditions, promptly return the Book and the unopened software packet(s) to the place you obtained them for a full refund.

1.License Grant. WPI grants to you (either an individual or entity) a nonexclusive license to use one copy of the enclosed software program(s) (collectively, the "Software," solely for your own personal or business purposes on a single computer (whether a standard computer or a workstation component of a multi-user network). The Software is in use on a computer when it is loaded into temporary memory (RAM) or installed into permanent memory (hard disk, CD-ROM, or other storage device). WPI reserves all rights not expressly granted herein.

2.Ownership. WPI is the owner of all right, title, and interest, including copyright, in and to the compilation of the Software recorded on the physical packet included with this Book "Software Media". Copyright to the individual programs recorded on the Software Media is owned by the author or other authorized copyright owner of each program. Ownership of the Software and all proprietary rights relating thereto remain with WPI and its licensers.

3.Restrictions On Use and Transfer.

(a) You may only (i) make one copy of the Software for backup or archival purposes, or (ii) transfer the Software to a single hard disk, provided that you keep the original for backup or archival purposes. You may not (i) rent or lease the Software, (ii) copy or reproduce the Software through a LAN or other network system or through any computer subscriber system or bulletin-board system, or (iii) modify, adapt, or create derivative works based on the Software.

(b) You may not reverse engineer, decompile, or disassemble the Software. You may transfer the Software and user documentation on a permanent basis, provided that the transferee agrees to accept the terms and conditions of this Agreement and you retain no copies. If the Software is an update or has been updated, any transfer must include the most recent update and all prior versions.

4.Restrictions on Use of Individual Programs. You must follow the individual requirements and restrictions detailed for each individual program in the About the CD-ROM appendix of this Book or on the Software Media. These limitations are also contained in the individual license agreements recorded on the Software Media. These limitations may include a requirement that after using the program for a specified period of time, the user must pay a registration fee or discontinue use. By opening the Software packet(s), you will be agreeing to abide by the licenses and restrictions for these individual programs that are detailed in the About the CD-ROM appendix and/or on the Software Media. None of the material on this Software Media or listed in this Book may ever be redistributed, in original or modified form, for commercial purposes.

5.Limited Warranty.

(a)WPI warrants that the Software and Software Media are free from defects in materials and workmanship under normal use for a period of sixty (60) days from the date of purchase of this Book. If WPI receives notification within the warranty period of defects in materials or workmanship, WPI will replace the defective Software Media.

(b)WPI AND THE AUTHOR(S) OF THE BOOK DISCLAIM ALL OTHER WARRANTIES, EXPRESS OR IMPLIED, INCLUDING WITHOUT LIMITATION IMPLIED WARRANTIES OF MERCHANTABILITY AND FITNESS FOR A PARTICULAR PURPOSE, WITH RESPECT TO THE SOFTWARE, THE PROGRAMS, THE SOURCE CODE CONTAINED THEREIN, AND/OR THE TECHNIQUES DESCRIBED IN THIS BOOK. WPI DOES NOT WARRANT THAT THE FUNCTIONS CONTAINED IN THE SOFTWARE WILL MEET YOUR REQUIREMENTS OR THAT THE OPERATION OF THE SOFTWARE WILL BE ERROR FREE.

(c) This limited warranty gives you specific legal rights, and you may have other rights that vary from jurisdiction to jurisdiction.

6.Remedies.

(a)WPI's entire liability and your exclusive remedy for defects in materials and workmanship shall be limited to replacement of the Software Media, which may be returned to WPI with a copy of your receipt at the following address: Software Media Fulfillment Department, Attn.: *CCNA INTRO: Introduction to Cisco Networking Technologies Study Guide (Exam 640-821)*, Wiley Publishing, Inc., 10475 Crosspoint Blvd., Indianapolis, IN 46256, or call 1-800-762-2974. Please allow four to six weeks for delivery. This Limited Warranty is void if failure of the Software Media has resulted from accident, abuse, or misapplication. Any replacement Software Media will be warranted for the remainder of the original warranty period or thirty (30) days, whichever is longer.

(b) In no event shall WPI or the author be liable for any damages whatsoever (including without limitation damages for loss of business profits, business interruption, loss of business information, or any other pecuniary loss) arising from the use of or inability to use the Book or the Software, even if WPI has been advised of the possibility of such damages.

(c) Because some jurisdictions do not allow the exclusion or limitation of liability for consequential or incidental damages, the above limitation or exclusion may not apply to you.

7.U.S. Government Restricted Rights. Use, duplication, or disclosure of the Software for or on behalf of the United States of America, its agencies and/or instrumentalities "U.S. Government" is subject to restrictions as stated in paragraph (c)(1)(ii) of the Rights in Technical Data and Computer Software clause of DFARS 252.227-7013, or subparagraphs (c) (1) and (2) of the Commercial Computer Software - Restricted Rights clause at FAR 52.227-19, and in similar clauses in the NASA FAR supplement, as applicable.

8.General. This Agreement constitutes the entire understanding of the parties and revokes and supersedes all prior agreements, oral or written, between them and may not be modified or amended except in a writing signed by both parties hereto that specifically refers to this Agreement. This Agreement shall take precedence over any other documents that may be in conflict herewith. If any one or more provisions contained in this Agreement are held by any court or tribunal to be invalid, illegal, or otherwise unenforceable, each and every other provision shall remain in full force and effect.

The Absolute Best CCNA: Introduction to Cisco Networking Technologies Book/CD Package on the Market!

Get ready for the Introduction to Cisco Networking Technologies (CCNA INTRO) Exam with the most comprehensive and challenging sample tests anywhere!

The Sybex Test Engine features:

- All the review questions, as covered in each chapter of the book.

- Challenging questions representative of those you'll find on the real exam.

- Two full length bonus exams available only on the CD.

- An Assessment Test to narrow your focus to certain objective groups.

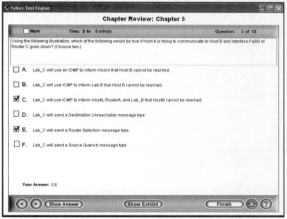

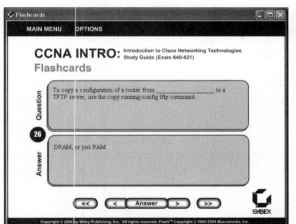

Search through the complete book in PDF!

- Access the entire *CCNA INTRO: Introduction to Cisco Networking Technologies Study Guide*, complete with figures and tables, in electronic format.

- Search the *CCNA INTRO: Introduction to Cisco Networking Technologies Study Guide* chapters to find information on any topic in seconds.

Use the Electronic Flashcards for PCs or Palm devices to jog your memory and prep last-minute for the exam!

- Reinforce your understanding of key concepts with these hardcore flashcard-style questions.

- Download the Flashcards to your Palm device and go on the road. Now you can study for the CCNA INTRO exam any time, anywhere.

Also includes almost an hour's worth of helpful audio and video files designed to enhance your learning experience.

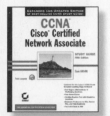
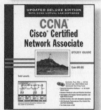